James Worrall is Associate Professor in International Relations and Middle East Studies at the University of Leeds.

'James Worrall has produced the most definitive account regarding the history of Anglo-Omani relations. Rich in detail yet nuanced in interpretation, this book will be invaluable to all those who want to understand why the Sultanate of Oman has developed in the way that it has, and how these ties – both strategic and economic – have managed to endure for so long.'

Clive Jones, Professor of Regional Security, Durham University

'Thoroughly researched and authoritative … an incisive diplomatic history covering a hitherto neglected aspect of postwar British foreign policy.'

Diplomacy and Statecraft

STATEBUILDING AND COUNTERINSURGENCY IN OMAN

Political, Military and Diplomatic
Relations at the End of Empire

JAMES WORRALL

Paperback edition published in 2018 by
I.B.Tauris & Co. Ltd
London • New York
www.ibtauris.com

Hardback edition first published in 2014 by
I.B.Tauris & Co. Ltd

Copyright © 2014 James Worrall

The right of James Worrall to be identified as the author of this work has been asserted by the author in accordance with the Copyright, Designs and Patents Act 1988.

All rights reserved. Except for brief quotations in a review, this book, or any part thereof, may not be reproduced, stored in or introduced into a retrieval system, or transmitted, in any form or by any means, electronic, mechanical, photocopying, recording or otherwise, without the prior written permission of the publisher.

Every attempt has been made to gain permission for the use of the images in this book. Any omissions will be rectified in future editions.

References to websites were correct at the time of writing.

ISBN: 978 1 78831 116 8
eISBN: 978 1 78672 382 6
ePDF: 978 1 83860 916 0

A full CIP record for this book is available from the British Library
A full CIP record is available from the Library of Congress

Library of Congress Catalog Card Number: available

In Memoriam

G.D.L, E.W & D.F.H

We set out thereafter for the land of Oman, and after travelling for six days through desert country we reached it on the seventh. It is fertile, with streams, trees, orchards, palm groves and abundant fruit of various kinds

Ibn Battutah

He is a tall, stout and noble looking man, with a benevolent countenance... and appears to wish to be considered as an Englishman in everything. The English, he says, he looks upon as brothers, and will willingly give them his country

Captain Henry Hart RN, on Sayyid Sa'id,
Sultan of Oman, r.1804-1856

CONTENTS

Acknowledgements xiii
Abbreviations xv
Gazetteer xvii
Glossary xxii
Maps xxviii

Introduction: Oman: Between the *Pax Britannica* and the World 1
   Britain's Post-War Position 4
   The Middle East (and the Gulf) 9
   Oman 11
   Statebuilding and Counterinsurgency 13
   Approach 15
   Defining Britain's Interests 16

1. The Context of Oman's Importance to Britain 20
   Themes in British Post-War Foreign Policy 21
   Britain, the Cold War and Problems in the Middle East 24
   Britain Under Pressure: The Suez Base and Palestinian
      Questions 25
   Ôte-toi de là que je m'y mette: Britain, the U.S. and
      Iranian Oil 27
   The Suez Crisis 29
   Attack or Retreat: Yemen and Aden 33
   Anglo-Omani Relations: An Historical Overview 36
   The Imamate Rebellion 39

2. Events and Policy Surrounding Britain's Increasing
   Involvement in Oman 43
   A New Era 43

A False Dawn	44
Growing Discontent	47
Oman Under the Spotlight	48
The Rebellion Grows	51
Ruling With the Rifle	54
Oil Bonanza?	56
The Retreat from South Arabia	57
The Impact of 1968	58
Family Opposition	61
Moribund Development	62
Changing Nature of the Insurgency	63
Review of Policy	65
Reasessing the Counterinsurgency Strategy	66
Between the Labour Government and the Conservative Opposition	69
Conclusion	75
3. The Conservative Ascendancy: Getting the Troops In	78
Introduction	78
Reassessment	79
Bureaucratic Troubles	86
Local Worries	88
Musandam Operations and the Cabinet	91
Luce, the Cabinet, National Interest and Implications for Policy towards Oman	96
Further Assistance	98
Contingency Planning: Operation 'Mahonia'	100
Conclusion	101
4. Britain & Oman's Internal/External Legitimacy Dilemma	103
Introduction	103
A New Dawn	105
Slow Development	109
The Establishment of the Government	111
The Internal/External Legitimacy Dilemma	112
Biding Time for Evolution	114
Policy Reassessment	115
Objections	121
Conclusion	126
5. The Search for International Recognition: Britain's Role in Securing Legitimacy	129
Introduction	129

Stage Management	132
The Return of Tariq	134
British Policy	137
British Representation in the Sultanate	138
Impact of the Review of Policy	140
Attaining Respectability: The Arab League	142
The Egyptian Key	143
Disappointment at the League	145
United Nations/Divided World?	151
The Application	154
On the Road Again	155
Omani-Saudi Relations	156
External Assistance	158
Conclusion	158
6. British Policy, Whitehall Debates & External Aid 1972–74	161
Introduction	161
New Strategy: Dominate the *Jebal*	162
Omani Exuberance: British Restraint	163
The Attack Proceeds	170
Financial Concerns and Additional Assistance	172
The November Review of Military Assistance	176
Outside Aid	182
Increasing U.S. Interest	192
The 1973 November Review	195
Conclusion	197
7. Continuity and Change: The Labour Government and Defence Reviews	199
Introduction	199
The 'Salalah Hook'	200
The Labour Defence Review	203
Defence Review in 1975	210
The Labour Government and Oman	212
Influence, Economic Interests and the Progress of the Campaign	213
Withdrawal from Salalah	215
The End of Major Operations: Dhofar is Safe for Development	216
Conclusion	218
Conclusion: Themes and Implications	221

Notes	230
Bibliography	264
Chronology of the Dhofar War	279
Key Personalities	290
Index	294

ACKNOWLEDGEMENTS

An undertaking of this nature requires the involvement and support of many people and it is a pleasure to acknowledge their help here. Firstly I wish to thank my PhD supervisors who inspired the research upon which this book is based: Professor Clive Jones and Dr Neil Winn have given me tremendous support and guidance from start to finish, and have continued to do so since completion. I could not have wished for better supervision and will remain in their debt. I also wish to thank Caroline Wise for essential help with the more practical administrative details of university life. The kindness of staff at archives and libraries will not be forgotten. Thanks also to Professor Alice Hills and Dr Georgina Sinclair for their help and advice. A *mis compañeros de oficina* Adam, Chris *y* Hector for the always enlightening discussions and general distractions from work. My other friends and fellow PhD students: Naomi Head, Wali Aslam, Helene Dyrhauge, Simon Mabon and Alam Saleh for the many and varied chats, help with everything under the sun and some great memories.

In Oman my friend Ali al-Hashli who gave me many insights into modern Oman, how Omanis see their own past and of course for taking me to see the places I was writing about. Omanis are said to be the most hospitable people on earth and Ali and his family more than lived up to that reputation. In Dhofar, my thanks go to Mahad for his kindness and hospitality. Those people who kindly agreed to be interviewed helped to bring the archive documents to life and added a new dimension to my understanding. My thanks especially to Sir Donald and Lady Hawley who were so welcoming and tolerant of my many questions.

I would also like to thank my grandparents who always remained interested in my studies and provided some of the financial means needed to embark on this project. Most of all though, my parents made this whole thing possible, without their support in all its myriad forms I would not have got to this point and would not be who I am. Thanks for everything, always.

At I.B.Tauris my thanks go to Jo Godfrey for seeing the potential in my book proposal and for getting it accepted with such alacrity and especially to my editor Maria Marsh for her kindness and patience when what should have been a matter of a few weeks to deliver the manuscript unexpectedly turned into many months. I would also like to thank Major D. J. Cuthbertson and Trish Sole for the permission to include photographs from their time in Oman during the 1970s.

This book is dedicated to those who fought in Dhofar when no one was looking and secured for Oman the stable future which it is still enjoying and is in memory of both Sir Donald Hawley, who played such a key role in co-ordinating the effort, and my grandfathers who sadly did not see this book published.

ABBREVIATIONS

ADDF	Abu Dhabi Defence Force
ADS	Air Defence Scheme
AIOC	Anglo-Iranian Oil Company
AL	Arab League
ANM	Arab Nationalist Movement
BATT	British Army Training Team
BBME	British Bank of the Middle East
b/d or bpd	Barrels Per Day
BFAP	British Forces Arabian Peninsula
BFPG	British Forces Persian Gulf
CBFG	Commander British Forces Gulf
CENTO	Central Treaty Organisation
CAT	Civil Aid Team (Dhofar)
CDS	Chief of the Defence Staff
CGS	Chief of the General Staff
CoS	Chiefs of Staff
CPRS	Central Policy Review Staff
CSAF	Commander Sultan's Armed Forces
CSOAF	Commander Sultan of Oman's Air Force
CSON	Commander Sultan of Oman's Navy
DCA	Dhofar Charitable Association
DIO	District Intelligence Officer
DOPC	Defence and Overseas Policy Committee
FO	Foreign Office
FCO	Foreign & Commonwealth Office
FST	Field Surgical Team
GPMG	General Purpose Machine Gun

HMG	Her Majesty's Government
IBRD	International Bank of Reconstruction and Development (World Bank)
IIBG	Imperial Iranian Battle Group
IITF	Imperial Iranian Task Force
IMF	International Monetary Fund
JIC	Joint Intelligence Committee
LFPG	Land Forces Persian Gulf
LSP	Loan Service Personnel
MFA	Ministry/Minister of Foreign Affairs
MoD	Ministry of Defence (London)
NDFLOAG	National Democratic Front for the Liberation of Oman and the Arabian Gulf (1968–71)
NLF	National Liberation Front (Dhofar)
ODA	Overseas Development Administration
OG	Oman Gendarmerie
OPEC	Organisation of Petroleum Exporting Countries
ORM	Oman Rebel Movement
PD(O)	Petroleum Development (Oman)
PDRY	People's Democratic Republic of Yemen
PFLO	Popular Front for the Liberation of Oman
PFLOAG	Popular Front for the Liberation of the Occupied Arabian Gulf (1968–71)
	Popular Front for the Liberation of Oman and the Arabian Gulf (1971–74)
PRPG	Political Resident Persian Gulf
PRSY	People's Republic of South Yemen (1967–69)
RA	Royal Artillery
RAF	Royal Air Force
SAF	Sultan's Armed Forces
SAS	Special Air Service
SEP	Surrendered Enemy Personnel
SOLF	Sultan of Oman's Land Forces
SON	Sultan of Oman's Navy
TOS	Trucial Oman Scouts (Trucial States)
UKMIS(NY)	United Kingdom Mission to the United Nations (New York)
UN	United Nations
UAE/UAA	United Arab Emirates/Amirates
WHO	World Health Organisation

GAZETTEER

Aden	Situated in Southern Yemen near the entrance to the Red Sea; a British colony until 1967 and the capital of South Yemen until merger with North Yemen in 1990; Britain's regional military headquarters were in Aden during the Jebal Akhdar War of the 1950s.
Batinah	Coastal region on the Gulf of Oman, running from Muscat to the United Arab Emirates border, which is the most densely populated region of Oman.
Bait al-Falaj	Fort and army camp just inland from Muscat and Matrah; the old fort was probably constructed in the eighteenth century and served as the headquarters of the Sultan's Armed Forces until the mid-1970s; it has been restored and serves as the SAF Museum. The Battle of Bait al-Falaj was fought on 11 January 1915 on the surrounding hills between tribal forces from the interior and Indian Army troops protecting Muscat on behalf of the Sultan.
Buraimi	Strategic oasis between al-Dhahirah region of western Oman and Abu Dhabi. Buraimi originally consisted of nine villages, six of which belonged to Oman and three to Abu Dhabi; the oasis was occupied at various intervals from the early nineteenth century by Saudi forces; a Saudi party occupied the village of Hamasah in 1952. Following a failed attempt at arbitration, the Saudis were evicted by the British-officered Trucial Oman Scouts in October 1955.
Capstan	Prominent feature below the escarpment at Sarfait on the western border of Dhofar; it overlooked enemy supply routes along the coast during the Dhofar War.

XVIII Statebuilding and Counterinsurgency in Oman

Dalkut	Small fishing settlement in western Dhofar and one of the last villages remaining in rebel hands during the War.
Dhofar	Southern region of Oman, its capital is at Salalah. Was once a colony of the Sultan later incorporated into the Sultanate.
Empty Quarter	Great sand desert lying between Oman, Yemen, Saudi Arabia and the United Arab Emirates. Known in Arabic as the Rub al-Khali.
Everest	Army position in western Dhofar.
Fahud, Jebal	Hill on the edge of the Rub al-Khali Desert where serious oil exploration began in the 1950s and the first oil was discovered in the 1960s.
Furious	Army position in western Dhofar.
Ghanam, Island	Small island off the Gulf coast of the Musandam Peninsula; formerly a British Royal Navy facility and a strategic Omani radar facility since the early 1980s, important because of its proximity to the Strait of Hormuz.
Habarut	Position on Dhofar-Yemen border; site of a Sultanate fort built in the late 1960s and destroyed by South Yemeni artillery in 1972.
Hauf	Town in South Yemen near the border with Dhofar, used as a base by the rebels.
Hormuz, Strait of	Only sea exit from the Gulf, connecting with the Gulf of Oman and the Indian Ocean, the principal route of oil tankers travelling to and from the Gulf; although the strait separates Oman and Iran, major maritime traffic passes through Omani territorial waters (see map three).
Jebal Akhdar	Mountain peak of around 7,800ft in the Hajjar range in northern Oman. Translates as the Green Mountain, due to the copper deposits found there. Formed the final retreat of the ORM and was assaulted by the SAS in January 1959.
Jasmine	Army positions on the vital Thamrait-Salalah road.
Kuria Muria Islands	Group of seven islands off eastern coast of Dhofar known locally as the Juzur al Hallaniyat; given by Sayyid Said bin Sultan to Queen Victoria in 1854 and returned to the Sultanate on Aden's independence, from where they had been administered, in 1967. The only inhabited island is Hallaniyah.
Mainbrace	Position within the army base at Sarfait along the Dhofar-Yemen border.

Gazetteer XIX

Masirah Island	Medium-sized island just off Oman's Arabian Sea coast and site of an airfield of the Royal Air Force until 1977 (and until recently the home of a British Broadcasting Corporation World Service relay station).
Matrah	Seaport and sister city of the capital Muscat; site of Oman's principal modern port in the 1970s, Mina al-Sultan Qaboos and an important trading centre.
Mirbat	Coastal town at the eastern end of the Salalah Plain in Dhofar; scene of the best-known battle of the Dhofar War (19 July 1972).
Mughsail	Coastal strip and beach in western Dhofar; southern end of the Hornbeam Line.
Musandam	Mountainous peninsula jutting north into the Strait of Hormuz; more properly known as Ru'us al Jebal, as the true Musandam Peninsula consists of just the very tip which almost forms an island; the Musandam belongs to Oman although it is separated from the rest of the Sultanate by territory of the United Arab Emirates.
Muscat	Prominent seaport first under the Kings of Hormuz in the fourteenth and fifteenth centuries. Then a Portuguese stronghold from 1540 until recaptured by the Omanis in 1650. Capital of Oman since the early nineteenth century.
Nizwa	The principal town of interior Oman, often serving over the centuries as the residence of the Imams.
Raykyut	Principal settlement of western Dhofar; claimed by the Popular Front during the Dhofar War as their capital of 'liberated Dhofar'. Its loss in the late 1960s left the SAF in control of only one major town in Dhofar.
Ras al-Hadd	Easternmost tip of Oman and the Arabian Peninsula.
Ras al-Khaimah	Emirate, now part of the UAE, bordering the Musandam Peninsula.
Rustaq	Town of the western Hajjar mountains one of Oman's oldest settlements; served as the capital of Oman before Islam and was a frequent seat of the Ibadi Imams.
Salalah	Principal town and only city of the Dhofar region, located on the Indian Ocean coast of the Salalah Plain a relatively fertile area; site of a Royal Air Force installation until 1977.

Sarfait	Strategic army base on the Dhofar mountains established by Operation Simba in 1972 and maintained with great difficulty throughout the Dhofar War.
Sharjah	One of the seven member states of the UAE. Before independence in 1971, Sharjah was the site of a Royal Air Force station from which aircraft carried out missions over Oman during the Jebal Akhdar War of the 1950s.
Shirshitti	Cave complex along a steep escarpment in western Dhofar and used by the Popular Front for central stores and medical facilities.
Seeb/Sib	Once a village at the eastern end of the Batinah coastal plain, site of the Agreement of al-Sib (26 September 1920), which created a modus vivendi between the Sultanate and an autonomous interior under an imam; also the site since 1973 of Seeb International Airport. Recently renamed Muscat International Airport.
Sohar	Main town of the Batinah coast an important trading centre and one of the largest towns in Oman.
Sur	Natural harbour and ancient seaport in eastern Oman, main town of the Sharqiyyah region.
Taqah	Town on the Salalah plain to the east of Salalah.
Thamrit	A site in the Dhofari Najd originally established by the John Mecom Oil Company under the name Midway. It later became an SAF post and was used extensively by Iranian military forces during the Dhofar War.
Trucial States	Name given to the group of principalities along the southern shores of the Gulf; the same area has been known variously as the Oman Coast, the Trucial Coast and Trucial Oman; in 1971–72, the seven Trucial States of Abu Dhabi, Dubai, Sharjah, Ras al-Khaimah, Ajman, Umm al-Qawain and Fujairah banded together to form the independent UAE.
UAE	United Arab Emirates: see Trucial States.
White City	Army position established on the eastern Jebal Dhofar as a result of Operation Jaguar in 1971; this became the first government centre on the Jabal under the name of Madinat al-Haq.

Yemen The mountainous southern or southwestern corner of the Arabian Peninsula; although consisting of a single historical and cultural unit, Yemen was divided into two countries until unification as the Republic of Yemen in 1990; South Yemen had been known as the Aden Colony and Protectorate, under British control until independence in 1967; the leftist government of the newly independent state first adopted the name of the People's Republic of Southern Yemen (PRSY), but changed to the People's Democratic Republic of Yemen (PDRY) in 1969.

GLOSSARY

Adoo	British Army slang for the rebels derived from the Arabic meaning enemy.
Alam, al-	Sultan's palace in Muscat.
Al Bu Said	Ruling family of Oman since 1749 and also the name of one of Oman's major tribes. The inner core of the Al Bu Said family is known as the Al Said.
Aqubah, Operation	Operation launched on 25 May 1972 against Popular Front stronghold at Hauf (South Yemen) with artillery and air strikes in retaliation for the South Yemeni attack on Habarut Fort.
Badri, Operation	Operation in western Dhofar during August 1975 intended to divert enemy attention away from main operations of the Final Push.
Bait al-Falaj	Fort and army camp just inland from Muscat and Matrah; the old fort was probably constructed in the eighteenth century and served as the headquarters of the Sultan's Armed Forces until the mid-1970s.
British Army Training Team (BATT)	Codename used for the insertion of British Special Air Service (SAS) teams in Dhofar to train and operate the *firqat*.
Civil Action Team (CAT)	Development teams created during the Dhofar War to complement military advances with a 'hearts and minds' campaign by setting up government centres throughout the region.
Damavand Line	Wired barrier built in early 1975 by the Imperial Iranian Task Force from Rakhyut onto Jebal Dhofar.

Glossary

Darb, Operation	Major operation of December 1974 and January 1975 to capture the opposition's stores complex at Shirshitti but failed with many casualties.
Diana	Set of army positions established during the Dhofar War on the mountains overlooking Salalah to provide protection for the airfield.
Dhofar Liberation Front (DLF)	Organisation formed in the early 1960s to fight for the independence of Dhofar. Was later transformed into PFLOAG.
Dragon, Operation	Launched in western Dhofar by the Jebal Regiment in the opening days of February 1973 to draw enemy troops and supplies away from Operation Simba; a full day of heavy fighting left numerous casualties on both sides.
Falaj (pl. aflaj)	Typical Omani water channel, generally originating in a mother well near the base of a hill or mountain and carried down the incline in a tunnel punctuated by additional maintenance wells until it breaks the surface just before cultivation or a village. Originally Persian in origin.
Firqah (pl. firqat)	One of a number of paramilitary groups established during the Dhofar War using surrendered enemy personnel from the *jebali* tribes and organised along tribal lines.
FN	*Fabrique Nationale*, modern Belgian rifle used by SAF.
Ghafiri and Hinawi	The two major tribal confederations of Oman.
Hedgehog	Set of small fortified positions built on the perimeters of RAF Salalah to protect the airfield and station during the Dhofar War.
Hammer Line	Series of patrol bases established in 1974 to counter enemy groups between the Hornbeam Line and Midway road.
Hilwah, Operation	Final operation of the Dhofar War which cleared the Dara Ridge, the last territory held in Dhofar by the opposition.
Hisn, al-	Sultan's palace in Salalah.
Hornbeam Line	Wired and mined barrier erected in late 1973 and early 1974, with regular manned positions, running north onto the mountains from Mughsail on the western Dhofar coast.

Hunter	British-built combat aircraft acquired by the Sultan of Oman's Air Force from Jordan during the War.
Ibadi	One of the earliest sects of Islam to emerge from the Sunni or orthodox mainstream; the Ibadis established themselves in Oman early in the Islamic era, and the Ibadi Imamate, under a succession of elected Imams, was the traditional form of government until the early nineteenth century; Ibadis constitute about half the Omani population today, including the ruling Al Bu Sa'id family.
Imam (and Imamate)	Elected religious and secular leader of the Ibadi sect of Islam; the Imamate constituted the traditional form of government in Oman until the beginning of the nineteenth century; Imam is also used to denote the leader of other Islamic sects and movements.
Intradon, Operation	Operation designed to reassert Omani sovereignty over the Musandam peninsula in the wake of reports of Iraqi backed insurgent activity and fears for the stability of the nascent UAE. Involved British troops, ships, armoured vehicles, the TOS and the SAS.
Jebal	Hill or Mountain.
Jebali	Person from the mountains.
Jaguar, Operation	Operation launched in October 1971 by two squadrons of the SAS with *firqat* support to clear the eastern *Jebal*. The Operation established the first permanent position in the area at White City.
Jason, Operation	Operation mounted to round up nearly eighty people in northern Oman in late 1972 and early 1973 in association with a Popular Front plot to cause disruptions in the north; a number of those arrested were executed.
Khareef	The local name for the monsoon which brushes the Arabian peninsula in Dhofar from June to September often causing dense fog.
King Charles Street	Synonym for the FCO.
Lakh	Indian unit of measurement: one lakh equals 100,000, 100 lakhs equal one crore.
Leopard, Operation and Leopard Line	Launched in late October 1971 to complement Operation Jaguar by establishing a stop-line of patrol bases between Mughsail on the coast and a position on the Najd near Haluf.

Glossary

Mahonia, Operation	British contingency plan for the invasion of the Sultanate if the PFLOAG got too close to victory.
National Democratic Front for the Liberation of the Occupied Arabian Gulf (NDFLOAG)	Radical organisation of northern Omanis with the goal of overthrowing the Sultanate government; the Front's attack on Izki in June 1970 was the immediate spur to the overthrow of Sultan Sa'id bin Taimur, but it was a military failure; the group was subsequently absorbed into the Popular Front for the Liberation of Oman and the Arabian Gulf.
National Liberation Front (NLF)	Radical organisation that fought the British in Aden and the Protectorates and formed the government of South Yemen upon independence in 1967.
PDRY	People's Democratic Republic of Yemen – see Yemen.
Petroleum Development Oman (PDO)	The main oil company of Oman. Sultan Sa'id bin Taimur granted a 75-year concession to the Iraq Petroleum Company (IPC). The exploration and production operations were to be run on behalf of the IPC by Petroleum Development (Oman and Dhofar) Ltd. The operating company had four shareholders, each with an interest of 23.75 per cent: the Royal Dutch/Shell Group, the Anglo-Persian Company (which would eventually become the British Petroleum Company, or BP), Compagnie Française des Pétroles (whose convoluted lineage would make it a predecessor of today's TotalFina-Elf) and the Near East Development Company (whose likewise convoluted lineage would make it a subsidiary of today's ExxonMobil). The remaining 5 per cent stake was held by a fifth shareholder, Partex. Lack of success, combined with worsening logistical problems and a glut of oil on the world market, led most of the partners to withdraw from the venture in 1960. Only Shell and Partex opted to remain in Oman to continue the search for oil. The first export of Omani oil took place on 27 July 1967. A month before, the Compagnie Française des Pétroles rejoined the partnership by taking over two-thirds of Partex's equity share, resulting in the following shareholding in the company that by then had changed its name to Petroleum Development (Oman): Shell 85 per cent, Compagnie Française des Pétroles 10 per cent and Partex 5 per cent.

Popular Front…	Radical development of the Dhofar Liberation Front; known variously as the Popular Front for the Liberation of the Occupied Arabian Gulf (PFLOAG, 1968–72), the Popular Front for the Liberation of Oman and the Arabian Gulf (PFLOAG, 1972–74) and the Popular Front for the Liberation of Oman (PFLO after 1974).
Provost	British-built aircraft used by the Sultan of Oman's Air Force in the 1950s and 1960s.
Rainbow, Operation	Elements of the Muscat Regiment travelled overland from northern Oman to Salalah to search for early rebels in the first SAF operation in Dhofar.
Rapier	British-built anti-aircraft guided missiles acquired by the Sultan of Oman's Air Force in the 1970s.
Riyal	Currency of the Sultanate of Oman, divided into 1,000 Baizas. The new currency was called the Riyal Saidi briefly during 1970.
Rupee	Indian currency circulating widely in Oman and the Gulf until 1970.
Sayyid	Used throughout the Islamic world as an honorific title for descendants of the Prophet Mohammed. Employed uniquely in Oman as an honorific for members of the ruling Al Sa'id family.
Shaikh	Head of a tribe or a section of a tribe, also used as an honorific title for religious figures and older notables.
Simba, Operation	Launched in 1972 to establish a strategic army position on the Dhofar-Yemen border at Sarfait.
Skyvan	British-built transport aircraft acquired by the Sultan of Oman's Air Force in the 1970s. Able to land on very short runways and very useful especially before sufficient helicopters were available.
Strikemaster	British-built combat aircraft acquired by the Sultan of Oman's Air Force in the early 1970s.
Sultan (and Sultanate)	After the Al Bu Sa'id rulers dropped their claims as Ibadi Imams at the beginning of the nineteenth century, they adopted the title of Sayyid and the ruler later became known as Sultan; the country was known as the Sultanate of Muscat and Oman. It was renamed the Sultanate of Oman in November 1970.

Tenable, Operation	Activities by a squadron of British Royal Engineers carrying out civil-development projects in Dhofar during the latter stages of the Dhofar War and until 1977.
Trucial Oman Scouts (TOS)	British-officered unit established to patrol the Trucial States in the 1950s and 1960s, and later forming the nucleus of the independent United Arab Emirates' Armed Forces; originally Trucial Oman Levies (TOL).
Wadi	Valley, ravine or dry river bed.
Wali	Governor of a town or district.
Wilayat	Region under the control of a *wali*.

MAPS

The Middle East

Taken From: [http://www.un.org/Depts/Cartographic/map/profile/mideastr.pdf]

Oman

Taken From:
{http://www.intute.ac.uk/sciences/worldguide/html/983_map.html}

The Strait of Hormuz

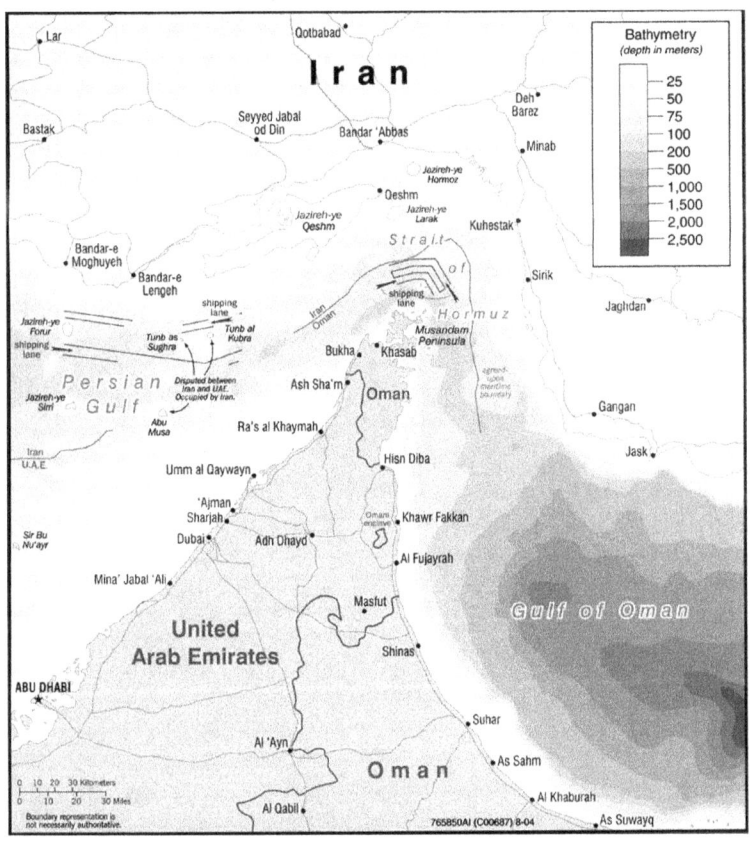

Taken From:
[http://www.lib.utexas.edu/maps/middle_east_and_asia/iran_strait_of_hormuz_2004.jpg]

The Musandam Peninsula

Taken From:
John Townsend, *Oman: The Making of the Modern State*
(London: Croom Helm, 1977), p.9.

Dhofar Including Lines

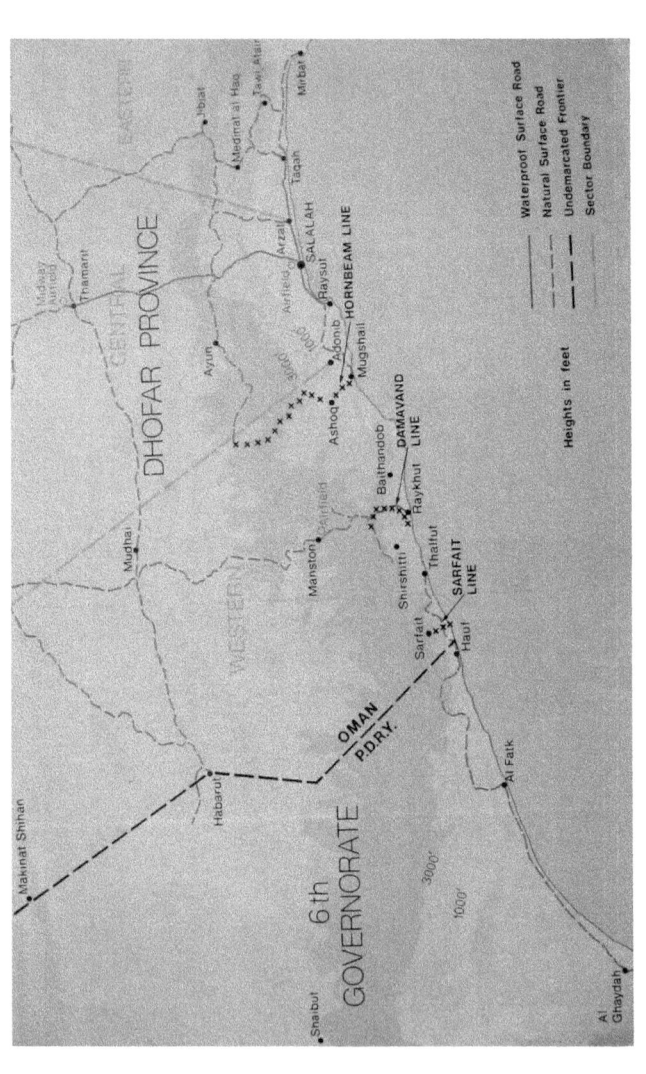

Taken from:
DEFE 13/779, Dhofar Campaign, Summary of Events.

INTRODUCTION

OMAN: BETWEEN THE *PAX BRITANNICA* AND THE WORLD

Un bienfait perd sa grâce à le trop publier
Pierre Corneille – Théodore

Situated at the end of the Arabian Peninsula and washed by the warm waters of the Indian Ocean, Oman is a land of history and tradition but it is also today a modern, peaceful, stable and prosperous place in marked contrast to its neighbour Yemen. Oman though, has had its fair share of conflict in its long history and especially in the twentieth century. This record of conflict is one in which Britain has often played a crucial role. It is Britain's role in the successful conclusion of Oman's last conflict, the Dhofar war, and the creation of a strong modern administration in Oman which is the focus of this book.

An understanding of Oman's strategic value is of crucial importance in order to comprehend the country's significance for Britain. The Sultanate occupies the entire south-eastern corner of the Arabian Peninsula with a coastline totalling some 1,200 miles on the Indian Ocean, the Gulf of Oman and even a short section within the Arabian/Persian Gulf.[1] Oman is adjacent to the sea lanes through which, shipping transiting the Suez Canal from Europe to Asia must pass. Of even greater importance is the fact that Oman holds sovereignty over the Musandam Peninsula, which juts out into the entrance of the Persian Gulf and forms part of the Strait of Hormuz, which is 'one of the world's most critical maritime chokepoints',[2] rivalling such places as the straits of Dover, Gibraltar, Malacca and the Suez and Panama Canals. Oman shares control over this strategic stretch of water with Iran and every year millions of barrels of oil are transported through the narrow passage on their way to supply the global economy. In addition, being one of just two Gulf states with an Indian Ocean coastline, Oman is a potential transit route for oil pipelines from the interior linking with terminals on the shores of the Indian Ocean should the Strait of Hormuz be closed for a long period. Therefore because of its geographical location, 'Oman, many would argue, might well be spelled with italics by geo-strategic cartographers'.[3]

As the price of oil increased during the early 1970s, Oman was rapidly becoming if not a major player in the oil world then a not insignificant one. It was only after decades of searching for oil in Oman that production began in 1967. In this respect Oman was the latest Gulf state to begin producing oil, with a mere 57,000 barrels per day (bpd) produced in 1967 and an export total for that year of 21 million barrels. By 1969 oil exports had reached 120 million barrels and production 328,000 bpd. Exports subsequently reached a high of 134 million barrels in 1976.[4] Given the prevailing oil market conditions in the 1970s a new source of oil on the world market would have augmented supply at a time when demand was increasing, thus removing some of the pressure for price rises. This would have been useful to Britain especially as the first oil shock hit. What is perhaps of greater importance is the role which British oil companies were playing in the opening up of the oil industry in Oman. Shell was the major shareholder in Petroleum Development Oman (PDO) and during a time of increasing competition from the big U.S. oil companies, a country where British oil interests could once again take the lead was important for British prestige, as well as for the health of one of Britain's leading companies. As Ian Skeet put it, Oman was 'a friendly and independent state in the South East corner of Arabia, where, with luck, oil [could] be found by a company that was not Aramco of Saudi Arabia'.[5] Here was oil coming from an Arab state with no ties to OPEC, with minimal consciousness of Pan-Arab unity and a friendly and trustworthy leader with extremely close links to Britain.

Britain and Oman have a long history; this link grew stronger during the 1970s when Britain gave significant support to Oman in its time of need, as she had done on numerous occasions in the past. Oman was suffering from a major insurgency in its southern province of Dhofar which had begun in 1965; a rebellion which was heavily influenced by Marxist ideology[6] and was supported by Communist controlled South Yemen, China and the USSR. By 1970 the counterinsurgency campaign was going badly, the rebellion threatened to spread to the north of the country and had the potential to destabilise the whole region and open it up to Soviet domination. What was needed was a change of approach, one which would undermine the basis of the rebellion and create a new era of hope. In July 1970 this new era arrived after Sayyid Qaboos bin Sa'id overthrew his father Sayyid Sa'id bin Taimur in a virtually bloodless coup. Britain then extended the existing, not insubstantial, assistance it already gave to Oman and over the following six years the tide of rebellion slowly turned.

What was different to previous British interventions around the world was the context, and in light of this, the extent of the British involvement. This was not the 1870s when European states were questing for ascendancy, new colonies and spheres of influence. This was the 1970s and the world had changed a great deal in just a century. Britain had fallen a long way from her pre-eminent position of the 1870s, having largely retreated from her empire she was no-longer the engine of the global economy. In a bi-polar world, under the shadow of the two superpowers, her once powerful military no-longer possessed a truly global reach. Indeed by 1968, London had declared that it would withdraw militarily 'East of Suez' including the Persian Gulf, the last bastion of British control and dominance, where she had enforced the peace for many decades.

Given this context, it is interesting to discover what made Britain take the apparently contrary step of committing a not insubstantial amount of her comparatively scant military resources and expending significant time and political capital intervening in Oman, while at the same time proceeding with the withdrawal of British forces from the wider Gulf region, where their presence had been welcomed and when there was no demand for them to leave. It is therefore important to ask questions about why the decision to intervene in Oman was made and how that decision was reached. This starting point naturally leads us to want to explore other questions surrounding the issue of this seemingly dichotomous British step, beginning in particular with the idea of national interest. If Oman was important enough to Britain for her to take such pains to come to her assistance, then Oman must have something to give Britain in return. In a world where altruism is a rare luxury, there must have been some benefit to London for it to commit its scarce resources to aid Oman.

This book therefore examines two specific areas. Firstly, what British policy was towards Oman, both during the period 1970–76 and before, how it changed over time and who the key players in the formulation of policy were. Secondly, it explores the extent of British involvement in Oman both materially and in terms of direction, influence and even control. Thus, the main focus of this work is Britain's foreign policy decision-making towards Oman and the subsequent implementation of those decisions. A lesser focus is upon the idea of the national interest, how a state decides what is in its interests, who within the state apparatus had inputs into decision-making over Oman and how the idea of national interest itself was used in the policymaking process.

What happened in the Sultanate during this period is particularly interesting because of the positive outcome that was achieved by those involved, principally Britain, in securing for Oman the prosperous and secure position it enjoys today. The example of what was achieved in Oman, during a difficult period of history both politically and economically for Britain stands as an example of what can be done given the right approach. By examining how Britain went about this process of combating an insurgency and helping build a state virtually from scratch during the retreat from its last major sphere of influence we can hopefully learn key lessons from one of Britain's least known foreign policy successes of the twentieth century.

Before moving on to the detail of the case it is important to examine the situation Britain was facing in the post-war period, especially in the Middle East, and more specifically the Gulf and Oman.

Britain's Post-War Position

Just as after the First World War, Britain seemed only to have gained as the victor of the Second World War with a seat at the top table as one of the 'Big Three'. Yet the foundations of this edifice of British power and dominance had been irreparably damaged by the total war which had been waged over the previous six years. There have been many studies exploring Britain's foreign policy and position during the second half of the twentieth century; much of them, for obvious reasons, detailing Britain's declining power, both economic and military, as well as the decolonisation of the British Empire. Many of these studies can be seen to be somewhat in response to the former U.S. Secretary of State, Dean Acheson's, comment of December 1962 that 'Great Britain has lost an Empire and not yet found a role'.[7] They chart Britain's loss of power and seek to understand how and why this decline came about. It is probably perfectly natural though that in the broad scheme of things 'shifts in the global economic balances, gradually impinge upon the political and military balances'[8] and that throughout history empires come and go. What is most interesting is how these changes in power balances were handled.

Easily the most striking development for Britain in the post-war world was the dissolution of the Empire. Going from an Empire controlling around a quarter of the world's surface, which had been built up over 300 years, to a few scattered remnants, was a process which took just three decades. Of course a country does not just 'lose' an empire and it is in part Britain's decline in pre-eminence in other areas which led to the loss of its colonial possessions and spheres of influence. This book deals with Britain's handling of its departure from its last sphere of influence – the Gulf – and in particular with how its engagement with Oman and its problems helped to facilitate Britain's exit from the region leaving behind stable, secure states. Since all of this occurred at the end of the empire an understanding of what led to the process of decolonisation and British decline is essential.

Many trace Britain's economic decline back to the late Victorian era and point to persistent concerns that Britain's economic performance was simply not good enough even at the height of Empire. Some conclude that in addition to nations which industrialised later than Britain swiftly eroding her head start, 'Britain's weakening performance in world trade stemmed from growing weaknesses in industry at home'[9] specifically a lack of investment and increasing inflexibility. While it would be absurd to suggest that by decline, Britain experienced a descent towards poverty, there was an increasing difficulty for Britain in maintaining a place among the major economies after 1945, 'the fundamental change was a loss of economic power: commercial power, bargaining power, financial power. Britain had become a much smaller fragment of the world economy with much less influence on the behaviour of that economy'.[10] The impacts of this fall in economic performance are key to understanding the reasons for British decline in other areas.

Clearly there is a correlation between a nation's income and its ability to pay for its defence and this was evidently the case for Britain, especially in the light of its dire economic situation in the aftermath of the Second World War. Thus Britain's economic decline described above is a major factor in the decline of British military power. It has also been argued that in addition to the economic situation it was imperial overstretch that led to difficulties for Britain in this sphere. Roger Tooze further suggests that some of Britain's economic difficulties were created 'largely as a result of government expenditure [especially on the armed forces] and the continuation of Sterling's reserve role.[11] Britain's responsibilities after 1945 were considerable and both Conservative and Labour governments displayed a willingness to carry out these responsibilities. Commitments though, plainly outweighed capacity. Thus the desire of government to continue to play a global role stretched both the economy and the armed forces to the limit.

In addition to this classic dilemma of scarce resources and unlimited requirements, the Cold War environment and the advent of nuclear weapons changed the nature of defence, as did the arrival of multilateral defence organisations like NATO. Policy was therefore shaped by a combination of responsibilities, financial constraints, politics, new technology and new military doctrines. All of these factors led to a number of changes in British Defence Policy including: the acquisition of nuclear weapons and the development of deterrence policy, increasing focus on the defence of continental Europe,[12] withdrawal 'East of Suez', a process of slashing defence budgets and consequently a massive reduction in the size of the armed forces and the cancellation of many modern weapons systems.[13] All of this left Britain much less of a military force than she had once been. As with economic decline however this was all relative to the military might of the superpowers and Britain remained an important power.

Declining economic and military power clearly also contributed to the process of decolonisation. The debates surrounding the reasons for Britain's retreat from Empire highlight a number of important themes. While the British Empire was clearly never the coherent entity its name suggests, comprising as it did formal and informal control and high levels of autonomy for some of its constituent parts even in its heyday, the beginnings of imperial decline can be seen even before 1945. Yet as John Darwin states 'if by "end of empire" we mean the final disintegration of an imperial system pivoted on British military and economic power, then it was in the post-war years that collapse began'.[14] In deciding the reasons for Britain's decolonisation the historiography has divided itself into four main areas: the economic, the domestic, the international and resistance from the colonised.

Clearly Britain's economic decline as detailed above played a role in decolonisation. Thus poor economic performance undermined Britain's ability to play a world role and in this very role – the devotion of resources and manpower to defence and to maintaining Sterling's position – took away resources needed for investment in the economic base, thus 'subjecting the economy to debilitating bouts of deflation'.[15] There is also a school of thought which stresses not a decline but a divergence of economic interests within the Empire with the colonies increasingly looking beyond Britain while at the same time Britain's economy was moving towards the continent, making the Empire less of an asset than it had been. A further school attempts to demonstrate that there was a switch to a form of neo-colonialism. As old-style colonialism no longer met the needs of business it became prudent to hand over power to locals perceived as moderates rather than radicals. As Darwin states, some see the end of empire 'not [as] the end of an era but merely a subtle and Machiavellian shift of technique'.[16] Cain and Hopkins see that 'neo-colonialism can undoubtedly be found in parts of the former empire but so too can a new form of post-imperial capitalism'.[17] Neo-colonialism is clearly a contentious theory, as Darwin states, 'far from having a single formula, and a single purpose... Britain had many other aims in mind besides promoting the interests of international capital'.[18]

Domestic causes behind decolonisation are often cited. There is a certain subset of the literature which names 'a sharp change of attitude in Britain towards empire and the burdens of the role'.[19] The possession of an empire came to be seen as an embarrassment even a moral wrong, especially when seen in the light of Hitler's attempt to gain an empire of his own. Others point to a change in public opinion, which reflected the fact that the majority of the British people had no interest in empire and were 'quite unwilling to see scarce resources preserving it',[20] although the public remained perhaps more concerned with British world power in its more abstract sense rather than the simple possession of colonies. Politicians, while cloaking themselves in rhetoric about Britain's continuing world role, tended to be more pragmatic than dogmatic. Yet they too wished to see Britain continue as a global power.[21] It is difficult though to see that there was a pure loss of will, but instead there was merely a more hard-headed sense of balancing expenditure with the benefit derived from the investment.

Changes in the international situation after 1945 undoubtedly offer a more convincing explanation for decolonisation. The change from a multipolar to a bi-polar structure was clearly a dramatic development. Britain was evidently dwarfed by these new powers and could not compete, either in terms of manpower, resources or weaponry.[22] Indeed both of these superpowers were proclaimed to be ideologically opposed to imperialism and the United States (U.S.) exhibited a degree of resentment towards supporting allies at massive expense while at the same time these allies maintained colonies from which the U.S. was economically excluded. While these are attractive arguments it is unclear that the rise of these two superpowers should on its own necessitate decolonisation. Empires in the past have continued to exist in the shadow of larger powers; this could also have been Britain's position. In the aftermath of the Second World War, Britain was able to recover all of its colonies and maintain an impressive level of power despite the changed circumstances. Even the Cold War soon persuaded the U.S. to revise much of its anti-colonial feeling. But the Cold War did change things for Britain. British leaders 'had to be prepared to take on new strategic burdens if necessary while being prepared to yield with as much grace as possible where American demands for a change of imperial policy became insistent'.[23] Clearly the defeat of the Dutch and French also gradually undermined Britain's colonial position. Yet the alliance with America also 'allowed Britain to remain a global power'.[24] Whilst the changing international environment undoubtedly placed new pressures upon Britain and served to strain an already overextended power still further, the U.S. had the ability to both undermine and strengthen Britain's position.

The fourth reason for decolonisation examines the challenge to British rule presented by colonial nationalism and rebellion. It is evident that the ability to maintain control can quickly break down when the acquiescence of the ruled disappears. Thus the international pressures experienced by Britain may well not have led to decolonisation if pressure for independence had not been exerted by the colonies themselves. New superpower sponsors clearly encouraged nationalism and gave colonies a new outlook and source of economic support. Nationalism though was a powerful ideological force in its own right and the doctrine of self-determination quickly became overwhelmingly accepted in both the colonies themselves and on the wider international stage.[25] In addition, the tactics used by nationalists from boycotts, civil disobedience, campaigning in the *metropole* to outright insurgency and terrorism undoubtedly added to the pressures placed on Britain's resources and made continuing occupation politically and materially difficult.

While it was in fact the combination of these four factors which led to British decolonisation, differing weight is given to each in the historiography. John Darwin in *Britain and Decolonisation: The Retreat from Empire in the Post-War World* attempts to give a balanced and complex account of decolonisation but he does suggest 'that it may have been changes at the international level – in particular the Second World War and its aftereffects – that served as the trigger for an infinite series of transformations that cumulatively destroyed the old pre-war relationships of the imperial powers with the regions of colonial rule and semi-colonial domination'.[26] While Wm Roger Louis and Ronald Robinson in their article *The Imperialism of Decolonisation* take a similar approach and question the simplicity of the idea 'of British enfeeblement as the prime cause of imperial demise' and the notion that the imperial centre caved in under the combination of 'infirmity in the metropole and insurgency in the provinces' since 'colonial emancipation is not necessarily a sign of metropolitan weakness'.[27] They also question the simple neo-colonial case and instead take an approach which places rising American power at its centre. They state that 'the post-war Empire was more than British and less than an imperium. As it survived, so it was nationalised and internationalised as part of the Anglo-American coalition. It acted more like a multinational company that after taking over peoples' countries was hiving them off again, one by one as associated concerns'.[28] Although in the end 'there was no American conspiracy to take over the Empire: American influence expanded by imperial default and nationalist invitation'.[29]

For Britain in particular, the ending of Empire in the post-war world was one of the major changes in her foreign policy. While many view the handover of Hong Kong to China in 1997 as the final symbolic end of Empire,[30] in reality Britain's withdrawal from the Gulf in 1971 marked the real closing of the final chapter of the British Empire story.

Yet, the post-war theme for Britain 'is not one of steady decline. Rather the motif is one of decline, revival and fall',[31] which is also true of the British position in the Middle East.

The Middle East (and the Gulf)

Britain's position in the Middle East and her retreat from that position in the post-war decades is one of the most important aspects of the end of empire.

Britain, as is explored in detail in the following chapter, faced many difficulties in the Middle East and by 1960 had been forced to retreat from Palestine, the Suez Canal Zone and its paramount position in Iran. In his important work, *The British Empire In The Middle East 1945–1951*, Wm Roger Louis highlights how the Labour government struggled to maintain British influence in the region by adapting to Arab nationalism, in order to maintain the broader edifice of empire. Faced with nationalism and American anti-colonialism he charts how this attempt failed, despite the fact that the Americans increasingly began to see the British Empire 'as a bulwark against Communism'.[32] The defining event for Britain in the region was without doubt the Suez crisis of 1956. Elizabeth Monroe's *Britain's Moment in the Middle East*, paints a portrait of inexorable decline in the region with Prime Minister Anthony Eden's policy over Suez marking the point when Britain's influence in the Middle East finally ended.[33] John Darwin states rather contentiously that Suez led 'to the abandonment of all British claims to manage Western interests in the Middle East'.[34] Ritchie Ovendale meanwhile paints a more cautious picture detailing a slow, ordered transfer of power in the region from the British to the United States especially in the aftermath of the crisis.[35] Keith Kyle sees that it was clear that 'the post-war assumption, not ever adhered to completely, that Britain could safely be left to take the lead when the West was dealing with the region, had abruptly ended'.[36]

Although the Suez crisis clearly damaged Britain and led to change in many areas, the extent to which it represented the turning point of Britain's fortunes in the region and the amount of damage it caused to Anglo-American relations is much debated. Undoubtedly Britain would be much more cautious after Suez but it was not entirely evident that Britain would simply be a 'junior partner'. There remained aspects of Anglo-American competition, yet according to Tore Petersen there was no 'American conspiracy to evict the British from the Middle East, but rather two great powers who were unwilling and unable to define their respective roles in the area...only when the Americans [saw] threatened what they considered their vital interest, did they censure the British'.³⁷ Others perceive the American role differently, seeing American fears of British mishandling of nationalism leading to Soviet influence that necessitated American political involvement coupled with 'mercantile ambition, as the United States government wanted to supplant British with American oil companies'.³⁸ While the transfer of power to the Americans highlighted by Ovendale has much merit for the Levant, especially after Suez, others take the more neo-colonialist line that instead of forcing an inexorable retreat, Suez in fact stimulated a rethinking and reformulation of the meaning of empire, its utility and costs. Gordon Martell suggests that the 'retreat from empire' was not so much a simple, reflexive response to demands from below but a conscious effort by those from above to find new ways of exploiting the opportunities that the world beyond Europe offered them. Retreat and abandonment may, on closer examination, turn out to be something more ambitious, an attempt to divest the imperial enterprise of unprofitable ventures and to reinvigorate others. In other words moving from overt political control towards political influence.³⁹ Martell even goes as far as to argue that 'neither the British nor the French regarded themselves as pawns of the Americans in the Cold War, but rather [involved in a game] in which they attempted to move the powerful new American piece around the chess board in the Middle East, Africa and Asia'.⁴⁰

In the aftermath of the Suez crisis and especially 'after 1960, the British were to commit themselves more and more to an east of Suez defence role'⁴¹ yet by 1968 that role too had been abandoned. As Wm Roger Louis suggests, this was 'because of the decision of Harold Wilson's government to rescue the British economy by taking severe measures including the evacuation of all troops'.⁴² The decision to withdraw 'East of Suez' and especially from the Gulf might also be seen to fit with conceptions of neo-colonialism. Ending a conspicuous scene of British dominance for one of influence, would naturally be a logical step, as a new relationship with vital oil producing states would attract much less unwanted attention, whilst still affording economic advantages. Equally the premise of lack of resources, economic crises and loss of will or as Saki Dockrell shows in *Britain's Retreat From East of Suez*, a combination of the above which had only worsened after Suez, led the Labour government to gradually move away from Britain's traditional commitment to the 'East of Suez' role.

Britain's role in the Middle East mirrored the decline, revival and fall pattern established in other parts of the Empire. As Britain was forced out of Palestine, Egypt and Iraq attention was instead switched to the Gulf where British influence was more secure, but this last remnant of the *Pax Britannica* could not remain immune from the events and pressures of the outside world forever. It was perhaps fortunate that the decision to withdraw from the Gulf came before those pressures became irresistible and Britain was able both to leave the region in its own time and to build capacity, legitimacy and stability before departure; in marked contrast to the withdrawal from Aden and the South Arabian protectorates.

This decision to withdraw 'East of Suez', whether taken because of economic pressures or a desire to convert dominance into influence, clearly left a lot of issues to be resolved and was to leave many of the leaders of the states of the region in a difficult position having never known anything other than British protection.

Oman

After the 1968 announcement of the withdrawal 'East of Suez' Oman was left hanging between the safety of the *Pax Britannica* and the dangers of the modern world. Having never been a protectorate, instead remaining an independent state, albeit with much British support, Britain could have walked away but instead, thanks to the commitment of officials and the clear national interest in assisting Oman with this difficult transitional period, Britain was to engage even more closely with the Sultanate.

Britain's role in Oman represents something of a challenge to traditional narratives of British decline and loss of will to maintain its ascendant position. The co-ordinated and calculated response to the situation facing Oman and the determination shown by both officials and key politicians demonstrates that when core national interests were threatened, a much more robust and determined British response would be apparent. This response though was different to that seen at the height of empire and was much more subtle and nuanced than previous interventions in the region.

In the scant histroiography on late twentieth century Oman, the main division over Britain's role is encapsulated by two writers whose books are actually about the Gulf but which have large sections on Oman and the British role there. Fred Halliday's *Arabia Without Sultans* is a highly critical account of Britain's role in Oman, originally published in 1974. Halliday spent time with the rebels in Dhofar and the People's Democratic Republic of Yemen (PDRY) and provides some fascinating details both of life with the insurgents and the nature of the campaign. The work is however hampered by having been written before the Dhofar war had finished and is marred by the deterministic and almost reductionist prism through which Halliday sees the conflict and the British role in Oman. Coming from a Marxist perspective and using that particular lexicography lends the book a feeling of its time, from which Halliday subsequently somewhat distanced himself.[43] The prediction encapsulated in the title of his book has clearly not come to pass, revolution did not sweep the Gulf and the traditional rulers in Arabia have further reinforced their position. Furthermore, in Halliday's book, Britain's role in the Sultanate is seen in a very deterministic manner, and is portrayed as a rather callous and rapacious actor, which is far from the picture painted by the archival sources.

At the other end of the spectrum J.B. Kelly, in his book *Arabia, the Gulf and the West*, criticises the British government for lacking the will to remain in Arabia, the precipitate retreat from Aden in 1967 arousing his particular ire. He conceives of the withdrawal from the Gulf as too rushed and he criticises the Conservative government for not fulfilling their commitment to rethinking the withdrawal. His book was written only a decade after the events he describes and so lacks a number of the sources now available. As such neither of these books contains that much in the way of factual description concerning the process of British decision-making regarding Oman, but both provide frequently ideological and thought-provoking analysis of Britain's role in the Gulf and Oman.

This book therefore aims to contribute to the existing historiography on Oman by moving away from contrasting pre- and post-1970 Oman, seen for example in the work of Ian Skeet. It also seeks to present a more balanced and nuanced view of British involvement in Oman than is currently seen in the literature, polarised as it is between those who are especially sympathetic to the revolutionary cause within Oman during this period and those who were in some way involved in the Omani administration, British establishment or in the thick of the action, fighting on the Dhofari *Jebal*.[44]

J.B. Kelly noted that a major problem was that: 'To describe in any detail the course of subsequent events in Dhofar, or even to compile a reasonably accurate summary of events is virtually impossible for want of adequate information'. He went on to say: 'a veil of secrecy was drawn over the war in Dhofar, for political as well as military reasons'.[45] J.E. Peterson has now supplied the details of the course of events in Dhofar in his work *Oman's Insurgencies*. Yet over 30 years after the events, there remains the need to look at Britain's involvement in Oman from the political perspective: how British policy was made, why was it made and what the real extent of Britain's influence in Oman was. This book aims to fill that gap. It is the first dedicated study of Anglo-Omani relations and British political, diplomatic, military and economic policy towards the Sultanate during this troubled period of change for Oman.

By exploring British government decision-making regarding Oman, this book examines how British interests were decided upon, how foreign policy was constructed and how it was implemented. Through the examination of this process this book aims to develop a better understanding of

INTRODUCTION 13

how and why Britain decided to forge a commitment to the protection of the Omani regime from what Halliday implies are 'the forces of progress and enlightenment',[46] while, at the same time, withdrawing from the Gulf and seeking membership of the European Economic Community. Whilst focusing on filling the gap in the literature on Oman and Anglo-Omani relations the analysis here also has other contributions to make to the historiography of the period.

By shedding more light on the extent of British decline, this book further challenges notions of Britain's loss of will, highlighting the reluctance of the U.S. to take over from Britain in the Gulf region and in particular questioning the extent to which the foreign policy of the Heath government was essentially Eurocentric. It is often assumed that entry to Europe was Heath's 'life ambition',[47] indeed David Sanders' states that 'the Heath government not only accepted the imposition of a discriminatory tariff against *all* non-EEC imports to Britain, but also acquiesced in the indefinite preservation of the C[ommon] A[gricultural] P[olicy]'[48] just to secure Britain's membership. Even Heath's memoirs concentrate extensively on Britain's entry to the EEC detailing the efforts he dedicated to gaining accession.[49] Yet as the case of Oman demonstrates, Britain continued to focus on interests beyond Europe. Importantly, this book also adds to our understanding of Omani history and in particular the early years of the modern Omani state by examining Britain's contribution to Oman's efforts in building a modern state and in defeating the insurgency in Dhofar.

Statebuilding and Counterinsurgency

Counterinsurgency (COIN) is suddenly fashionable again in the aftermath of the interventions in both Iraq and Afghanistan. There has been a resurgence in interest in the subject in both academic and policymaking circles, and yet there have only been a couple of recent examinations of the COIN campaign in Oman[50] and there is a strong focus on tactics. This work therefore stresses the political elements of a successful COIN campaign and highlights the importance of combining good COIN strategy with a thorough engagement with the construction of a modern state.

Britain was not just focused on winning the counterinsurgency campaign in Dhofar through the application of the tested principles of winning 'hearts and minds' that had been so successful in other theatres, with Malaya being the prime example. There was a broader strategy to undermine the rebellion than just a technical process of simply following the rules laid down by scholar-practitioners of good COIN from the period. Men such as Thompson[51] and Kitson[52] were foremost in the conceptualisation of this, focusing upon creating enough security for the population so that the rebels became isolated and legitimacy could be built through development projects. Britain's strategy in the Dhofar war went far wider than just this and combined a revised COIN strategy, a thoroughgoing policy of development and a plan to secure legitimacy both within and outside the Sultanate. Ultimately though, while the defeat of the insurgency was the catalyst and focus for much of this activity, it can be persuasively argued that the real aim of Britain's involvement in Oman was to create a secure state which could stand on its own two feet without needing Britain's assistance.

This book therefore focuses on how Britain decided upon the strategy and then went about helping the Omani state to build both physical and institutional capacity and to transform itself in a remarkably short period from a medieval space into a nation able to function effectively in the late twentieth-century's globalising world. This process would now be known as 'statebuilding'. There is a vast literature on the evolution of the modern nation state and more recently on the process of building nation states after conflict and intervention by western powers in particular. While this book does not directly engage with these debates, it is related to them and it aims to show that given the right circumstances and strategies, building a successful state in the modern world is possible.

Statebuilding is currently defined as 'constructing or reconstructing institutions of governance capable of providing citizens with physical and economic security'.[53] This is a definition which has strong resonance for what Britain ultimately wanted to see in Oman. There is also however, a link with an older form of statebuilding which is drawn from ideas of how modern states emerged and is neatly summarised by Charles Tilly: 'Statebuilding provided for the emergence of specialized personnel, control over consolidated territory, loyalty, and durability, permanent institutions with a centralized and autonomous state that held the monopoly of violence over a given population'.[54]

The idea of a state and the notion of statebuilding are underpinned by core structures and institutions and are clearly western notions rooted in the Weberian notion of the state. It is perhaps natural therefore that the type of state envisaged for Oman was based on this Weberian conception of a state[55] given that Britain had already exported the idea to its areas of influence and that Sultan Qaboos had been educated largely in Britain. That the modern state has rooted itself so well in Omani soil demonstrates perhaps that an effective idea can cross cultural boundaries and be adapted and customised to suit the local environment.

The rapid construction of a new state is one of the most challenging of tasks which requires co-ordination, determination and co-operation.

Introduction

The realisation that statebuilding is largely an endogenous process but one which can be cajoled, advised and assisted by exogenous forces is a reality which many intervening powers find difficult to adapt to. Britain's approach to *helping* to build the Omani state therefore contains important lessons for more recent attempts at statebuilding showing what many of the key elements of a successful statebuilding programme look like.

It seems that T.E. Lawrence's much quoted dictum from his *27 Articles* may be as true of statebuilding as it is of counterinsurgency:

> Do not try to do too much with your own hands. Better the Arabs do it tolerably than that you do it perfectly. It is their war, and you are to help them, not to win it for them. Actually, also, under the very odd conditions of Arabia, your practical work will not be as good as, perhaps, you think it is.[56]

Except that while this offers a guiding general principle, the role that an external actor can play in these processes can be crucial. Britain's strategy pursued in Oman during the 1970s involved engagement and support on all fronts – diplomatic, political, economic, military and developmental – in order to assist the Omani authorities with the implementation of a proper counterinsurgency strategy and to begin to build the structures, capacity and legitimacy of the Sultanate.

Approach

This book takes a broadly historical approach, towards exploring how Britain went about formulating and implementing this strategy. It uses primary source documents and interviews to establish the views of those with inputs into the foreign policymaking process. Of course, the events in Oman remain a somewhat sensitive subject even after more than thirty years. Despite the wealth of material available in the National Archives as a result of both the thirty year rule and the Freedom of Information Act of 2000, there are still some files which are subject to longer or indeed indefinite closure and of the files that are available, redactions are a not uncommon occurrence. Even those who were there and were kind enough to be interviewed, remain subject to the conditions of the Official Secrets Acts. Yet the range of material that is available still allows for a much more detailed picture of the attitudes, perceptions, arguments and agreements that went into producing British policy towards Oman to be painted. While essentially being a work of diplomatic history, an awareness of the concept of national interest will help inform the assessment of how foreign policy was made in this instance.

Defining Britain's Interests

While this book is not a theoretical one, the idea of the national interest is one which occurs throughout and it is useful to briefly mention some conceptualisations of the phrase. This overview of the concept of national interest provides an awareness of the role of the concept and affords us a clearer idea of how in general terms national interest was thought of by decision makers in Whitehall.

The 'national interest' is an oft-used phrase, although few in society give much thought to exactly what the term means and fewer still question its use. Joseph Frankel describes national interest as 'the key concept in foreign policy, [which] in essence, amounts to the sum total of all the national values'.[57] There are of course a range of feelings as to what the phrase, the national interest, means, since as Fred Sondermann says, 'many doubts and reservations attach to the concept and its use'. Yet 'the term has clearly retained currency among practitioners of foreign policy'.[58]

Frankel in his seminal analysis of the concept sees two ways in which the concept is employed; firstly, by those who use it to 'explain and analyse the foreign policy of nation-states and [secondly by] those who employ the term to justify or rationalise state behaviour'. He further divides the idea into *objective* interests which are independent of but discoverable by foreign policy-makers, these can be permanent or semi-permanent and *subjective* interests which are those which depend on the preferences of 'specific governments or elites'.[59] Those interests which are based on subjective interpretations can, and do, change as governments alter. It is of course often difficult to decide when an interest is an immutable one or is simply perceived to be so. National interest is an important concept then, because it is through this concept:

> [T]hat policy-makers understand the goals to be pursued by a state's foreign policy. It thus in practice forms the basis for state action. Second, it functions as a rhetorical device through which the legitimacy of and political support for state action is generated.[60]

It is apparent therefore that the term 'national interest' has many difficulties and complexities 'some...suggest it will not be much used in the future [by scholars]' but 'the term clearly remains a part of the rhetoric of foreign policy'[61] and as such obviously means something to those who construct foreign policy.

Since this work is ultimately concerned with British foreign policymaking in relation to Oman, it follows that we must understand what British foreign policy decision makers themselves believed the national interest to be. According to Frankel 'all statesmen are governed by their conceptions of national interest'.[62] Policymakers certainly believe national interest to be an important consideration. When asked what a definition of the essential skills of a diplomat to be, Emyr Jones-Parry who entered the FCO in 1973 replied 'I think the major one would be to identify national interest, then to work out the best way of furthering that interest'.[63] Since the term national interest is a human construct and different people can and will read different things into it depending on their experience and personal beliefs, it is important to develop a framework within which we can unpick what policy makers believed Britain's national interests to be. It seems very likely that British foreign policy makers would have erred far more towards a 'Realist'[64] way of thinking about the national interest, albeit with a more nuanced approach. The reasoning behind this supposition is derived from the international climate prevalent in the 1960s and 1970s and the patterns, codes, education and norms to which the decision makers had experienced and become accustomed. The experiences and memories which many would have acquired during the Second World War and the earlier years of the Cold War, could have done little other than convince them of the existence of an anarchic international system, the importance of Britain's continued security and therefore the necessity of pursuing and defending Britain's interests which would enable that security.

Perhaps the best combination of national interests likely to be relevant to Britain is found in Holsti's definition of 'four purposes common to all states' which he describes as 'security, autonomy, welfare... and status/prestige'.[65] This combination of purposes seems apt for Britain during this period and would likely reflect the opinions and concerns of policymakers most of whom, it seems certain, shared concerns over power and sovereignty, whilst also being aware of the importance of the welfare needs of the population at large and having a greater interest in issues of economics and a better understanding of the interdependence of the world. This is perhaps best seen in the views of Julian Amery, the Minister of Aviation in Macmillan's government and later Minister of State in the Foreign Office for part of the Heath government, who noted in the 1950s that:

> The prosperity of Britain rests on the oil of the Persian Gulf, the rubber and tin of Malaya, and the precious metals of south and central Africa. As long as we have access to these, as long as we can realise the assets we have there, we [the people of the United Kingdom] will be prosperous. If the communists take them over we will lose the lot.[66]

While issues such as these were, and indeed still are, undoubtedly the concerns of policymakers, policymaking is far from a unitary activity but something composed of competing bureaucracies, which can result in decisions which are sometimes less than fully coherent. It must also be recalled that ministers are not necessarily the ones who have all the power, 'any civil servant worth his salt will know how to steer a minister to a desired conclusion by careful briefing'.[67] Equally it is also clear that Britain has its own individual and particular interests which remain fairly constant and upon which there is widespread consensus, despite the fact that the 'national interest' may indeed shift with successive governments.

In order to explore how British policy towards Oman was developed, how it was implemented and how Britain was able to organise a successful counterinsurgency campaign while assisting in the construction of a modern state, this book is divided into seven chapters. The first, provides much of the all-important historical backdrop, against which British policy was made. The chapter begins by briefly examining some broad themes in post-war British foreign policy before focusing more closely on the security setting of the Cold War and events in the Middle East. This is followed by an examination of the historical relationship between Britain and Oman, particularly in the post-war period. The chapter thus provides the essential context to the formulation of British policy towards Oman. In chapter two, the book examines in more detail the years before 1970 and in particular Britain's decision to withdraw 'East of Suez', the structure of her relationship with Oman and how British policy towards Oman changed and evolved over this period. Chapters three, four and five cover the initial post-coup period from July 1970 until the resignation of Tariq bin Taimur as Prime Minister in December 1971. This is the most important time for Britain's relationship with Oman. London faced no competition for influence but there was a great deal to achieve in a short space of time and the inexperienced Sultan was reliant on British advice, expertise and resources. Since British policy had three broad pillars these are examined during these critical first 18 months in more detail. Chapter three is primarily interested in the debates in Whitehall surrounding the military and financial aspects of this period and shows how policy was made and implemented during this time. On the military side the reshaping of the counterinsurgency strategy and direct British military assistance to the Sultanate is explored. There is also a particular focus upon the formation of formal stated British national interests in Oman which then guide policy creation. Chapter four is focused on political and economic reform, especially the British preoccupation with development as the centrepiece of policy and the emergence of structures of governance in the Sultanate. Britain knew that while it may be easier to do everything alone, it was not a long term solution. Instead it would help build state structures and the ability to administer these. This chapter explores the difficulties and dilemmas of that approach. Chapter five is concerned with diplomatic issues and the policy of securing international recognition for the new regime in Oman and how Britain was involved in this process. Chapter six deals with the remainder of the Conservative government's period in office, from 1972–74 and the changes in British policy towards Oman during this period, focusing especially upon why Britain sought wider regional help in Oman and how it went about facilitating the process. Finally, chapter seven deals with the impact of the change of government in Whitehall on Britain's policy towards Oman, the effects of the defence review process of 1974–75, the eventual victory in Dhofar and Britain's military disengagement from the Sultanate. The book concludes with a summary of the main themes and the contribution this work makes to our understanding of Britain's role in Oman, the process of policymaking in this period and how Britain was able to help defeat an insurgency and aid the building of the modern Omani state.

CHAPTER 1

THE CONTEXT OF OMAN'S IMPORTANCE TO BRITAIN

> Le profit de l'un est le dommage de l'autre
>
> Montaigne, *Essais*

> There is more respect to be won in the opinion of this world by a resolute and courageous liquidation of unsound positions than by the most stubborn pursuit of extravagant and unpromising objectives
>
> George Kennan

In order to provide context and an understanding of why Oman was important to Britain, a familiarity with some of the broad themes in post-war British foreign policy is essential. Undoubtedly, the most important issue for the British government was the Cold War confrontation which had emerged by 1948. Most of the post-war events in the Middle East, an area of traditional importance for Britain, have the Cold War as their crucial backdrop. But it is also important to be aware that the Middle East in this post-war period also saw a number of the growing Anglo-American tensions, as Britiain tried to cling to its preeminant position in the region. This traditional ability to dominate the region was gradually reduced after 1945, leaving the Persian Gulf as Britain's main sphere of influence. This process was paralleled by an increase in the intensity of Britain's centuries old interactions with Muscat. Without an understanding of Britain's historical links with the Sultanate, the general regional situation facing Britain and London's post-1945 commitments to Oman, much of what is to follow would lack proper perspective.

Themes in British Post-War Foreign Policy

Britain, despite a dramatic decline in capability and power since the end of the Second World War, still felt it needed to exercise a role on the world stage. While no longer a member of the 'big three', Britain's 'task was to maintain the appearance of at least being as equal as possible with the remaining 'superpowers'. In hierarchical terms, this meant claiming a special position for Britain, just 'below' the U.S. and the Soviet Union perhaps, but definitely 'above' the other European allies.[1] Both Britain and France had much to gain in terms of national interest and self-perception in maintaining a world role and in talking up that role.

Shorn of much of her former power, Britain was left to rely upon her influence and prestige in numerous international fora to win people around to her way of thinking and to get other nations to act in ways which were beneficial to her interests. The hangover from Britain's glory days was a pool of respect and positions at the top tables of power in world politics. It now became of vital import to utilise the tools of 'soft power' – influence and prestige – to precipitate change through the use of activities such as agenda setting.[2]

Britain had three main aims in her foreign policy during the 1960s and 1970s, aims which were broadly similar to those of other powers. Firstly, Britain saw it as important to use its influence to ensure that the agreements and actions of others were in its favour. Secondly, it had also to fulfil Britain's needs by ensuring security and economic prosperity, which meant alliances and trade agreements, protecting Britain's overseas investments and ensuring the free flow of raw materials into the country. Thirdly, it needed to protect and improve its status and prestige 'to generate deference, respect and sometimes awe among others'.[3] The use of influence and negotiation to protect British security and economic progress became increasingly important.

Naturally, British foreign policy is, in the words of the 1907 Crowe Memorandum, 'determined by the immutable conditions of her geographical situation on the ocean flank of Europe, as an island state with vast overseas colonies and dependencies, whose existence as an independent community is inseparably bound up with the possession of sea power'.[4] Much of this analysis remained true even after Britain had divested itself of its colonial empire, which it had largely completed by the mid-1960s. In the light of this position, Britain's foreign policy outlines were laid out in 1948 by, none other than, Sir Winston Churchill. His famous 'three circles', with Britain at the centre, showed that the country could play a role 'not as a regional power but emphatically as a global power with global interests to defend'.[5] Britain could, and should play a leading role in all three circles without concentrating on just one, thus increasing its influence and prestige as a power which straddled three areas of major importance. These 'three circles' enabled Britain to maintain its 'special relationship' with the U.S., which as a true superpower, offered Britain a great deal of security. The European circle had always been important to Britain because of the need to prevent one power dominating the continent and in the modern era, because of the increasing economic ties to the rapidly expanding West European economies. Finally, the third circle represented Britain's former colonies now embodied in the Commonwealth and also Britain's leading position in international groupings such as the United Nations.

From the mid-1960s a great deal was happening in all three circles, as Britain slowly shifted away from the global and Atlantic circles and moved closer to the previously marginalised European circle. The Atlantic relationship had been repaired by Macmillan after the damage done by Suez. The signing of the Partial Test Ban Treaty in August 1963 was seen by President Kennedy and Prime Minister Macmillan 'as a peak in their partnership'.[6] Yet 'less than three years later the relationship was looking distinctly 'normal', and the precipitating issue was Vietnam'.[7] The British decision to withhold support for the U.S. position and her choice to withdraw East of Suez 'made Britain less useful in its [the U.S.'] efforts to contain the Soviet Union'.[8] Relations were not significantly improved when Edward Heath replaced Harold Wilson in 1970, 'Britain's emphasis was on being a good European',[9] and as such the 'special relationship' appeared to be of lesser importance.

With the end of Empire, Britain had hoped that the Commonwealth could play a useful role in providing prestige and an alternative to Empire, which had originally been the foundation of Britain's global role. Unfortunately, the Commonwealth quickly lost 'whatever coherence it had possessed as an economic and diplomatic block'.[10] Two major nails in this aspiration's coffin were the handling of Ian Smith's Unilateral Declaration of Independence of Rhodesia in 1965, which greatly upset many of the recently independent African members of the Commonwealth, and the rather humiliating retreat from Aden in 1967, which was followed with the announcement of Britain's decision to withdraw East of Suez in 1968. Eventually the Commonwealth became 'little more than a forum in which ex-colonial states could express their disapproval of the British government's domestic and foreign policies and at the same time seek to secure special concessions from Britain's overseas aid budget'.[11] The lack of real benefits, aside from ensuring continued access to raw materials, naturally enough, saw Britain move away from this circle, while still being heavily involved at the United Nations.

By the late 1960s the post-war concentration on the Commonwealth and Atlantic circles was largely coming to an end. This process would, however, take some time. Britain began looking to move back towards the European circle as early as the end of the 1950s, when London led the effort to establish a rival to the European Economic Community (EEC) in the form of the European Free Trade Area (EFTA) which was agreed in 1959. A few short years later in November 1961 negotiations began to join the EEC 'and continued until January 29, 1963, when, on French insistence, they were finally broken off'.[12] Having been rebuffed by De Gaulle, Britain retreated from the idea of Europe somewhat and did not reapply until May 1967. This attempt was again opposed by De Gaulle, who remained unconvinced 'that Britain had become sufficiently European in orientation to be prepared to give up its special links with Washington'.[13] In 1970 Edward Heath's Conservative government was elected and vigorously pursued a third British application for membership of the EEC. The case for British membership of the EEC rose as the value of the Commonwealth declined, but was essentially an economic one. Britain's trade profile changed 'dramatically, with the focus...shifting away from the Empire/Commonwealth and towards Europe'.[14] At the end of the 1940s 'Britain conducted about half of her foreign trade with the Commonwealth and with other members of the Sterling Area, and about one-quarter with Western Europe; by the early 1970s this position had been reversed.'[15] Heath's efforts culminated in the signing of the UK-EEC accession treaties in January 1972, with Britain entering the Community on 1 January 1973.

Denis Healy stated in 1969 that Britain had been transformed 'from a world power into a European power'.[16] Yet despite the rhetoric and the moves back into the European 'circle', it is clear that 'Europe was never seen as an *alternative* to the other two circles'.[17] The British accession to the EEC was seen as adding to British influence, not at the expense of the Atlantic or Global roles but in addition to them. This is seen in the behaviour of successive British governments towards Europe and the fact that Harold Wilson called a referendum on Britain's membership of the EEC in 1975. Britain would continue to play a role in all three areas, as envisaged by Churchill. London had merely evened up the balance of the circles by moving a little further into the European sphere. By doing this, Britain would gain economically and politically and thus its interests would be better served. The three circles idea helped make British policy more pragmatic and gave Britain greater influence and prestige in the world, which is arguably exactly what its national interest required. Yet throughout this period of change and transformation the Middle East would still remain of vital import to Britain.

Britain, the Cold War and Problems in the Middle East

In the post-war world, Communism, and more specifically the Soviet Union, represented a direct threat to that most important of national interests: the very security of the state. The thought of hundreds of thousands of Soviet troops sweeping across Europe in armoured columns was a prospect which filled people with dread in the immediate post-war years. This alarming idea was only to be replaced by something much worse, the detonation of Moscow's first nuclear weapon in 1949. The idea of multiple nuclear strikes on British cities was, without doubt, a powerful stimulant upon the government not only to expend considerable amounts of time, effort and resources on preparing to protect the state, but also on attempting to avert a conflict in the first place.

Along with the more fundamental aspects of the Cold War, London also faced a lower level threat to other interests.[18] This took the form of Communist inspired and often supported insurgencies in British colonies, such as Malaya. These insurgencies affected British interests in a number of ways. Firstly, they were costly in terms of 'policing' and combating. Secondly, if successful, the new Communist government would naturally look to Moscow rather than London for its imports and exports, thus depriving Britain and the West of markets and often, more importantly, essential sources of cheap raw materials which were crucial to economic growth. It was not only British colonies which were subject to insurgencies, left wing rebellions swept the globe, from Vietnam to Cuba and seemingly everywhere in between.[19]

Britain saw itself menaced on two fronts. Its political and economic ties with the developing world were threatened, and the British nation was potentially minutes away from a nuclear holocaust. Of course though, aside from the insurgencies and revolutions in the third world, the Cold War never became a 'Hot War' but crises such as Cuba in 1962 merely added to the perception that war could very well break out. Proof of a Soviet intention to attack was not really necessary, in order to create 'a sense of vulnerability and fear'.[20]

Somewhat separate from the issue of broader East-West relations which were, of course, of vital import to Britain's national interests, was the potential for the spread of communism/nationalism in the former empire and other traditionally important spheres of influence. The most significant of these spheres was the Middle East. In this region, Britain was to face constant threats to its interests and its position as the pre-eminent power in the region. At the end of the First World War, Britain and France had been the paramount powers in the Middle East.[21] By 1945, France was no longer a viable force in the Middle East, leaving Britain as the undisputed power in the region. British dominance stretched from the deserts of Tripolitania in the west, through Egypt with the massive concentrations of troops along the Suez Canal, into Palestine, Trans-Jordan, Iraq and southern Iran, across India to the jungles of Burma. Yet the foundations of this edifice of British power and dominance had been irreparably damaged by the total war which had been waged over the previous six years. This was not immediately recognised in the Middle East and many in Whitehall also failed to identify the extent of the damage, seeing Britain's enfeeblement 'in the immediate aftermath of the war as temporary'.[22] This proved to be illusionary.

The postwar Labour Government with its perilously limited resources found itself facing a huge range of difficult decisions and problems. At home these included: reconstruction, demobilisation and economic stagnation. Britain also faced numerous complex foreign policy decisions including, the partition and decolonisation of India, the first frosts of the coming Cold War and the reconstruction and reordering of the British sector of Germany. In addition to these, were the demands of the British electorate who voted for the Labour Party on the basis of its promised implementation of the expensive conclusions of the Beveridge Report, which were, what the British public saw to be their reward for six years of blood, toil, tears and sweat.

Britain Under Pressure: The Suez Base and Palestinian Questions

Britain had been severely weakened by the war, and the many conflicting demands on its budget meant that the weakness of its position would soon become apparent. Yet, 'the Middle East, to the British Military mind, had an importance second only to the United Kingdom...the security of the British Commonwealth depended on protecting the United Kingdom, maintaining vital sea communications and securing the Middle East as a defensive and striking base against the Soviet Union'.[23] Tensions were however, growing, not just between the Western allies and the Soviets but also between the Western allies themselves.

The first source of this had its roots in the pre-war era, when Britain had decided to limit Jewish immigration into its already fractious Palestine mandate, the Zionists decided to focus their efforts on getting Washington on their side through threats of electoral punishment. On 30 April 1946, the day of the publication of the Anglo-American Committee of Inquiry, President Truman endorsed the report's main proposals including the admission of 100,000 Jews into Palestine, without consulting Britain. This was just the start of a period of Anglo-American disagreement over the issue. The Palestine question was not the only matter which clouded the atmosphere between the two powers in the Middle East and elsewhere. The U.S. had cancelled co-operation with Britain and Canada in the arena of nuclear development and 'some Americans were worried that Britain was securing too large a share of the world's potential oil reserves'.[24]

Britain was also coming under pressure in other areas of the Middle East. Egypt formally requested the renegotiation of the 1936 Anglo-Egyptian Treaty on 20 December 1945. In the ensuing negotiations the Egyptians asked for much more than the British had expected. London had thought that the renegotiation of the Treaty would in the end result in British withdrawal *to* the Canal Zone. But Egypt was demanding nothing less than total British military withdrawal. After discussions within the cabinet, Britain agreed to withdraw and to inform the Egyptians of this at the outset of the second round of talks. This was quite an incredible position for Britain to take considering the historic importance of the Suez Canal for the British Empire. It caused a great deal of heated debate in the Commons and the newspapers. For Churchill, it was 'a very grave statement, one of the most momentous I have ever heard in this House'.[25] Despite this major concession, the negotiations for a new Anglo-Egyptian Treaty failed, in large measure due to misunderstandings over the future of the Anglo-Egyptian Condominium of Sudan: the Egyptians wanting union and the British insisting that the Sudanese retained their right of self-determination.

Egypt was not the only place where relationships with Britain were being renegotiated; Jordan became independent on 22 March 1946 – albeit with continuing British subsidy of £2 million per annum and a Defence Pact with Britain, including the right to station troops there. Britain's Anglo-Iraqi treaty of 1930 was also subject to renegotiation, the result of which, the 1948 Treaty of Portsmouth, was greeted with political upheaval in Baghdad and the rapid repudiation of the document by the Iraqi regent.[26] This in turn led Britain and Jordan to negotiate a new treaty in early 1948 which would give the agreement an appearance of being one between equals. At the same time, Britain was attempting to gain the mandate for the former Italian colony of Cyrenaica in the hope of using it as an alternative Middle Eastern base after the withdrawal from Palestine and the Suez Base.

It had not taken long for the British position in the Middle East to be challenged, with perhaps the only satisfactory resolution being found in Britain's relations with Jordan. These challenges also undermined Britain's standing in the region and showed the weakness of the British position. Perhaps the worst event for Britain's reputation was the withdrawal from Palestine and the subsequent establishment of the State of Israel. Against this background, 'Britain had difficulty in negotiating alliances with Arab states'.[27]

Despite these pressures, the Middle East remained of vital importance to Britain. The rapid freezing of the Cold War in the aftermath of the Berlin Crisis of 1948, soon led Washington to modify what seemed to be its earlier rather anti-British stance in the region. This had been caused by a post-war return to traditional U.S. anti-colonialist attitudes[28] and differing interpretations of the Atlantic Charter,[29] whose provisions were 'deceptively vague'.[30] 'After 1947 [though] even the United States acknowledged the need to maintain the British presence there' it being agreed that, 'the Middle East was to be a British and Commonwealth area of responsibility'.[31] This change in U.S. attitude coincided with a quieter period for Britain in the Middle East. The Egyptian dispute had entered a standoff phase. With no negotiations taking place, the British garrison remained firmly entrenched in the Canal Zone. Relations with the U.S. over the Middle East continued to steadily improve, with informal political and strategic talks taking place in Washington in the autumn of 1948, after which the American delegation 'recommended that their government strengthen the British strategic, political and economic position throughout the Middle East'.[32]

Elsewhere in the late 1940s, Britain and the U.S. were increasingly working together in a manner not dissimilar to that seen during the Second World War, with the establishment of NATO in 1949 and extensive combined planning in case of a Soviet attack on the Middle East.[33] There was also close collaboration in the intelligence sphere, as well as in the Korean War, with the dispatch of the Commonwealth Brigade which was one of the largest troop contributions to the UN-sanctioned intervention aside from that of the U.S. itself.

Ôte-toi de là que je m'y mette: Britain, the U.S. and Iranian Oil

The threat posed to British interests by nationalism in the Middle East is perhaps clearest in Iran. The proposed nationalisation of the Anglo-Iranian Oil Company (AIOC) was symptomatic of an Iranian desire to rid themselves of foreign influence and gain control of their country. British and American approaches to this crisis were clouded by the Cold War and economic rivalry between the two powers. The economic significance of Anglo-Iranian oil for Britain is difficult to overstate, with the refinery at Abadan representing Britain's largest single overseas asset. The tax revenue paid by the company was extremely important in the context of Britain's post-war economic recovery, as was a cheap source of oil priced in sterling. On 28 April 1951 the Nationalist, Mohammed Mossadeq, became Prime Minister. Just three days later the Shah gave Royal Assent to the nationalisation of the

Anglo-Iranian Oil Company, which had for so long been Mossadeq's dream. In the early days of the crisis Britain seriously considered military intervention[34] but President Truman and the U.S. government remained entirely opposed to the use of force. The U.S. Secretary of State Dean Acheson suggested negotiations with Mossadeq, indeed the U.S. worked hard to encourage Britain to make concessions. The Permanent Under-Secretary at the Foreign Office, Sir William Strang said: 'The main difference between us and the Americans in this affair seems to be that to the Americans, in the fight against communism in Persia, the Anglo-Iranian Oil Company is expendable... It is not possible for us to start from this premise'.[35]

At length, Britain persuaded the Shah to replace Mossadeq. This act was greeted by intense public anger and the Shah was forced to reappoint him. He then felt bold enough to reject settlement proposals by Churchill and Truman. By this stage the Americans were coming around to Britain's way of thinking and began to see Mossadeq as a threat. Helped by the change of administration on both sides of the Atlantic, with the election of President Eisenhower and the return of Churchill as Prime Minister, a more interventionist policy began to take shape. In the U.S., the anti-Mossadeq plan 'Operation Ajax' and in Britain 'Operation Boot' were hatched, which were both parts of the same plan. These paid off on 19 August 1953 when Mossadeq was toppled, arrested and imprisoned for three years. With Mossadeq gone, Sir William Fraiser the head of Anglo-Iranian Oil tried to restore the company's exclusive position in Iran. Washington and Fazlollah Zahedi (the newly appointed Iranian Prime Minister) considered this to be unacceptable. The new U.S. Secretary of State, John Foster Dulles, described the company's position as 'completely unrealistic' he even threatened a decline in Anglo-American solidarity if the company pushed for the status quo ante. Fraiser had 'taken Anglo-American harmony to the brink of destruction'.[36] In February 1954 the U.S. Government put together proposals for the formation of a new consortium to produce Iranian oil. Under the terms of the plan the Anglo-Iranian Oil Company would have a 40 per cent share; another 40 per cent was to be in the hands of the five major U.S. oil companies with the remaining 20 per cent to be shared between Royal Dutch Shell and the French company CFP. This was, while better than nothing for Britain and the AIOC, rather less than they had hoped for. In this crisis then, Britain had initially received little help from Washington, even earning American disapproval of its 'Plan Buccaneer': the invasion plan to protect the refinery. The U.S.' attitude then changed dramatically, demonstrating the fickle nature of the relationship. The final result of the U.S. gaining a 40 per cent share in what had once been a 100 per cent British concession also further demonstrates the importance placed by states on securing their interests.[37]

Even during the Iranian crisis the tide of events elsewhere threatened British interests in the Middle East. On 8 October 1951, Egypt unilaterally abrogated both the 1936 Treaty and the 1899 Condominium Agreement. The Treaty had formalised Britain's presence in the Canal Zone and the Agreement had provided for the joint Anglo-Egyptian administration of the Sudan. Egypt wanted the British out and the unity of the Nile valley. Sir Ralph Stevenson the ambassador in Cairo, commented in a minute to Foreign Secretary Herbert Morrison in October 1951 that 'the effect of the evacuation of the British oil personnel from Abadan suggested that Egypt might draw a lesson from Iran's firm stand, since it had been proved that the British could not stand up to force'.[38] The abrogation 'strained Anglo-Egyptian relations almost to a state of war'.[39]

U.S. fears over the Communist threat in the Middle East led Washington to look for a more solid bulwark and reliable ally in the region. It was quickly realised that this could not be achieved bi-laterally and that a collective defence agreement along the lines of NATO would be more appropriate. The formation of a 'Northern Tier' of states, initially envisaged as including Turkey, Iran and Iraq, as a shield for the rest of the region was seen as a solution. Pakistan also expressed interest in the idea. Turkey's NATO accession in 1952 persuaded Britain of the idea's worth. Progressively, over the course of 1954 and 1955 agreements were made between Turkey, Iraq and Pakistan. Britain too adhered to the Baghdad Pact agreement in April 1955, partly seeing it as a way of maintaining influence in Iraq after the collapse of its influence elsewhere. As the Northern Tier concept took shape in the form of the Baghdad Pact, 'Washington while endorsing the move suddenly became aloof and declined to become part of the arrangement'.[40] Washington was fearful of imperilling its 'Project Alpha' plan to secure Israeli-Palestinian peace.[41] It was also worried that Israel would expect a defence guarantee and was concerned that Washington's involvement might be taken as a red rag to the Soviets. 'London was increasingly infuriated over what it saw as ambivalent American policy, difficult to discern and continually changing... which appeared in part to be dictated by American oil interests'.[42] The U.S. only became more involved in the region after 1957 once the events at Suez had further undermined British influence in the Middle East.

The Suez Crisis

If relations with Washington over certain issues in the Middle East had been strained, what was to come next would bring the tension to the surface for the whole world to see. The Suez Crisis precipitated one of the most serious breaches in Anglo-American relations. Washington not only refused to support Britain but also openly condemned Britain and France at the United Nations.[43] This was in large part because the British government had kept Washington in the dark about the operation and had ignored frequent American warnings about not using force.[44]

On 19 July 1956 the U.S. withdrew finance for the Aswan Dam project, largely because Nasser had recognised Communist China.[45] The Dam project formed the centrepiece of Nasser's plan to industrialise Egypt using cheap hydro-electric power. In response, on 26 July 1956 Nasser nationalised the Suez Canal as a way of raising revenue to fund the dam. Britain was outraged and protested vociferously. The Suez Canal was, after all, half owned by Britain after Disraeli had bought the bankrupt Khedive's shares in November 1875, partly to prevent the French from obtaining full control but also because since the construction of the Canal, which Britain had attempted to prevent. Britain quickly came to rely upon it to speed up shipping and connect the Empire,[46] indeed over time the Canal came to be seen as Britain's 'jugular vein'. President Eisenhower however, observed that until Egyptian administration of the Canal proved to be incompetent or unjust then there was nothing to do.

Despite American warnings, Eden planned for military action. An elaborate plot was hatched which would enable Britain and France to retake control of the Canal and to do so in the guise of peacekeepers. It is clear that while Britain feared the loss of the Canal, Nasser's rising influence throughout the Middle East also played a role in the decision to resort to force. In a Cabinet meeting on 24 October 1956 Prime Minister Eden stated: 'It is known that [Nasser] is already plotting coups in many of the other Arab countries; and we shall never have a better pretext for intervention against him than we have now as a result of his seizure of Suez'.[47] France had been working with the Israelis on a plan and after much suspicion was overcome by Israel who had major misgivings about Britain's reliability after their difficulty in obtaining arms which had been frequently delayed[48] and traditional French concerns about *perfide Albion*, Britain too was drawn into the plot. At Sevrès, just outside Paris, on 22 and 23 October 1956 it was agreed that Israel would provide the pretext by invading Egypt and menacing the Canal. Israel had sufficient excuse to take such action because of the raids which had been carried out on its territory by the *fedayeen* and Egypt's insistence that there was a state of war in existence between the two states. Britain and France would consequently invade Egypt in order to protect the Canal Zone and separate the two belligerents.[49]

In the two weeks before the Israeli invasion, there was a virtual blackout of information between the U.S. and Britain. The action at Suez was an unwelcome distraction from the Presidential and Congressional elections on 6 November. The attack also derailed a plot to install a pro-Western government in Syria and deflected attention away from the brutal suppression of the Hungarian uprising which almost destroyed the Warsaw Pact. It seems that the two sides had rather different priorities. Britain wanted the Canal to be secure for British shipping and Nasser taken out of the picture so that he could do no more damage to Britain's regional interests. The U.S. on the other hand wanted to attract Nasser into the anti-Soviet camp.

The Americans realised the extent of the Anglo-French-Israeli collusion, when the French Foreign Minister Pineau informed the American Ambassador Douglas Dillon what had been going on. The U.S. response was twofold. Firstly they distanced themselves from the British and French at the UN and secondly they put considerable economic pressure on Britain and in particular did nothing to prevent the run on Sterling. On 12 November 1956 the Chancellor, Harold Macmillan, had to inform his colleagues of a loss to British reserves of $328 million[50] – approaching 20 per cent of total overseas currency stocks. There were fears that Britain might go bankrupt. Anglo-American relations had been taken to the brink. Britain and France were forced to withdraw their troops from Egypt with military victory in sight, leaving a jubilant Nasser more powerful than ever. Overall, 1956 had not been a good year for Britain in the Middle East. In March, Sir John Glubb, the British commander of the Arab legion in Jordan was dismissed from his post; Britain feared it was losing yet more influence. The fall out from the débâcle at Suez, both to Anglo-American relations (temporarily) and to Britain's standing in the Middle East as a whole cannot be underestimated. At a time when Arab nationalism and in particular President Nasser appeared in the ascendant, Britain seemed moribund in its ability to protect its regional interests.

On 14 July 1958, the pro-British Hashemite Monarchy of Iraq was overthrown and a hostile Republican regime established. The shockwave from the Iraqi revolution was felt across the region, but this was especially so in Lebanon and in Jordan. Lebanon had been experiencing upheaval prior to the events in Iraq but in the aftermath the situation further deteriorated. In January 1957 President Eisenhower had promised help to those states in the Middle East menaced by Communism. This announcement, supported by a joint resolution of Congress, became known as the Eisenhower Doctrine. Soon after, Jordan, Iraq, Lebanon and Saudi Arabia openly adhered to the Doctrine. Thus when Lebanese President Camille Chamoun was forced to appeal to the West for help because of rioting and threats of civil war caused both by his adherence to the Doctrine and the fall out from the Iraqi revolution, the U.S. could not risk the collapse of a friendly state and on 15 July 1958 sent in the Marines.[51] Britain supported this move. At the same time, the shock wave from the revolution in Iraq was felt strongest in Jordan, which, in response to the formation of the United Arab Republic between Egypt and Syria on 1 February, had formed the Arab Union between Iraq and Jordan just a fortnight later. The new Iraqi government promptly withdrew from the Arab Union and King Hussein of Jordan fearing that his would be the next Hashemite throne to be toppled, requested British intervention.[52]

A clear divide had been opening between states in the Middle East which had republican and Arab Nationalist regimes and those which were ruled by dynastic regimes which feared Nasser's popularity and expansionist tendencies. This trend, which later became known as the 'Arab Cold War',[53] led to great tension between Egypt and Saudi Arabia. Washington increasingly began to see Nasser's growing relationship with the Soviet Union in Cold War terms and was increasingly less conciliatory towards Cairo.[54] Consequently just two years after the damage caused by Suez, Britain and America were working together again in support of common interests – namely showing both Arab revolutionary forces and the Soviets that the major Western powers were willing and able to support pro-Western regimes.[55]

With the final loss of the Suez Canal zone, Britain was in need of a new base in the Middle East. This formed part of a broader review of Defence needs and spending which was contained in the 1957 Defence White Paper. This, among other things, ordered the development of the V-Bomber force and ended conscription. It also focused Britain's defence needs on three key areas outside of Europe. Singapore as the focus of Britain's interests in the Far East, Kenya in Africa and it 'identified Aden as the lynchpin of British power projection east of Suez'.[56] From then on, Aden with its perfect natural harbour, vast British Petroleum (BP) refinery, status as a vital bunkering port for ships of all nations and a strategic position as a base became increasingly important to British interests: this was soon demonstrated by events in Kuwait.

In 1961 Kuwait gained its formal independence from Britain. Within days it was menaced by the threat of an Iraqi invasion and Britain was asked to send troops to protect the Emirate's territorial integrity. In dealing with the Iraqi threat in 1961 London and Washington were able to co-ordinate a joint policy, with the White House prevailing upon the Saudis to mediate in the Iraqi-Kuwaiti dispute; they also gave Britain their full diplomatic backing and offered to send a small U.S. Naval force to the area to assist Britain and to show their support. The Aden base was used as an important staging post for 'Operation Vantage'[57] the code name given for the deployment of British troops to protect Britain's interests in Kuwait. The reasons

THE CONTEXT OF OMAN'S IMPORTANCE TO BRITAIN   33

for U.S. support for Britain on this issue are clear: they too did not wish to see an anti-Western regime controlling Kuwait's vast oil reserves and needed to reassure their Saudi partners that Iraq would not pose a similar threat to their territorial integrity. There have since been questions raised about the true nature of the Iraqi threat but the episode clearly shows the extent to which both major Western powers were still willing to support what they saw to be friendly nations and protect their interests in the Middle East.[58] Despite this willingness to work together, British and American interests in the region would not always coincide.

Attack or Retreat: Yemen and Aden

In September 1962 a Republican coup in Yemen came to directly threaten British interests in Aden and Southern Arabia. This was especially the case when Nasser sent Egyptian troops soon after the coup, to prop up the fledgling Republican government which faced a growing fight-back from Royalist forces.[59] By 1965 Cairo had committed approximately 55,000 troops to the campaign. This move was clearly seen by the British government, under both the Conservatives and Labour, as damaging to Britain, despite the Foreign Office urging caution.[60] In March 1965 the newly appointed Labour Foreign Secretary, Michael Stewart, noted that 'Nasser had as an objective to eliminate the Western influence in the Middle East... as an immediate aim he wished to expel us from Southern Arabia and thus render untenable our position in the Persian Gulf'.[61]

The U.S. was among the first states to recognise the revolutionary government in Sana'a, despite opposition from their Saudi allies. Indeed, the Saudis were providing aid to the Royalist forces of the deposed Imam. The U.S. then proceeded to put 'the strongest pressure on the British Government to follow their example in a move so plainly contrary to British interests that it is surprising that the Foreign Office even considered it'.[62] General von Horn, the Swedish commander of the UN observer mission sent to Yemen said of Washington's move, that 'beneath this apparently logical decision by the Americans lay a baser policy aimed at embarrassing the British in Southern Arabia, linked with a desire to further their own oil interests in the Arabian Peninsula'.[63]

Britain had, in the early 1960s, been working hard to form a federation of the protected states of Southern Arabia and Aden, an effort which came to fruition with the establishment of the Federation of South Arabia in January 1963. In addition to the problem of whether or not to recognise the Republican regime in Yemen, Britain was also facing a growing insurgency sympathetic to Nasser inside South Arabia in the Radfan mountains, as well as intense trade union activity inside Aden.[64] With the growing influence of Arab nationalism and rising disaffection in South Arabia, 'supported both materially and ideologically by President Nasser', 'the scene was set for a sustained programme of subversion and revolt against British rule'.[65]

Britain confirmed in 1963 that it was her intention to 'lead the people of South West Arabia as soon as is practicable to sovereign independence',[66] but with the retention of a sovereign base area in Aden. This soon became a pledge to grant independence by 1968. The new Labour government of Harold Wilson elected in October 1964 appeared much less interested in the problem as 'in the end it seemed to matter little to HMG whether or not the Federal government survived'.[67] In the 1966 Defence White Paper the pledge of independence by 1968 was reaffirmed and it was also announced that 'we do not think it is appropriate that we should retain defence facilities there after that happens'.[68] This decision angered many, especially since the Royalist forces were in the ascendant in the Yemen and attacks in the Federation were relatively small in scale. The British decision in part led to Nasser breaking an agreement to reduce the number of troops in Yemen. This, in the words of the former commander of the Federation's army, 'was like giving burglars advance notice of one's intention to be away from home'.[69] The decision led J.B. Kelly to say that 'Britain betrayed her trust and ran away from her responsibilities in South Arabia'.[70] As the Labour MP Anthony Crossman wrote in his diaries, the Foreign Secretary George Brown was 'passionately determined to get out of Aden at all costs'.[71] The situation in Aden and the protectorates continued to deteriorate, from 1963 onwards 57 British personnel were killed and 651 wounded.[72] As order collapsed in South Arabia and the Federal government disintegrated, Brown informed the cabinet on 7 September 1967 that this fact meant that Britain no longer had to honour the commitments it had made to that government. British troops subsequently withdrew from Aden without formally handing over power on 29 November 1967 in what J.B. Kelly describes as 'an abandonment...a shameful end to British rule'.[73]

After what J.B. Kelly calls, 'the débâcle in Aden',[74] it was necessary to reassure the rulers in the Gulf that despite the decision to quit Aden, 'Britain was fully determined to continue fulfilling her treaty obligations'[75] towards the Gulf States. To this effect the Minister of State at the Foreign Office, Goronwy Roberts was dispatched to soothe any fears. A statement was made by Denis Healey, the Minister of Defence, in which he said, 'It would be totally irresponsible for us to withdraw our forces from the area'.[76] Yet two months later Goronwy Roberts was back in the Gulf to inform the rulers that due to 'financial stringency' the British government was 'now compelled to rescind the assurances given to them only two months previously about the continued maintenance of a British military and naval presence in the Gulf to fulfil Britain's treaty obligations'.[77] Britain would now be removing her military presence from 'East of Suez' by the end of 1971. In reality, the decision to withdraw was, in Kelly's eyes, taken not just for economic reasons, mainly the devaluation of sterling but also because 'Labour party leaders, whether or not they wholly shared it, were increasingly exposed to the hostility of party ideologists to the practice of empire'.[78] Even Wilson admitted that 'the economic argument, though strong was not necessarily conclusive'.[79] Some believe that 'Europe played a major role in determining Britain's role East of Suez'.[80] It is clear that although there are a variety which led to this momentous decision, what it signified was that the race was now on to prepare for Britain's withdrawal from the Gulf.

This meant attempting to leave the region in a position to take care of its own affairs and face the outside world alone. Britain therefore began a complex process of boundary delineation, dispute resolution, accelerated modernisation and, since the states in question were so small, the attempt to create a federation of the nine lower Gulf States. This was to be a lengthy and fraught process which would eventually lead to the formation not of a federation of nine but of seven states, which went on to form the United Arab Emirates.[81]

A great deal had changed for Britain in the Middle East, following the end of the Second World War. Initially Washington had allowed Britain to maintain its paramountcy in the region during the early post-war period. Over time though, the U.S. became increasingly concerned to secure for itself greater influence in the region, often at Britain's expense. There was a gradual ratcheting up of tension and rivalry between the two powers throughout the period. Yet there was also a not inconsiderable amount of co-operation. In operations where goals were shared the U.S. was quite willing to back Britain up, this is especially evident during the Kuwait incident in 1961.

But, while it appears that Britain was often concerned primarily with practical matters and its economic position, Washington was increasingly anxious about the Communist threat in the Middle East, whilst equally, seeking to both secure and expand its influence, both political and economic. The U.S. was quite content for Britain to shoulder burdens, especially in the Gulf, but was less willing for Britain to get in the way of U.S. economic interests.

The post-war period in the Middle East was filled with a mixture of Anglo-American mistrust followed by co-operation. Anglo-American discord was merely a symptom of the gradual loss of British influence in the region and the slow but steady takeover by the U.S. of the dominant role in the Middle East and Britain's confinement to the status of junior partner. This change was always likely to be turbulent. What prevented it from permanently turning sour was the ever-present Soviet threat and the need of both parties to contain communism. The change of dominance is one of the most important themes in post-1945 Middle Eastern history. But this change was not linear and, as the case of Oman demonstrates, it was Britain that in some areas continued to play the predominant role.

Anglo-Omani Relations: An Historical Overview

In pre-Islamic times Oman formed part of an extensive commercial network and invested the profits from trade into sophisticated irrigation systems called *aflaj*. Subsequently agriculture became highly developed. In 796 CE Oman fell under the rule of Ibadi Imams who managed to control tribal rivalries and founded commercial colonies in India, Aden and Iraq. Under the Ibadi system the Imam is nominated by the elders and holds power for as long as he upholds the law and maintains the confidence of the elders.[82] The Imamate was a tribal state, containing a complex mosaic of tribes given unity by a religious authority.[83]

After centuries of patterns of rise and fall of its economic fortunes and conflict with the Portuguese, during the seventeenth and eighteenth centuries Oman experienced a revival in its fortunes begun by Imam Ahmed Bin Sa'id (1744–83) who was the founder of the Al Bu Sa'id dynasty which rules Oman to this day. He was elected Imam after defending Sohar from attack and driving the Persians from their last stronghold in Muscat.[84] Imam Ahmed was a remarkable man who on his death in 1783 'handed down a strong mercantile state with a powerful navy and control over important trade routes'.[85] His son Sa'id, however, was unpopular and was forced to step down after just one year, handing power to his son Hamed (1784–92) who moved the capital from Rustaq to Muscat. But Sa'id continued to be Imam and it is at this point that the positions of Sultan and Imam split.

Hamed's successor Sultan bin Ahmed had difficulty in managing the competing claims for power with the family and was killed in 1804 in a mutiny at sea.[86] He was succeeded by his nephew Badr who ruled until 1807, when he was in turn assassinated by his cousin Sa'id Bin Sultan.[87] Sa'id focused his attention on unifying his domains and quashing all dissent. By 1829 though, Sa'id was expending much more energy upon his empire along the East African littoral, this led to some loss of control of the interior of Oman. But during this period a new Omani golden age was born[88] with the Sultanate becoming 'a major maritime force in the Indian Ocean on a par with the European powers in the area'.[89]

Britain and Oman have a long formal relationship dating back to 1798,[90] although contact with the East India Company began as far back as 1624.[91] With Britain's growing power in India, in order to maintain lucrative Omani links with the subcontinent, the Sultan was obliged to enter into a formal Treaty of Friendship with Britain.[92] It should be noted that Anglo-Omani association was somewhat different and began much earlier than Britain's formal interactions with the tribes which would eventually come to form the other Gulf States of Kuwait, Bahrain, Qatar and the UAE. Oman would later, while choosing to have Britain conduct its foreign affairs on its behalf, remain a sovereign nation unlike the semi-protectorates of the Gulf.

The death of Sultan Sa'id in 1856 began the 'rapid decline of Al Bu Sa'id fortunes'.[93] Sa'id wished to split his dominions between two sons, Majid and Thuwayni, and made this clear in a letter to Lord Aberdeen sent in 1844. The two sons and their disinherited brother Hilal were quickly at loggerheads. It seemed that Sa'id's 'letter to Aberdeen amounted to nothing less than an open invitation to mediate in his family disputes',[94] although at this point Britain preferred to see the continuation of a unified Omani state. After years of fighting between the brothers, Rigby, the British Resident in Zanzibar, stepped in, when in 1859, Thuwayni and 2,500 men set sail to capture Zanzibar, a British warship was sent to intercept Thuwayni's force. In May 1860 the Coghlan Commission was established to arbitrate the competing claims, this resulted in the Canning Award of 1861.[95] The award led to Oman's African possessions being given to Majid and Thuwayni becoming ruler of Muscat with compensation for the loss of Zanzibari riches of 40,000 Maria Theresa Thalers paid per annum as a subsidy.[96] Later Britain was forced to take over responsibility for this payment. Aside from this however, Britain only intervened in Omani affairs when they threatened to damage British interests and so concerned itself mainly with issues of commerce and the abolition of the slave trade. Although the usual factors of the protection of British Indian subjects and 'the almost pathological fear of the French' clearly both also played a role.[97] With Oman's power and economy in decline after 1861 and a series of internal squabbles in Muscat, Britain was not greatly occupied with the country, contenting itself with security guarantees for the Sultan and the dispatch of the occasional warship.

The Sultan's control of the interior remained precarious and in 1913 the Government of India was forced to dispatch troops to Muscat to prevent the fall of the capital to the forces of the newly elected Imam Salim who was supported by the newly reconciled two main tribal factions.[98] In 1915 Muscat was attacked and although Muscat did not fall the rebellion, unlike previous attempts, did not subside. This led to the *de facto* division of the Sultanate into the interior beyond the control of the Sultan and the coast which remained under his writ. The next major intervention came in 1920 when Britain was forced to step in after the situation had descended into what Ian Skeet describes as 'virtually a state of civil war' between the Al Bu Sa'id controlled Sultanate on the coast and the Omani interior controlled by the Imam. Britain was increasingly concerned that it was only a matter of time before they became further enmeshed in Oman's difficulties. The Treaty of Sib[99] largely negotiated by the British was ambiguous and was designed to convince the Sultan that the British had 'not derogated from his overall sovereignty', while the interior tribes (the Imam was forced to recognise the agreement *ex post facto*) were led towards 'believing they had their independence'.[100] The Treaty though ensured that the *Pax Britannica* remained unbroken.

In the aftermath of the Sib Treaty, Britain took more control of the Sultanate attempting to overhaul the administrative structures especially customs and finance. Taimur Bin Faisal had become Sultan in 1913 but had no appetite for the job and asked the Viceroy in Delhi for the right to abdicate, which was refused. As such he took little interest in government and ran up debt.[101] In 1932 after Taimur's son had attained his majority, Taimur was finally allowed to abdicate and Sa'id bin Taimur was crowned Sultan. He had been educated at Mayo College, the so called 'Eton of India' and later completed his Arabic and Islamic studies in Baghdad, and the British had high hopes for his coming rule. He had inherited a state with many serious problems. There were signs of unrest in Sur and Sohar and the economy was in tatters. There was a period of drought and Muscat had significant debts with Britain, indeed 'the state was practically bankrupt'.[102] The new Sultan devoted himself to solving the problems of the country – its finances and the deep division between Imamate and Sultanate, littoral and *jebal*. He therefore expended much effort on balancing the budget, which was no easy task considering the size of his debts and the paucity of his revenues. He imposed new customs duties on goods coming from the interior to be exported, curtailed investment projects and drastically cut expenditures – including those of other members of the royal family. With these measures and the signing of an oil exploration agreement with a subsidiary of the largely British owned Iraq Petroleum Company in 1937, the Sultanate's economy was placed on an even keel. His next task was to properly reconcile Sultanate and Imamate; this was to prove much more difficult to achieve.

This task was further complicated when in August 1952, the Saudis dispatched an armed party to occupy the Buraimi Oasis, a strategically important point, which was under the rule of the Sultan of Oman and the Sheikh of Abu Dhabi. Saudi Arabia had a number of border disputes with the British protected states of the Arabian littoral but the dispute at Buraimi in the 1950s was by far the worst and would have the most severe repercussions for Anglo-American relations. The Saudis were supported in their desire to gain sovereignty over the Buraimi Oasis by ARAMCO, the American company which held the concession for Saudi Arabian oil. Indeed, 'no one was greatly surprised that the [armed] party travelled in transport provided by ARAMCO'.[103] The support of an American company for the Saudi action could have been ignored by Britain; what could not however, was the intervention of the U.S. Government who requested, when the Sultan gathered forces to eject the Saudis from the oasis, that 'both sides should remain where they were and refrain from acts of provocation'.[104] The British agreed, and ordered the Sultan to disband his forces. It was decided to negotiate with Riyadh. This led to the Saudis remaining in the oasis for more than two years whilst negotiations took place.

Eventually in July 1954 agreement was reached to submit the dispute to arbitration. Meanwhile, Saudi Arabia had been busy in the oasis and its environs 'doing its best to suborn the local sheikhs and tribesmen into denying their traditional allegiances and pledging loyalty to the Al Saud'.[105] On 17 September 1955 the British delegate withdrew from the arbitration process citing Saudi attempts at bribery. On 26 October Britain did what the Sultan of Muscat & Oman[106] had planned to do more than two years previously. It ejected the Saudis from the oasis and reoccupied other disputed border areas. This provoked what Halliday describes as 'a wave of inter-imperialist vituperation'.[107] Britain had not informed the U.S. of its plans for fear that they might inform the Saudis. This whole situation had the potential to put the Americans in a very awkward position, if, as the Saudis desired, the dispute were to be brought before the UN. Washington 'knew that the British accusations against the Saudis were true'[108] and they could either, risk not supporting Britain in the Security Council to the further detriment of relations or they could support Britain and upset the Saudis with the potential damage that could cause to the extensive American interests in the country. The Buraimi dispute not only showed the growing Anglo-American tension but also its results. The eight-year severance of diplomatic ties between London and Riyadh, 'effectively marked the end of Britain's once paramount influence with Ibn Saud'[109] and the formal handover of residual British influence in the Kingdom to the Americans.

The Imamate Rebellion

Whilst the Buraimi dispute was reaching its climax, a greater threat to Muscat and Sultanic authority was emerging, which was to create further

Anglo-American tensions.[110] When, in May 1954, Imam Mohammed Bin Abdullah Al-Khalili died, the vacuum this created led to the release of long contained feuds. Two great tribal leaders, Sulaiman Bin Himyar Al-Nabhani (Amir of the *Jabal Akhdar* and Bani Riyam) and Salih Bin Isa (Amir of the Sharqiyya and the Hirth), decided to appoint Ghalib Bin Ali Al-Hina'i as the new Imam, he was seen as a compromise candidate who would bring stability to tribal relations. The new Imam's brother, Talib, was however the power behind the throne and convinced his brother to take steps almost immediately, backed by the Saudis, which attacked what had been agreed at Sib. In November 1954 it was announced that the Imamate would issue passports, petitioned the Arab League for recognition as an independent state and cancelled the 1937 concession given to Petroleum Development Oman to prospect for oil in the area.[111] This was a direct challenge to the Sultan's authority and could not be tolerated with so much at stake. It was time to consolidate the Sultan's control over the interior before the Saudis could create any more mischief. In December 1955 the Muscat & Oman Field Force captured Nizwa and the Batinah Force captured Rustaq. In a swift operation the Sultan had regained control of the interior and was quickly given the allegiance of the tribal sheikhs, with many showing 'dissatisfaction with the Imam Ghalib'.[112] The Imam posted his resignation in the mosque and retired to his house. Sulaiman bin Himyar was placed under house arrest in Muscat, but Talib fled to Saudi Arabia where he set about raising a force he named the Oman Rebel Movement (ORM). The 'Saudis [who] had used their occupation of Buraimi to send arms to the Imamate forces'[113] were increasingly worried by the growing power of the Sultan and his desire to unify his domains. This episode had though further stirred up Anglo-American bitterness, although Britain had informed the U.S. that a major offensive was under way to defeat the rebellion in December 1955. Secretary of State Dulles 'complained that had he been informed earlier he would have urged Britain to restrain the Sultan. He also said that Saudi Arabia might now consider asking the Security Council to examine Buraimi and Oman', a response that apparently 'threw Foreign Office officials into a rage'.[114] To cap his *reconquista* of the interior Sultan Sa'id embarked on an epic journey from Dhofar to Muscat, taking in Nizwa along the way.[115]

The defeat of the rebellion was just a temporary reprieve however; as in 1957 Talib returned to the Omani interior and led a further rebellion against the Sultan, 'the situation quickly got out of hand, the Sultan asked for assistance from Britain and was given it'.[116] But Suez had shaken Britain and as Macmillan wrote in his memoirs 'to embark single-handed upon a further military enterprise, even of a modest character, seemed at first to some of my colleagues hazardous and even foolhardy'.[117] But proceed they did because 'the inescapable conclusion was that so long as the Sultan's sovereignty over Oman was not recognised, the validity of the [oil] concession he had given the British would remain in doubt. The Imamate-Saudi co-operation was liable...[to] result in the transfer of the concessions to American oil companies'.[118] It was clear that the Saudis were once more backing the rebellion, with further assistance from ARAMCO. The 'rebels, by August 1958, had received substantial supplies of weapons, ammunition and money from Saudi Arabia, and some Saudi subjects had served with them'.[119] When the British tried to stop the flow of American mines into Oman which were killing British troops, 'the Americans were brutally unsympathetic. Their reply was that they supplied the mines to Saudi Arabia under their Military Aid Programme, and it was not their concern how the Saudis chose to employ them'.[120] Tension over Oman was causing further damage to the Anglo-American relationship, Britain saw the American pressure on the issue as 'an example in the purest form of U.S. policy: it is to take no action which could possibly offend an enemy, but not to worry about the interests of friends'.[121]

The ineffectiveness of the Sultan's Armed Forces at crushing the new rebellion necessitated a significant a British commitment, including the deployment of two squadrons of the Special Air Service (SAS), RAF jets from Sharjah, elements of the Cameronians, the Trucial Scouts and a squadron of Ferret armoured cars.[122] By 1959 after a prolonged campaign, British and Omani forces prevailed and the rebellion was quashed. 'The power of the Imamate was broken and in practice, a situation was created whereby Muscat and Oman were ruled together by the Sultan'.[123] While the U.S. did little to help Britain in Oman, it also did little to prevent Britain from helping the Sultan, ultimately perhaps not wanting to push Britain too far when 'Britain was clearly assisting an anti-communist ruler'.[124] The war had exposed Britain to difficult questions at the UN, had cost significant sums of money and had strained Anglo-American relations. But once the conflict was won, it was time to consolidate and construct a more sustainable peace.

The British wanted to reinvigorate the Sultan's Armed Forces, establish an air force and linked to this, introduce a programme of civil aid and development. While it was easy to get the Sultan to agree to the further empowerment of his armed forces, the development side was rather different. The Sultan clung to his traditional way of doing things and wanted minimal development. Increasingly he came to view the British vision of how the state should be organised as being at odds with his own Sultanic version and attempted to slow the attempted British injection of new ideas and methods into the country.[125] The Sultan, after his struggle to balance the budget in the 1930s disliked unnecessary expenditure and was reluctant to fund the British development programmes. Taimur came to be described as a ruler whose 'tight-fisted policy did not even budge when his revenues increased'.[126] While the Sultan clearly cherished his British links and was thankful for Britain's help he disliked interference in Oman's internal affairs. His 'attitudes towards civil and military development were worlds apart. He opposed the implementation of a broad, unified development plan'.[127] The Sultan was especially opposed to extensive education programmes and advocated instead education for the sons of sheikhs and very limited technical training for the chosen few.[128] There were developments however, with 'important changes in the agricultural and fishing infrastructure'.[129] Taimur also continued to work hard to secure the unity of his state, his 'authority had [by the mid 1960s] become more extensive and efficient than ever before',[130] this, along with the limited developments permitted by the Sultan all 'helped in the creation of a more congenial and stable atmosphere in Oman'.[131]

Britain's foreign policy moved increasingly towards Europe in the postwar world but it was a process which was not preordained. During the same period its position in the Middle East declined. Faced with a combination of Arab nationalism, humiliation at Suez, a weakening economic position and increasing competition from the U.S. it is little surprise that Britain lost much of her earlier power in the region. The story though is not one of straightforward British decline. Throughout the period efforts were made to shore up the British position. British interests were not always simply abandoned, policies were reshaped and over time Britain focused increasingly on Arabia. Here the U.S. found the British more willing to defend their interests as exemplified during the Buraimi incident, its refusal to recognise the new Yemeni regime and the crushing of the Imamate rebellion. The U.S. when faced with British resolution stood back, 'the underlying assumption being that Britain [itself] was a *major* American interest'.[132]

During the 1950s in particular Britain became increasingly involved with Oman. This was not however a new relationship, as the exploration of the character and origins of the Anglo-Omani relationship above demonstrates; the nature of the association between the two nations was long and intertwined and would only become more so during the 1960s and 1970s. Having provided the essential background and context to Britain's overall foreign policy, her fortunes in the wider Middle East and her history in Oman. It is now important to take this analysis further by looking more closely at Britain's position in the Gulf, her relations with Oman during the 1960s and the rise of the rebel movement in Dhofar.

CHAPTER 2

EVENTS AND POLICY SURROUNDING BRITAIN'S INCREASING INVOLVEMENT IN OMAN

Hope leads us on; we may succeed or fail. The wind's not always fair that fills the sail

Al-Mutanabbi

Il faut être prudent, mais non pas timide

Voltaire

A New Era

When on 2 November 1964, Shell announced that it had discovered commercial quantities of oil in Oman, things were bound to change, Oman could soon be richer than it had ever been. But the excitement of discovering oil was somewhat tempered by an altogether more serious challenge to the Sultan's rule.

What had been a very minor rebellion against the Sultan's rule by a few disgruntled Dhofari tribesmen in Oman's southern protectorate of Dhofar, became something more serious when in June 1965 after its first conference; the newly formed Dhofar Liberation Front (DLF) launched an attack which 'officially began the revolution'.[1] The situation became much graver when in September 1968 'the Marxists displaced the more moderate nationalists in the DLF's leadership'.[2] From that time on the conflict began to escalate, as the new leadership wanted to make some real progress and not just in the Dhofar struggle. The organisation 'now aimed to liberate the entire Gulf from Imperialism, and altered its name from the Dhofar Liberation Front to the Popular Front for the Liberation of the Occupied Arabian Gulf'.[3] The British would be now faced with a fully fledged Marxist inspired rebellion with a stated aim of removing them from the Gulf. The situation was made considerably worse because 'the British retreat from Aden gave the DLF a secure ally on their south-western flank and for the first time provided a sure supply of food and equipment'.[4] A Marxist government in Aden was a sobering prospect but one which supported a movement whose aim was the eradication of imperialism in the whole of the Gulf was something which threatened British investments, regional stability, the flow of oil and worse still, could encourage the Soviet Union to take advantage of the situation and increase its influence. A proliferation of Marxist governments in the region would give the Soviet Union the opportunity to gain a foothold in that most strategic of regions: the Persian Gulf. A Communist insurgency was undesirable enough in Vietnam or Malaya but because of the importance of oil to Western societies,[5] its potential impact in Oman could not be exaggerated enough. Oman then, became increasingly key to Britain's national interests throughout the period, even as Britain's interests were on the wane elsewhere in the Middle East.

Throughout the 1960s British government thinking on the Sultanate evolved. At the same time though, mounting international attention was increasingly fixed on Oman, its system of dynastic rule generally and more specifically on Britain's role in that country. The most important period for Britain in terms of its decision to become more closely involved in Oman was undoubtedly after the announcement of withdrawal 'East of Suez', accordingly these years will be examined in greater depth and contrasted with the policy attitudes of earlier years. In addition, it is important to consider the Conservative opposition's policy towards the Gulf and the key role of bureaucrats in the formulation of policy; this in particular, is done through an examination of the perceptions of national interest and how these ideas came to inform policymaking. It was undoubtedly the changing nature of the situation in Dhofar which in the end caused the change of pace in the British involvement, consequently it is important to discern the chronology of the growing insurgency within the country and the extent of the British involvement in the Sultanate until the transformational year: 1970.

A False Dawn

In the years after the crushing of the Imamate rebellion, immediate threats to the continuance of dynastic rule appeared to be considerably lessened.

Nevertheless, neither Britain nor Sultan Sa'id were inclined to rest upon their laurels. In 1958 there was an Exchange of Letters, a method of international agreement chosen, 'in order [both] to avoid pressure for ratification and the inconvenience of unwanted publicity'.[6] In the post-Suez era, with Nasser at the height of his powers, it paid Britain to conduct her business in the Middle East more discreetly than in previous years. The agreement was designed to follow a twin track of both strengthening the Sultan's Armed Forces (SAF) and providing funds for a civil development programme, a classic strategy of increasing the number of carrots as well as the reach and weight of the stick. Under the accord Britain agreed to, 'at your Highness's request make available regular officers on secondment from the British Army, who will while serving in the Sultanate, form an integral part of your Highness's armed forces'. The agreement also provided for assistance in the establishment of an Air Force for the Sultanate, the improvement of roads, agricultural research, health and education. In return for these British-funded civil and military programmes, the RAF was given use of the airfields at Salalah in Dhofar and Masiriah Island on a 99 year lease.[7]

The 1958 Exchange of Letters put what was already a close relationship on an even firmer footing. If further proof of the Sultanate's importance to Britain was needed after Britain's role in preserving Muscat's sovereignty over Buraimi and defeating the Imamate rebellion with British troops, then the Exchange of Letters provided this. Britain was willing to risk criticism and commit new resources at a time of continuing budgetary pressure to support its ally. The Exchange of Letters was aimed in part though at reducing the likelihood of further insurrections and at giving the Sultan the strength to put down any future rebellion with his own forces, thus reducing the risk of a further potentially costly British intervention on his behalf. If this could be achieved then the value of a secure ally who did not need direct British military support to stay in control would be more than worth the costs incurred.

By the early 1960s then, the Sultanate was experiencing a 'period of relative tranquillity';[8] of course there were still various problems to contend with though. The Sultan had become the frequent target of *Saut al-Arab* radio propaganda from Cairo and as the attention began to lift the first shadows from the country, a citizen's committee headed by British MP Judith Hart[9] was formed and began to ask questions about civil rights in the Sultanate, focusing particularly (in the tradition of Wilberforce) on the issue of slavery. Naturally, of somewhat greater concern was the fact that Saudi Arabia remained bitter about the Buraimi issue. The leader of the Imamate rebellion, Imam Ghalib bin Ali, who after the final defeat of the Imamate rebellion in 1959 was now in exile in the Saudi city of Dammam, the Saudis evidently neither forgiving nor forgetting their ejection from the oasis. The Imamists were largely restricted to issuing propaganda from their bases in the radical Arab capitals of Cairo and Baghdad, although as Halliday says, by '1959 active military resistance by Imamist forces had ceased, mine laying continued into the early 1960s'.[10] None of this was however, much more than an inconvenience.

In 1962 Shell began to drill for oil in Oman. This of course excited everyone, not least British officials who thought that oil revenues would put Oman on the path to development upon which many other Gulf States had embarked. The problem was, as Political Resident Persian Gulf (PRPG) William Luce, highlighted, that even if the Sultanate became financially independent 'it would still not solve the problem of creating indigenous and effective administration and security organisations'. He stressed that the Sultanate 'can not become viable in any proper sense of the word, within the next ten years'.[11] While the prospect of oil held out hope for the future it was clear that Britain's role in Oman as the Sultan's advisor, protector and financier would continue for many years to come. If the situation remained calm as it was in the early 1960s, it would simply be a case of introducing proper administrative structures, commencing a well researched development plan and strengthening the SAF as the Exchange of Letters had envisaged in order to bring Oman into readiness for efficient self-government in the twentieth century.[12]

This plan though was already experiencing some teething troubles with the attitudes towards development held by British officials contrasting with the more reluctant and cautious attitude of the Sultan. With a budget of £250,000 per annum from Britain,[13] Colonel Hugh Boustead had been appointed to head the new Development Department.[14] He had a very difficult job indeed, and in his own recollections; '[B]efore I could start on anything, I had to organise the Department and find trained staff'. He also had to contend with the fact that 'the Sultan was, I felt very half-hearted about plans for health, education, agriculture and so on'.[15] He stayed in Oman for three years of hard won successes, and since 'his plans had to be approved by both the Sultan and the British'[16] his progress was all the more remarkable. His replacement lasted just a few months and when a more permanent alternative was found, 'the difficulties which Boustead had found in getting the Sultan to take an interest in the work of the Department multiplied... Major Ogram [Boustead's second replacement, from December 1962] could do little more than maintain what had been started'.[17] As a result development fell far behind the level of progress expected by Britain.

The reasons for the Sultan's unwillingness to develop can be put down to two main factors. The Sultan was worried about debt and did not like spending money unless it was absolutely necessary. This was because when he took over Oman in 1932 'he assumed responsibility for a pretty unattractive economic mess.' In his own words 'the Sultanate's Treasury was completely empty.'[18] Worse, the Sultan's father owed large sums to Muscat's merchant class. When the situation improved the Sultan retained a deep dislike of debt. While being fiscally conservative, the Sultan was also socially conservative and in the context of revolutions occurring across the Arab world from Egypt in 1952 to Iraq in 1958, was fearful that increased educational and economic activity would allow Arab nationalist and Communist ideas to spread and put his rule in jeopardy. The Sultan once stated the reasoning for his attitude to education to Boustead as: 'that is why you lost India... because you educated the people'. He told another of his officials when pushed on the education issue: 'where would the teachers come from, I cannot afford to pay for good teachers from England, and so they would come from Cairo and spread Nasser's seditious ideas among their pupils'.[19]

John Townsend, who was Economic Advisor to the new Omani government from 1972–75, questions why it was that during the 1960s Britain did not put much pressure upon the Sultan to become more actively engaged in development and did not do more to ensure aid given for this purpose was more properly used.[20] The Sultan was clear in his reasoning and it is unlikely that British pressure would have achieved much, as the Sultan was zealous about his political independence. It should have been more than evident that there was a problem on this score when the Sultan's reform minded brother Tariq bin Taimur left the Sultanate for Germany in November 1962. Still, Britain did comparatively little to encourage the Sultan to engage with development.

Growing Discontent

The period of relative quiet enabled the Sultan to extend his control into the interior, improve his armed forces, impose peace and stability, and for the rudiments of a development programme to emerge. Under the calm exterior however, the Imamate rebellion was beginning to have other effects. Many Omanis had moved abroad to find work in the booming oil economies of the Gulf, an even higher number of men from the southern province of Dhofar had trodden the same path. Dhofar was the personal colony of the Sultan. It is separated from the rest of Muscat & Oman by the *Jaddat al-Harasi* desert and is different in terms of its climate and is populated by a mixture of tribes distinct often in terms of ethnicity and language or some mixture of these from the tribes of the north.[21] The region has over the centuries, despite this, been heavily penetrated by Arab culture and traditions, as well as by Islam. The region is brushed by the southwest monsoon and is dominated by its own *jebal*, this means that for three months of the year it is shrouded in heavy mists known as the *khareef* which make this the most verdant corner of Arabia for part of the year.[22] Despite spending much of his time in the province, and in the later years of his rule hardly deigning to go to Muscat at all, Sultan Sa'id appeared to dislike the region's people and offered little material incentive to encourage their loyalty.

Working in the oil fields of Kuwait, Qatar, Bahrain and Abu Dhabi these Dhofaris were exposed to various left wing ideologies and saw the effect of frequent protests and strikes. They also felt the impact of both Immamate hostility to the Sultan and the various brands of Arab nationalism promoted by Baghdad and by Nasser from Cairo. Being exposed to this volatile mix of ideologies combined with the lack of progress at home it is little surprise that some were seduced.

As early as 1962 the Dhofar Charitable Association (DCA) was formed, initially under the pretence of being a humanitarian organisation. In reality it had an aim similar to that of the Imam, simply the removal of Sultanate authority, in this case from Dhofar. Little happened initially but the rapidly changing regional environment was to provide some impetus. In September 1962 civil war broke out in North Yemen[23] and early in 1963 an anti-British uprising commenced in Aden. Soon there were minor incidents of sabotage and ambush occurring in the Sultan's domains, the first instance of armed rebellion occurred in April 1963 with an assault on a truck belonging to the John Mecom Oil Company, followed up by mine laying around the province.[24]

By 1964 the DCA had combined with other radical elements in Dhofar including the local branch of the Arab Nationalist Movement (ANM) to form the Dhofar Liberation Front (DLF). In reality all of these groupings had been small and even coming together to form the DLF could only muster a number of men thought to be in the low hundreds. In the spring of 1965 the DLF suffered setbacks when around 40 of its members were captured.[25] It was at this time that the DLF held its first Congress and issued its first statement, aiming simply to destroy the Sultan's power and remove the imperialist influence. From this small base the DLF set about regrouping and to this end began active recruiting. At this stage its military activities were confined to ambushing SAF troops and minor sabotage. During this period Britain continued to regard the highly vocal Imam Ghalib as the main threat to the Sultanate.

Oman Under the Spotlight

At the same time, Oman was increasingly coming to the attention of the outside world, where a great deal had changed since the end of the Imamate rebellion of the late 1950s. The rebellion had drawn attention to Oman and the Arab nationalist states had attempted to cause trouble for Britain at the United Nations over the issue. Since Oman was not a member of the UN and the Sultan was not interested in sending someone to represent him in New York, it fell to Britain to defend both his rule and its own involvement in the country. Initially there were successes, as when on 14 December 1962 a hostile resolution calling for Omani independence and British withdrawal failed to attract the necessary two-thirds majority in the General Assembly.[26] While denying the right of the United Nations to discuss the internal affairs of the Sultanate, the Sultan did invite a UN representative to meet him. This happened in May 1963. The UN however, under the influence of the radical Arab states and eastern bloc nations always on the lookout for ways of causing 'imperialist' states pain, continued to discuss Oman. At the same time, Britain's ability to defend the Sultan in the UN General Assembly was diminishing, as increasing numbers of Asian and African states gained their independence and entered the UN, Britain and its allies found themselves outnumbered by nations who had just emerged from colonialism and wished to put as swift an end as possible to all remaining instances of the practice.

The problem here was also that the Imamate had the backing of the radical Arab states and was still very active in terms of propaganda. Nasser for example gave frequent airtime on *Saut al-Arab* and this kept international attention on Muscat & Oman generally. But it also had the effect of focusing UN debates on the complaints of the Imam, thus further enhancing his image in the eyes of Arabs and the potential threat he posed to the Sultan in the eyes of the British. Indeed a Ministry of Defence (MoD) summary of the development of the trouble in Dhofar in the period December 1962 to May 1965 states that 'the main preoccupation in the UK and in the Sultanate was the threat in Northern Oman (where incidents were still occurring) aggravated by ORM [Oman Rebel Movement] propaganda and the UN debates on Oman'.[27]

With annual attempts to pass resolutions condemning Britain's role in Oman and demanding immediate Omani independence, Britain had increasing difficulty in halting General Assembly resolutions. After holding off unsympathetic resolutions in 1963 and 1964, on 17 December 1965[28] a hostile resolution condemning Britain's presence there was finally adopted just as global attention was being focused on Britain's problems in South Yemen. On 20 December 1966[29] a further condemnatory resolution was agreed.

Britain's attempts to defend itself and Oman from UN criticism, both in the General Assembly and the Committee of 24, the UN body for ending colonialism, centred on the assertion that Oman was in fact a fully sovereign state and was in no form of colonial relationship with Britain unlike the other Gulf States. Additionally Muscat & Oman had chosen not to become a member of the United Nations and had merely requested that Britain represent it there as a matter of convenience.

The international and media pressure on Britain and Oman continued, while Britain's protestations of Oman's sovereignty fell on deaf ears. On 12 December 1967 the United Nations General Assembly adopted resolution 2302 (XXII), which, like its 1965 and 1966 predecessors took a strong stance towards the British presence and its influence in Muscat & Oman. The resolution included many strong phrases condemning British involvement in Oman and deplored 'the policies of the United Kingdom which, by installing and strengthening unrepresentative régimes in the territory, without regard for the basic rights of the people', considered both that the 'concessions granted to foreign enterprises without the consent of the people constitute a violation of the rights of the people of the territory' and also that, 'the military presence of the United Kingdom and the existence of military bases in the territory...are prejudicial to peace and security in the region'. The resolution not only went on to call for immediate British withdrawal from the Sultanate but article nine went as far as to call 'on all member states to render all necessary assistance to the people of the Territory in their struggle to obtain freedom and independence'.[30]

It should be remembered that despite such strident calls for withdrawal and direct support for assistance to help 'liberate' Oman, these resolutions were issued by the General Assembly and therefore had little real significance. Even if they had been draft resolutions put before the Security Council, Britain would have been able to use its power of veto to prevent such a resolution being passed. By the time the issue of Oman returned to the itinerary for the plenary session of the General Assembly in 1968, the Foreign Office had decided on a change of tactics: it would now simply ignore the issue at plenary and not speak 'unless there is an unexpected change in Arab tactics'.[31] The new approach appeared to pay off. Although the resolution was still passed by the General Assembly, the 'new policy of non-participation has in no way reduced votes against the resolution, nor indeed prevented sizable inroads into the vote in favour, nor a considerable increase in abstentions'.[32]

It appears that a combination of this tactic and the fact that many of the Arab delegations at the UN were supportive of Britain's efforts to create a union of the lower Gulf States and did not wish to 'disturb the nascent UAE in its present delicate state' and that 'King Faisal of Saudi Arabia was instrumental in trying to get the Oman item disposed of quietly this year'.[33]

By 1969 however, Britain had fixed on its new policy of not addressing the issue and was increasingly much less concerned by the General Assembly resolutions. In the Muscat & Oman review for 1969, the resolution of 12 December 1969 is reported simply as 'routine hostile resolutions adopted by United Nations'.[34] This marks something of a change from earlier years when in the run up to the General Assembly and Committee of 24 meetings, lengthy exchanges clarifying facts and tactics were entered into between the UK Mission in New York, the Arabian Department, the Political Resident in the Gulf and the Consul in Muscat.[35] After the shock of the first resolution of 1965, when the hostile resolution had little appreciable impact, and after the change of tactics for the 1968 session, it was recognised that there was little point fighting a losing battle against something which caused little appreciable damage. Moreover, after the final withdrawal from Aden in November 1967, the world's media had moved on to the next crisis and had lost interest in Oman once more.

The Rebellion Grows

It was during 1965 that the Dhofar rebellion really began to take on a greater seriousness. On 27 May 1965 the Sultan's Armed Forces (SAF) established a permanent presence in Dhofar. Until this time Dhofar had been policed by local troops and *askari*. This was followed on 9 June 1965, by the official commencement of the DLF campaign. An MoD report on this first phase of the conflict, which is specified as being from December 1962 to May 1965 states that, 'it is worth noting just how much took place in this period (including the first British casualties) even before the DLF claimed the campaign began'.[36] With the beginning of the DLF's campaign the threat posed by the rebels would only grow. By August 1965 the *wali* (governor) of Dhofar was warning that the RAF camp at Salalah had become a target. The response was to send a platoon from Bahrain to help defend the base, though 'British involvement [at this stage] was very much concerned [only] with the security of RAF Salalah'.[37]

In 1966 the rebellion was almost over before it had begun, when on 26 April some of the Sultan's own troops from the Dhofar Force, formed in 1955, attempted to assassinate him during a military parade.[38] Miriam Joyce suggests that eight days prior to this the Middle East News Agency carried a report of the Sultan having been wounded; she contends that Cairo had foreknowledge of rebel plans.[39] A number of *Jebalis*, men from the mountains of Dhofar who were serving in the Dhofar Force, had mutinied while others from the Salalah Plain remained loyal to the Sultan. The mutiny was suppressed by loyal troops, 22 *Jebalis* were arrested and a further 19 fled to the hills.[40] The British reaction to this attempted coup was simply to suggest that the Dhofar Force be disbanded. The Sultan declined since the loyalty of the remaining troops had been proven by their reaction to the incident. This initial response to the near death of their ally is rather surprising, especially considering the potential for chaos which Sa'id's sudden demise would have provoked.

The Sultan's handling of the escalating rebellion was repressive: he was unwilling to respond with anything other than force. But as the rebellion became an insurgency it was becoming increasingly clear that force alone could not break the insurgents. Indeed there have been some damming criticisms of Sultan Sa'id bin Taimur in much of the literature, with Townsend stating:

> Sultan Said's tyranny was not that of the history books, a harsh rule imposed by naked force, but a tyranny of indifference to want and suffering backed up by a very genuine threat of punishment if his people complained. This remote old man...had instilled such a fear in his people that very few of them dared defy him.[41]

Others, such as Halliday are even more strident in their criticism of the man and his rule:

> In 1970 Oman had an infant mortality rate of 75 per cent. It had three small primary schools, one hospital, no press and a literacy rate of 5 per cent...Trachoma, venereal disease and malnutrition were widespread. Said bin Taimur was one of the nastiest rulers the world has seen for a long time...[he] prevented Omani's from leaving the country; discouraged education and health services and kept from the population a whole series of objects, including medicines, radios, spectacles, trousers, cigarettes and books.[42]

The image of Sultan Sa'id bin Taimur as despot has in more recent years been revised. Without doubt he achieved a great deal in paying off his country's heavy debt burden and ensuring that he balanced the books. He also unified Sultanate and Imamate and ensured that mechanisms of rule were reinforced. While he did not institute a wholesale development programme, he reinvigorated and modernised his armed forces and introduced the first tentative steps towards modernity and development for his people. He is now shown not to be the remote and untouchable ruler historiography has built him up to be, 'he did not operate in a vacuum; his keen understanding and responsiveness were often utterly at odds with the image with which historical research has tagged him'.⁴³ Rabi even challenges the orthodoxy over the prohibition on radios and sunglasses, 'Radios... were not banned. Moreover, during the 1950s transistors were given as special gifts to the tribal rulers who came to the capital... As for sunglasses, rank and file Omanis as well as government officials and even the Sultan himself all wore them'.⁴⁴ That said, his ideas of development did not match up with those of Britain and he was clearly increasingly unsuited to ruling a newly wealthy oil state. A senior British officer working in the Sultan's intelligence service – G2Int stated that: 'He is fiddling while Rome burns and no one will change him'.⁴⁵

It is worth considering what HMG's policy was towards the Sultanate. In July 1960, Selwyn Lloyd, the then Conservative Foreign Secretary, in a paper presented to the Cabinet stressed that 'it is important that the Sultanate should remain effectively controlled in friendly hands'. He then highlighted the main British interests in the Gulf area and that Britain 'must retain the confidence of the rulers in our will and ability to protect them, and we must maintain the military facilities needed for successful intervention'. Lloyd then went on to examine options including 'strategic disengagement from the Sultanate as a whole, and support for a British protected state in inner Oman. These were all argued against on the grounds that they would erode the British position in the Gulf'.⁴⁶ This left British policy in the early 1960s based on the accepted importance of a friendly regime in Muscat & Oman, the need 'to maintain rights over Masiriah Airfield, [as] this is likely to grow in importance'⁴⁷ and therefore the need to protect the Sultanate.

Given the recognised importance of Oman and the necessity of having a friendly and reliable ruler in power, it is strange that Britain thought so little about contingency planning for the Sultan's death and neglected the development of an insurrection against his rule in Dhofar. Perhaps by keeping such a close eye on Inner Oman and the Imam's activities, the government took its eye off the ball in those critical early years of the Dhofar rebellion. The MoD report on phase one of the conflict states that: 'The seriousness of the threat in Dhofar emerged only gradually. Perhaps it was truly not very great to begin with, although the rebels were getting outside aid very early on'. It goes on to ask the pertinent question of whether the rebellion could have been 'nipped in the bud' if among other things 'the character of the Sultan and his advisors' had been different and if 'the limitations on UK's freedom of action' had been less.⁴⁸ At this stage the British government was relying on the strategy endorsed after the suppression of the Imamate rebellion and based upon the 1958 Exchange of Letters – development and SAF expansion.

It was of course during phase two (May 1965 – December 1967) of the Dhofar conflict that the attempt on the Sultan's life occurred and while little appeared to change in the handling of the rebellion there was at least some attempt by certain officials to think about what would have to happen in the event of the assassination of the Sultan in order to secure an orderly handover.[49] On 8 May 1966 the British Consul-General in Muscat, Bill Carden, met with the Sultan's son Sayyid Qaboos in Salalah where he was by all accounts a virtual prisoner, isolated from the affairs of state, while his father declined to use his talents to assist him in the administration of the country. Indeed Sa'id was described as having an 'almost pathological inability' to delegate responsibility. Yet Qaboos, as a Sandhurst graduate had served in Germany with the Cameronians, who had themselves served in Oman during the Imamate rebellion in 1957. He had also made an extensive tour of Europe and North America and had spent time studying civic administration in Birmingham.[50] Qaboos' could therefore have helped in many areas of state from Defence and Foreign Affairs to the development of municipal structures in Muscat/Matrah, Salalah or elsewhere. Yet the Sultan continued to keep him isolated and even refused to name a successor.[51]

Qaboos told Carden that he was afraid that the next attempt on his father's life would be successful and asked him what he should do in this eventuality. It was clear during the course of this meeting that Qaboos had concerns about the lack of development and expressed dismay that 'the present situation necessitated ruling Dhofar with the rifle'.[52] Carden informed Qaboos that he should have reliable people around him and that, in the event of his father's death, he should not delay in securing SAF and family support and that one of his first acts should be to announce a development programme.

Ruling With the Rifle

It was clear to all, that by this stage Dhofar did indeed need to be ruled at the point of a gun. From the period when the DLF announced the beginning of its campaign to liberate Dhofar until the end of 1967 'the rebel threat and SAF commitment both increased'.[53] By July 1966, perhaps buoyed by the narrow escape experienced by the Sultan in April, the number and scale of DLF attacks increased, leading to what Halliday calls a 'larger scale confrontation...where the DLF lost two men but blew up seven military vehicles, killed or wounded 59 of the enemy and captured supplies of weapons'.[54] The response to these increased attacks was to seal off 'Salala [sic] with a barbed wire fence...and trying to resurrect the economic blockade practised by previous Sultans in an attempt to starve the mountain people'.[55] With fewer arms coming into Dhofar from the north, south and east, the main supplies of weapons for the DLF were now captured weapons and those coming across the border from South Yemen. These were supplied by the National Liberation Front (NLF) the Communist inspired force which would go on to defeat its Nasserite inspired rivals, the Front for the Liberation of South Yemen (FLOSY), in the wake of the British withdrawal from South Yemen. It was at this stage that Britain began to take a more active role in the conflict. British sources 'verified that the rebels had an Egyptian supported base in Hauf'.[56] This was a Yemeni village near to the border with Dhofar but on the Eastern Protectorate side. In October 1966, according to Halliday, 'the British from South Yemen attacked and sealed the border village of Hauf'.[57] This is borne out by a MoD document reviewing this phase of the campaign, in which the author says that the 'October 1966 Hauf Operation damaged the Jebalis (I believe however, that the grab was less successful than it might have been, since some rebels were living outside the village).' The report's author goes on to say that 'it is unfortunate that it could not have been repeated'.[58] This perhaps indicates that such direct assistance in quashing the rebellion in Dhofar was more of a by-product of operations against both the NLF and the Egyptian influence in South Arabia itself and thus consistent with policy in the protectorates rather than the more *laissez faire* approach taken towards the DLF rebellion. It is apparent that there was little policy co-ordination in strategy between the protectorate administration and those with links to Whitehall on the Dhofar side of the border. It must have been clear that links between the two rebel groups were fuelling the trouble and yet little was done on a policy level to coordinate counter-insurgency action. This can in part be put down to the small-scale nature of the Dhofar problem and the time and energy absorbed by the problems in South Yemen.

British policy towards Oman generally seemed to be following more established procedures which were common to the whole of the Gulf[59] during this period, with attempts to push forward development and to foster 'better relations among the Gulf rulers'. In following these policies some limited successes were achieved with cordial relations between the two Buraimi states being established. The Sultan even appeared to finally grasp the necessity to at least be seen to be in favour of development when he commissioned a firm of consultants from London to commence a development plan for the capital area.[60]

Despite the difficulties in Dhofar during 1965 and 1966, by 1967 'it seemed as if SAF were getting on top, although they had to deal with many extraneous commitments (e.g. escorting oil company vehicles, the takeover of the Kuria Murias [islands, which having originally been given to Queen

Victoria as a gift, were returned to Oman before the withdrawal from Aden] and the building of the fort at Habrut)'.[61] While the SAF were able to, despite their other duties, keep a lid on the rebellion they were not able to put a stop to it. It is clear though that the Hauf operation disrupted the rebels, giving the SAF the chance to keep control of the situation in Dhofar for another year.

Oil Bonanza?

Drilling for oil began in 1962 and commercial quantities were found in Yibal and Natiah but it was not until there was a further find in northern Oman at Fahud in 1964 that the decision was taken to develop and export from the fields. Before 1967 oil exports from Oman were irregular and it was only on 1 August 1967 that regular commercial crude exports commenced. Oman only managed to export 20,907,029 barrels of oil[62] in 1967 which was a small amount by comparison with the medium size Gulf players of Dubai and Qatar. But with oil on the horizon, Britain decided that continuing financial assistance could not be justified and all of the £250,000 'subsidy from the British government was stopped at the end of March 1967'.[63] At once development halted as the debt-sensitive Sultan moved to live within his means. Since oil revenues were expected to arrive in his treasury in March and it was not until August that the first exports were begun, the Sultan faced a cash flow crisis. One must question why London made such a pre-emptive and hazardous move. With the rebellion growing in seriousness and a policy of development and increased SAF strength in place to tackle that rebellion, the last thing which would appear sensible was to cut off funding. Yet with apparently little thought, the supply of funds was cut off with no immediate prospect of replacement. This withdrawal of funding could however, to some extent, possibly be explained, either as part of the endless search for savings. Indeed, subsidising a state pumping oil would on the face of it seem somewhat bizarre, or an early example of trying to prepare a state for a possible British withdrawal from the Gulf. Whatever the reasons behind the withdrawal of the subsidy the effects were both unfortunate and entirely predictable. According to the MoD report 'the Sultanate's finances were at a very low ebb between the ending of the British subsidy on 31 March 1967 and the first oil revenues some months later'. This meant that, 'the combination of actual financial stringency and the Sultan's character seriously retarded the build up of [the] SAF'. The report subsequently asked the question of whether 'a more forthcoming British attitude during this period [May 1965 – December 1967] might not have considerably shortened the war'.[64]

The explanation for this move and the failure to provide more support to the Sultanate is the need for savings to be made in the context of economic difficulties at home (*viz* the 1966 Defence White Paper) and the perception that oil was an immediate source of wealth. The Foreign Office was not fully aware of the effects the delay in oil exports would have. At this stage as well, the challenges both to the Sultan and to the British presence in the Sultanate were of a relatively small magnitude when compared to many of the other challenges which London had faced in recent years such as Malaya, and especially when contrasted with the increasing anarchy in Aden and the Federation of South Arabia.

The Retreat from South Arabia

In the Defence White Paper of 1966, the withdrawal from South Arabia was planned for the end of 1968. In the aftermath of the decision taken on 30 October 1967 to bring forward the date of withdrawal from Aden and South Arabia to November 1967, the Minister of State at the Foreign Office, Goronway Roberts, made a trip to the Gulf to reassure the increasingly nervous rulers that Britain remained committed to their defence and that it would not allow the situation in Aden or the planned withdrawal to prevent Britain from continuing to carry out her obligations towards the Gulf States. According to J.B. Kelly 'the reassurance was highly necessary, for the Gulf sheikhs had watched the development of the débâcle in Aden with mounting dismay and apprehension'.[65] Roberts stated his objectives in visiting the area as: '(a) to reassure the Rulers that the British presence would continue as long as it is necessary to maintain peace and stability in the area. (b) to urge the Rulers to speed up the modernisation of their administrations and to expand popular participation. (c) to encourage them to cooperate among themselves and to resolve their differences'.[66]

While on his tour of the Gulf, Roberts had a meeting with Sultan Sa'id. In his report to the Foreign Secretary, George Brown, he stated that he was 'concerned about the future of the Sultanate'. Roberts thought it possible that Oman 'rather than the Gulf States, will be the next target of revolution in the Middle East'.[67] It seemed that the British government was waking up to the increasing threat to Oman. Roberts commented on the Sultan's 'fairly benevolent despotism', his fears that the Sultan would use his newly arriving oil revenues in 'the loyal areas of the Sultanate at the expense of the disaffected' and that the Sultan 'is impervious to the dangers of denying participation in his administration except to a few nominees of his own'. Nothing Roberts could say to the Sultan would 'budge him from this visionless policy'.[68] The concerns that the Sultan was intransigent, unwilling to placate those not demonstrably loyal to his rule and reluctant to countenance relinquishing control even of minor details of government were to be echoed and amplified by many on the ground in Oman and in future government reports. The fact that these concerns were now expressed at the highest levels of the British government is significant, but it did not lead to any immediate policy changes. Despite his recognition of the Sultan's obstinacy and short sightedness and the potential problems this could bring, there was no mention of the rebellion in Dhofar in the report. Roberts chose instead to focus on the 'points of friction on his northern frontier'[69] giving as examples Buraimi and a minor dispute with the Trucial State of Ras al Khaimah. He also mentioned the NLF governed South Arabia as a potential problem but it is clear that although he has a general sense of unease he was not at all clear as to where the threat to the Sultan truly lay. He concluded his section on Oman with the words; 'for the moment I can only sound a note of warning but I am sure we must examine afresh the future of the Sultanate'.[70] He was right to be uneasy; the chaotic withdrawal from South Arabia[71] was to change the nature of the conflict in Dhofar, as Halliday says, 'with the victory of the revolution in South Yemen the struggle entered a more militant phase.'[72]

The Impact of 1968

That the events of 1968 brought changes in Britain's policy towards Oman there is no doubt, but these changes in policy were not to be immediately apparent. So much occurred during this year that it is essential to examine several major events separately and assess their impact on British policy. Unquestionably the most important event of 1968 came at the very beginning of the year, when on 4 January 1968 the Cabinet took the decision to withdraw 'East of Suez', with the date for withdrawal fixed for March 1971. The reasons for this sudden *volte-face* are usually stated to be purely economic. At the end of 1967 Britain had faced a run on the pound after a massive growth in the balance of payments deficit. This led to Britain having to approach the IMF for a loan and the devaluation of Sterling from $2.80 to $2.40 to the pound announced on 18 November 1967. The IMF demanded cuts in public spending as a condition of the loan. Negotiations began soon after to decide where the axe would fall, and under a Labour administration defence was an easier target politically than other public services.[73] In addition, 'Labour party leaders, whether or not they wholly shared it, were increasingly exposed to the hostility of party ideologists to the practice of empire',[74] and the Gulf and South East Asia represented Britain's last major non-NATO commitments.

Roberts duly had to return to the Gulf on 7 January 1968 to inform those concerned. It is safe to say that few rulers in the Gulf were happy with the bombshell which had just been dropped on them. On 27 January 1968, Sir Stewart Crawford the Political Resident Persian Gulf (PRPG) sent a report to the Foreign Secretary, George Brown, on the reactions of Gulf Rulers to the news. He reported that the Sultan 'has in no way attempted to query our decision to withdraw' but that 'the decision must have disturbed him greatly, for it is bound to complicate the security situation within and on the borders of the Sultanate, and he has very little time to prepare for the final shock to the whole area which our withdrawal will cause'. Crawford then stressed that 'the stability of the Sultanate is as much in our interest as that of the Protected States, for one is linked to the other, both in the particularly sensitive point of Buraimi and more generally'. He finally affirmed that Britain should 'continue to help the Sultan through the difficult period of adjustment which the Sultanate like the Protected States will have to face'.[75] Despite the complete absence of even a mention of the increasing troubles in Dhofar, it is plain that although Britain recognised the importance of the Sultan, policy would continue as before to be based upon the strategy outlined in the Exchange of Letters. Later in the report Crawford suggested that 'we should continue our policy of giving practical support to the Governments of the Gulf States, to the extent that they wish it, in building up their administrations, developing their economies and improving their security forces'. He then extended this to Oman, when he stated 'this applies not only to the Protected States but also to the Sultanate where we should continue to give personnel, administrative and logistic help to the Sultan's Armed Forces within our capabilities and on repayment.'[76]

Here, perhaps, two subtle but quite far-reaching changes appear. Firstly while Britain would continue to give help, it would not be of a financial nature as it had been in the past. If the Sultan did not have the means to pay, he would get short shrift from Britain. Secondly, any support from Britain would only be within British capabilities, which seems rather obvious, until Crawford added that 'British forces will of course continue to avoid getting directly involved in Sultanate defence and internal security commitments'.[77] This represented a real diminishment in the British commitment to the Sultan. Crawford effectively stated that there would be no direct British military or financial commitment to Oman in a time of need. This of course reflects the natural consequences of the decision to withdraw. While in the past there had been no British commitment to intervene militarily on behalf of the Sultan but in practice Britain had done so, this new statement appeared to rule it out completely.

If this was the view from the Gulf then, attitudes elsewhere to the Sultan's plight in a post *Pax-Britannica* Gulf were harsher. A report by the Defence Review Working Party, on long term policy in the Persian Gulf of September 1967, which was already discussing timescales for withdrawal and potential difficulties arising from this process, claimed that: 'Muscat is a simpler case in some ways because we have no commitment to give military help. On the other hand, Muscat's position is complicated by her involvement in the Buraimi dispute'. There is no mention, yet again, of Dhofar; the concern is wholly on a resolution of the oasis problem, which of course affected not only Muscat but Abu Dhabi as well. In a single paragraph on Oman the only other concern was that Britain's ability to continue seconding officers to SAF 'would not of course be affected by our general military withdrawal'.[78] In April 1968 in what was very much standard policy for all the Gulf States, a background paper by the Foreign Office Planning Staff prepared for the Joint Intelligence Committee (JIC),[79] declared that: 'we should encourage the Sultan to improve his international standing'. The paper went on to explain that the 1958 Exchange of Letters 'under which we enjoy staging rights (which we wish to retain) at Masiriah and Salalah, obliges us *inter alia* to second personnel to the Sultan's Armed Forces' but that 'it should be made clear [to the Sultan] that it does not imply a commitment to intervene militarily on his behalf if things go wrong'. This somewhat frosty and rather downbeat approach was echoed when the paper continued to explain that 'we should also recognise that his regime is not very secure and that if the Sultan falls a successor government might well denounce the Masiriah agreement. We should not however allow our need for Masiriah to draw us into a position of commitment to protect the Sultan from internal or external opposition'.[80] It seems that British policy here is clear. Help would continue to be offered based on the old strategy, but it had to be paid for. It should not involve British troops in action and Britain should not get drawn into giving direct military assistance to support the Sultan, even if important British national interests, such as, continuing access to the Masiriah staging post, were put in jeopardy. This new policy was adopted despite the fact that earlier British policy, at the beginning of the Labour government, had stated that 'the continuing stability of the Gulf area, including Kuwait and the Sultanate of Muscat and Oman, is an important British interest'.[81]

Whereas in the 1950s Britain had been willing to defend the Sultan against all comers, in the aftermath of the decision to withdraw, the Labour government's policy was to offer some limited assistance but to keep the Sultan at arms length. Perhaps this seemingly dramatic change was down to the psychological break made by the reality of announcing withdrawal. Even as late as October 1968 London remained confident that the SAF were capable of securing the ruler's territory and that after their departure in 1971 the Sultan would maintain control.[82] This optimistic assessment undoubtedly contributed to the clear change of policy brought about by January's announcement. The demoralising influence of the recent devaluation of Sterling by 14.2 per cent,[83] the associated economic malaise and the influence of a Labour government ill at ease with the idea of protecting autocratic monarchs were also contributory factors in the change. However, policy towards Oman was in effect merely crystallised by the decision to withdraw; it had in reality been slowly building for years with the withdrawal of the subsidy in 1967 being a key example of the distancing trend.

Despite the new more distant attitude to Salalah, Sir Stewart Crawford, the Political Resident in the Gulf, stressed the importance of the survival of the Al Bu Sa'id dynasty to Britain. He examined the pros and cons of alternatives to Sultan Sa'id. Sir Stewart stated that it was up to the family to decide who would succeed Sa'id and it would be unwise for London to get involved. Yet for the years ahead 'whatever his shortcomings' Sultan Sa'id should in his opinion remain in post.[84]

Family Opposition

While the Sultan was facing his troubles in Dhofar, members of the Al Bu Sa'id family were becoming increasingly disenchanted with the Sultan's reluctance to delegate and to begin the development of his country in earnest. While Sultan Sa'id engaged in correspondence with Shaikh Zaid of Abu Dhabi he was rather reluctant to meet him. The Sultan's self-exiled brother Tariq however, was only too willing and in November 1966 visited Abu Dhabi. Evidently frustrated both with the lack of change in his homeland and with the life of an exile, Tariq had come to the conclusion that his brother needed to be removed from power and that he should be the regent for Qaboos. He even went as far as to ask for Shaikh Zaid's assistance with his plan, though Zaid refused. In April 1967 the Sultan's brother Fahr, who had been accorded some administrative duties, also left the Sultanate frustrated with the pace of change. This was deemed by Britain as a 'blow' to the Sultan, who thought that it would raise Tariq's standing. Britain did not want to give any appearance of supporting the brothers' stance against the Sultan, although it was clear that the British Consulate thought their treatment at the hands of the Sultan 'shabby'.[85] One would have thought that with the obvious discontentment even of his own family the British government would have attempted to persuade the Sultan to be more conciliatory and to engage more with development issues. Instead, Britain was reluctant after the withdrawal announcement to get involved in internal aspects of the Sultan's rule despite the fact that if it was turning members of his own family against him, it was likely to have similar effects on his subjects.

Moribund Development

Until the removal of the subsidy the development programme was of a very small scale but even this was halted by the Sultan's fear of debt. His advisors though, had clearly been working at making him understand the importance of bringing at least some elements of modernity to his domains. It was simply an inbuilt conservatism which held the Sultan back from engaging in development or indeed from spending any money unless it was absolutely necessary. It was something of a surprise therefore when on 28 January 1968 the Sultan issued a statement entitled: *The word of Sultan Sa'id bin Taimur, Sultan of Muscat & Oman, about the history of the financial position of the Sultanate in the past and the hopes for the future, after the export of oil*.[86] This document which appears to be aimed as much at the British as at his own subjects laid out the Sultan's view of the history of his reign so far. He described the terrible financial state in which he inherited power with the words 'when we took over the reigns of power the Sultanate's Treasury was completely empty'.[87] He went on to describe the beginnings of a development programme after 1958 with the help of 'our friends the British Government', and stressed that things would be different 'now that we know that revenue from oil will be coming in steadily can we consider and estimate how to put into effect the various projects which the country needs'.[88] The rest of the document outlined in relative detail how oil revenues would flow and what they would be used for, with some of the first projects being water and electricity systems for Muscat and Matrah and development for the tribal areas from which the oil was flowing. The envisaged development was very much focused on infrastructure and on Muscat, Matrah and Salalah. The Sultan obviously maintained antipathy towards development in the *jebal* of Dhofar and extensive educational and healthcare expansion, providing schools for the sons of sheikhs only. Overall, this pronouncement would seem to be very much out of character for the Sultan and in many ways its mere existence in this form is unusual but its contents to some extent challenge the traditional view of the Sultan as someone who opposed development outright. Many accounts of this period rail against the Sultan, John Townsend being a good example when he said that in 1967 'a development department existed in name, it did a little useful work, but it was not allowed to go further'. He goes on to describe 'a marked reluctance on the part of the Sultan to support their endeavours'.[89] Miriam Joyce describes the Sultan's view as being 'that he could not develop one area before he was able to provide the same amenities to all areas'.⁹⁰ While it is true that development was moving very slowly indeed, there had been progress, but it clearly did not match the expectations of either the British who worked in Oman, those in the Foreign Office or many of the Sultan's subjects.

Changing Nature of the Insurgency

The year 1968 was also to mark an important change in the nature and dynamics of the rebellion in Dhofar, which would subsequently impact upon British policymaking towards Oman. Between 1 and 20 September 1968, the DLF held its second congress at Hamrin in central Dhofar. At the congress only three of the eighteen leaders from 1965 were re-elected.⁹¹ According to Halliday the congress also 'carried reappraisal of the Front's experience in every field – theoretical, organisational, strategic and political'. The Congress decided that the solution to its problems was to 'adopt "scientific socialism" and build a revolutionary organisation, launching a social revolution in the liberated areas and tying the Dhofar revolution to the struggle in the Gulf and the world-wide combat against imperialism, reaction and their allies'.⁹² As a result the Congress adopted organised revolutionary violence as the sole means of struggle and changed its name from the DLF to PFLOAG – the Popular Front for the Liberation of the Occupied Arabian Gulf. The emphasis was now firmly placed on class as the driving force of the rebellion. This was made clear in the Front's new 'National Charter' first formulated at the second congress. This placed the rebellion in the context of the 'oppressed masses on the one hand and the feudal rulers and the various capitalist forces on the other',⁹³ whereas in the past the DLF had classified its enemy as simply 'despotic and corrupt'. Interestingly, the Communist takeover of the DLF was not entirely successful as a number of rebels, feeling aggrieved at both their loss of control and the antipathy to Islam expressed in Communist ideology refused to join PFLOAG and continued to fight as the DLF.

The radicalisation of the ideological nature of the challenge can be put down to a variety of factors including of course, the rise to power and subsequent influence of the equally radicalised NLF movement in neighbouring South Yemen. The chaotic nature of the British retreat from Aden could also do little but offer encouragement to such movements. Equally though, the effects of the Arab defeat of June 1967 (in the Arab-Israeli war) which was to encourage many towards radicalism also played a part.

The change further energised the rebellion and an offensive was launched in autumn 1968. The SAF plan had been to try and block the supply route from South Yemen but due to a combination of lack of resources and the intensity of the new rebel offensive the plan failed and by mid-1969 the SAF were confined to just two towns in the whole of the west of Dhofar. By early August only Rakhyut, the administrative centre of western Dhofar remained under the Sultan's control. Yet even this town was taken on 23 August during a heavy storm which prevented SAF reinforcement from air or sea. The SAF could no longer aspire to preventing supplies and volunteers flowing from South Yemen and were falling back on Salalah, their own supply road from Salalah to Thamrit and the, as yet only partially affected, eastern side of Dhofar. The PFLOAG continued to push their advantage through 1969. The rebels' new energy and increasing success not only came from ideological change, but also from Soviet and Communist aid, both materially and in terms of training. Halliday notes that the Chinese and Soviet influence was visible during his trip to the region in early 1970 and that 'dozens of militants had visited China and had been trained there'.[94]

The deteriorating military situation in Dhofar combined with the change of nature of the rebellion into one which was Communist inspired and aimed at the whole of Oman and the Gulf, had a dramatic effect over the course of 1969–70 on those making British policy towards Oman. After all, the new PFLOAG charter highlighted the NLF role in having 'prepared the favourable conditions for a similar revolution in Dhofar' and described Dhofar as an 'intermediary link' between Yemen and the Gulf.[95] The intentions of the PFLOAG and its NLF, Chinese and Soviet backers could not have been much clearer, while the military situation in the province slowly demonstrated that their intentions could well prove to be more than just rhetoric.

The concerns of officials about the new nature of the conflict were matched by their worries about the Sultan and what were described in one Foreign Office telegram as his 'unrealistically punitive and parsimonious policies', which in the initial draft read 'his unrealistic and almost inhumane policies'.[96] The concerns of officials were threefold: his unwillingness to engage fully with development, his direction of and excessive interference in the counterinsurgency campaign and his slow responses to requests for the expansion and modernisation of SAF. A good example of these concerns came in the first quarter review for 1969 which stated in relation to the idea of a Navy for the Sultanate: '[H]e has yet to set in motion the machinery for its creation. By contrast he has ordered a ship which will primarily be for his personal use but will also carry guns. This is being built in the U.K. at a cost, I am told, of over £900,000.' The review also bemoans the fact that 'the Commander of SAF has got some of the increase which he sought from the Sultan... yet he has not got other things which he has wanted as much or more'.[97] In particular a pressing need for a fourth regiment of infantry was identified to ensure that two regiments could be permanently deployed in Dhofar. It was not until the following year under intense pressure that the Sultan assented to these demands.

On the development front officials claimed some successes. Progress was made in the construction of a harbour at Matrah, a water system for Muscat and in April 1969 equipment for a power station and electricity grid was landed at Salalah. Despite these advances, the Sultan's views on development and those of British officials remained rather different, with one official commenting: 'staid is the word, there are no new developments to report...other plans continue to lumber ponderously forward'.[98] While British officials were able to secure some movements towards the fulfilment of the old strategy of development and SAF expansion and modernisation, the pace and extent of change was very slow and was clearly damaging the chances of a successful termination of the rebellion. Sultan Sa'id was also disinterested in intelligence matters and did 'not believe that there was a risk of external subversion from elements outside of the Sultanate'. He 'thinks that the British use outside subversion as a pretext for interference in the internal affairs of the Sultanate and for giving him gratuitous advice'.[99] With all these concerns it is clear that many officials were coming to see him as part of the problem itself.

By early 1970 the rebels were able to conduct mortar attacks against RAF Salalah, one telegram stated that 'it is difficult not to avoid being impressed by the capacity of DLF to irritate an extremely sensitive nerve'.[100] With the increasing numbers of military problems and the slow pace of development, officials began a major review of policy towards Oman, with the sanction of the newly appointed Labour Foreign Secretary, Michael Stewart.[101]

Review of Policy

The initial documents produced by the Foreign Office examined British interests in Oman and the seriousness of the current situation. They then proceeded to outline possible strategies including: immediately increasing the military commitment in Dhofar, withdrawing British military support or threatening to withdraw, attempting to change the regime, retaining the same policy and hoping the Sultan would see the light or making a major attempt at a high level to try and jolt the Sultan into action. The latter suggestion was quickly adopted as the only realistic option and work began on the details.[102]

Much of the review of policy looked primarily at civil issues and not the expansion of SAF. This was in large part because the military issues were more likely to be accepted by the Sultan and officials did not want the whole package they were working on to be rejected. The new policy would therefore eventually be put to him in two separate tranches. Despite this practical decision, the two were seen as very much part of the same overall strategy of increasing the capacity of the Sultan to govern through a process of modernisation and statebuilding. Given the deteriorating situation though, for most of the early part of 1970, the focus was on ways to expand and support the Sultan's Armed Forces.[103]

On the military side the need for the expansion of SAF, at the very least to create a fourth infantry battalion,[104] and the creation of a navy were envisaged along with the purchase of modern equipment including modern FN rifles, armoured cars, artillery, helicopters and skyvan transport planes. If the Sultan agreed to the expansion and modernisation proposals, then because of the time this would take to come to fruition, British officials decided that 'we are ready to discuss with him steps needed to hold the military position [in the meantime]'.[105]

On the civil side, the idea of a new post of Chief Secretary was floated, the new role would entail having control of the day to day running of the government. The Sultan insisted that this new role be confined only to the 'modern' departments of government i.e. development. British officials accepted this because as one commented 'we would be unlikely to get anything else'. Also envisaged was the need to 'employ more Omanis and give his people greater freedom' a report stated however, that 'it is not easy to see how they could be put into precise terms which could expect his agreement'.[106]

As can be seen, officials were very concerned to obtain the agreement of the Sultan but they were not willing to immediately promise committing British forces directly or increasing the numbers of British loan service personnel without having first secured some concessions. Equally it was considered important to be generous in the levels of assistance in all areas, as this would 'put us in the best possible position to justify whatever course of action we adopt in the event of the Sultan rejecting the package'.[107] However, at this stage officials worried that, 'threats... would be counterproductive with the Sultan. While the effect of carrying them out would be seriously damaging to our own interests'.[108]

Reasessing the Counterinsurgency Strategy

It seems strange that options of how Britain could give military assistance were being seriously contemplated in the review of policy that was instigated under the very same Labour government which was so keen on withdrawing troops 'East of Suez' – not sending more. But it is a clear indication of the seriousness of the situation in Dhofar and the threat to Britain's interests. The contemplation of how Britain could assist militarily came as part of the wider review of policy, which in effect was only reinforcing the older policy of strengthening the SAF and encouraging development. In addition though, direct military assistance was designed to support a radical re-evaluation of the failing counterinsurgency strategy adopted in Dhofar.

The main suggestion for British military assistance was the use of the SAS, but it was stressed that 'it should not, repeat not be regarded as the main element' of the overall strategy for defeating the rebellion.[109] The problem with the need for more direct aid to the Sultan was that direct British military intervention in the Arabian Peninsula was seen as a rather undesirable option. The intervention would have to be as low key as possible and that of course meant using the SAS. This was however seen as very much complementing the proposed expansion of SAF. In early February 1970 Britain sent an inspection team, at the request of Sultan Sa'id, to examine the SAF and their capabilities with the implicit goal of improving their capacity to fight the rebels. This team was led by Major General J.B. Dye who had served in both Egypt and Aden. The Sultan's Defence Secretary, Colonel Oldman was pleased to be receiving external advice and in a meeting with General (Roly) Gibbs, Commander British Forces Gulf, Oldman was asked what material help he might wish for from Britain. The reply was a relatively modest list of mostly technical and logistical aid but also included SAS assistance, in particular to improve intelligence gathering.[110] General Gibbs in a report based upon his visit to Oman proposed using the SAS in a 'hearts and minds' role in Dhofar as well as discussing broader strategy in the Dhofar campaign, the expansion of SAF and other types of British assistance.[111]

The SAS idea was catching on quickly and was well received by officials in the Foreign Office who had in fact tentatively floated the idea some months before.[112] The SAS themselves were also keen to be involved. To this end a small team from the SAS visited Dhofar during Easter 1970 with the aim of making a full assessment of the situation and advising on both how the SAS could help and how the counterinsurgency strategy itself could be fine tuned. Until 1970 the counterinsurgency strategy remained almost exclusively military in focus and had scant regard for the population of the *jebal*. The Sultan wanted no quarter given to anyone who opposed him or who had sympathy for the rebels. This dislike of the Dhofaris was summed up by one FCO official, who when faced with the SAS idea of organising some *jebalis* into a militia commented: '[T]he Sultan...must be expected, I imagine, to be even less ready to arm the Jebalis than [he is] to feed them'.[113]

The SAS report stated that effectively the SAF's main focus was on preventing the rebels from descending onto the Salalah Plain, simply containing the threat and not aiming to eliminate it. When SAF patrols were carried out and the rebels opened fire at long range, the SAF troops always tried to engage but this was 'always without success'. The report also said that '[l]imited sorties are made onto the jebal but no attempt is made to hold ground. Ambushes are laid at night with no reported good fortune'. In short the SAS viewed the current military tactics and the lack of engagement with the people as disastrous.[114]

By early April 1970 the regiment had drawn up a comprehensive strategy for restoring peace to the province. It examined the strengths and weaknesses of both sides in the conflict and stated that:

> [T]he SAF are overstretched and tired... the methods used by the rebels, so far, are effective and they have seized the initiative and are dominating the *jebal*. There is a feeling of abandonment among the uncommitted *jebali* and the operations by the SAF are hampered by interference from the Sultan, no clear long-term aim, no overall direction and poor intelligence.[115]

The SAS plan insisted on the Sultan making dramatic and permanent changes in policy towards his people. It demanded that overall control of operations should be passed to the SAS commander and broke the operation into phases and five specific fields: Overt Military Operations, Civic Aid, Veterinary Aid, Psychological Operations and Intelligence and Covert Operations.

None of this of course was particularly new or groundbreaking, it simply represented the lessons learnt from decades of colonial warfare and the successful conclusion of counterinsurgency campaigns in Kenya and Malaya as well as some of the lessons learnt from more recent operations in Aden and Borneo. There were, during this period, real attempts to learn the lessons of these operations and many British service personnel had direct experience of these conflicts – the SAS in particular. There was also a small body of literature written by British practitioners of counterinsurgency who had fought during these campaigns which was appearing during the late 1960s and early 1970s and which must have had an impact on SAS and wider British Army thinking.[116]

The things proposed by the SAS team, while having some situationally specific elements, are at the core of all good counterinsurgency strategy with the fundamentals being engagement with and protection of the population, development, good intelligence,[117] good public relations, the integration of civilian and military efforts, good planning and the development of indigenous security forces. All of these were clear lessons from British operations in the past and all of these things form the core of current U.S. counterinsurgency doctrine in Field Manual 3–24.

By April 1970 the Sultan had actually agreed to most of the military aspects of the review.[118] The problem was that the situation was so bad that officials saw a need for the commitment of British forces in support of the Sultan even before the review was fully complete. It was obvious that approval for this move would not come without reference to a ministerial committee or even the full Cabinet and that approval was very unlikely to be forthcoming. The reasons for this were stated as: 'the possible openended nature of commitment... to a regime which looks increasingly wrong in the twentieth century... we are also moving into a situation where it is increasingly difficult to get unpalatable decisions made in a pre-election period'. The document concluded that it would be 'tactically unwise' to go to the Defence and Overseas Policy Committee of the Cabinet in advance of the review being completed, although the fact that it was considered at all suggests the nature of the situation on the ground in Dhofar. The document also stated that 'we should operate within decisions which can be taken by the F.C.O and M.O.D alone. If we start getting involved with the Treasury or O.D.M [Overseas Development Ministry] for provision of new money for assistance to the Sultan we will be bogged down forever'.[119]

Before the review of policy was even finished, officials were examining ways of pushing forward with direct financial and military assistance to the Sultan. This occurred despite the fact that policy in 1968 had been that the Sultan could expect neither of these things. The evidence strongly suggests that this newly interventionist attitude was being driven by officials at the Foreign Office and to a lesser extent by the Ministry of Defence. The perceived reluctance of many in the Labour government to endorse the new attitude can be accounted for by the unease about the nature of the regime in Salalah and the increasing media spotlight being shone upon the country.

Between the Labour Government and the Conservative Opposition

The general image, which is sometimes presented, of the Labour government being unwilling to become too heavily involved in Oman or indeed in any foreign adventurism can be challenged on a number of accounts. Events in Borneo and Malaya during Wilson's premiership saw at one point 68,000 troops and a third of the British surface fleet committed to the protection of the Malaysian Federation.[120] The reluctance to authorise intervention in Dhofar can be understood in relation to the decision to withdraw 'East of

Suez' and its timing in the run up to a general election. But the image of the Labour government being hostile to this sort of intervention on principle is much less clear than is usually thought. While Labour backbenchers were unlikely to support such actions Labour ministers, especially those in the FCO and MoD, were much more willing to entertain alternative perspectives. They too were increasingly concerned about the ramifications of Britain's withdrawal from the Gulf and the consequent threat that the Dhofar rebellion could pose to the whole region. Certainly, they did not want a repetition of the debacle that had marked Britain's withdrawal from Aden.

If the Labour Government was inching towards a more robust policy towards the problems of Oman then the Conservatives were even more prepared to play a fuller role in the region. The Conservatives had been strongly hinting that some British military presence might be maintained in the Gulf if the Conservatives were to win the next election and if the Gulf rulers wanted Britain to remain. The Conservatives clearly wanted to challenge the idea that Britain was in terminal decline and had lost its place in the world.[121] This idea had grown with the loss of the mass of the British Empire by the late 1960s and the economic difficulties faced by Britain which appeared not to afflict neighbouring France and Germany. Edward Heath, accompanied by the then head of the Foreign Affairs section of the Conservative research department, Douglas Hurd, even went as far as to make a tour of the Gulf region. In March 1969 the pair visited all of the lower Gulf States along with Oman, Iran, Saudi Arabia and Kuwait. It was evident that the Conservatives were minded to either reverse the 1968 decision to withdraw or at least retain some sort of presence in the Gulf. Conservative opinion, despite the fact that they were not in power, still prompted the Foreign Office to assess the feasibility of a reversal of policy. There was however a good deal of resentment among some in the Foreign Office about Tory proposals with one official criticising the 'current unhelpfulness of Mr. Heath's public statements'.[122]

Nevertheless, the FCO did examine the possibility of reversing the decision and also looked at alternatives to withdrawal. These included: simply reducing troop numbers or rather than withdrawing at the allotted time quietly failing to meet the deadline and simply remaining for an extended period. A final idea was to withdraw militarily from the Gulf but move a reserve of troops to Masirah, thus retaining some teeth in the region.[123] The FCO however, worried that 'talk of a change of policy can take the Rulers' eyes off the ball and do damage'.[124] After expending so much effort to ensure a Federation of the lower Gulf States and to encourage the establishment of adequate administrative structures it is easy to see why the Foreign Office would not want to give the rulers hope that they could slip back into their familiar British protected groove and avoid the challenging issues that oil wealth was bringing to the fore.

On 19 June 1970 the Conservatives under the leadership of Edward Heath took office in Britain. The election of the Heath government would on the face of things seem to suggest some sort of a radical rethink of British policy towards the Gulf would now take place. The Conservatives had, after all been somewhat less than content about the idea of withdrawal from the start. Yet the 1968 decision had produced some seemingly unusual results within the Conservative Party itself. It is very much the accepted view that the Heath government's main foreign policy aim was to reorientate Britain's foreign policy towards Europe and secure British entry to the EEC. Heath is therefore remembered as the single-minded premier who secured what had previously been an elusive goal. In his quest for Britain's entry to the EEC it follows that any potential obstacles to this goal, such as Britain's 'East of Suez' role would be sacrificed on the altar of EEC entry. Heath came to be seen as a pragmatic centrist politician. Yet from 1968, he took what to our eyes may be seen as a stand based more on traditional Conservative convictions of British prestige and place in the world. He opposed the Wilson government's decision to withdraw even when some unlikely members of his own party, Enoch Powell being the prime example, were in favour.[125]

Throughout the election campaign Heath included in his platform and manifesto the commitment to re-examine the government's decision to withdraw. This then was bound to have some impact upon British policy towards Oman. By 1970 though, the chance of the British being able to reverse the decision of January 1968 was unlikely. Having announced withdrawal there could realistically be no way of reversing it. At the end of July 1970 the new Foreign Secretary, Sir Alec Douglas-Home, appointed the retired former Political Resident, Sir William Luce, to investigate opinion in the region and the possibility of Britain remaining in the Gulf. By the end of September he had informed Home that neither a reversal of the withdrawal decision nor a postponement was possible. The Heath government acknowledged this in a statement to the House of Commons on 1 March 1971 and a date for the final withdrawal of troops was set for 1 December 1971. But while there could be no direct change in policy of withdrawal there were many other ways of ensuring that Britain was able to retain an influential role in the region, albeit a more discreet one.

The realities of Britain's involvement in Oman fits into this idea. It represented not a reversal of the decision to withdraw from the Gulf but instead, a modification or readjustment of that decision. Home's statement of March 1971 gave the strong impression that the Gulf would not be treated as any other region of the world but would continue to have very close diplomatic, commercial, military and political links to Britain. In his statement, although referring to the nascent United Arab Emirates (UAE), Home spoke about 'continuing links and assistance', making available 'British officers and other personnel on loan to the Union's forces' and assisting with the supply of equipment. He also stated that 'elements of British forces could be stationed there on a continuing basis to act in a liaison and training role' and that HMG 'is ready to consider ways of assisting local police forces if so requested'. He was also 'prepared to help the Union in development and other appropriate fields'. He concluded his statement with the words 'I believe, Mr Speaker, that arrangements of this kind will form a sound basis for a continuing and effective British contribution to the stability of the area, and a new and up to date relationship between Britain and the States concerned'.[126] This clear readjustment of the policy of withdrawal was also applicable to Oman and was visible there earlier.

By taking a more active role in Oman the Conservatives could ensure that their policy readjustment would be successful. There are two main reasons for this. The first is the increasing involvement in Oman which was taking place or was envisioned under the Labour government: to make the Gulf safe to retreat from. Secondly, and in some ways just as importantly for the readjustment of policy, Britain's involvement in Oman would signal not just to Muscat but also to other Gulf States and Kuwait that although Britain was overtly leaving the Gulf, she was securing her allies' position and may well be willing to offer them similar assistance and protection in the future without the need for treaties and permanently stationed forces. Britain's increasing role in Oman can therefore be seen as a signal of Britain's continuing commitment to the region and a symbol of how valuable continuing British friendship could be.

When comparing the policies and attitudes towards Oman of the Labour and Conservative governments in 1970 there are a great number of similarities. Both were committed to development, both were frustrated with the Sultan's attitude and both were (albeit to differing degrees) ready for more direct British involvement in the Dhofar conflict. Where the differences in the two governments can be seen are not in terms of policy but in the level of commitment and determination and the lengths to which they were willing to go. The Conservatives were far more willing to move things along.[127]

Within six weeks of the Conservatives coming to office, a coup took place in Oman. After months of planning among a small group of conspirators a plan was eventually hatched. The conspirators included: Sa'id bin Taimour's son Qaboos, his friend Timothy Landon with whom he had been at Sandhurst and who was then serving as the Sultan's intelligence officer in Dhofar, along with input from Ray Kane,[128] Colonel Hugh Oldman, the Omani Defence Secretary (who had only recently moved from being CSAF to Defence Secretary), and others, almost certainly including CSAF John Graham. On 23 July 1970 a number of conspirators entered the palace in Salalah whereupon; the Sultan's abdication was requested by the son of the *wali* of Dhofar, Sheikh Breik bin Hamoud. Sultan Sa'id refused and shot the Sheikh in the shoulder leading to a stand off and a firefight. In the ensuing *mêlée* the Sultan accidentally shot himself in the foot whilst reloading his pistol and was also injured in the stomach. Eventually realising that further resistance was futile, he insisted he would only surrender to a British officer, who was soon called from RAF Salalah. He, along with some loyal retainers, was then flown by RAF plane to Bahrain that same evening and then on to London arriving at 9.30 am on 25 July.[129] That he had been deposed by his son Qaboos, who had been under virtual house arrest in Salalah for many years, was ironic since the house arrest was imposed precisely because Sa'id feared a coup. Clearly that isolation had not been sufficient, for Qaboos had been able to organise events with the help of seconded and contract officers.[130]

Accounts of events surrounding the coup negate any direct British participation in its execution. The planning and sanctioning of the coup are however a different matter. While many key files remain closed, recent research suggests that there was some British involvement in the coup's orchestration and clear tacit British approval.[131] The Arabian Department of the FCO evidently became aware of the possibility of a coup at least two months before it occurred and were clearly kept in the loop by the Consul-General in Muscat, David Crawford who was told of the plans by some of the conspirators, most likely Oldman.[132] The FCO reacted in their usual way by thoroughly analysing the possibilities. That there was sympathy for the coup is not in doubt given the prevailing issues and difficulties. In an interesting report entitled 'Sultanate of Muscat and Oman Possibility of a Coup', Anthony Acland the Head of the Arabian Department wrote in early July 1970 that the information he had received from Crawford in Muscat was that contingencies clearly needed to be drawn up in the event that the coup was to go ahead, Britain could not afford to be caught off-guard.[133] Crawford suggested the adoption of Oldman's idea of instructing CSAF to prepare two contingencies. The first was that should a coup be successful 'whereupon the Sultan's Armed Forces would align themselves with Qabus and facilitate his constitutional sucession to the sultanacy as fast as possible'. The second was that if 'the coup fails, whereupon the SAF would assist Qabus in gaining control of Salalah town and in deposing his father'. Clearly Britain had foreknowledge of the coup and had to make plans for it either being successful or failing. On 12 July the Chiefs of Staff reported that Oldman 'has now changed his mind and has suggested in effect that British seconded officers in the SAF should take part in the overthrow of the government to which they were seconded'. This was met with some reluctance in the FCO however who wanted a much more cautious approach. The logic of the coup and the contingency plans proposed nevertheless seemed to tread the right balance. The Political Resident Persian Gulf, Sir Stewart Crawford, noted in a telegram on 13 July that: 'I also accept the logic of Oldman's contingency b). We should of course maintain the public position that we had no foreknowledge. The correct forms should be observed so as to enable the coup to be presented as an internal matter, with the British hand concealed or at least deniable'.[134]

In the immediate aftermath of the coup J.J. Bannerman of the Middle East Section of the FCO's Research Department was sent to meet the former Sultan's flight which was arriving into RAF Brize Norton to act as an interpreter for the four retainers which Sa'id had brought with him. An entire wing of the hospital at the RAF base had been reseved for the former Sultan and his retainers, one of whom was also injured, and an RAF security detachment detailed to guard them. The Sultan underwent two operations and was reported to be 'taking a fairly philosophic view of events... it may be worth noting that he found the cartoon in the "Daily Sketch" of Tuesday 28 July [that depicted the Sultan in hospital] amusing'.[135]

In the event, of course, the second contingency was not required and the coup was a success. That Britain effectively approved the coup by both not preventing its execution and by putting in place the contingency of essentially ordering British seconded personnel to support it were it to fail, is clear. Yet there is still no evidence in the public domain that implicates Britain in the orchestration or planning of the coup or indirect British government involvement in the execution of the coup on the 23 July. Indeed, as late as 4 June 1970, officials were still planning for the next 'landmark' in the process of putting pressure on Sa'id to reform, which would be 'a Ministerial visit to the Sultan in the second half of October to assess the development of the position'.[136] Clearly though, the FCO were pleased with the outcome but their treatment of Sa'id was excellent after the coup and Qaboos himself was generous in offering financial support to his father. Sa'id remained in exile at the Dorchester in London, dying two years later.

By removing the Sultan, who had long frustrated British strategy and replacing him with his modernising son, Sayyid Qaboos, Britain would finally be able to tackle the insurgency head on and transform Oman into a modern state. By August 1970 the SAS were in Dhofar and administrative reform and development plans were moving forward at pace.

With Qaboos, Britain finally had a Sultan who shared London's views on development and how to tackle the insurgency. The strategy to defeat the problem was the same as that outlined in the 1958 Exchange of Letters and the plans used were those that had been drawn up by officials during the Labour government. An interesting parallel can be drawn here between the overthrow of Sultan Sa'id and the removal of Shaikh Shakhbut of Abu Dhabi in 1966. Both rulers had stood in the way of progress and both had eventually been removed. Yet the deposition of Shakhbut had occurred while the Labour government had been in office and on this occasion he was asked to step down directly by the Deputy Political Resident, Glenn Balfour-Paul,[137] who had acted at the request of Shakhbut's family and would clearly have had to receive approval for his actions from the highest levels of Whitehall.[138]

Conclusion

Clearly, British policy towards Oman over the decade or so from 1958 experienced a degree of both continuity and change. As has been demonstrated, British policy changed a great deal from the 1950s and especially during the years 1967–70, but belief in the overall strategy of development and strengthening the SAF endured. The reasons for these changes were many. In the aftermath of the events of 1968, the announcement of British withdrawal initially cooled relations with the Sultan somewhat. But the radicalisation and escalation of the conflict in Dhofar from September that year meant that officials and politicians were to realise that vital British interests were at risk and that Britain needed to do something to protect them. There are many conclusions which we can draw from Britain's involvement in Oman during this period. One of the most important of these is that it does not mark a reversal of the decision to withdraw East of Suez; rather, it marks an evolution of the policy. The announcement of the decision shocked many and created the impression of a sudden termination of the long-standing Anglo-Gulf relationship. The determination of the Conservatives to retain more influence in the region than had been initially envisaged under the Labour government, highlights what was in fact a double readjustment of policy. There would be the expected political readjustment in the Gulf in the aftermath of military retreat but also a full re-evaluation of the extent to which Britain would in fact retreat from the Gulf, which had, under previous government, been accepted as being of a more extensive nature. British involvement in Oman was therefore a reflection of the evolution of wider Gulf policy. A deeper commitment than had been imagined under Labour took place but the evidence strongly suggests that Labour were also moving along the path to greater intervention. Labour ministers were aware of the threat to British interests that could arise if the rebellion was not dealt with and they had already witnessed the disasterous consequences of a rushed withdrawal and the absence of a friendly regime to take over the reigns of power.

Britain's movement towards greater involvement in Oman over this period also demonstrates that British national interests, in particular the free flow of oil and the defeat of Communist movements in areas of the globe which had strong British links or interests, were still given a high priority. The standard historiographies of Britain during this period paint an image of inevitable and inexorable decline. Britain's retreat from Empire is blamed on a variety of factors from economic malaise, U.S. usurpation of Britain's traditional role to a loss of British will. The historiography of Britain's role in the Middle East is also painted as one of decline from Suez onwards.[139] Events in the Gulf and Oman do indeed to some extent reinforce these views. There was some loss of will and worries over Britain's financial ability to maintain a role. These traditional views do not however tell the whole story. What happened in Oman does not show that Britain was either unable or unwilling to protect her national interests or that she was in inexorable and inevitable decline. In the post-War, post-Suez nationalist era Britain could no longer rely on the traditional mechanisms of influence and control. Changes were needed and Britain's withdrawal from the Gulf reflects this. For this change in political relationship to come about though, the states from which Britain formally withdrew had to remain stable, prosperous, well governed and well disposed towards Britain. After seeing in South Arabia what could happen if these conditions were not present upon departure, Britain was willing and able to ensure a different outcome in the Gulf and Oman.

The prominence of ideas and conceptions of the national interest in much of the discourse between officals and politicians is clearly the reason why involvement in Oman came to be seen as so vital in an era of withdrawal. It could also be said that Conservative policy on Gulf issues helped to focus attention on the issues, yet this chapter clearly demonstrates that the role of bureaucrats in attempting to reshape policy under the Labour government, was clearly vital. Officials both on the spot and in Whitehall exercised a great deal of power. They were able to explore avenues and push policies which were often in opposition to what had been clear government policy just months previously. In Oman's case this meant moving from an increasingly distant relationship, in which the commitment of British forces was ruled out, to extensive planning to send in British special forces. The ability of officials both to take action and shape policy was extensive. In the case of

Oman they were able to draw up plans for British financial support for the Sultanate and direct British military intervention there and were willing when the right circumstances presented themselves to persuade and cajole ministers to support the new direction. This rapid change of policy however could not have come about without the radicalisation of the insurgency and the dire nature of the military situation in Dhofar which in the face of imminent British withdrawal from the Gulf placed key national interests in danger. In the end it is national interest which shapes debates over policy in government circles and it is this, along with attempts to get direct support to Oman under the Conservative government which forms the basis of the following chapter.

CHAPTER 3

THE CONSERVATIVE ASCENDANCY: GETTING THE TROOPS IN

Here begins the Great Game

Mahbub Ali
Rudyard Kipling

Introduction

The Conservative government, which came to office in June 1970, led a change of emphasis on defence and 'East of Suez' matters which was also, naturally, to affect policymaking towards Oman. This change in the development of British policy towards Oman was especially important for Britain's involvement, particularly here in terms of military support. This process reveals a number of disputes between government bureaucracies and also impacted upon policymaking. Given that officials had had a high degree of influence over the previous government it is essential to assess the extent to which officials were able to mould and influence policy under the Conservatives. It is important also to examine how the protection of British interests was redefined under the Heath government to include the bolstering of local elites and the maintenance of British influence through less direct means. Changing perceptions and articulations of the national interest during the initial phase of the Conservative's period in office and how they came to inform policymaking were to have a real effect on both policy and the extent of British involvement which would last well beyond the Heath government. The twin initial concerns for the new British government and its officials were financial management of Omani revenues and military assistance in the initial post-coup period and the provision of British help to Oman in these two key areas.

Reassessment

As demonstrated in the previous chapter, the Conservatives had been against the idea of a British withdrawal from the Gulf. Their election manifesto stated that: 'By unilaterally deciding to withdraw our forces from these areas by the end of 1971, the Labour government have broken their promises to the governments and peoples of these areas and are exposing these British interests and the future of Britain's friends to unacceptable risk'.[1]

There is of course a degree of difference between the political rhetoric used while in opposition and actual policies implemented when faced with the realities of power. This is because an opposition has less access to information with which to inform policy and has an election to win, which can, of course, lead to some exaggeration. The Conservative approach to the withdrawal when in office was to be no exception. It was soon to become clear that the departure of British forces would not be halted by the new government.

The election of the Conservative party in June 1970 did however; bring about a number of changes and reviews in defence and overseas policy, especially with regard to 'East of Suez' strategy. On 29 June, just weeks after coming to power, Foreign Secretary Alec Douglas-Home circulated a paper, in preparation for a meeting of the Cabinet's Defence & Overseas Policy Committee (DOPC) scheduled for 1 July. This document examined a number of Foreign Policy issues not least of which was the Persian Gulf and the declared withdrawal from the region by the end of 1971. The Foreign Secretary stated that the aim is 'to establish a stable political situation' before withdrawal. He also asserted that 'even if we withdraw completely by the end of 1971 we would retain major economic interests in the Gulf area...and a special and potentially embarrassing relationship with Muscat and Oman'. He concluded by stating that: 'I am considering in consultation with the Shah, the Saudis and the Americans, as well as the Rulers what contribution we can make by a political and/or military presence'.[2] It is clear from this reference to Oman that the Conservative government, despite the impending withdrawal which it was clearly going to push ahead with, was also considering ways to continue to protect British interests in the area and had no intention of leaving what was, at this stage, a pre-coup Oman to fend for itself.

At the end of July 1970 Douglas-Home appointed Sir William Luce as his special representative in the Persian Gulf. Luce, a former Political Resident in the Gulf (1961–66) and Governor of Aden (1956–60), had been against a premature retreat from the area and had deplored the manner in which the previous government had announced its decision to withdraw.[3] He also however, recognised that now the genie had been released it could not be forced back into the bottle and that the decision could not 'be reversed, nor the withdrawal postponed'.[4] Holding these opinions he would appear to be a strange choice for such a position, when the new government was publicly committed to a rethink of the withdrawal. Luce, however, effectively reflected Conservative government attitudes and was the perfect appointee for the role both because of his distaste for the original decision and because of his pragmatism and expertise on Gulf matters. For despite the public stance of the Conservatives as Kelly asserts, '[T]here was hardly an official to be found either in London or in the Gulf in the late summer of 1970 who was prepared to entertain the possibility of postponing, even for a day, the withdrawal from the Gulf'.[5]

The new government could not fail to be influenced by the overwhelming weight of opposition to a rethink on the part of officials but to assume that this was the only factor in the seeming change of heart in the new government would be mistaken. During his earlier tour of the Gulf in spring 1969 Heath would have undoubtedly been influenced by the view in Kuwait and Iran especially, that there was no going back on the decision to withdraw. It would have been very difficult for Britain to openly retract its decision in the face of opposition from Iran. It is also hard to see how Kuwait could have openly advocated a reversal of the decision, considering its role in pan-Arabist politics and with the heady political atmosphere in the region after June 1967.[6] Douglas Hurd perhaps puts it best when he wrote at the time that 'we [the Conservative Party] are isolated from everyone on this, and can only persevere if there is a real change of nerve over the next few years – dubious'. He went on to write in his memoirs that '[B]y the time Ted became Prime Minister the withdrawal from the Gulf had gone too far to be reversed... the east of Suez controversy was [soon] forgotten as if it had never been'.[7]

If the Conservatives had come around quickly to the prevailing view of the Foreign Office that the military withdrawal from the Gulf had to go ahead there was little need for officials to apply much pressure over the Oman issue which both agreed needed attention. The Conservatives clearly had a different conception to the Labour government of the extent and nature of a continuing 'East of Suez' role despite their acceptance of military withdrawal. In a speech to the Conservative party conference in September 1970 Heath stated that:

> We are leaving behind the years of retreat – we are determined to establish the reputation of Britain once again, a reputation as the firm

defender of her own interests and the skilful and persistent partner of all those working for a lasting peace. We do not propose to reap the benefits of a peace kept by others without making such contribution as we can afford to make ourselves. Limited resources we have; but those resources can be used to good effect. We shall, therefore, use them in areas which Britain knows and where we have had experience.[8]

While Kelly is scathing in his criticism of the rhetoric coming from Heath and Home and their lack of corresponding action when it comes to the reversal of the retreat from the Gulf, the fine words coming from the Conservatives, as explored in the previous chapter, do in fact represent a new willingness to protect British interests but in a different manner to that which Kelly would have wished. Kelly clearly desired that the announcement of withdrawal had never been made and that Britain could and should have had the backbone to stay the course and show no weakness. In this sense he fails to recognise that the era of empire was over and that Britain's position in the Gulf was seen from the outside as an anomaly and one which was likely to cause Britain increasing trouble. While the Conservatives were willing to play more of a role than Labour they were still unwilling to reverse the decision. This change of attitude can especially be seen in the Defence Policy paper issued for discussion at the Defence & Overseas Policy Committee on 14 October 1970 in preparation for a Defence White Paper. In this document, as well as a clear commitment to NATO, it was also stated that:

> There are also serious threats to stability outside the NATO area. Britain will be willing to play her part in countering these by continuing: a. to honour her obligations for the protection of British territories overseas and those to whom she owes a special duty by treaty or otherwise... The government intends in addition: b. to continue discussions with leaders in the Gulf and other interested countries on how Britain can best contribute to the maintenance of peace and security in the area.[9]

The intention to use Britain's 'limited resources' to play a role outside the North Atlantic theatre is clearly transferred from mere words in a speech to concrete policy proposals. This is of course especially true for Oman and the new government's response to the situation there. Home's report on Foreign Policy issues to the DOPC on 29 June, in which, he states that the special relationship with Oman will be retained after withdrawal is a fairly unambiguous declaration of the Conservative government's intention to use the resources at its disposal to maintain British interests and not entirely abandon its 'East of Suez' role. This intention can also be seen in the government's decision to take part in the Five Power Defence Arrangements for Singapore and Malaysia. The Defence policy paper of 14 October 1970 stated that:

> Britain has long-standing associations with the Commonwealth countries of South-East Asia and shares their interest in the stability of the area. The Government believes that the total withdrawal of forces planned by the previous Administration would have weakened the security of Malaysia and Singapore; and that a continuing British military presence on the spot will have an important deterrent value and a stabilising influence.[10]

Clearly the new administration was determined to continue to play a global role albeit in a different guise. It was not slow in authorising action either. The situation in Oman was growing more serious by the day. In June 1970, attacks in central Oman, well away from Dhofar, took place against the SAF. On 12 June the SAF camp at Izki[11] was attacked unsuccessfully, while the garrison at Nizwa was also assaulted soon after,[12] by elements from a new opposition group; the National Democratic Front for the Liberation of Oman and the Arab Gulf (NDFLOAG). In July further NDFLOAG cells and caches of Chinese weapons were found at Matrah, Sur and Mutti along the northern coast of Oman.[13] The existence of this new resistance group was proclaimed in a press release in Beirut which expressly stated that the new organisation would 'operate along the same lines as PFLOAG in Dhofar'.[14] The danger of a second front was stark, particularly whilst the SAF were so overstretched in Dhofar. The 1969 review of events in Oman stated that, 'the Commander [SAF] had, in fact, by the end of the year been placed in the difficult position of seeing his commitments grow faster than his resources'.[15] If, as seemed likely, there was to be co-ordination between the two groups the position would be far worse. The fact that Sultan Sa'id had already proven unwilling to listen to proposals from the British for the 'hearts and minds' campaign proposed by the SAS in April 1970[16] now appeared even more grave. With the revolution spreading and becoming ever more incessant, Britain could not allow another Aden situation to develop so close to the vital Gulf oil supplies while it was in the process of withdrawing British forces from the area.

Days after the coup of 23 July, a formal request was made by the 'Sultanate authorities for SAS assistance in the 'hearts and minds' role and to help train a bodyguard for Qabus'. According to a report drawn up for the visit of the Oman Defence Secretary, Colonel Hugh Oldman, to the MoD on 14 October

1970, 'As a stop gap four SAS soldiers were loaned to advise and give ["]on the job["] training to the Sultan's bodyguard'.[17] Clearly Britain was willing to ensure that the new Sultan remained alive to secure his country's future. The document goes on to outline the further planned SAS assistance to Oman including more SAS bodyguards, 'a light SAS squadron (approximately 40 strong) to operate in detachments training the two SAF battalions stationed in northern Oman' and finally 'an SAS troop reinforced with interrogators, intelligence collators and a psyops trained NCO to operate on the Salalah plain gathering intelligence, supervising the training of auxiliary forces by SAF and assisting with the rehabilitation of the inhabitants of the Salalah plain'. The document also notes that 'Ministerial approval has been given... and the necessary deployments have taken place into Oman'.[18]

At first glance it would appear that the Conservative government were taking clear decisive action based upon their conviction of the need for Britain to continue to play a global role in ensuring stability. In reality however, the decision-making process meant that the Omani request was filtered through several levels of bureaucracy.[19] Officials on the ground in Muscat had to prepare advice for those in the FCO, the Foreign Secretary had to be brought on board and negotiations with other bureaucracies, in particular the MoD, needed to be conducted. Finally any significant request had to gain Cabinet approval. In the specific case of the Sultanate's request for SAS assistance one must remember that the suggested use of the SAS was made months before the coup and had been pushed by officials at the time. It is no surprise that the Sultanate's request came with a recommendation for an immediate response from the British Consul in Muscat, David Crawford. On 5 August this was supported by the Commander of British Forces Gulf and Michael Weir the Deputy Political Resident Persian Gulf (DPRPG).[20] By 6 August the MoD had asked for and received clarification from the Consul-General that the request was for 'Hearts and minds type activity'.[21] The obvious support from the Gulf had played its part because on 7 August a telegram from the Vice Chiefs of the General Staff to the Commander of Land Forces Gulf stated that:

> The Army department would be pleased to provide SAS to assist in the training of SAF and to assist in a 'hearts and minds' operation in the Salalah area and we appreciate the dividends which will accrue from acting expeditiously. However the agreement of Chiefs of Staff and Ministers is necessary before we can deploy troops to Muscat and Oman. Your signal... does not contain sufficient information on which to prepare a case for submission [to] Chiefs of Staff and Ministers.[22]

It was therefore proposed to send Brigadier Semple, the commander of SAS group, to the Gulf to decide 'what is needed to be done, by whom [and] where in Muscat and Oman'.[23] By 13 August, Semple had returned from the Gulf and had written up his report. In a minute circulated among officials at the FCO and MoD his recommendations were stated, along with a section detailing 'Whitehall Procedure' which was in effect the strategy proposed in order to get the Brigadier's proposals adopted. In this section it was stated that:

> Should you agree to the recommendation of this minute, the FCO will be asked to prepare a note from the Foreign Secretary to S of S [for Defence], copied to the Prime Minister. The note will be based on the suggestions contained in this minute and will be cleared through Chiefs of Staff before going to S of S.[24]

After further cordial discussion between the FCO and MoD, it was decided that one of Semple's four suggested missions for the SAS, that of direct support on the *jebal* for the planned 1971 SAF offensive, should be downgraded. This was because of unknown factors at this stage not least the lack of intelligence on the strength of PFLOAG and that 'were an incident to occur involving casualties it could lead to parliamentary and public concern'. As such it was suggested that 'for the present therefore we believe no final decision should be made about the Jebal operation, but we should agree to give it favourable consideration later in the year in light of developments'.[25]

On 24 August 1970 a note was circulated among both officials at the MoD and the Assistant Permanent Under Secretaries of the Secretary of State and Minister of State explaining that 'The Department has been working with the FCO at the official level to clarify and formulate in terms likely to be acceptable to the Chiefs of Staff and Ministers, a request made for military assistance...by Sultan Qabus'.[26] The note explains that the proposals have been submitted to the Foreign Secretary and that if his agreement is given he will write to the Defence Secretary and the Prime Minister for their agreement.

By 4 September Alec Douglas-Home, the Foreign Secretary, had sent his note to Lord Carrington, the Defence Secretary. In what is a very carefully worded submission, no doubt drawn up by FCO officials, he is careful to state the benefits to Britain from the mission and to assuage any doubts. In terms of cost 'acceptable financial terms for this assistance have been worked out'. In terms of time frame it was stressed that, 'it is important to ensure that a decision to send SAS personnel to the Sultanate does not become an open ended commitment. However, I note...that, in all three cases, SAS personnel would be in the Sultanate for strictly limited periods'. Another potential concern, that of potentially negative public opinion was addressed in the words that, 'it should be possible [to keep their presence secret] since the SAS would be under operational command of CSAF [Commander Sultan's Armed Forces], would wear SAF uniform and would be accommodated in SAF camps'. Finally some useful persuasive phrases such as 'your officials and mine are agreed that' and 'Commander British Forces Gulf... Political Resident... H.M Consul General in Muscat have strongly recommended that we should agree to the Sultanate's request',[27] were used to convince Carrington of the validity of the appeal for SAS assistance.

The note from the Foreign Secretary to convince his colleague and the Prime Minister is then, a crafted piece of writing designed to assuage any fears, convince of the benefits and reinforce the depth of opinion within the two key departments of state in favour of the recommended action. It appears to fit with the trend seen in the last chapter for officials to plan for more decisive action and shape opinion on the Oman issue without the input of ministers. But while it is clear that a great deal of work was conducted at the official level in the MoD without the knowledge of ministers, it is a very different story at the FCO where Douglas-Home was more involved. His endorsement of the plan is clear from the note to the Defence Secretary of 5 September but he was also personally involved much earlier in the process leading up to the formulation of this document. On 6 August, very soon after the request was made, he personally sent a telegram to the Residency in Bahrain. He requested that in the light of the MoD requesting the CBFG, [Commander British Forces Gulf] General Gibbs, provide more details of the requirements in Dhofar and for recommendations on the units likely to be needed. An 'early reply would facilitate a decision here on the Sultanate request for SAS assistance'.[28] The Foreign Secretary was clearly convinced from an early stage of the necessity for direct British military assistance to the Sultanate and was willing to help facilitate rapid agreement on the matter. He would already, of course, have been *au fait* with the circumstances surrounding the transfer of power in the country, having been fully briefed, and direct British military assistance was the next logical step in stabilising the situation there. Agreement with the proposals from Downing Street came on 7 September in a note in which the Prime Minister commented, 'I strongly support [the proposals] – and the Sultan has plenty of money with which to pay for all this'.[29]

After the Prime Minister's support was expressed so clearly, the Defence Secretary's response came on 11 September, with the words '[I] have arranged for the first of the party to arrive in Oman early next week'.[30] The Prime Minister certainly seemed to have a degree of influence over such decisions.

Whether bureaucracies always need No.10's support is however, open to question. Though it appears that No.10's support was very important. This becomes clearer in the light of a letter from D.J. McCarthy to Sir Stewart Crawford sent in May 1969 a year before Heath's election in which he states: 'Mr Heath seems to operate a Shadow Presidency rather than a Shadow Cabinet'.[31] This is reinforced by much of the literature on the Heath government. Indeed, 'the style and personality of the Prime Minister was even more than usually central to the government's working'. It was, 'in public and in private a Heath government throughout.'[32]

The clear support given to the request for assistance from the Sultanate by the Foreign Secretary throughout raises questions as to the extent to which officials were able to direct and lead policy towards Oman under the Conservative government. It must be borne in mind that officials had been working on these issues for many months before the election of the new government. A clear consensus had emerged among both the men on the spot and in Whitehall about the necessity of a change of strategy in the Dhofar conflict. Equally, frustration at the lack of progress in development projects and the rapidly deteriorating military situation in the southern province had convinced many important actors of the need for, 'regime change' and for more active British support to counter the growing rebel successes. This consensus and the policy ideas, developed while the Labour government was still in office could not have failed to influence Conservative thinking when they entered the corridors of power. The fact that plans and strategies were in place no doubt made it easier, in a rapidly deteriorating situation, to decide on a course of action. In that sense then, the agenda and possible responses were indeed set in large part by officials. Yet the Conservatives had come to power with an agenda of their own, to secure British interests and continue to play a role 'East of Suez'. Officials were pushing at an open door with the new government, which was amenable to their concerns, shared their conception of national interest and were easily convinced by their plans.

Bureaucratic Troubles

While officials at the FCO and MoD were largely willing to co-operate closely in securing a positive reply to the Sultan's request for assistance, the Treasury's response to the change of rule in Muscat was much more mercenary. Since 1861, under the Canning Award, the Government of India and after 1948 the British Government had paid an annuity termed the Zanzibar Subsidy to the Sultan of Oman. This came about after the 1856 separation of the Omani empire into two separate dominions for rival siblings with Oman being compensated for the loss of Zanzibari riches in an agreement brokered by Britain to avert a confrontation.[33] By 1966 when oil was being extracted in commercial quantities in Oman, the Treasury was anxious to attempt to negotiate the end of the subsidy.[34] They were rebuffed by the FCO with the words 'although it is certainly something of an anomaly... there is no doubt in our view that Her Majesty's Government have a continuing liability to pay it', although the hope was held out that when Oman began to receive substantial oil revenues 'we would then hope that it will be possible to secure his agreement to its termination'.[35] Not willing to be dissuaded for long, on 2 October 1967 the Treasury tried again. On this occasion the request was passed on to the Sultan through Bill Carden the Consul in Muscat and received a very hostile reception. The reply from the Residency in the Gulf to the Arabian Department of the FCO stated: 'The Sultan's reaction is as we expected... he can be expected to stand by his own understandings, and will expect us to stand by ours... if we now default, our interests are likely to suffer more than we gain by the cost of the subsidy'.[36] These arguments were enough to dissuade the Treasury yet again but the issue certainly seemed to exercise them and cause the FCO no small amount of trouble.

Less than a month after the coup on 12 August 1970 the Treasury sent a letter to the FCO to raise the matter yet again in the light of the expected withdrawal and the changed circumstances of the coup aftermath. The letter contained the less than conciliatory phrases 'we agreed to let the matter drop for the time being: but we would have far less to lose in the post-withdrawal period' and 'might it not be a convenient ploy to say to the new Sultan that since we are withdrawing in 1971 we hope he can agree to its being the terminal payment'.[37]

The Foreign Office response to the letter came on 24 August and while diplomatically written, was a clear rebuttal to the Treasury's demand. The letter agrees about the principle of termination of the subsidy but stresses that it can only be achieved with the consent of both parties. It points out that the issue of timing of a potential request is difficult and advises against any immediate approach to the Sultan since 'he is preoccupied with the urgent tasks of unifying his country, setting up a governmental machine and initiating much needed development'. It stresses that relations with the new Sultan are 'as good if not better than those we enjoyed with his father and we would not wish to harm those relations at this early stage'. The response continues with a rejection of the Treasury logic of the withdrawal of the subsidy being linked to the withdrawal from the Gulf with the words: '[I]ncidentally, I do not think there is any logic in linking together [the two]' since '[T]he military facilities we enjoy in the Sultanate are not connected with the presence of British Forces in the Gulf... and we do not wish to provoke a request for payment for the use of these facilities by precipitous action over the subsidy'.[38]

The annual subsidy at this time amounted to £6,480[39] an insubstantial amount of money for the British government compared to its value in Oman at this time, yet for the Treasury the issue was clearly an irritant. That such effort would be expended on such a minor matter seems to be rather odd, considering British interests in the region and against the backdrop of the Cold War and a serious insurgency in the country. Far from being a petty dispute however, the Zanzibar Subsidy disagreement is helpful in highlighting some of the fault lines within Whitehall during this period.

It is clear from the correspondence between the Treasury and FCO that relations were far from cordial and that the FCO became deeply frustrated with the Treasury's obsession with the subsidy over this period. The Treasury clearly had very little conception of the realities on the ground in Oman, the need to maintain good relations with the Sultan and the serious nature of the problems facing the ruler. Even when the FCO used its trump card of the effects of the withdrawal of the subsidy potentially leading to greater costs being imposed upon the exchequer than would be saved, the Treasury continued to press the matter. One would expect this financial argument to be persuasive to a department so concerned with saving money but the prospect of long term costs in this case appeared to exercise little influence over the chance of short term gain.

This whole episode is illustrative of the attitudes of the Treasury and why the MoD and FCO were so keen to allow the Treasury as little involvement as possible in decisions about Oman. This fact was clearly recognised as the situation in Oman deteriorated in the months before the coup when in an internal FCO memo between two high ranking officials, it was stated that '[I]f we start getting involved with the Treasury for provision of new money for assistance to the Sultan we will be bogged down forever'.[40] The logical way around engaging in a prolonged bureaucratic struggle was, of course, to gain funding for assistance from the Sultanate itself and there can be little doubt that once this was achieved it helped facilitate the positive response to the Sultanate's request for assistance.

Local Worries

In the days after the accession of Qaboos it was clear that he would need assistance in many fields and especially with Financial Affairs. To this end it was decided to appoint a Financial Advisor and quickly. Indeed in a telegram putting forward a name pressed upon him, David Crawford the Consul in Muscat states that, 'Oldman [the Omani Defence Secretary] said to me last night that this was one post that had to be filled quickly so I would be grateful for ideas soon'. The telegram forwarding the name of the candidate, David Trefry [sic], who had formerly worked in a financial post within the Aden government and was recommended to the ex-Sultan the previous year by Sir Kennedy Trevaskis the former Governor of Aden,[41] also expresses Crawford's reservations. He states that:

> [S]peaking quite personally, I am hesitant to see too many of these ex-Adenis here, however good they might be, for the reason that they might smack too much of the old colonial image. I would far prefer to see forward looking professional advisors with overseas experience yes, but not tarred into this colonial background.[42]

It was difficult to appoint an advisor at such short notice when the need was so pressing and so it was agreed a temporary appointment would suffice in the interim. The Arabian Department subsequently managed to find an experienced man for the job but David Crawford reported that Muscat was unenthusiastic, '[T]heir reluctance stems from his age (Qabus literally winced when I consulted him) which does not conform to the philosophy of the era'. The Consul goes on to suggest that because of this reluctance and 'the pressure to which I am currently being subjected by the influential quote Aden Colonial unquote lobby here', it might be better to go with Treffry. He continues to state that, 'Oldman is much in favour of Treffry and we might avoid future strains if he is given his chance now'.[43]

While officials in the Gulf and London shared doubts about the candidate which was being pressed upon them they were careful not to engage in a battle over the issue and were wary of taking on Oldman if it could be avoided. David Crawford in a telegram on 20 August again emphasised his misgivings about the desirability of Treffry's appointment which were shared in Bahrain by Sir Stewart Crawford. However, he now amplified his uncertainties about pursuing their objection with the words: 'I wonder whether it would now be tactically wise to confront the growing influence of the Aden Club here on this issue when they could quite easily circumvent us. Hopefully Tariq's new government will put an end to this nonsense'.[44] This is a reference to the embryonic government being formed under the new Prime Minister, the Sultan's uncle Sayyid Tariq bin Taimur.[45]

The obvious concerns about the level of control of the 'Aden Club' in the operation of the new regime and their particular style of government, which, '[H]owever efficient, might be thought equally out of keeping with the new era as advanced years',[46] demonstrates that the FCO feared a certain loss of control in Muscat. Yet it is also clear that officials were concerned with potentially alienating the increasingly powerful group surrounding the new Sultan. These officials were however, clearly well versed in the bureaucratic game and did not engage in open battles that could not easily be won.

On the 21 August 1970 a telegram direct from Foreign Secretary, Douglas-Home, to officials in Bahrain and Muscat informed both, that:

> We have now heard indirectly that Treffry now has a permanent appointment with the IMF and is returning to Washington in a fortnight's time. He has heard about the job in Muscat direct from the Sultanate authorities but does not apparently wish to resign from his IMF appointment. However he would be willing to consider the Muscat job on a short term basis provided we approach the IMF with a view to securing his temporary release. It would seem from the above that, Treffry himself does not want the Muscat job on a long term basis and is not too keen on it on as a short term proposition.[47]

This slightly cryptic telegram raises a number of interesting questions. The fact that it comes directly from the Foreign Secretary is especially curious since the appointment of a short term financial advisor does not seem much like the kind of issue which would normally be dealt with by him. Equally the question of how the information about Treffry's intentions could be obtained by the Foreign Office 'indirectly' is unclear. Finally, although there is no evidence to suggest that the IMF appointment was somehow engineered by the FCO, it is indeed very convenient timing. This telegram was followed swiftly from Weir in Bahrain who asked London '[I]n order to avoid a confrontation... ask Washington to go through the motions of consulting the IBRD about Treffry, with a view to enabling the Consul-General to say that... [he] appears not to be immediately available'.[48] Conveniently then, the Foreign Office was able to get its way in this instance without causing offence in Muscat. This episode is illustrative both of the desire of the FCO to maintain its influence in Muscat against its rivals and to shape the new Oman so as to avoid the outward impression of colonial control.

These doubts about loss of control initially seem somewhat unfounded in the light of the report of a meeting on 2 December 1970 between Qaboos and Geoffrey Arthur who had by then moved from the Arabian Department to became the Political Resident in the Persian Gulf, in which he states that the Sultan was: '[F]orthcoming and decisive – so forthcoming, indeed, that an Arab nationalist might have been forgiven for thinking that he was a British puppet'. However, towards the end of the meeting when Arthur moved the conversation towards financial matters, the Sultan, 'immediately became cautious and reserved... the contrast with his attitude on every other subject that I raised with him was most marked'.[49] This, coupled with some of the difficulties encountered by the temporary Financial Advisor Mr Aldous, although his contract was later extended for a further year; suggest that the FCO had reason to worry about a loss of influence over financial matters.

Musandam Operations and the Cabinet

While the FCO had been experiencing difficulties with the Treasury and the 'Aden Group' in Muscat, the war in Dhofar had been continuing and the fear of it spreading to northern Oman remained. When on 2 November 1970 the Joint Intelligence Committee (JIC), FCO and MoD received a report from HQ British Forces Gulf of infiltration of the strategically important Musandam Peninsula by Iraqi backed insurgents it appeared that officials' worst fears were being realised. The report stated that recent information collected confirmed information passed by the ruler of Ras al-Khaimah to the Political Agent there about rebel activity and the sighting of groups of men in uniform being landed on the coast of Fujariah. Upon returning from leave on 14 October the District Intelligence Officer (DIO) heard the rumours and conducted further investigations. On 27 October the DIO purchased six sacks of weapons and explosives from local tribesmen which were said to have come from rebel arms caches.[50] There were also rumours of attempts to suborn local tribesmen. The report, while unsure of numbers or the exact nature of the threat either to Britain or the Sheikh of Sharjah, stated that the naming of a possible target of a German cement factory was 'interesting, the situation of this factory has always been a bone of contention... any move against it would no doubt rally many of the local tribesmen behind the rebels'. The report also stated that the most recent development in the situation was the fact that the DIO's main sources of information 'have been drying up, and have claimed that they are on the rebel quote list unquote'. In its summary the report states that there were about 80 rebels likely to be in the area, a significant number of them foreigners, that they were well armed, possibly with mortars, and that they are 'supplied by sea possibly from Iraq... [and] in a position to mount terrorist operations at any time'.[51]

On 4 November Commander British Forces Gulf (CBFG) reported to the MoD that after local discussions with the residency and the Sultanate authorities, certain measures would be taken to gain more intelligence and warning that in any future operation, British Forces may need to be used to back up SAF and the Trucial Oman Scouts (TOS).[52] By 11 November CBFG and his team had drawn up a nine page report entitled 'Appreciation of the Musandam Situation'; examining three options to remove the dissidents from the Peninsula, combined with a naval blockade to prevent reinforcements. The intelligence information attached to the report stated that it 'seems likely that the group is part of the NDFLOAG organisation'.[53]

Just a few days later on 14 November CBFG informed the MoD that he had 'directed CLFG [Commander Land Forces Gulf] to prepare urgently contingency plans to include use of TOS and, if absolutely necessary, other British forces to eradicate dissidents from the peninsula'. He went on to state that 'clearly we cannot allow the Musandam Peninsula to become as the Yemen was to the South Arabian Federation'.[54] In addition, insurgent control of Musandam could place in jeopardy the oil tankers' route through the Strait of Hormuz.

By 16 November David Crawford in Muscat had briefed the Sultanate authorities on the situation and informed them that he was under instructions to seek the agreement of the Sultanate to a military operation, which if they wished could be a joint operation with SAF. Initial agreement from both Tariq and Qaboos was given on 18 November.[55]

It is worth noting that the groundwork for the conducting of a not insignificant operation was very much underway and all the running was taking place in the Gulf between the Residency in Bahrain, CBFG and David Crawford in Muscat. It is they who saw the danger that the reported dissident activity posed both for Oman and the soon to be independent Trucial States and they were the ones who attempted to construct the foundations as swiftly as possible for an operation against the rebels.[56]

By 23 November 1970 CBFG's plan for the operation against the rebels, code named 'Intradon', was with the MoD and two days later it was passed to the Secretary of State for Defence having been approved by the Vice Chiefs of the Defence Staff (VCDS). The plan envisaged the blockade of the coast with minesweepers, the use of TOS and SAF at battalion strength with a squadron of SAS to seek out the dissidents, along with the use of the Royal Irish Regiment to seal off the Peninsula. Air cover would be provided by RAF Hunters and helicopters would be used for troop lifts. CBFG specified that the SAS squadron and an SAS interrogation team as the only reinforcements that would be needed from Britain. Some questions were asked about it being 'judicious to use that kind of force' in reference to the Hunters and whether it would be prudent to take as the aim of the operation merely to disrupt the dissidents rather than to eliminate them. The VCDS also insisted that the operation last no longer than 14 days and that the use of the Royal Irish should not extend into Sultanate territory.[57]

The Vice Chiefs in their report for the Chiefs of Staff reported that 'The FCO have been in on this from the start...at a desk level meeting on

Tuesday the FCO representatives were keen for speedy action and supported CBFG's line'. The VCDS were unhappy about the lack of intelligence and suggested a 'hearts and minds' alternative. The army representative had 'strong reservations about an operation at all at this time' given the number of troops available. Despite their concerns however the VCDS recommended that the CDS support the revised version of the plan and that a draft submission to the Defence Secretary be drawn up, since not to take action now 'could result in a major problem later'.[58]

CBFG's plan then underwent quite extensive redrafting in terms of language used, although the content was broadly left untouched. The VCDS clearly wanted the document to be less certain and more cautious in its approach, as one passage in the annotated version of the plan makes clear: 'We also feel that some indication of the doubts which we hold about the concept as a whole should be included and offer the following new paragraphs as replacements for the existing'.[59] MoD officials were clearly unhappy with CBFG's plan and appeared to be less than amused with his replies to the specific questions about intelligence and the use of the Hunters. The supplementary brief for the upcoming meeting with CBFG stated that:

> You may find that General Gibbs will feel that he has had less than 100% support from the Chiefs of Staff... and that [the further questions] had really invited CBFG to give you extra 'ammunition' rather than merely a reply to your specific questions. His stark signal was to say the least, unhelpful therefore.[60]

By 27 November, the Chiefs of the Defence Staff had however, agreed to the amended plan and to the VCDS' suggestion of an operation with a second major aim of assistance over the introduction of an administration in the area and had written to Lord Carrington, the Defence Secretary, to inform him of their support for the operation. The report of the Chief of the Defence staff stated that: 'The Foreign and Commonwealth Secretary will minute the Prime Minister probably to-day... alerting him to the situation and mentioning that we may need to seek his agreement'.[61]

Once again the Foreign Secretary appeared to be leading the way and not only at the highest levels of government. On 30 November in the light of CBFG's meeting with the CDS, Douglas-Home sent a telegram to the Political Resident in Bahrain informing him that 'all concerned here greatly prefer the change of emphasis from a purely military operation to assistance over the introduction of an administration' and that the plan had now been approved by the Chiefs of Staff. The Foreign Secretary then asked the Resident to 'please press the Sultan hard to release the money [for the operation] from his own resources', that the Sultan should be seen to request the help and that this presented a good opportunity to stress the need for adequate intelligence in Musandam.[62]

On the same day as the Chiefs of Staff were meeting CBFG, the original plan, with the VCDS' amendments inserted simply to provide an element of uncertainty as an insurance policy, was discussed by the full Defence and Overseas Policy Committee. The meeting found 'a general acceptance of the necessity of the operation' to proceed sometime in mid-December but wanted to ensure that publicity was kept to a minimum and that the Sultan requested the operation to go ahead. The Prime Minister agreed with the operation but stated that 'he would wish to be consulted again when the details had finally been worked out'.[63]

The Foreign Office worked swiftly to obtain the reassurances sought by the Foreign Secretary and Cabinet. On 3 December the reply came from the Gulf stating that: 'The Sultan agreed that the new plan was much better than the first' and confirmed that 'The Sultan, who is grateful for our help, has met all our requirements'. The reply continued to state that 'Tomorrow I must go through it all again with Tariq...I expect him to be grumpy but I do not (not) think he will try to upset the agreement'.[64] The problems between the Sultan and his uncle had been causing officials in the Gulf some difficulties and the following day Tariq stated that unlike the Sultan he preferred the original plan. He wanted to blame everything on Ras al Khaimah who would have to call in the British to sort out the mess, which would of course look better in the Arab world. The official disputed the idea and reported that after that '[W]e wallowed in an ocean of words (mostly irrelevant) for nearly an hour...I have no little doubt that Tariq will acquiesce. This is the way that business is done in Muscat'.[65]

Effectively the door was now open for Operation 'Intradon' to commence after 16 December when the UN General Assembly had ended and the chance of trouble being made there much diminished. On 8 December the Foreign Secretary wrote to the Prime Minister informing him of the changed nature of the plan and that all the necessary concessions from Muscat had been obtained. He stressed that the operation would not go ahead until after the end of the General Assembly session and stated that 'I believe this new plan is the best which can be devised in the circumstances. I remain of the view that action should be taken soon'.[66] Both the Prime Minister and the Secretary of State for Defence replied the following day, agreeing that the operation should go ahead.

From 2 November, when the first proper intelligence reports were received in Whitehall until the final authorisation of the operation on 9 December, little over a month had elapsed. The somewhat startling speed with which Operation 'Intradon' was planned and authorised tells us a number of things about the policymaking process with regard to Omani issues at this time. The role of the 'men on the spot' in the Gulf and Oman was key to the success of the drive for an operation to confront the rebels in the Peninsula. Without the intelligence gathered by the DIO and the support given to him by CBFG and the Political Resident the threat could have gone unremarked in Whitehall. The combined efforts of CBFG, the Political Resident and the Arabian Department allowed the situation in Musandam to be quickly pushed up the agenda in London. CBFG was also quick to try and set the nature of the agenda with his outline plan for an operation on 11 November. Foreign Office officials were able to ensure by their conviction of the need for action over the issue, that the VCDS meeting approved action despite their concerns about elements of the plan. The role of officials on the spot was also later important in gaining the support of the Sultan and other local rulers for the operation and more importantly, in swiftly securing the funds and direct request for British assistance from the Sultan which was required by the Cabinet and the Chiefs of Staff before they were willing to commit to action.

The role of Douglas-Home here is also an important one for the ultimate adoption of the policy. He, as with other issues to do with Oman at this time, involved himself early on in the process and his clear support of the policy was surely instrumental in bringing the Secretary of State for Defence and the Prime Minister on board. The fact that he himself wrote the telegram requesting certain assurances from the Sultanate suggests his strong commitment to the adoption of Operation 'Intradon' as policy.

It must also be noted that unlike the response to the Sultanate request for assistance of August and September 1970 there was no plan already in existence and it cannot be said that the policy was inherited by the Conservatives from plans drawn up under the previous Labour government. In this instance the policy was shaped from scratch and subsequently adopted in little over a month in response to what was clearly perceived by all involved as a serious threat which needed to be nipped in the bud. The adoption of this policy does however tell us something about the attitude of the Conservative government and Heath and Douglas-Home in particular. That is to say that while care was taken to minimise the risk of adverse publicity and reaction in the Arab world, despite a lack of intelligence they swiftly saw the benefits of a speedy reaction and the clear dangers of not doing so. Britain's interests were fully appreciated and the appropriate action was taken to defend them.

Although, it was later discovered that there was little evidence of insurgents in Musandam,[67] the operation, which began on 16 December 1970, was instead swiftly converted into an exercise in extending the Sultanate's administration, with the SAS using their time on 'hearts and minds' work and honing their mapmaking skills in this underexplored corner of Arabia.[68] While it was clearly important to try to better integrate the peninsula into the Sultanate, operation 'Intradon' also had the convenient by-product of helping to stabilise and give confidence to the Trucial States as well.

Luce, the Cabinet, National Interest and Implications for Policy towards Oman

In the aftermath of the decision to intervene in Musandam, the Defence and Overseas Policy Committee met on 8 December to discuss the recommendations of Sir William Luce's report on the Persian Gulf. This document, while agreeing that the military withdrawal from the Gulf should go ahead in 1971, stated that British aims in the Gulf were:

(a) to contribute by all possible means to the creation of conditions which will ensure peace and stability;
(b) to preserve as much influence as possible with a view to maintaining that stability and to limit communist influence in the area to the greatest possible extent;
(c) to maintain the uninterrupted flow of oil on reasonable terms;
(d) to increase British exports to a rapidly growing market.[69]

These statements of Luce's feelings of what comprised British national interests in the Gulf accorded with the Conservative government's conceptions of British national interest in the region. The bold statement of these goals, which often tend to be assumed,[70] and which were easily adopted by the government, were complimented by Luce's proposition that in spite of withdrawal in 1971 there were still ways in which these interests could be promoted.

In his report Luce was clear that the main threat to the Gulf and thus these four British interests came from 'subversion and revolution from Arab nationalist and left-wing elements against the remaining traditional regimes, and their encouragement and exploitation by Russia and possibly by China'.[71] He went to say that: 'It would certainly not be in British interests to let it be thought by friends or potential enemies that after 1971 HMG would have no further direct concern with the peace and stability of the Gulf area'. On the contrary, he suggests that maintaining influence, stability and preventing the spread of communism cannot '[B]e done effectively solely by economic and cultural means; for a further period some politico-military manifestation will be a contribution to stability and an important means of maintaining influence'.[72]

Luce made it absolutely clear again later in the report stressing that:

> It would certainly not be in British interests to let it be thought that after 1971 H.M.G. would have no further direct concern with the peace and stability of the Gulf area; on the contrary, it will be very much in our interest to keep as much influence as possible in the area after the withdrawal of our forces.[73]

He also stated that 'we should go some way to towards meeting their [Gulf Ruler's] desires for continuing British support in ways which will not be harmful to our mutual interests'. His report recommended a strong naval presence which should make regular visits to the area and some sort of formal treaty relationship with guaranteed consultation with the rulers in the event of an emergency. Although stopping short of full military support, continued assistance in training of local forces, in particular through the continuing secondment of British forces personnel, should be provided. These proposals were subsequently adopted by the government and made clear in Douglas-Home's statement to the House of Commons on 1 March 1971.

These sentiments can be said to be important in shaping Cabinet conceptions of national interest to some extent, and also policy towards Oman, since the main threat was clearly identified as Communist/Arabist insurrections and the main recommendation was that Britain should continue to use political and military means to ensure stability in the area in the short term. However, while these recommendations from a respected Gulf expert cannot have failed to have had some influence one wonders if the choice of Luce, whose views appeared to fit with those of the Cabinet already, meant that the recommendations in his report substantially matched the existing opinions of the government. The previous chapter examined the attitudes of Heath on the issue of Gulf withdrawal before the election, to which he and many others in the party were opposed. When the Conservatives came to power and realised that the policy could not realistically be revoked it is natural to assume that some sort of compromise would be reached. Thus allowing for withdrawal to continue (for which Luce's recommendation on this issue provided important political cover) while at the same time being able to hang on to influence in the region and continue to support friendly rulers whose continuation in power remained vital to the protection of national interests. The very fact that even before Luce's report was delivered to the Cabinet for discussion, the coup had taken place in Salalah, SAS involvement in the country had been approved and Operation 'Intradon' had been given the green light strongly suggests that as far as Oman was concerned the Conservative government had already made up its mind about its interests in the region and the best means to protect them.

In this sense then, any hint that the Conservative government was in some way distracted by other issues, such as the more direct Soviet threat, the many economic problems at home, especially the constant wage negotiations, or in the foreign policy sphere with the considerable work which was required to gain Britain's entry to the EEC, can largely be dismissed. While there is no doubt that the role of officials was crucial in shaping policy both before the Conservatives were elected in June 1970 and again at later stages under the new government, without the comprehension of the threat coupled with the interest in Oman and the conviction shown by Carrington, Heath and especially Douglas-Home, it would have been difficult to get these policies adopted and even more so with the alacrity with which they were approved. Heath was evidently, due to the pressures of leadership, less engaged in Gulf affairs than Douglas-Home but he clearly maintained an interest and was later to meet Qaboos on a number of occasions. Douglas-Home, as a former Prime Minister and Foreign Secretary, was able to dominate policy in this area; he maintained a much greater interest than Heath and was surprisingly 'hands on'.

Further Assistance

With British interests in the Gulf framed so concisely and with SAS assistance and Operation 'Intradon' already approved, it was clear that British military aid was still required in a number of other areas. Before the coup, the situation had become so bad that RAF Salalah had come under attack, necessitating the deployment of an additional detachment from the RAF Regiment accompanied by mortars. In March 1970 defences had been further strengthened with 'Green Archers' and a new type of experimental radar.[74] What was now needed was: a reinforcement of the SAS to assist with the planned 1971 offensive (a decision which, as seen above, had earlier been postponed), Royal Engineers to assist with speeding up the 'hearts and minds' operations and also interrogation experts. The last of these was achieved at the end of December when the interrogation team attached to Operation 'Intradon' but based in Sharjah were transferred to Muscat in a move, authorised by the CoS. It came with stern caveats, including: strict cover, they were to be known as No. 1 Holding Unit and were issued with orders to conduct interrogations according to a clear set of rules designed to uphold the highest ethical standards.[75]

During autumn 1970, Muscat with the support of PRPG requested assistance from the Royal Engineers. From 15 to 30 November, three separate reconnaissance parties visited Oman, who presented their findings to Oldman during a conference in Muscat from 21 to 23 December. The focus was on developing water resources on the Salalah Plain, Northern Oman and Masirah Island. In a detailed report which laid out the tasks to be completed, the officer in charge of the teams concluded that there would be great benefits to Royal Engineer involvement but that administrative support would have to be provided by SAF since BFG was in the process of being run down in preparation for withdrawal.[76] CBFG asked that consideration be given to the proposal to offer the Engineers on an 'extra costs' only basis. This would mean that the Sultanate would at least not have to bear the full cost. David Crawford while supporting the use of the RE was concerned that the Sultanate might not be able to provide the administrative backup required and that some of the tasks envisaged may be overtaken by building contracts issued to private firms by some of the ministries.[77]

His fears were realised when the CoS decided that the RE assistance should not go ahead 'because neither the FCO not ODA can offer financial assistance'[78] and because of uncertainties over SAF administrative support and lack of clarity as to the Omani government's planned development activities. Accordingly it was asked that all activities planning for the operation be halted until the Omani government could provide assurances and had decided if they would be willing to pay the full costs.[79] This was a disappointing development, on the other hand though, there were more positive developments with regard to the expansion of the SAS role in Dhofar.

During a tour of the Gulf and Oman the CGS after extensive briefings with CBFG and PRPG sent a telegram to the MoD stating '[A]m convinced of need for further SAS deployment in the Gulf area... existing two troops in Salalah to be reinforced soonest by remainder of squadron, troops there doing magnificent job but too thin on the ground'.[80] With so many people seeing the crucial role of the SAS (who numbered around 25 at this time), it was almost inevitable that the mission would be expanded. The SAS had indeed been very busy in both training and psychological operations roles, having established a radio station in Salalah, a propaganda poster campaign, air leafleting[81] with a clever strategy of appealing to Islamic sentiments and portraying the rebels as godless, a campaign which the rebels willingly reinforced by among other things comparing Marx to the prophet Mohammed.[82]

On 4 February Douglas-Home formally wrote to Lord Carrington to ask that the SAS be reinforced to around 65 men, that their operations should be extended to the *jebal* and their mandate be extended until at least the end of 1971.[83] This was duly approved by both Lord Carrington and the Prime Minister. Heath however was concerned that the Defence Secretary's minute assumed for planning purposes that 'the SAS assistance will not continue after the end of this year, the Prime Minister has questioned whether it is right to limit the assistance in this way. He has commented that the ruler wants us to stay and that Oman is a key place'.[84] Once again the Prime Minister was showing a real interest in Oman and an understanding of its importance. The MoD wrote to explain their position to No. 10 stating their unwillingness to get drawn into an open ended commitment but agreeing that rigid time limits were not useful.

Contingency Planning: Operation 'Mahonia'

As is standard in military matters contingency plans had been drawn up and were regularly updated. In the case of Oman however, the situation before and in the aftermath of the coup looked bleak. To this end a detailed plan, codenamed 'Mahonia' was made in the event of a serious deterioration of the situation in Oman or from an external threat from the PDRY. In their directive to CBFG the CoS stated that they would from time to time be willing to authorise the deployment of detachments from British Forces Gulf to Oman to support SAF. This was to be the first resort if the situation deteriorated. In addition though 'should a serious internal threat develop in the Sultanate which posed a threat to its general stability or that of the Trucial States, it may become necessary to provide substantial military assistance in open support of the Sultan'. While this assistance would need CoS and government approval, the amount of work which clearly went into the preparation of the plan and the 24–72 hours readiness of British forces to assist indicates that the planning was taken very seriously indeed. An updated version of the plan, which envisaged substantial numbers of troops, at least 22 aircraft and a frigate, was approved by the CoS on 15 February 1971.[85] While it is hypothetical to enquire if the government would have approved the enactment of the plan, especially with the political risks involved, the option was there and both the Prime Minister and the Foreign Secretary, as demonstrated above, had a keen appreciation of the importance of Oman and the key role the Gulf played in Britain's national interests.

While the plans were never needed, there remained throughout 1971 increasing pressure from officials and the Sultanate for Britain to provide more military assistance. As we have seen throughout this chapter, ministers and most officials shared the sense of urgency and the desire to assist Oman as far as possible. It is then of little surprise that in August 1971, ministers authorised the deployment of a second squadron of SAS until March 1972.

This was followed by the dispatch of a Field Surgical Team (FST) which was a great boost to morale for British and Omani troops alike, the defences at RAF Salalah were further strengthened, a Royal Artillery detachment known as 'Cracker Battery' was deployed and finally the Royal Engineers arrived to assist with development.[86] All in all, this represented a not inconsiderable package of military aid, coming as it did in the final few months before the withdrawal of British forces from the Gulf.

Conclusion

The immediate post-coup period until the end of 1971 represented a time of intense activity and considerable concern about the strength of the insurgency. There was a great deal of change in the way the insurgency was dealt with and the SAS undoubtedly influenced both strategy and tactics in Dhofar. This chapter has demonstrated how the key triumvirate of Ministers (Heath, Douglas-Home and Carrington) showed themselves to be highly sympathetic to the Omani cause and demonstrated a keen understanding of the area's importance to British interests. The authorisation of Operation 'Intradon', the incredibly swift dispatch of the SAS and their subsequent reinforcement clearly shows that significant action was considered necessary. It has also revealed the importance of officials in shaping the policy which was so rapidly approved by the government. Clearly the Heath government and officials worked well together to bring assistance to Oman.

This initial period is also interesting in the financial sphere with the Foreign Office concerned with focusing especially on getting some semblance of order installed in Muscat. Knowing the previous Sultan's rather *ad hoc* system and the need for the Sultanate to pay for much of its assistance from Britain, either in whole or in part, meant that fiscal discipline would be critical to the success of the campaign. The issues arising from the choice of candidate for finance minister further show that officials did not want Muscat to be controlled in the old manner nor to be seen to be a colony. Moreover, FCO officials, while preoccupied with other more important matters, were forced to fight with the Treasury over the Zanzibar Subsidy and also had to work hard sometimes to convince the MoD to be more flexible on issues of timing, scope, duration and scale of reinforcement of the campaign. This further demonstrates the vital role of FCO officials.

By exploring the beginnings of active British military and financial involvement through the arrival of the SAS and operation 'Intradon' and the issue of the financial advisor this chapter has illustrated the growing extent of British involvement in the Sultanate. During this critical early period of the new era for Oman, through Luce's report to the cabinet, perceptions of the national interest were crystallised and increasingly provided an unquestioned background against which policy towards Oman was formed. As is highlighted in chapters six and seven, these interests identified by Luce, which finally put on paper what many in the government, Whitehall and in the Gulf already believed Britain's interests to be, went on to be used to justify policy towards Oman for years to come. Britain's policy evolution towards Oman in the military and financial spheres, was at times quite rapid but always retained an element of caution. If in the early post-coup period British military assistance was essential, it is also vital to explore the evolution of British policy and the extent of the British involvement in respect of the internal political dimension. Namely, the establishment of an internal administration, difficulties with the essential development programme and issues between Qaboos and Tariq. At the same time though, the diplomatic dimension was also pursued, the quest for external legitimacy and recognition for the Sultanate would be just as important as the internal dimensions of power, legitimacy and efficient administration.

CHAPTER 4

BRITAIN & OMAN'S INTERNAL/EXTERNAL LEGITIMACY DILEMMA

Pitié pour nous qui combattons toujours aux frontières de l'illimité et de l'avenir

Guillaume Apollinaire

Essential though it is, the military action is secondary to the political one, its primary purpose is being to afford the political power enough freedom to work safely with the population

David Galula

Introduction

There is little doubt that the coup of 23 July 1970 brought hope both to Omani citizens and to those foreigners who were closely involved with the country. Indeed in the words of the outgoing British Consul-General, David Crawford in 1971, there was now at least no longer 'the smell of despair and inevitable defeat which clogged the air of Oman when I arrived here in September 1969'.[1] As demonstrated in the previous chapter the initial focus of officials was to be on the difficult task of changing the counterinsurgency strategy and securing active British military support, since Britain was the only country which could come to the new regime's aid. This was even more important as PFLOAG's response to the coup, was 'to escalate the struggle' aiming to cut the Sultan's only land link to the outside world from Dhofar – the Thamrit road, something they had achieved by early 1971. A press report stated that PLOAG 'mobility, equipment and tactical skill have all improved'.[2] There were in addition to this intensification, however a number of other important issues which required the attention of both the new government and British officials. The most pressing of these was the establishment of an effective administration, since the only two coherent entities in the post-coup era were the SAF and Petroleum Development Oman (PD(O)). In addition to this, the new state needed to cement its legitimacy both in the eyes of the Omani people and those of the rest of the world. Both Sultan Qaboos and Britain therefore faced great challenges.

While it is true that Qaboos had been allowed no access to power during his father's rule it is not true that he was completely unprepared for the role he assumed in July 1970. He had a sound knowledge of military affairs, experience of the wider world, had a spell of observing local government administration in Britain and had managed, despite his isolation in Salalah, to acquire a knowledge of the situation and power structures of his country. Qaboos had also had the time to think about the future he desired for his country and the benefit of widespread popular support. Despite these undoubted advantages he still required considerable British and expatriate advice and assistance in the running of the country. Ian Skeet however asserts that despite this need for advice: '[T]he British authorities, however, having helped Qaboos to take over the country henceforth deferred to him as a ruler who, by some innate instinct or some process of osmosis, was assumed to have developed overnight presidential wisdom and virtue'.[3]

This statement suggests that Britain was unwilling to give help and advice and gives the wrong impression of the actual extent of British assistance. Moreover, it fails to understand the reasoning behind not extending to the Sultan the level of direction or constructive criticism which Skeet implicitly believes was required. Aside from the clearly essential British military backing described in the previous chapter, Qaboos plainly required support in a number of other spheres – political, diplomatic and economic. He was to receive from Britain a great deal of assistance in these areas. This assistance was provided initially along similar lines to previous help but it was also recognised that the long-term British interest was in creating a country which could govern itself and would also be less reliant on British aid and advice. In order to assess the extent of British involvement in these spheres, the nature of British efforts in the immediate post-coup months to assist in the establishment of a stable, legitimate and effective administration marks a key juncture in the process of statebuilding. These efforts are underpinned by the policy review process towards Oman, conducted in the spring of 1971, shows how policy developed and demonstrates how official conceptions of Britain's national interests shaped this policy.

British policy towards the stability and modernisation of Oman, especially in terms of political authority within the country, international legitimacy and the programme of development so necessary to the Sultanate's future was viewed as being as crucial as military assistance in securing Oman's future by officials in both Whitehall and the Gulf.

A New Dawn

In this new era British policy towards Oman continued to rest, as it had under Sa'id, on the principle of development and a change in the way in which the Dhofar war was fought. In addition to this however, the need to bring Oman into the international community was recognised. In many respects Oman was a blank canvas upon which a modern state could be drawn. It is helpful at this point to bear in mind that there were, however, remnants of the old regime, the most important of which was the continuing respectful attitude of officials towards Omani sovereignty. Sultan Sa'id had been zealous in his insistence of respect for his sovereignty and Britain tended to be careful to emphasise Oman's independence and to comply with his wishes. This attitude, as this chapter will explore, was to continue under Qaboos' rule.

In addition, while there exists in much of the literature a common assumption that 23 July represented Oman's year zero, especially in terms of development, Britain had in fact been encouraging Sultan Sa'id to engage in development projects for a number of years with London suggesting appropriate experts to use. Sa'id belatedly responded to British exhortations albeit in his typical cautious and parsimonious manner, and as such there were only a small number of development projects in train prior to July 1970. These included, among others, an electricity system for Sur and the development of Mutrah port,[4] an essential requirement for the traditional merchant enclave there and a potential economic driver for the future prosperity of the capital area.

In the days following the change of ruler it was only to be expected that with the excitement and confusion the British and Omani authorities had little time to focus on development issues, especially with the rather desperate security situation. The post-coup confusion lasted for quite some time. In a dispatch on 19 August Consul-General Crawford made the difficulties he was having quite plain:

> I have been inundated by visitors, consulted at all hours of the day and night by government and bombarded by telegrams... in the first few nights following the coup we did not have disturbed nights, since we never got to bed at all... after four or five weeks of round the clock

working, some of us here are just a little tired. I have also made a conscious effort to slow up on my telegraphic traffic until I had something tangible to say.[5]

It is remarkable therefore that with the confusion and workload placed on the British officials on the spot that the foresight displayed and actions taken by these men occurred at all. It is also important to recall that in the years prior to the coup Qaboos had not been the only candidate in the picture to take over from Sultan Sa'id. Tariq bin Taimour, Sultan Sa'id's younger (half) brother, also had significant credentials which allowed him to be viewed as a potential successor. He had, after service in the Muscat Municipality and the SAF during the 1958 *Jebal Akhdar* campaign, grown disillusioned with his brother's unwillingness to engage in development and had left Oman for voluntary exile in 1962.[6] Since that time he had settled in West Germany (he had a German wife) and became increasingly active in Omani exile politics. In August 1967 he announced formally that he would fight against Sultan Sa'id, an announcement which gained him support amongst fellow exiled Omanis.[7] He was after this regarded somewhat warily by British officials who initially suspected him of holding left-wing ideas.

It was recognised by those plotting the coup however, that there was merit in having him on board if only to avoid his use as a rallying point for dissent against the new regime. British officials also saw the danger Tariq posed, stating that, 'he could present a serious challenge to Qaboos if he was unwilling to work with him'.[8] It was therefore agreed by all that Tariq needed to be involved in the new Oman. The necessary overtures to Tariq were made, according to Townsend,[9] through Hugh Oldman the Defence Secretary. J.E. Peterson, however, states that it was Malcolm Dennison the Chief of Intelligence in Oman who secured Tariq's support in a meeting in Dubai on 5 May 1970.[10] Happily for all involved, Tariq agreed to return as Prime Minister in the new regime, arriving in the Sultanate on 2 August where according to *The Times* he received a 'rousing welcome...and verse after verse of the song My Country, My Country'.[11]

In the period between the execution of the coup and Qaboos and Tariq's formation of a new government the day to day running of the Sultanate fell to a largely expatriate committee, the self-styled 'Interim Advisory Council'. The membership of this council consisted of Oldman, as chair, along with John Graham CSAF, several development officials, some Omanis who had been involved with the coup, Francis Hughes of Petroleum Development Oman (PD(O)) and Peter Mason of the British Bank of the Middle East (BBME).[12] While this group would undoubtedly have been viewed by some as a colonialist device for exercising British dominance over the Sultanate, in reality Consul-General David Crawford was anxious, despite its 'vital vacuum filling function' to see it 'subsumed into an Omani government structure run by Tariq'. He wanted no unnecessary reason for the 'Arab world to regard the Sultanate as a...client of quote British military and oil interests unquote'.[13] Crawford, however, despite his desperation for the council's disappearance was clear that there were also a number of obstacles to the swift establishment of a government run by Tariq. These included the remaining euphoric feelings, enjoyment of newfound freedoms and much receiving of supporters and relatives. Oman remained a largely tribal society and the pledging of allegiance and corresponding hospitality involved was an important part of the mix as far as the internal legitimacy and consolidation of Qaboos' rule. The 'hesitations' between the two key figures of Qaboos and Tariq who barely knew each other and finally, the daunting task of building a functioning state, further delayed progress in establishing a proper Omani government. Crawford had, despite these initial hold-ups, had been 'urging a faster momentum to this process'.[14] In the event it was not to be until the end of August 1970,[15] when the new Prime Minister returned from putting his affairs in order in Germany, that the Interim Advisory Council was wound up, which, considering the situation in Oman was still remarkably swift.

The Consul-General made it absolutely clear that he believed that 'Omani government with the Sultan and Tariq clearly seen both inside and outside the country to be running it is thus the number one priority'.[16] Despite this insistence upon making the new rule as legitimate as possible the Consul-General also made plain that 'the back-up of British advice and assistance to give government substance and to make it work is essential'.[17] He made it clear that without British help 'the risks that the real enemies of the Sultanate will take advantage of their failure are equally considerable'.[18] It seems that Crawford was already by 7 August aware of the danger of Britain being distracted by military matters and complacency over the new regime's ability to govern. As touched upon previously he stressed the urgent need of the Sultanate authorities for a Financial Advisor, a need which was expressed by Colonel Oldman to David Crawford 'with a certain hint of desperation', Crawford believing that the arrival of such an important figure could be 'the catalyst to credible Omani government'.[19] The appointment of this advisor was, as was explored in the previous chapter, carried out with relative haste by the FCO and even enjoyed the active support of the Foreign Secretary. London, too, obviously saw the need for sound advice for the new government.

The British interest in financial matters, which were to be so important to a country with a modest oil income, extensive military spending and a desire for rapid development, also extended to more technical issues and especially the idea of establishing a central bank, a necessary pre-requisite for a country whose main unit of exchange remained the Maria Theresa Thaler. As such both the FCO and the Bank of England were keen to advise the new regime on such issues. A letter from the Bank of England to the Arabian Department states that '[T]he Bank has wide experience and specialised knowledge of monetary affairs, which he [Qaboos/Tariq] might find it useful to call upon as the economy of Oman develops'.[20]

When Tariq returned to Muscat at the beginning of September the initial post-coup problem of an overly formal, wary and difficult relationship between Prime Minister and Sultan quickly came to pass once more. In addition to this was a new problem – the lack of activity on the part of the Prime Minister. It appeared to officials that these two problems were interrelated. In a dispatch of 13 September J.C. Kay of the Consulate-General used the allegory of a game of cards which had previously been used by Crawford to describe the 'game' being played by Qaboos and Tariq. He described Tariq's inaction since his return, a view backed by the merchants of Matrah who were to be of increasing importance in the new oil dominated[21] rentier state,[22] as part of the 'long cool and skilful game of cards' envisaged by Crawford. In his opinion though, 'in my Bridge you at least play something when it is your turn'. This situation meant that 'the effect of this lack of government is emphasised by the withdrawal back into their own jobs of the British officials who have been running the country until now...as a result, the country is collectively waiting for Godot'.[23]

At this moment, despite the problems, there was still optimism that the spheres of influence of Tariq and Qaboos would be reconciled after they had spent more time working together. Indeed it was also reported that Col. Oldman was attempting to get Qaboos to be more forthcoming in his attitude towards his new Prime Minister. It was recognised though that 'the danger of a vacuum is worrying a lot of people here'.[24] The lack of co-ordination and exact definition of responsibilities of the two roles led to Tariq becoming frustrated with the Sultan's reluctance to allow him any say in matters of finance and defence. In an interview with Crawford on 15 September Tariq said he would be 'holding the two portfolios or (wryly) so he thought'.[25] In the same meeting he also said that he wished to see Colonel Oldman continue in his job for as long as he wanted to and that he had great respect for him. He also however, stated his preference that most of the other expatriates would be replaced by Omanis fairly soon, stating in particular a desire to remove a number of prominent figures. In the margins of this dispatch someone from the Arabian Department has written: 'looks like the Aden club's days are numbered!'[26]

Clearly, like Crawford there was worry elsewhere in the FCO that the presence of these men was creating the wrong image. John Townsend certainly concurs with this evaluation when he states that their presence 'gave rise to much adverse propaganda in the Arab world... that "the British" were ruling Oman for their own commercial and political benefit and that Qaboos and Tarik were "British puppets"'.[27] The Deputy Political Resident Persian Gulf (DPRPG) Michael Weir said that he could understand Tariq's desire to reduce the number of Britons in the administration. He stated that in none of the other developing Gulf States 'was there an "Old Guard" British element as conspicuous and notorious as that in Muscat'. He did however, see the value in having high quality Britons in financial positions while avoiding appearing 'to be out for grabs'.[28]

It is interesting to discover here that officials in other postings felt able to contribute to the debate which was going on about the desirability of appointing British citizens to important posts. C.J. Treadwell, the Political Agent in Abu Dhabi, argued that experiences in his posting should not dissuade the British government from encouraging the appointment of Britons to key positions. Indeed he reports that there was some criticism within Abu Dhabi that Britain did not bring in enough men of sufficiently high calibre in the early period of Sheikh Zaid's rule. Anthony Acland wrote across the top of this opinion piece, '[G]ood points. For Oman we probably need a few men of really high quality rather than a quantity of lower calibre British expatriates'.[29]

Officials were clearly aware of the dangers in terms of internal and external legitimacy if there were too many British members of the new administration. At the same time they were also cognisant of the difficulty of finding suitably qualified Arabs 'with all the manoeuvring, intrigue, corruption and avoidance of responsibility that can so often result from their greed and sense of insecurity'.[30] The balancing act that this dilemma entailed was mainly concerned with the formation of a new government under Tariq rather than in what Townsend describes as the 'three vital areas, petroleum affairs, finance and defence'.[31] Indeed, Weir explicitly stated in his report on Oman, that, 'it is in the Armed forces that the regime can least afford to take the risk of pushing a policy of Omanisation'.[32] Despite a continued strong British presence in these three areas elements of the old guard had already left Oman and were followed on 12 October by the hugely influential General Manager of PD(O) Francis Hughes who was replaced by a Swiss, a Mr R. Jäckli.[33]

Slow Development

Whilst the problems of deciding the appropriate number and visibility of British officials in the new government and the division of labour between Sultan and PM occupied a large amount of government and Consular time, there was a worrying lack of focus on the material benefits expected by the Omani people – the 'coup dividend'. A number of large contracts had been awarded by the Interim Advisory Council for such projects as road building, yet there had been little focus on the less glamorous types of development which could have an immediate and very welcome impact upon the everyday lives of Omanis especially in the interior of northern Oman. It is fitting then that in line with the British policy of encouraging development and the new idea of Civil Action Teams, which were envisaged as part of the strategy to win over the *jebalis* of Dhofar, that in October 1970 the Engineer in Chief of the British army, Major General R.L. Clutterbuck, visited the country to assess development progress and to propose areas in which the Royal Engineers could make a difference. In his report submitted at the end of October 1970 he highlighted the fact that 'it was hardly fair to have expected much within three months, though major construction projects... had already been started, many people are disappointed that there is still little sign of rural development'.[34] He highlighted the pressing need for smaller scale development projects both in Dhofar and the interior of Oman and suggested a number of projects which the Royal Engineers could provide assistance. He specified the need for proper town planning and the construction of housing in Salalah, the possibility of an irrigation and water storage system to utilise the Salalah plain for agriculture, the building of dams in the wadis of northern Oman for similar purposes, the construction of schools and clinics and the training of locals to do this in the interior. He also expressed concern over the SAF's lack of an engineer unit.[35] He further suggested that experts in irrigation and drilling should be sent to survey the areas he proposed in more detail.

The head of the Arabian Department, Anthony Acland, certainly saw no problem with the proposed assistance stating 'I should have thought that this was an activity which should be supported'.[36] Britain wished to provide as much help as possible in the speeding up of the delivery of immediate benefits of the new regime to the people in order to increase the regime's legitimacy and reduce the likelihood of rebellion spreading. This assistance remained, however, within the parameters of previous policy in that the MoD required assurances that the Sultanate authorities wished them to carry out these activities and that they were willing to pay for them. To this end, before the suggested hydrologist was sent out to conduct his survey, David Crawford in Muscat received an urgent telegram from the Foreign Secretary stating that the visit 'would be on the understanding that it in no way committed the MoD to the implementation of the proposals... please also confirm that the Sultanate authorities i.e. political as well as military agree to this visit and are prepared to meet its "full costs"'.[37]

The Establishment of the Government

The whole process of establishing an administration almost from scratch was undoubtedly a considerable challenge. By 17 August 1970 four ministers had, by agreement of Tariq and Qaboos been appointed in the areas of Health, Education, Justice and Home Affairs.[38] While British officials were keen for the new government to be established, little could happen until Tariq returned from wrapping up his affairs in West Germany, at the beginning of September. At this point though, David Crawford was not yet too concerned about the lack of agreement on responsibilities of the Sultan and Tariq. It seems that Oldman had attempted to create a more precise formulation of the new government structure which would have put the ministries of finance and defence under the Prime Minister's control leaving Qaboos as the initial recipient of oil revenues and as the CinC of the Armed Forces. Crawford reported however that 'the Sultan remains unpersuaded about the need for Tariq to have a significant say over matters of finance and defence'.[39] Qaboos did however wish Tariq to have more power in the sphere of external affairs which Tariq was unsure about because of his lack of knowledge of written Arabic.

At this stage British officials appeared willing for Oldman to attempt to broker, somewhat unsuccessfully, a deal between the two figures. It was also reported that both 'appear to have accepted the principle that Government should emerge organically in an Omani way, without precise guidance on "structure" from their British advisors'. Crawford certainly seemed to like the two men's reaction to Oldman, stating in a report that: 'I find this gentle but polite reaction to advice based on sound military and Aden colonial precepts rather healthy'.[40] By the end of August though, Crawford could already see that the differing visions for Oman of the two leading personalities could lead to a prolonged game between the two participants. Tariq's vision of Oman was some form of constitutional monarchy with a chamber of deputies, while Qaboos believed that such a dramatic change of ruling style would confuse his people and create more problems. He wished instead to get systems of administration in place and to focus on development.

Just a few months later, at the beginning of November, Crawford would see the organic emergence principle in a rather less favourable light and what were seen as initial teething problems between Tariq and Qaboos as a much more pressing concern. The initial British attitude of allowing things to settle down and allowing a natural system to develop appeared to be a sensible one. It is far better for a *modus operandi* to appear in this way rather than to risk being seen to be imposing a structure and enforcing a delegation of powers, especially in a sovereign state.

Despite the continuing need for this balance to be achieved, by the end of October there were signs reported by Crawford that the power relationship was moving in the direction of a resolution. He describes the growing confidence, stature and authority of the Sultan and the growing indications that Tariq is 'neither as popular, effective or as certain of his ability to cut the Sultan down to size as he was some weeks ago'.[41] Qaboos remained concerned about Tariq's desire for a constitution and had thought long and hard about the issue. He had also consulted far and wide and had become convinced that it was 'an irrelevancy at this stage', since many tribal sheikhs and *walis* had stated that they would only take orders from him and no one else.[42] Crawford reported on the Sultan's new determination that his voice would predominate in the areas of finance, defence, external policy and the awarding of large scale contracts. There were growing concerns about Tariq's inability to get a grip on his new government, with Crawford noting that '[G]overnment here is incoherent since it is not co-ordinated from the Prime Minister's office'. He reported on the good work being done by the energetic minister of Health Dr Jamali but stated that apart from that 'the rest of the government remains inert'. Indeed it appeared that Tariq had not even visited the Ministry of Education.[43]

The Consul-General questioned whether this purposelessness in the government should be causing the British government concern but stated that the new rulers retained a large degree of goodwill from the lifting of the restrictions of the previous regime but that it was essential to get good quality advisors in place in the economic and financial fields to ensure revenues are spent wisely and to 'avoid the chaos of development Abu Dhabi style'. Despite these problems he believed it difficult to 'think how the birth of effective government in the Sultanate could be other than untidy'.[44]

The Internal/External Legitimacy Dilemma

British officials were, by this point, increasingly becoming aware of a serious dilemma. The Sultan had a great deal of internal legitimacy, partly because of the sense of relief the new era inspired, partly because of his extensive tours, made since his assumption of power and the contact with his people this engendered[45] and most importantly because of the hope for future development and prosperity he had promised. The difficulty which faced both the Sultan and the British was the need for the new regime to be seen to be run by Omanis for Omanis when so few Omanis had the education and skills to create an effective indigenous administration which could provide the development craved by the people. There was also a desperate need to avoid the mistakes of other Gulf States in the throes of swift modernisation. Since Oman could not afford to waste the meagre resources with which it had been blessed, this necessitated good management, which was at that stage sorely lacking in the Sultanate's new administrative structures and could only be provided by expatriates.

In addition to the need to cement in place the internal legitimacy which had been built by Qaboos, there was also a need to create secure external legitimacy for Oman. This meant a further series of dilemmas for Britain as external legitimacy rested upon the deconstruction of the firm belief, in the Arab states in particular, that the new regime was controlled by 'the British'. External legitimacy also rested albeit to a lesser extent on the visible progress in development which was also so important for internal legitimacy. Britain was therefore placed in something of a quandary. The new regime needed to reduce British influence to appear legitimate but also needed British expertise to be able to create an effective and developing state.

There appears to be little question of the British wanting to create a colonial administration in Oman although that was the only way that Crawford could envisage the 'muddle and uncertainties' facing the government being remedied. He therefore reasoned that the present situation was tolerable 'since it is our wish that Omanis should govern themselves'. This, then, was longer term British policy. Omanis should, develop the structures of self-government, as had been occurring in the rest of the Gulf, with some British guidance so that Britain would not have to administer Oman for decades to come. Crawford was even able to see a potential benefit for legitimacy in the present situation due to the fact that, 'Ironically, it could be argued that because there is a muddle...we have a more familiar Middle East situation on our hands that may even persuade outside Arabs that colonialism is a thing of the past'.[46]

Perhaps though, the prescient reason for Britain giving the new government the space to evolve, albeit with advice when clearly essential, was the protective presence of British-controlled Armed Forces. Crawford admitted that 'there remains the comforting fact that the Army, with our support, provides a firm shield, behind which government will, we trust, become more coherent'.[47] This willingness to let things proceed with as little involvement as possible did not however prevent the Consul-General and the Arabian Department from keeping a close eye on proceedings. The Consul-General provided lists of new appointees in the four ministries and Anthony Acland was quick to note that the list 'seems to include a number of people who given their background and credentials cd [sic] be potential troublemakers'.[48]

In the focus on the teething troubles of the essential Tariq-Qaboos axis and the problem of slow development it is interesting to see that Crawford was able to provide a different perspective from these twin obsessions. This is manifest in a report from the Consul-General on the occasion of the Sultan's official birthday on 16 December 1970, which was the scene of some flamboyant displays of pageantry:

> It is prudent that a European observer should look with jaundiced eye upon the muddle and lack of real progress in government, but at the same time, it must be acknowledged that the opportunity to take part in public occasions may be as important to Omanis as is the provision of schools, hospitals and roads. Pomp and ceremony served the new regime well this week and may help to give them the time they need to bring modern and effective government to Oman.[49]

David Crawford reported that the difficult relationship between Sultan and Prime Minister however, 'was not as it might have been destructive'. At least 'the degree of disorder bordering on chaos' in the areas of government appointments, structure and economic development did not affect the SAF and oil extraction, since Qaboos had reserved these issues solely for himself. Skeet suggests that 'perhaps it should have been the business of the British Consul General to have tried to bridge the gap' between the two men.[50] Essentially though, what Skeet failed to understand in his criticism of the British for not offering the new regime the advice and assistance it required and in not using its extraordinary influence to create an understanding between the key players, were the reasons behind the desire of officials to avoid doing exactly that.

Biding Time for Evolution

Oman was treated by officials as a sovereign state as far as possible and permission for activities such as the proposed hydrological survey was always requested (as too, most often, were the funds to pay for it). There was always a desire in official minds to limit as far as possible the impression of Britain running the new regime. The opportunity for a more secure future for British interests in the Gulf presented by the new era in Oman meant that the long term legitimacy of the new regime was of almost equal importance as winning the war in Dhofar. The impression that the Sultan was not able to develop his own governing structures could have had long term consequences for Qaboos' internal legitimacy. In addition, if Britain wanted to leave the Gulf at the end of 1971 and Oman as soon as possible thereafter, the country would need to step onto the world stage and to do that with a reinforced image as a British stooge would have seriously damaged the process. Crawford alluded to this dilemma when he wrote 'the place of the British in a country seeking international "respectability" will be a matter which will have to be treated with delicacy by both ourselves and the Omanis'.[51]

It could be argued that with the already extensive British presence in the SAF and the oil industry, Britain had nothing to lose in imposing a definition of their roles on Qaboos and Tariq. This, though, could easily have had negative consequences for Britain's influence and longer term national interests in the country. It is always better to allow a solution to emerge naturally and endure the intervening difficulties than it is to impose a solution which may be unsuccessful and which has the potential to alienate both sides and the political capital which has been carefully accrued spent at no benefit to yourself. In the Omani situation it was clear that this was an option of last resort as two factors were present which allowed Britain the luxury of letting nature take its course. The goodwill of Omanis and the existence of the SAF enabled Britain to maintain a respectful distance from Omani sovereignty.

It must also be remembered that the impression Skeet gives of British officials believing that Qaboos was suddenly endowed with the skills to rule and therefore did not need advice is also somewhat at odds with the evidence. Both Qaboos and Tariq had regular meetings with the Consul-General at which advice was offered. In addition there were frequent visits to the Sultanate by officials from both Bahrain and London and help was given in finding for example the new Finance Advisor, Mr Aldous, from the Bank of England on currency and reserve matters and in the development sphere.

Policy Reassessment

Despite the willingness, especially on David Crawford's part, to allow a natural solution to develop in the Qaboos-Tariq relationship, some of the concerns expressed in the Consul-General's reports began to sound some alarm bells elsewhere within the system. British policy from July 1970 to March 1971 while dynamic in the military sphere, remained in the political sphere a mixture of wait and see, help where needed and the previous stress on the need for rapid development which had been the consensus among officials for a long period. This could be described in some senses as policy drift but there were good reasons why policy remained like this. In the early spring of 1971 however, the increasing concern over the difficulties being experienced by the fledgling administration and the imminent change of Consul-General in Muscat prompted the decision to provide some policy guidelines so as to be able to offer the new Consul-General, Donald Hawley, who had previously been the chancellor at the British Embassy in Baghdad, some idea of his remit. It was seen that 'the time is opportune to take stock of the situation in Oman and of our relations with the Sultanate'.[52] A decision was therefore taken between Bahrain and the Arabian Department to produce a policy paper.

The ensuing policy review was to look at both the future prospects of Oman and both the short and medium term British interests there, so as to formulate a clear set of policy objectives. Towards the end of March 1971 Mr J.M. (Ian) Blackley of the FCO submitted an in depth examination of British interests in Oman, a summary of recent events, a series of possible future developments in the Sultanate and a list of policy ideas. This of course was just the beginning of the policy review process but the contents of this initial examination were to have a bearing on the course of future debates on the issue.

Ian Blackley identified five key areas of British interest. These were: a) to prevent the Sultanate from disintegrating or falling to a regime hostile to the stability of the Gulf and Britain's oil interests during the withdrawal from the Gulf, b) in the long term to ensure the Sultanate was a stable, internationally recognised and pro-British state, c) to maintain the flow of high quality oil from PD(O), d) to maintain the RAF facilities and BBC relay station on Masirah at least for as long as commitments to Malaysia and Singapore continued, and e) to keep to the minimum, British military activities in the Sultanate without damaging the other objectives.[53] He then went on to assess the future validity of these traditional assessments of British interests agreeing that a) and b) were essential. He qualified the need for Oman to be universally recognised however, and suggested that failure to join the Arab League and UN in the next five years meant that 'British interests need not be endangered and we may be able to use the further period of isolation to consolidate our commercial and political position'.[54] Oil too was judged to remain an important interest not just for Britain but as an energy source for all developed countries. Of greater interest were the sterling reserves generated by oil held in London and the future potential market for British banks and financial sector in the country. The short term need to retain RAF Masirah was judged 'a pillar of our policy'. The immediate increase in British military engagement was regarded as 'a valid policy which does not invalidate the medium term policy of disengagement'.[55] In essence then, British interests in the Sultanate remained constant.

Next were examined a number of potential internal factors which might affect future policy. A setback in the Dhofar campaign and the spread of rebellion was seen to have potentially major consequences and Blackley believed that the temptation to reinforce SAF in this instance would be very strong. British intervention he thought though 'would create more problems than it would solve', if it was on a large scale then it could cause Britain much expense and casualties, as well as 'opening us to the charge of blatant imperialist aggression and ruining the Sultanate's chances of international recognition'.[56] Once again the dilemma of the need for British involvement versus the potential costs to Oman's long term legitimacy became apparent and would provoke disagreement among officials as to the correct balance.

Other potential internal factors included: the possible disillusionment of returning exiles with lack of external recognition, which may be blamed on Britain, how the Sultan may react to this demand and indeed how the Sultan may develop as a ruler were also considered to be a potential future difficulty for British policy. Blackley judged that 'although he has yet to make a serious mistake, he is already showing ominous signs of inheriting many of his father's characteristics'.[57] The possible outcome of a serious power struggle between Sultan and Prime Minister was also considered.

External factors were next assessed. These included potential subversion of the nascent UAE and then of Oman from the Trucial States after Britain's withdrawal, a potential Greater Oman incorporating these states, Saudi expansionism to include other Gulf states, increased subversion from Iraq or the newly renamed People's Democratic Republic of Yemen (PDRY),[58] the political and economic activities of the Communist bloc in the rest of Arabia, especially Sino-Russian rivalry, and finally, future British commitments to the defence of South East Asia that had the potential to impact upon the interest in retaining the facilities on Masirah.[59] All of these possible events would have had important ramifications for Britain's policy.

Blackley noted 'HMG's policy has served British interests very well up to the present and has been rejuvenated by the change of regime in Oman. It is, however, if not an imperialist policy, certainly that of a possessive mother towards a difficult child'.[60] He recognised that the next 12 months would be crucial for the next five years and as such suggested a number of policy proposals. These included, continuing with the current levels of support, meeting all reasonable short term requests for assistance, renegotiating and extending the secondment of service personnel, trying to discover the real intentions of the Saudis towards Oman and offering diplomatic support to the Omanis to fit the situation, to avoid as much as possible appearing to be the Omanis intermediary or 'post-box', refusing to act on behalf of nations or bodies which are reluctant to contact the Sultanate authorities for political reasons, changing the Consulate in Muscat to an Embassy and finally 'to investigate ways of destroying the present National Front regime in Aden, or, failing that to dissuade it from operations against SAF' as well as jamming or destroying Aden Radio.[61]

These preliminary assessments and policy proposals contained in Blackley's extensive initial report were to provoke a great deal of debate and some disagreement within the Arabian Department and amongst the Residency staff in Bahrain and the Consulate-General staff in Muscat. It is therefore interesting at this juncture, to follow how the policy review was conducted and future British policy was decided upon. From this examination it is possible to see which personalities and departments had the upper hand in deciding the future of British policy towards Oman.

Ian Blackley's 24-page initial policy paper was sent to Anthony Acland the head of the Arabian department and Mr Robert McGregor. By 14 April 1971 McGregor had read the draft and commented that it was 'too long, ambitious and speculative'.[62] He had therefore written a shorter draft paper with two assumptions, that in the absence of a reply from the MoD as to the future of Masirah that it would continue to be required and secondly that 'HMG genuinely wish to treat Oman as an independent country and not as a fall-back base, when our special treaty relationship with the Gulf States comes to an end'.[63] His paper was less than half the length of Blackley's and was sent to Anthony Acland, who sent it on to William Luce and Anthony Parsons for comment, with the words that if they agreed 'the next step would be to send it to Mr Arthur [Political Resident Persian Gulf] for his comments and then to clear it in Whitehall. There is no point trying to clear a document with which Mr Arthur fundamentally disagrees'.[64]

Anthony Parsons was not altogether happy with the draft policy paper and stated his concerns in a letter to William Luce on 21 April. While he agreed with the need for Oman to make its move onto the international stage and that too obvious a British presence in the country could prevent this, he also thought that 'on the other hand the stability of Oman in the short and medium term is an important British interest in the context of our interests in the Gulf'.[65]

Just eight days before writing this letter, after a brief trip to northern Oman, the PRPG Geoffrey Arthur had sent a dispatch to the Arabian Department. In his message Arthur stated that 'the trip was extremely depressing from the political, economic and sociological points of view. Absolutely nothing has been done in Oman since my last visit there six months ago. Not one brick has been laid on another.' He reported that 'everybody is complaining that the Sultan and his ministers sit in Muscat and neither know nor care what is happening in the interior'.[66] Arthur's shock at the lack of progress in inner Oman and the rumblings of discontent there led him to speak directly to the Sultan about the problem during his meeting on 9 April and to suggest that 'some token development be done in Oman immediately – outside the normal development programme'.[67] The

Sultan was shocked, and was sympathetic to Arthur's idea stating that he would provide £100,000 from the Privy Purse for the construction of a medical centre at or near Nizwa. On 11 April David Crawford in Muscat sent a telegram to Geoffrey Arthur in Bahrain reporting a meeting with the Health Minister Dr Jamali who had been told on 10 April to build a dispensary in Nizwa no later than 23 July using £100,000 which had been released by the Sultan for the purpose. The telegram also stated that Jamali 'welcomed your initiative and understood why you had not had time to discuss Health matters with him'.[68] Geoffrey Arthur concluded his dispatch with the words 'It looks for once as though my interference in the only independent country with which I deal may bear some fruit. But the fruit will be symbolic only. I feel pretty depressed as a result of my recent trip'.[69] It is clear then that if a situation was of serious magnitude, British officials felt able to raise matters with the Sultan and the Sultan would take these concerns seriously.

The concerns expressed by Geoffrey Arthur were to have an impact beyond Oman itself however. In his letter to William Luce on 21 April 1971, Anthony Parsons went on to state that 'recent correspondence from Mr. Arthur suggests a really alarming degree of stagnation under the new Sultan; we might have the power, if we use it appropriately, to galvanise him into action'.[70] The suggestion in the review, that the priority was for Muscat to gain international recognition and therefore that there would be a need to lessen the obvious British presence was challenged by the reports of stagnation and the need for development to ensure stability – development which could be encouraged and facilitated by Britain. This meant that the dilemma of which path to choose was becoming more acute. Anthony Parsons went on to state in his letter to William Luce that 'I am not sure that the paper reflects this dilemma vividly enough or that it comes to the right conclusions'.[71]

Before much more work on the policy paper could be conducted, the Arabian Department was to receive two dispatches from its men on the spot, both of which were to emphasise the dilemma in a much more vivid way. On 24 April, Consul-General David Crawford sent his valedictory dispatch to Political Resident Geoffrey Arthur. In what was not an especially optimistic message he described Oman as a 'sick country' and laid out the problems which Oman faced; he also stressed his opinions of where things could be improved. The lack of suitably trained and experienced Omanis in all fields was highlighted as a major problem. Crawford emphasised the need for outside expertise with the words:

> The thin red line of European expertise which, if reinforced, could strengthen government at a practical level (thus protecting Omani

ministers from their own inadequacies and from the growing discontent of their people), is in danger of snapping through overwork.[72]

Later in the dispatch he highlighted the problems between the Defence Secretary Colonel Hugh Oldman and Prime Minister Tariq bin Taimur and suggested that on his return from a trip to Europe in June the Sultan might 'be faced with the task of persuading two prima donnas to cooperate or of reluctantly deciding that one must go'. He then used this potential problem to illustrate the challenge which Britain faced. The Sultan could rely extensively in the short term on British advisors and security and damage his regime in the eyes of the world leading to the arrival 'sooner or later of the Kalashnikov carrying liberators'. At the opposite extreme he could have an Oman badly governed by Omanis thus gaining outside approval. Yet without the British shield the 'day of the Kalashnikov carrying liberators' would still have come. So neither extreme of behaviour would be good for Britain 'if we wish to see a stable, western inclined but sovereign and independent Oman at the end of this decade'. The Consul-General therefore suggested the continuing policy of 'tactful and unobtrusive, (in as far as our military presence will permit it) handling of our relations with Oman'.[73]

It is clear that David Crawford believed that Britain still had a role to play in Oman and that while development was slow it was discernable. He also thought that the international recognition of Oman was important. This could bring mixed blessings however, and while Britain would be 'rid of an international embarrassment which has gone on for far too long; . . . the pressure that may then be placed on Oman from many directions could ultimately erode our special military position in the country'.[74] UN membership could be useful for Oman both in terms of access to the specialised agencies but also because it would allow the use of article 2(7) of the Charter to shelter behind when facing examination of her internal affairs. He also pointed out that there was a real and natural desire on the part of Omanis for recognition and that 'Sayyed Tariq is the man most likely to succeed in persuading a suspicious world that a united Oman is now ready for international recognition'.[75]

Coincidentally, at the same time as David Crawford was working on his valedictory dispatch Geoffrey Arthur was also drafting a memo on his impressions of Oman and its future. In a lucid and entertaining dispatch overflowing with imagery Geoffrey Arthur highlights the dilemma facing Britain and the Sultan. He states that 'we cannot afford to let things go too wrong. If we leave things to the Omani government they will go wrong; but if we step in too often to straighten things out, we shall show up the Sultan as our puppet'. It would have been better to keep the patient, 'isolated as before, but under treatment and not neglect; for treatment is difficult when the patient has too many visitors or insists on walking out in the world. But this choice was probably never open to the Sultanate or to us: it is certainly not open now'.[76] Like David Crawford, Geoffrey Arthur suggested that 'we must be discriminating in our help and intervention'. Where he parts from Crawford's opinion is in what he later describes in a covering letter sending both his and Crawford's reports to the Foreign Secretary as 'not in the diagnosis, but in the remedy, for I suspect that Mr. Crawford's prescription contains more Arab and less British drugs than mine'.[77] He was not wrong in his assessment. While he stressed the need to remain committed to the war in Dhofar by providing 'the fullest possible aid' he also suggested that 'if we see that the security of the state is being put at risk by the lethargy or folly of the Prime Minister or other Ministers, we should not hesitate to warn the Sultan, who will lend a ready ear'.[78] The two separate dispatches on Oman received a somewhat mixed response in London; an unidentified hand has written 'It is a pity that we have been presented with two dispatches covering... much the same ground'.[79] Yet the document upon which it has been written states that 'both dispatches have arrived usefully at a time when a new paper was being drafted on HMG's policy towards Oman'.[80]

Objections

After having seen the second draft of the paper both Anthony Parsons and William Luce expressed their opinions on the piece. Anthony Acland, the head of the Arabian Department, made some changes to the original draft based on their and his own concerns. Undoubtedly one of the most important of these changes was the addition of a new paragraph under the British interests section. This section stated in the original draft that British interests were: to maintain good relations with the present and any successor regime, to maintain continued production of and search for high quality oil, to increase British exports, to retain staging facilities for the RAF. It then stated the general British interest in maintaining stability in the area. Acland has changed the emphasis of this section entirely by deleting this paragraph and adding:

> These can only be achieved however, against the background of the continuing stability and integrity of the Sultanate of Oman. This is therefore the first British interest from which the others follow and is relevant not only in the context of Oman itself but in the context of our even greater material interests in the Gulf States.[81]

This is a serious change of emphasis and makes it very explicit where British interests are seen to lie in the eyes of senior officials: Anthony Acland, William Luce and Anthony Parsons. On 28 April the further revised draft policy paper was sent by Sir Anthony Acland to Bahrain for PRPG Geoffrey Arthur's approval accompanied by a covering letter which suggested that while Britain's influence in Oman was still strong 'probably the most fruitful action... is to spur the Sultan and his government to get a move on with development (on the lines of your recent talk with Qabus about the situation in the interior)'.[82] It appeared that the coming change of Consul-General to Donald Hawley was going to be accompanied by a greater willingness to press British opinions on important matters and as such marks a slight change of emphasis of British policy towards greater involvement. It appeared that all concerned with the policy review saw it as a temporary measure which would require a further review later in 1971 because of the number of uncertainties and the evolving situation in the country.

By 4 May Geoffrey Arthur had read the draft policy paper and had agreed with its general direction although he did attach four pages of detailed comments. These comments are interesting as they show the perception of British interests from Bahrain. Arthur believed that the concentration on having Britons in key posts alone may not safeguard British commercial interests and warned that 'we shall have to watch Tariq and his German connections'. He pointed out that British relations with the current regime were so close that it would be difficult to have good relations with a successor regime, effectively all of Britain's eggs were now in the one basket. He also asked for any reference to the withdrawal of the SAS in 1971 to be removed. Equally any doubt about the renewal of the agreement about the secondment of British officers due to expire at the end of 1971 should be removed. There was no option in his opinion other than the subversion of the PDRY regime as they were not likely to voluntarily stop supporting the Dhofari rebels. Geoffrey Arthur's comments are clearly motivated by his strongly held view that British interests lay in protecting the Sultanic regime to the upmost. Indeed later in his letter to Acland one can feel his frustration that some in London have not fully grasped the importance of supporting the Sultan. Paragraph 14 in particular seemed to annoy him most. He described it as 'too facile' and that:

> [T]he sentence I object to mostly is the one which reads [']If the Sultan and his Government were divided on this, or indeed any other major issue, our underlying aim would be to support the side most likely to win in the long term[']. I do not think that we should be able to conduct

a policy on this basis. In the near future (which is what this paper is about) the side which will win is the side which we support.[83]

In the final part of the letter Geoffrey Arthur attempted to end the dilemma which had been stressed elsewhere. He clearly believed that the level of British civilian presence in the Sultanate had no effect on the widely held belief that Oman remained under British control. He did not even think it was the British bases at Salalah and Masirah, but because:

> SAF is regarded as a British army. We are stuck with this position and we might as well accept it... We must either withdraw the British officers, and that means the end of the Sultanate, or accept our identification with the Sultanate and be prepared to appoint more civilian officials... since the sooner civilian government begins to work in the Sultanate, the sooner SAF can confine itself to purely security duties.[84]

It is interesting to note how much influence the PRPG had. This is clearly visible in how Anthony Acland saw little point in trying to clear the paper if Geoffrey Arthur disagreed. Arthur clearly felt able to express his opinions to Acland frankly and in the expectation that they would carry weight. Although the PRPG's opinion mattered, Acland still felt able to write on the letter 'some good points, some which may be questionable'.[85] As we have seen then, there were a number of people to be consulted as part of the process, most of whom were unhappy with the first and second drafts of the paper. The key personalities were clearly Anthony Acland and Geoffrey Arthur with serious input from David Crawford and Anthony Parsons. While they all had slightly differing views, in his reply to Geoffrey Arthur, Anthony Acland summed things up nicely saying 'I think in fact we all know what we are aiming at and broadly speaking what we should do up to the end of the year'.[86]

The problem now was that Donald Hawley was now *en poste* in Muscat and still had not received the policy paper which was intended to guide him. On 24 March 1971, the Arabian Department had asked the MoD for its opinions on the future requirement of Masirah. Having had no reply by mid May the Arabian Department wrote again, this time enclosing a copy of the policy paper amended to take into account Arthur's views.[87] On the same day a letter was also sent to the Overseas Development Administration (ODA) along with a copy of the paper asking for comments.[88] John Rowley of the ODA replied by 26 May with one correction that Technical Assistance 'can only be a help in the long term'.[89] There was still however, no reply from the MoD. A holding letter was received on 27 May from Air Commodore Brian Stanbridge, the secretary of the Chiefs of Staff Committee, stating that MoD staff were now carrying out a study of the defence aspects of policy.[90] Finally on 3 June the MoD replied to the Arabian Department stressing that Masirah was not just needed for staging facilities but that 'maintaining full and free use of the airfield' was the requirement. The MoD was also keen to stress the threat to the Sultanate but that some doubt should be expressed about the extension of the SAS term. '[T]his is not to say that we are against extending the SAS – merely that... we shall of course need to consider carefully with you the military requirement... and the financial basis on which they might be made available'.[91] Equally the MoD was concerned, as well as Arthur and others in the FCO, about the over rapid Omanisation of SAF and also wished to see a reference to the value 'to be obtained by indirect military measures such as the Royal Engineer assistance.[92] As ever then, the MoD was concerned with maintaining its own interests in Oman and in being paid for its services.

Finally on 16 June 1971 the new Consul-General Donald Hawley received the completed copy of the policy paper which was supposed to guide him in his new appointment. The letter to Hawley stated that 'we have limited the paper's scope to the short term. I hope that it will provide you with some guidelines for at least the next few months, we shall have to review the situation again in the autumn'.[93] The whole process had taken a little over three months and would have to be examined again at the end of the next quarter.

There are however a number of interesting themes which the policy review highlights. The first of these is that the extensiveness of the process demonstrates how importantly the issue was viewed. The debates during the process indicate who the most important people within the FCO were in shaping policy towards Oman. The lesser officials are given the responsibility of producing the first draft and were in this instance, more pessimistic about Oman and Britain's ability to maintain its interests there. At more senior levels people like Anthony Acland and Geoffrey Arthur were much more willing to stress the need for Britain to focus on its main interest of stability and take a much more positive and forceful role in protecting British interests.

One of the most important themes to come across from this examination of the review of policy is the perceived dilemma viewed both by Ian Blackley in his initial draft, by David Crawford in his valedictory dispatch and by Anthony Parsons who wanted it to be stressed more strongly. While the dilemma was vividly expressed by some including Geoffrey Arthur, his later reaction to the policy paper stressed that in reality Britain had no other option but to remain committed to Oman and the SAF in particular. Arthur's reaction demonstrates that some in the FCO held much more strident and forceful opinions about Britain's role and the need to defend national interests and were able to express these views to good effect in influencing policy decisions.

It is plain that all concerned with the policy review had the same objective of seeing a stable and pro-British Oman emerge onto the international stage. It was only in terms of how to balance the difficulties of gaining recognition with the need for stability, which only Britain could guarantee, that caused disagreement. The final policy adopted held a good degree of continuity with the previous policy of more active involvement in the military sphere (with as much paid for as possible) and attempting to keep the visible British role to a minimum so as to allow Oman to make progress in joining the international community.

While there is visible continuity there is also a change of emphasis which became visible on the ground in the Gulf and in the policy paper itself. While David Crawford in Muscat had been willing to allow Qaboos and Tariq time to work out their relationship and for Tariq to develop a government, with advice from Britain when requested, the continuing difficulties and lack of swift progress increasingly led to a more direct approach being taken. There was after all a war to be won and while great strides forward had been made with the SAS and turned rebel groups named *firqah*, there was much still to be done.[94] This new approach was pioneered by Geoffrey Arthur who raised the issue of healthcare in the interior and got a quick response from Qaboos, who immediately made funds available. This lesson convinced Anthony Acland to ask both Arthur and Donald Hawley to pursue this tactic again when required. This change was to lead to trouble with Tariq however, who stated to David Crawford that 'this was a panic measure...urged upon the Sultan by those, like British intelligence officers, who did not understand Omanis'.[95] In response Acland noted of Tariq that, 'many of Tariq's views are sensible if he did something about them but there is always an undercurrent of resentment'.[96] Geoffrey Arthur's views were much more forthright. In a letter to Acland in early June he stated that 'I sometimes think people think I exaggerate the administrative and political ineptitude of Tariq and that collection of orators who call themselves the government of Oman'. Later in the letter he goes on to say that:

> So far (touch wood) Tariq seems not/have shown [sic] even the ability to cause havoc in Oman. That he is a brilliant linguist there is beyond doubt. That he is an utter nincompoop, and dangerously so, I regard fairly well established. What I am not sure about is his skill in conspiracy.[97]

Clearly the difficulties between Sultan and Prime Minister and Prime Minister and Defence Secretary Hugh Oldman were still as bad as ever and consequently British tolerance of Tariq was running very low in some quarters. With David Crawford soon to leave and Geoffrey Arthur's strong opinions slowly being shared by others in the Arabian Department, British officials were showing a new willingness to intervene in order to get things moving again, even if it meant bypassing Tariq.[98]

Conclusion

During this initial post-coup period of the development of government in Oman, while Britain was intent on becoming more actively engaged in Dhofar, London was content to use the time afforded by the popularity of the new regime and the shield provided by SAF to allow a system of government to develop organically. Sadly, the difficulties faced by the new rulers in evolving their relationship and nurturing the structures of government showed little sign of improvement. During the first six to eight months of the new regime David Crawford was able to follow a relatively hands off approach both to increase the international legitimacy of the new Sultan's regime and because he believed that a *modus vivendi* between Qaboos and Tariq was possible. Yet as government in Muscat remained confused and inefficient, the dilemma facing London became more acute. Should Britain become more involved in trying to impose a working relationship on Qaboos and Tariq, raising its concerns directly and getting experts appointed so as to make government more efficient and to get development back on track? Or should London focus more on reducing Britain's visible role and encouraging Oman to join the international community as quickly as possible? Both options held attractions but thanks to the views of Geoffrey Arthur and the increasingly difficult and lazy attitude of Sayyid Tariq, British policy began to move away from its initial *laissez-faire* attitude. The policy review undertaken in the spring of 1971 stated in its final version that 'British interests in the Sultanate in particular and in the Arabian peninsula[r] as a whole are important enough to justify this [policy review] exercise'[99] as it was agreed in Whitehall by both the MoD and FCO that Britain's interests in Oman were significant.

The only other thing to decide upon was how to overcome the dilemma facing British officials. Even David Crawford had moved away somewhat from his belief in the more hands off approach and suggested that Britain must remain engaged in Oman while maintaining a low profile to help with recognition. While Geoffrey Arthur endorsed this position he could not see any way of resolving the dilemma and encouraged King Charles Street to commit further to Oman since any lessening of the British role would court disaster. What emerged from this in the policy review was a move away from the old approach towards a more active engagement by officials in trying to encourage co-operation and action. The need for an improvement in relations between Tariq and Qaboos was recognised and policy became a compromise between the two extremes with Britain willing to intervene more often and to countenance the appointment of more British officials even at the risk of appearing to be the colonial power. By examining the policy review process we once again see that officials had a large amount of control over the direction of policy, especially in this area. Clearly, the definition of Britain's national interests highlighted in the previous chapter had a role to play in underpinning the continued commitment to Oman and formed the basis of the review of policy. British policy evolved in this vital area of governance and development from a relatively passive position to a cautiously active one during the course of the crucial first year after the coup.

What this chapter has demonstrated is that Britain had good reasons for not exercising its extraordinary influence during the first six months of the post-coup period. It was important that Oman was seen to be making its own mistakes and for government to evolve rather than be imposed. Ian Skeet fails to see the fact that Britain did not leave the new regime entirely to sink or swim, advice was offered, advisors and administrators suggested and support given in practical fields. He also ignores the reasons why London followed a more hands off approach when he denounced Britain's unwillingness to assist in the establishment of the government. As the situation worsened the British approach changed to something closer to what Skeet clearly wished for and Britain began to risk being denounced by Arab Nationalists and Marxists as the colonial power. This too was clearly not the intention of British Officials, who both wanted to avoid the charge and were willing, despite their influence, to have a hands off approach wherever possible, even after the change in policy during the Spring of 1971. Writers like Halliday have claimed that:

> The pretence of Omani *independence*, like the *complexity* of the relationship, is meant to hide what is in fact a pellucid arrangement. Britain supports the Sultan and has told him what to do when it needed to; otherwise it has allowed him to rule as he likes, providing he keeps Oman tranquil and defends British strategic interests. The Sultans are British collaborators.[100]

This statement on the surface appears to be what British policy had become by 1971. This was not, however, the case. It was only after attempts had been made to allow systems to evolve naturally that officials felt obliged to intervene. When intervention was required it was conducted sensitively and often had the effect of speeding development and improving people's lives. Indeed the efficacy of intervention in the case of the dispensary at Nizwa surprised many in the Arabian Department, indicating that officials were unaware of the true extent of their influence. These are hardly the actions of an uncaring Imperial power. Like Skeet, Halliday appears unaware of the nuances of the situation and the extent to which officials wanted there to be a different relationship with the new regime. While clearly realist conceptions of national interest were at the forefront of official minds it was always recognised that Oman was a sovereign state and Britain attempted to behave in a correct manner towards Muscat. Any intervention in Omani affairs was carefully considered and a surprisingly high degree of reticence was present in official thinking about the concept. When intervention did occur it came in the form of advice and requests similar to those that would be made to any government. In investigating the extent of British involvement the evidence has shown that it is perhaps remarkable that in 1970–71 with political stability in Oman still precarious and the rebellion in Dhofar remaining formidable there was not far more British interference. After all, Oman was hardly tranquil and British interests were under threat. Britain therefore had much to be anxious about and to achieve, the most important being to remain focused on winning the war and to gain international legitimacy for the Sultanate. Neither of these was going to be easy to accomplish and help from other states with an interest in a stable Oman was to be required. In order to do this, achieving international recognition and membership of two key organisations, the Arab League and the United Nations was essential, for which further British assistance was required.

Exit Gate from Salalah 1974.
Photo by kind permission of Major D J Cuthbertson.

Supplies for Operation Hammer 1974.
Photo by kind permission of Major D J Cuthbertson.

One of the Defensive Lines in Dhofar.
Photo by kind permission of Major D J Cuthbertson.

Firqah Fighters, Dhofar 1974.
Photo by kind permission of Major D J Cuthbertson.

Cattle Watering at Tawi.
Photo by kind permission of Major D J Cuthbertson.

Defensive Positions on the *Jebal* in Dhofar.
Photo by kind permission of Major D J Cuthbertson.

The ubiquitous Skyvan, workhorse of the SOAF, unloading medical supplies as part of a medical mission to the Kuria Muria Islands.
Photo by kind permission of Trish Sole.

Sultan Qaboos inspecting positions from a *sangar* in Dhofar.

CHAPTER 5

THE SEARCH FOR INTERNATIONAL RECOGNITION: BRITAIN'S ROLE IN SECURING LEGITIMACY

Oh mankind! We made you male and female, and made you into nations and tribes, that you may know one another
Qur'an, Chapter 49, Verse 13

Introduction

While the immediate focus of both British and Sultanate policy was upon the prosecution of the war in Dhofar and the construction of a state almost from scratch, the prospect of securing international recognition and perhaps even some help in the task of nation building, remained both a tantalising prize and a policy of increasing importance. The policy was eventually to pay off, leading to 'twenty one states being represented in Muscat by late 1975 in a significant contrast to Sa'id's time when only Great Britain and India maintained representatives there'.[1]

Until the drive for recognition, which was a result of the *coup d'etat*, Oman had existed in a strange twilight zone between those states which formed the international community and were members of international organisations participating in the full panoply of diplomatic intercourse, and those national identities which were still under either direct colonial control or protection. Oman was recognised as a sovereign state by Britain and had also been recognised in the past by France[2] and the U.S.[3] In Oman's twilight zone, differences existed in its *de facto* and *de jure* position. There is no doubt that Muscat maintained a particularly 'special' relationship with Britain but Oman was never in the same position as other Gulf States and it is generally agreed that 'little in the treaties subjected Oman either explicitly or implicitly, to a protectorate status'.[4] On the other hand, the 1958 Exchange of Letters had openly acknowledged that Britain was committed to Oman's security.[5] Omani Sultans had agreed in treaties with Britain not to engage in the slave trade (1822 and 1845), not to dispose of Omani territory without British consent (1891) and in 1902 and 1923 not to give oil concessions without British approval.[6] All of these dispensations were reflected in Britain's relations with other Gulf States, all of which were considered to be under formal British protection. In addition, a further indicator of the nature of the relationship with Britain was the fact that the British representative in Muscat was not described as a Political Agent, as in the other Gulf States, nor was he an Ambassador; he was instead a Consul-General. Despite this distinction in nomenclature, the Consul-General in Muscat reported to the British Political Resident for the Persian Gulf in Bahrain, in the same way as did the Political Agents.[7] This was seen as a logical idea by Britain in terms of communication and logistics but also to ensure some co-ordination in the area. This anomaly, while logical to bureaucrats in Whitehall, did not exactly help with the promotion of the idea of Omani independence in the eyes of others.

In addition, Britain had retained its extraterritoriality arrangements for a further ten years under a new Treaty of Friendship, Commerce and Navigation signed with Oman in 1951. It was not until January 1967 that Britain finally relinquished its extraterritorial rights and even then not for British service personnel. The issue of extraterritoriality is a somewhat illuminating one. Many would see the very existence of a protection from prosecution under local law for foreigners as an abnegation of Omani independence. A state cannot be sovereign unless it has full legal jurisdiction over every person on its soil. Those countries such as China and Siam (Thailand) which had had such arrangements imposed upon them during the nineteenth century had clearly been penetrated states forming at best a part of other states' informal empires. Jürgen Osterhammel's work on informal empire states that informal empire 'rests on the three pillars of: (1) legal privilege for foreigners; (2) a free trade regime imposed from outside; and (3) the deployment of instruments of intervention such as the gunboat and the 'imperial' consul.[8] In Oman then, there were clearly elements of all three of these pillars. Yet Oman still did not quite fit the mould.

While its status in many ways seemed to reflect those of the other Gulf States there remained a number of important differences. Firstly, unlike the

Gulf States, British treaties with Oman were 'classified – published in the same way as those with independent states'.[9] This is a fine legal distinction but remains an important one. Secondly, the existence of a treaty giving Britain the right to interdict Omani vessels suspected of engaging in the slave trade, while seemingly giving Britain great power does not mean some sort of colonial control. Britain did not stand to gain anything from stopping the Omani trade in slaves (Britain was hardly likely to want the trade for itself). Additionally, at the time of signature there were no international organisations like the UN to pass resolutions authorising member states to take action to stop the trade. Thirdly, while in practice the Sultan was generally happy for Britain to act for him in the arena of Foreign Affairs, the agreements which he had entered into with Britain contained 'the Sultan's specific instructions that such representation would be undertaken only when specifically requested'.[10] This was unlike similar agreements in other parts of the Gulf which gave Britain much more latitude. Fourthly, it was clear that London itself considered its relationship with Muscat to be different to that with Dubai or Qatar. As argued in the previous chapter Britain was careful to respect Oman's sovereignty and to give advice, not orders. Finally, Oman's long and distinguished history, its past importance as a regional sea power and its days of empire in East Africa and elsewhere gave the country a different outlook and gained the Sultanate a different degree of respect from Britain.

Francis Owtram concedes that 'in legal terms a case could be made out that the Sultanate of Muscat and Oman was a fully independent and sovereign state which had accepted some limitations on its external relations though treaty relations with Britain.'[11] Fred Halliday however, cannot agree with the *de jure* recognition of Oman as an independent and sovereign country. He states that: 'It is power, not treaties, that determines history. Only writers blinded by a fog of legalism and imperialist ideology can doubt the fact that Oman has been a *de facto* British colony.'[12] While this claim may be true, it raises three important questions, a) the word colony implies a very significant amount of control, how much control was Oman under in the field of foreign affairs, b) does the legal status of a country have no importance, and c) does the recognition of independence by the dominant power in the region affect how it treats that state. These questions will be an important underlying theme in this chapter.

As was demonstrated in chapter two, Britain had great difficulty in persuading Sultan Sa'id to invest in development projects and to change the way in which he prosecuted the counterinsurgency campaign in Dhofar. Again in chapter four the difficulties British officials experienced in persuading Qaboos and Tariq to work together and the slow pace of change show that while Britain had influence it often lacked control. While the *de facto* state of affairs in a state is clearly important, the *de jure* status of a country is also of great relevance. Why else would so many states seek the legal trappings of statehood if it did not carry any significance? Talking about the United Nations, Sir Anthony Parsons states that 'it became virtually automatic for newly independent states to seek membership'.[13] Oman was to be no exception.

With the British withdrawal 'East of Suez' and the sweeping away of the architecture of protection in the Gulf, Muscat could no longer afford to retain its somewhat ambiguous position. The time was approaching when Oman would have to step out into the Society of States and standardise its relationship with the world.

Stage Management

The *coup d'etat* of 23 July 1970 presented Britain with a golden opportunity to ensure that the Sultanate would be viewed in a new light on the international stage. The very day after the *coup* a telegram was sent from Foreign Secretary Alec Douglas-Home to the Political Residency in Bahrain explaining that the Foreign Office, 'propose to telegraph tomorrow to HM representatives in certain Arab capitals, explaining developments to them in strict confidence and seeking their views on how best the governments to which they are accredited can also be encouraged to express support for Qabus'.[14] This attempt, coming as it did such a short time after the coup, demonstrated Britain's concern to secure a different more regularised future for the Sultanate. As seen in the previous chapter, part of securing support for the new regime from other countries meant that a new impression of Oman needed to be created, one of irresistible momentum and progress towards development, prosperity and independence. As such, officials were concerned about the possible effects of abrupt recognition of the new Sultan by Britain. J.M. Edes of the Arabian Department cautioned 'a short delay, if only to avoid strengthening suspicions, which are no doubt bound to arise, that HMG engineered the coup'.[15] Equally though, too long a delay might undermine the new regime which 'certainly needs H.M.G's full support'.[16] It was therefore not until 29 July, six days after the coup and three days after the coup was announced to the world that Britain formally recognised Oman's new ruler. Messages of support and good wishes had arrived on 27/28 July from the smaller Shaikhdoms of the Trucial States and from Qatar, Abu Dhabi and Dubai. By 3 August the Sultan had sent messages to non-regional states including the U.S. and France as states with which Oman already had a special treaty relationship. In addition to this, messages were sent to West Germany, the Netherlands, Australia, Canada,

New Zealand, Denmark, Japan, Pakistan and Austria.[17] By 8 August the Sultan had received a telegram from King Hussein of Jordan expressing his 'fullest greetings and sincere expressions of affection and brotherhood',[18] and by 18 August was expecting an emissary from the Amir of Kuwait.[19] This seemingly stage managed cascade of recognition however appears not to have been controlled by the Foreign Office. On 12 August H.M. Ambassador in Tehran reported a conversation he had had with the Acting Foreign Minister indicating that the Iranian Government 'were somewhat hurt and puzzled that there had been no approach [from Muscat] so far'.[20] In reply Douglas-Home stated that 'it is not yet clear to us whether Qabus has yet sent such messages [to Iraq and Egypt]'.[21] The Foreign Office was exercising little control over such an important process. On the exact same day Michael Weston of the British delegation to the UN in New York reported a conversation in which a Kuwaiti delegate spoke with a Syrian delegate about his government's message from Qaboos to which the Amir had replied. The Syrian delegate spoke with Weston after the departure of the Kuwaiti to say that he did not think his government had received such a message and volunteered to pass it to Damascus if there had been some difficulty.[22] So on 15 August, Michael Weir of the Political Residency in Bahrain sent a telegram to Muscat urging them 'on the assumption that messages to remaining Arab states and to the Shah have not yet been sent' to 'suggest to Sultanate authorities that they should now complete the operation'.[23] The response from Consul-General David Crawford on 16 August explained the view of Qaboos, which had been given on 13 August, was that he wished to send short non-committal messages to states like Syria and Iraq but that he was concerned not to go 'too fast or too far... while the Sultanate is so inadequately equipped to deal with such relations'. Crawford reported that there 'is a powerful body of opinion here... which would support the Sultan's concern' and that he had been trying to convince Colonel Hugh Oldman the Defence Secretary 'to see the need for a series of messages... I have got him to the stage of accepting the need but he believes that such messages might be more appropriate... next month when the new Sultanate government will be properly installed'.[24] The Consul-General's suggestion to those British officials in foreign capitals who were asked about the lack of direct contact with Qaboos was that they should refer to the Sultan's earlier statements desiring good relations with other states and that once the Sultanate's new government was in place events could progress more quickly.

It is clear from all this that while the Foreign Office was monitoring the situation they in effect had very little idea of what was happening during these initial weeks of the new regime. This did not however prevent them from ensuring that those things which they did have some control over were handled to create the right impression with other states. So, on 12 August when a note from the Prime Minister arrived in the Arabian Department asking if it would be appropriate both to send a personal message to the new Sultan and a gesture to his father, the reply stated that 'it would be preferable if the Prime Minister did not send a message to the Sultan at this stage'.[25] The reply also stated that 'It is politically desirable that the Sultanate should now emerge from its former isolation and achieve recognition from as many Arab and friendly non-Arab states as possible.' The fear was that a message might be counter-productive and not 'encourage other states to reply favourably to Qabus.'[26]

The situation inside the Sultanate was hardly conducive to a co-ordinated and planned foreign policy. Thus it fell to the Foreign Office to try and keep some level of coherence and co-ordination not to mention one eye on the future. By 21 August there had still been no reply to the extremely friendly telegram of 8 August from King Hussein. This and other matters prompted Douglas-Home to send a telegram to Muscat requesting that a further attempt be made to get messages sent to 'recipients discussed in earlier telegrams without further delay'. He also stressed the need for such messages to 'amanate [sic – emanate] from the Sultan himself rather from Tariq's initiative. Moreover Tariq might wish to give a different, and more political, flavour to the messages which would not be appropriate at this stage'.[27] It was not until 24 August that a warm reply to King Hussein was sent.

At the beginning of September the Sultan expressed his concern to Sir William Luce, that he had not had any reply to either of his messages to King Faisal of Saudi Arabia. Luce who had just come from Saudi Arabia had had discussions with Saudi officials and King Faisal about the possibility of an exchange of courtesy visits between the Kingdom and the Sultanate. The Sultan readily agreed to receive a Saudi delegation at Salalah and Luce suggested to the British Embassy at Jedda that they should begin work 'pursuing this idea with Faisal's advisors'.[28] It was becoming increasingly clear that Britain was going to have to maintain a delicate balance between using the extensive knowledge, contacts and influence of the Foreign Office to help facilitate Oman's move onto the world stage and trying to ensure that Britain's essential assistance did not at the same time damage the image of Oman as a newly energised and independent state deserving of serious consideration.

The Return of Tariq

The appointment of Tariq to the post of Prime Minister was an important one as far as foreign affairs were concerned. Having left the Sultanate in protest at the lack of development under his brother and been active amongst Omani exiles, Tariq had a good deal of credibility in Arab capitals. His return was to have a more positive outcome in the field of foreign affairs for Oman than it had in other areas. According to Skeet, both Qaboos and Tariq 'had the objective of integrating Oman into the mainstream of Arab and international affairs... [the responsibility for] foreign affairs was... shared between Qaboos and Tarik but with no great clarity as to where the dividing line resided'.[29] In this sense then, the views of the two key men in Oman also coincided with those of the Foreign Office but the lack of defined responsibility between Qaboos and Tariq was to cause London some considerable concern.

Soon after his return, Tariq advocated the dispatch of delegations or 'Goodwill Missions' to all fourteen Arab states as well as India, Pakistan and Iran. Yet Tariq still felt the need to ask British officials in Muscat for advice on how to go about his goal of sending out these delegations.[30] The reply to advice sought on this by officials in Muscat came direct from Foreign Secretary, Douglas-Home, 'We presume that Tariq is not thinking of using our channels: we would not want to be involved and such messages should be sent directly by the Sultanate'.[31] Once again London was concerned about projecting the wrong message concerning the nature of its influence. The Foreign Office still, however, wished to give advice to Tariq as to how to handle the delegations, an idea which was 'welcomed'.

With one eye on the future, the Foreign Office foresaw that the proposed delegations 'could be useful in securing Arab support for deferment of discussion of the Oman item at the UN'. This of course was the annual discussion by the 'Fourth Committee' (on Decolonisation) which in November each year discussed 'The question of Oman' and decried its lack of independence.[32] Additionally it was suggested that while:

> [W]e do not wish to press too much advice on Tariq we hope that you will be able to suggest tactfully to him... that it seems desirable that the delegation should visit Saudi Arabia first. If but only if Tariq is in a receptive mood you might also suggest that [taking advantage of the momentum of improving Saudi-Omani relations] he himself can pay a brief visit on King Faisal.[33]

Michael Weir in Bahrain was reluctant to have Oman rushing into anything and stated that 'in my view Tariq would do better at this early stage to employ the scarce talent at his disposal on urgent domestic tasks'. He also suggested that the major Arab states would be too busy to give Oman a proper hearing because of the Black September[34] crisis in Jordan and the limited time before Ramadan. He did however recommend that Britain should not oppose the mission.[35] While all officials agreed on the need for the missions to go ahead the timing was causing some mild disagreement.

The new vigour brought about by Tariq did not however mean that Britain's role was diminished quite yet. In a meeting on 21 September with the Shah, Sir William Luce, who was acting as the Foreign Secretary's personal representative for the Persian Gulf, was able to talk around a rather reluctant Shah who had by now received a message from the Sultan but who was concerned about 'the question of Oman' on the UN agenda and was rather lukewarm about the Sultanate. Luce explained that he had encouraged Qaboos to send a message of goodwill and that Iranian support for him would be most welcome. The Shah immediately instructed his Foreign Affairs minister that 'there should be a complete reversal of Iranian policy towards Oman',[36] from wait and see to more active engagement. Britain was clearly willing to go in to bat for Oman in areas which were behind the scenes, and with a fair degree of success.

The death of Nasser not only marked the end of a momentous era in the Arab world, but it also provided the Omanis with a golden opportunity to increase their contacts throughout the Middle East and show solidarity with their fellow Arabs. The Omani mission to the state funeral was warmly welcomed, so warm in fact that the Egyptians recognised Oman and agreed to allow Muscat to establish a consulate in Cairo.[37] In his early months in office Tariq made one appointment that was to play an important role in helping Oman's move onto the world stage. He took on as an advisor on foreign affairs a former minister and diplomat of the deposed Libyan King Idris, Mr Omer Barouni, whose job was 'specifically to help in preparing Oman's application to join the Arab league'. Moreover, he was also to prove useful in persuading other Arabs that Oman was not under British control. Skeet puts it mildly when he says that 'they had a large job of information and persuasion in front of them'.[38] By the end of November little had been done about Tariq's proposal of sending out Goodwill Missions, the Sultan though, approved of the scheme and Tariq was reported to be 'seized' of the idea. Tariq proposed sending the mission first to the Yemeni Arab Republic and proceeding to the People's Democratic Republic of Yemen (PDRY) and Saudi Arabia and from there moving on to more northern Arab states. A member of the delegation though, told the Consul-General that the mission would begin in the Gulf. Clearly the idea was not progressing well, and the suggestion of going to PDRY was met with disbelief by officials. Michael Weir in Bahrain wrote 'This is crazy!' and Anthony Acland wrote 'I see no harm in briefly stressing again the importance of not offending SA'.[39]

The Foreign Office was growing increasingly concerned at the lack of progress in Saudi-Omani relations and was becoming slightly anxious about remaining the middleman between Muscat and Riyadh. By 30 December 1970 the Goodwill Mission was finally approaching readiness to leave Oman; it comprised five members led by the Minister of Education, Saud bin Ali al Khalili. Tariq informed Consul-General Crawford that telegrams were to be sent over the following two days seeking invitations for the mission and that both he and his advisor Barouni had planned arrangements for the tour with the delegation. More importantly he added that 'in the light of my [Consul-General's] comments on Saudi attitudes to Oman the mission would plan to go there first'.[40] The Foreign Office had all along seen the importance of the Saudis and had been careful to use their influence in Jedda and Riyadh to ensure that the Omanis had chances to further their relations with the Kingdom. In addition, officials had been assiduous in attempting to persuade Qaboos and Tariq of the need both for patience with the Saudis but also of making them aware of the need for Saudi goodwill.

The Saudis were clearly important for Oman, being a large, powerful and rich neighbour who could if they so wished add to the instability in the Sultanate. Relations between Oman and Saudi Arabia had been bedevilled by two issues for the previous 20 years. The first problem remained the undemarcated frontier that had encouraged Saudi expansionism, culminating in the Buraimi Oasis crisis of the 1950s. This issue continued to be a problem but as Hawley said 'it was the question of the Imamate, which really divided the two countries' who should have been natural allies, being both dynastic regimes opposed to the PDRY. During the Imamate insurgency of the late 1950s, the Saudis aided the rebels both materially and ideologically and when the rebellion was put down offered sanctuary to the leaders of the Oman Rebel Movement (ORM), Talib and the Iman Ghalib. As Hawley put it 'face was involved, as the Saudis have been backing the wrong horse since the middle 1950s'.[41] This made the Saudis reluctant to recognise a different government of Oman despite the acceptance of the new Sultan by most of the Arab World.

British Policy

The year 1970 had ended with some progress towards international recognition having been made but with a long way to go before Oman was truly part of the international community. Most of the achievements of the first five months of the new era can be put down to a number of factors. One of the most important of these was that the momentum produced by the coup and the sense of hope and progress created, infected not only

Omanis and British officials but also excited exiles and a number of neighbouring countries. Without the new atmosphere little advancement could have been made. The determination of both Qaboos and especially Tariq to secure international recognition as soon as possible gave the impetus needed for diplomatic recognition not to get lost amongst the many other issues which were facing the new government. Events in the region can also be said to have played a role in the improvement made during this period. Black September in Jordan distracted Arab attention away from Oman and made the first phase of entering the international arena easier to bear for the new regime, giving them more time to prepare the diplomatic ground and making any mistakes less apparent. Equally the death of Nasser and the rise of Sadat gave the Sultanate a chance to identify with Arab causes.[42] The installation of the more moderate Sadat ensured the support of Egypt, the most influential of the Arab states, which would prove vital in the future. Finally, without British support many of the achievements made in the initial period would have been much harder to secure. British information gathering from its network of embassies, contacts and experience in the region was indispensable and something which Oman with its meagre resources could not have hoped to achieve. In addition it was British officials who tried to rectify Omani mistakes and who were able to lobby directly and discreetly with Iran and Saudi Arabia to at least secure the Omanis opportunities to win round these two vital states to their side.

Britain's formal policy towards the Sultanate's external affairs was essentially invisible. Instead, what characterised London's policy were both its rather *ad hoc* nature and the fact that all officials shared, almost instinctively, the desire to see Oman gain greater recognition. It seemed clear to officials that while Britain should help wherever feasible, it remained essential that this help should be as unobtrusive as possible. Perhaps it was the lack of dissension towards these views which meant that a formal policy was not spelt out at this early stage. It may also have been, as seen in the previous chapter, that development, needed to gain both internal and external legitimacy could only be accomplished with British help, and that this very help could damage the Sultanate's legitimacy. This made the need for discretion clear to officials as a similar tightrope had to be walked in the field of external affairs and whilst British help was still essential to gain legitimacy, it was unlikely to aid in that process if it was too obvious.

British Representation in the Sultanate

One of the more obvious symbols of the British role in Oman was the fact that the British representative in Muscat was a Consul-General and not an Ambassador (as was normal with Britain's relations with all other independent states). In a meeting between the Political Resident Sir Geoffrey Arthur and the Sultan on 9 April 1971, the Sultan informed Sir Geoffrey that the Indians had asked the Sultan if their Consulate-General could be upgraded to Embassy status. The Sultan informed Sir Geoffrey that he wished to agree and that he very much hoped that Britain would convert their mission to an Embassy. Sir Geoffrey told the Sultan that 'we should certainly wish to be the first to have an Ambassador in Muscat'. The Sultan however was slightly worried about a rush to upgrade the British representation to Ambassador level. He had two objections:

> a) Oman was to have a Consul-General in London: he was not prepared to appoint Shebib [Tariq's brother] Ambassador yet b) he wished to retain his links with the Political Resident in Bahrain so long as British forces remained in the Gulf. He therefore proposed that we should follow the precedent which he hoped to establish with Egypt... and would apply to India: that is, we should announce that diplomatic relations had been raised to Embassy level and that Ambassadors would be appointed later.[43]

Sir Geoffrey pointed out to the Sultan that unlike the Egyptians, Britain would have somebody resident in Muscat and therefore if it was announced that the status of the mission had been changed that person would have to be an Ambassador or Chargé d'Affaires and that in the latter case someone else would have to be appointed Ambassador, most likely the Political Resident himself. This would hardly be ideal as any change would draw further attention to the anomalous role of the PRPG. Sir Geoffrey thought that the solution would be for the proposed replacement for the existing Consul-General David Crawford, Donald Hawley, to be appointed Ambassador upon arrival.

The Sultan's suggestion had not come out of the blue for the British who had been discussing a change in the nature of representation in Muscat as a result of the withdrawal from the Gulf for some time. The previous year it had already been 'agreed in principle' that the post would be upgraded to Embassy status and that it would be discussed with Sultan Sa'id during the 1970 review of policy. Sultan Sa'id had however demanded a grade 1 Ambassador rather than the grade 3 Ambassador proposed.[44]

While one would have expected officials to want to get an Ambassador *en poste* as soon as possible so as to reduce the impression of British control, the Sultan's 'strong desire (shared by Hugh Oldman) to retain his links with the military in Bahrain through me' was enough to prompt Sir Geoffrey

Arthur to think of an alternative. To try and secure something of a compromise he suggested that 'the answer surely lies with the appointment of Donald Hawley as Ambassador and the simultaneous negotiation of a special status for me which will guarantee the same sort of access to the Sultan and his government as I enjoy now'.[45] He concluded his letter to Anthony Acland the head of the Arabian Department with the words that 'in the Gulf of all places we should not be afraid of what is anomalous'.[46]

This compromise, which would only be in place for a few months, until the end of 1971, was tolerable in that it would regularise relations while retaining co-ordination and efficiency. The opportunity provided by the change from Crawford to Hawley in Muscat which was scheduled for May 1971 provided the ideal opportunity to effect the change. By 23 June all had been arranged and the Sultanate announced that 'desiring to strengthen...friendly relations' both governments had agreed to raise the level of their representation to Embassy level.[47] Thus on 22 July 1971, Donald Hawley presented his credentials to the Sultan and became both the first British Ambassador and the first Ambassador to the Sultanate. Reporting the event Hawley stated that: 'The ceremony went very smoothly by any standard and considerable credit is due to Shaikh Omar Barouni...and to Major Landon the Sultan's Equerry...The Omanis themselves are almost embarrassingly delighted to have a British Ambassador here.'[48]

On 25 August the Indian mission was also raised to the status of an Embassy.[49] While one would have expected the issue of representation to have been decided by the desire of officials to minimise British exposure in the new era so as to promote Oman's chances of the widest possible recognition, the influences on policy in this area meant that this desire took a back seat. Officials were willing in external affairs as they had been in internal affairs to take the risk, where necessary, of damaging Oman's external image by risking reinforcing the image of British control, in order to maintain efficiency and to keep the Sultan satisfied. The gamble in part paid off when the Sultanate was admitted to its first international organisation: the World Health Organisation in May 1971.

Impact of the Review of Policy

As discussed in chapter four a review of policy towards Oman took place during the spring of 1971. The review also covered Britain's policy towards Oman's external affairs. The review effectively formulated British policy in this area with relation to the general understanding of priorities which had developed among officials after and in some cases before the coup. The document resulting from the review, 'HMG's Policy Towards The Sultanate

Of Oman', stated that 'it is both the wish and the logical course for the Sultanate Government to emerge from isolation and seek Arab and international recognition. This process is inevitable, and we cannot and should not seek to prevent it, although it may create difficulties both for Oman and for us'. While this course was consistent with the *ad hoc* policy thus far, the policy statement still expressed concern that 'the change in Oman's external status could have a bearing on the Dhofar rebellion'.[50] The benefit however of denying the rebels the propaganda tool of the Sultan's government being a British puppet would be valuable.

The document went on to formalise the perception, which had been clear among officials, that Saudi Arabia was an important consideration for British policy in this area. It stated that 'another factor of the first importance affecting the stability and security of Oman is the relationship with Saudi Arabia'. The paragraph continued to stress that 'it is very desirable that Saudi Arabia's claims to parts of the Sultanate's territory...should be satisfactorily disposed of'.[51] The focus on Saudi Arabia was not simply one of securing recognition but one of resolving disputes and tying up loose ends so as to create 'the best "insulation" for Oman'.[52]

In the final section of the paper a series of short term priorities for British policy objectives in Oman were laid out. These included impressing upon the Sultan and the Prime Minister 'the importance of initiating without delay economic and social measures and projects', encouraging the Sultan to appoint British officials to 'key' posts and to help 'discreetly and unobtrusively to working out a *modus operandi* between the Sultan and the Prime Minister'. It was further suggested that in addition to these three key lines of policy Britain could best contribute to the stability of Oman and 'to the maintenance of our interests there' by continuing to second British officers while continuing with Omanisation at a pace which would not damage effectiveness, responding positively to other requests for help, maintaining British influence through British personnel and developing technical assistance and cultural links through the British council.[53] It was also stated that:

> We should in the immediate future take full advantage of the unique advisory role and influence...which we still enjoy but will progressively lose as Oman develops relations with other states to:...f) encouraging Oman to join international organisation at the right pace, to establish relations with western and friendly Arab countries and to obtain expertise and assistance from such bodies (for example the IBRD [World Bank] and FAO [Food and Agriculture Organisation of the UN]) and states.[54]

As such, formal British policy was mirroring the informal policy consensus which had developed in the months following the coup.

Attaining Respectability: The Arab League

While the initial focus of Oman's campaign for international respectability had focused on obtaining recognition from other states, it had been clear to both the Sultanate authorities and the British that this would not be enough. Membership of international organisations was also essential and in Muscat's case this meant the League of Arab States (Arab League) and the United Nations. Yet the desire of both sides for this process to occur was not communicated at a formal level for many months.

The year 1971 began with the dispatch of the Omani Goodwill Mission around the Arab world and beyond. The mission turned out to be something of a success as the impression they left in Jordan in particular testifies. A reliable informant of the British Ambassador reported that the King and others were impressed by the 'true Arab bearing and brotherly simplicity of these bearded Sheikhs'. The leader of the delegation, the Minister of Health Dr Asim al Jamali, was even given a chance to address the Jordanian people on national television and the delegation left Amman with Jordanian promises of teachers, training and technical assistance with establishing radio and television networks.[55] The telegram concluded with the words 'there is no doubt that the mission have [sic] made a good and dignified impression on the Jordanians, although the Foreign Minister asked me (with a twinkle in his eye) if I had noticed the small Union Jack on their aircraft. I had.'[56] While the reception from the Anglophile King Hussein was somewhat to be expected, the impression made by the mission on the Arab Nationalist population of Jordan was equally important. The light hearted observation at the end of the dispatch of course proves that while the result was all Omani, the advice and facilitation needed to secure it remained British.

By March, the Sultan had been able to turn his attention to the issue of Arab League membership. He had consulted with Barouni, who despite being appointed by Tariq had become increasingly trusted by Qaboos, about the prospects of accession. Barouni was optimistic especially after the success of the Goodwill Missions. Qaboos therefore decided to put forward an application for membership for consideration by the League on its next meeting, scheduled for 13 March 1971. During the course of a discussion with the PRPG on 6 March the Sultan informed him of his decision. Sir Geoffrey Arthur counselled caution, as while 'the Goodwill Mission had indeed been well received in the Arab countries'[57] the process was clearly not going to be as easy as Barouni had suggested. The difficulties posed by the certain opposition of a hostile PDRY would have to be overcome and 'Oman would need Egyptian help in this matter'. Indeed it was rumoured that the Egyptians were considering sending an emissary to Muscat. The Sultan replied that he would '"put it on the table" if it [the application to join the League] failed it would be clear where the responsibility lay'.[58]

While Geoffrey Arthur was cautiously realistic in his assessment of Oman's chances of admission R.A. Beaumont, the British Ambassador in Cairo (where the League is based), was pessimistically downbeat. In a telegram to the Arabian Department two days before the Arab League meeting he stated, 'I fear that the Omanis will not have helped their cause by applying so soon for Arab League membership'. He also informed London that Imam Ghalib, the leader of the Imamate rebellion against Sultan Sa'id in the 1950s who had been in exile claiming to be the legitimate ruler of Oman, was due to arrive in Cairo as part of his own tour of Arab capitals. 'One can assume', he stated, 'his major aim will be to persuade league members not to accept Oman. He may well succeed'. Beaumont continued to offer his advice that 'I hope that if it is not accepted this time, the Sultan will agree to continue to work patiently for acceptance rather than attempt to rush his fences and come a cropper'. A hand that looks like Acland's wrote next to this comment 'Yes but it is up to the Omanis!'.[59] This is an illustrative comment, in that it shows that while some officials were a little frustrated with the Omanis, others recognised that it was Oman's decision and that Britain's role was to advise and facilitate, not insist and enforce. Despite his pessimism, Beaumont went on to lobby his contacts in the Egyptian government with some success to persuade them that 'there might therefore be a case for cutting corners in admitting Oman to the League before the end of 1971'.[60]

The Egyptian Key

It was clear to officials that the positive response of the Egyptians to the Omanis at Nasser's funeral needed to be reinforced and that as well as a focus on the Saudis an Egyptian focus could also go a long way to securing Omani recognition in the Arab world. The Goodwill Mission in early 1971 made a good impression in Egypt. Beaumont in Cairo therefore began to use his contacts to explain why it might be in Egypt's interests to assist Omani acceptance on the Arab stage. On 26 February he was invited to a meeting with Saad Afra the under-secretary at the Egyptian Ministry of Foreign Affairs, who informed him that 'the UAR government was inclined to take a "positive attitude" to the Omani question'[61] following the visit of the delegation and Beaumont's talks with officials. Afra however informed

Beaumont that Cairo would have to be quite sure before reversing its position and asked five specific questions about the relationship between Britain and Oman. Beaumont answered off the cuff but promised a fuller reply. On 1 March after talks with the Egyptian Foreign Minister, Beaumont recorded the fact that he had been assured that 'the specific questions... were designed to allow the UAR to play a positive role and not for the purpose of attacking Oman'.[62] Officials were quick to take advantage of the chink of light coming from Cairo and prepared a full package of information, albeit carefully constructed. Acland replied to Cairo with the words, 'while we certainly want to co-operate with the Egyptians to encourage them to be helpful to Oman... we must avoid arousing their suspicions to such an extent that they in turn waken a whole lot of sleeping dogs which would be much better left asleep'.[63] Beaumont reported further conversations with Afra who was probing for information. In the event the Egyptians were quite happy with the information provided. Interestingly Afra was hopeful that Britain would give Oman much aid and financial support 'and not to leave them (presumably like PDRY – though he did not say so) exposed to soft loans and technical aid on easy terms from the Soviet bloc or the Chinese'.[64] The Egyptian attitude, although cautious, was looking promising especially if even they were concerned about the Soviets. This change in Egyptian attitudes of course reflected the general changes taking place in Sadat's Egypt in the wake of Nasser's death.

Opinion in the Arab world appeared to be turning decisively in Oman's favour when news from the British Ambassador in Baghdad, Glenn Balfour-Paul, arrived stating that a senior director in the Iraqi Foreign Ministry had told him that 'the Omani delegation had made a good impression here and that the Iraqi government was disposed to help them get over the legal difficulty concerning Ghalib'. Considering Iraq's status as a centre of radical Arab nationalism this was quite a turnaround. Although Balfour-Paul cautioned that the radicals may once again gain the upper hand, 'with luck Iraq will leave the running to other Arab states'.[65]

That such Republican regimes as Egypt, Iraq and later Syria[66] should have been so surprisingly co-operative and positive towards Oman is somewhat surprising considering the enmity felt in previous years between them and the dynastic regimes of the Arabian peninsula. That this situation, fortuitously for Oman, should have come about can perhaps be ascribed to a number of factors including the Arab humiliation in the June 1967 War[67] making a new recruit to the cause an interesting prospect. Oman, being an oil producing state might also have meant financial contributions to the 'front line states'. After Nasser's death, tension between Egypt and dynastic regimes and between Nasserism and other forms of Arab nationalism in the Middle East was somewhat lessened, this created a better environment in which policies could be less ideologically driven. Finally the fact that moderates or pragmatists (as far as was possible for these to exist in the Ba'ath party) temporarily held the upper hand in Baghdad and that Sadat was pursuing a more balanced Foreign Policy were clearly important factors in this new attitude.

Disappointment at the League

At the League meeting on 13 March the PDRY, as expected, stated its opposition to Oman's entry. The Council decided to postpone the discussion of Oman's application until the next session, scheduled for September. The Council requested that the Secretary-General of the League visit Oman and draw up a report.[68] Beaumont in Cairo reported to the Foreign Office that 'the UAR [Egyptian] Foreign Minister adumbrated to me... that Oman would have to sweat it out a bit and produce practical evidence of its independence'. Beaumont suggested that the delay was not meant obstructively and that 'we should take comfort from the fact that Oman's application was not rejected'.[69] The howl of protest at the sending of an Arab League mission to Muscat was reported from Aden by Arthur Kellas. The PDRY denounced the application as a 'new imperialist trick' and that 'it was the new imperialist strategy to complete "the political encirclement" of the Revolution'.[70] The PDRY were fully aware of the danger of anything which would give Muscat international legitimacy. If Oman succeeded in joining the League and the UN, the PDRY would not only lose a valuable propaganda tool it could use against the Sultanate but membership of these organisations would make winning the war in Dhofar significantly more difficult. If Oman was successful in joining the UN its sovereignty would be greatly enhanced, it would be protected by the notion of collective security and could claim its right to self defence under article 51. In addition this recognition would give the Sultan immeasurable legitimacy and make it much easier for states to assist the Sultanate. Britain of course knew this too, which is why the campaign for membership of these organisations was considered to be so important.

The Omani delegation arrived back in Muscat on 22 March 'by no means despondent about the decision... commenting that... the delegation had received a cordial reception, most notably from UAR officials'. Qaboos (and Tariq) however were concerned that the League visit to Oman should not be presented as some kind of 'quote inspection unquote of the Sultanate's independence'.[71]

Despite the positive outlook of the delegation, British officials were growing increasingly concerned about Ghalib and his claim that he represented the real Omani government. The problem for a number of Arab states was that legally the Arab League had previously 'recognised Ghalib as the legitimate ruler of at least parts of Oman'.[72] In addition, Beaumont in Cairo reported a conversation he had had with Sabri al-Kholi, President Sadat's personal representative to the Gulf, in which al-Kholi stated that 'a tactical mistake had been made by rushing the second mission in and for membership of the Arab League virtually before the first mission's message had had time to sink in. These pressure tactics had given offence, especially to the Saudis'.[73] This was a worrying development for British officials who had stressed caution and the importance of Saudi support again and again. By the end of March reports suggested that Oman had the firm support of Tunisia, Morocco, Kuwait, Lebanon and Jordan in its bid to join the League.

During April al-Kholi made a trip to the Gulf States and Oman and in conversation with Beaumont upon his return, stated that 'he had been much impressed with Qabus'. He also offered the valuable advice to Britain that the Sultan should appoint a Foreign Minister and 'push Baruni [sic] into the background'. If there was no suitable candidate then Tariq should get the job and proceed to visit Arab capitals. He also stated that 'the Sultan had to do something about Ghalib and square this with the Saudis, who apart from Southern Yemen were the only Arab state which had reservations about Oman'.[74] Al-Kholi was proving to be a valuable ally; he even asked Beaumont to 'convey his thanks to H.M. Consul-General and the British officers who had helped and entertained him during his stay'!'[75] Once again Omani charm backed up with British support proved its worth.

By 30 April acting on this advice and similar prompting from Kuwait, Sir William Luce broached the topic of a conciliatory gesture towards Ghalib with the Sultan. Qaboos was enthusiastic but Luce got the impression that little would happen quickly.[76] A further delegation arrived in Cairo on 5 June apparently hoping to get Oman's application considered at an emergency June meeting of the League (ostensibly to discuss the question of exports from the Gaza Strip),[77] when the Oman issue had been formally postponed to be discussed at the normal September meeting. Advice on taking things slowly was not being heeded, thankfully for Oman; the emergency meeting was postponed at Syria's request with the issues to be discussed at the scheduled meeting in September.[78]

Despite their formal position of support for the Omani position both Kuwait and Lebanon continued to insist to British officials that some sort of compromise with Ghalib was still required. The Lebanese Minister for Foreign Affairs, Khalil Abu Hamad, told the British Ambassador in Beirut, Mr Edden, that while he had spoken of the issue to the Omani mission 'they had merely said that he [Ghalib] was free to return to Oman. This formula was too vague to be helpful'. As he saw it 'some kind of deputation should go [to] Ghalib and inform him of the "conditions" of such return. What was needed was some kind of "moral compensation". He suggested the title of Mufti as he believed that 'something more than a simple "return" was essential... particularly from the point of view of Saudi Arabia [sic] position', Riyadh having offered Ghalib exile and a stipend. The British Ambassador pointed out that the Foreign Minister 'clearly felt that we were in a position to advise the Omanis usefully on the subject, in the interest of smoothing their path to recognition'.[79]

It was obvious to British officials that little was going to happen with this issue unless it was consistently put to the Omanis. The Sultan had been in London during early summer and on 14 June had met with Foreign Secretary, Douglas-Home, and Anthony Acland of the Arabian Department. The issue of Ghalib was raised, with Acland arguing that 'the attitude of countries of the Arab League, and particularly Saudi Arabia and Kuwait, might depend on there being a settlement with Ghaleb'. The Sultan 'confirmed that he would allow Ghaleb to live honourably either in Oman or outside it and agreed that it might be necessary to make the Saudis and Kuwaitis more specifically aware of the offer'. Acland replied that 'the matter was becoming more urgent if a settlement had to precede Oman's entry into the Arab League which in turn had to precede consideration of the UN application'.[80]

D.G. Allen of the Arabian Department communicated to Donald Hawley in Muscat that 'we do not know whether the Sultan will act on this advice'; in addition to British counsel, the Sultan had also received a suggestion to write to King Faisal to explain he was willing to offer Ghalib the title of Mufti and a generous financial allowance. Allen stated that 'the main difficulty seems one of communication. The Sultan appears to take the line that Ghalib is aware of his offer and that in any case it is up to Ghalib to make the first approach'.[81] Allen stated that it was also important that other Arab states were aware of the offer and suggested to Hawley that perhaps the Arab League could be used as a means of communication between Ghalib and the Sultan and this would make the wider Arab world aware of the efforts the Sultanate was making. He suggested a letter to the Secretary-General or if this was not good for reasons of face, sending an emissary to express the offer to the Secretary-General in person. Better still, the position could be put to him when he visited the Sultanate, although there was no idea as to when this might take place. He suggested that Hawley should 'try out this idea in whatever way you think best i.e. at Tariq/Barouni level as you see fit'.[82]

The difficulties with the Ghalib situation were not to be the only hurdle to Omani admission though. A letter from Cairo at the end of July stating that after informal talks with several members of the League's administration it did not look likely that the proposed visit by Secretary-General Dr Hassuna would take place. Without this trip and a clean bill of health the Saudis, the PDRY and possibly the Iraqis would be able to insist on further deferral. One of the sources suggested that if only one country objected then the absence of the Hassuna Mission 'may be quietly forgotten' but that if two or more states raised objections then this 'would be enough to block Oman's membership for the time being'.[83] P.J. Dun of the Arabian Department wrote on this dispatch that 'this is, if true, a great pity: and underlines the urgency of an arrangement over the Ghaleb question with the Saudis'.[84]

In the meantime British officials in Kuwait had, on prompting from the Arabian Department, taken the initiative and informed the Kuwaitis of the Sultan's offer to Ghalib and asked them to use their influence to suggest that this might be the best offer available.[85] This soon had the desired effect of making the Sultan's offer known to all, aided by a *Financial Times* report 'Ruler of Oman to accept Imam' on 11 August. On 12 August the Arab League began efforts to get the Sultan and Imam into face to face discussions, sending invitations to both men to 'choose an Arab capital in which to hold a joint meeting'.[86] By 18 August the Sultan had not received the invitation and Greaves of the Embassy in Muscat was informed by Sayyid Fahd bin Massoud the director of the Omani Ministry of Foreign Affairs, that 'in any case it would be out of the question for Qabus to attend such a meeting'.[87] While this position was logical to British officials, it underestimated the difficulty of establishing direct communication of any kind between the two sides. On 20 August Jedda reported that Ghalib was willing to accept an offer to be Mufti 'since that was what the Saudis advised'. Morris in Jedda stated that the 'position therefore seems to be that Ghaleb is willing to accept what Qabus has for the last four months been prepared to offer but failed to communicate to Ghaleb'. Morris asked if there was any possibility of getting Muscat to agree that the offer be communicated by either the British Embassies in Jeddah, Kuwait or Cairo. 'I understand' he continued, 'the objections to our becoming involved, but if we do not there seems serious danger that Qabus will fail to pick up the key that we, Saudis and every other Arab state except PRSY want him to take'.[88]

The response to this suggestion came the same day direct from Douglas-Home. While the essential next step was to ensure that the Sultan's terms were communicated to Ghalib, 'we do not favour the suggestion...that HM Embassies should communicate the offer to Ghaleb. This would be playing into Ghaleb's hands if negotiations subsequently fell through. It must remain an Arab undertaking'.[89] He suggested that since the Arab League seemed keen on getting a resolution its auspices should be used and Oman should send a representative to meet with Ghaleb. He also stressed the danger of Oman risking isolation if other Gulf States entered international organisations and Oman failed. By 25 August a meeting under Arab League auspices was arranged between an Omani delegation and the Imam's representatives led by Talib in Beirut.

The talks were a complete disaster. Talib had insisted on shared authority with the Sultan and the termination of British influence. The Arab League representative had told the Omani delegation that he had 'lost patience with Talib' and that when he reported the talks to the League he would 'emphasise the fact that Talib had made no serious attempt to come to terms'. He was also 'hopeful that the Beirut meeting would demonstrate that... reconciliation with Ghalib and Talib was impossible... and that consequently Oman's application would go through in September'.[90] Greaves also reported that the Sultan had sent a letter to King Faisal before the meeting explaining the terms he was offering. Similar opinions were expressed to Kuwait and Saudi Arabia, the Kuwaitis thought Ghalib's demands 'excessive' and that the 'Sultan had showed himself [to be] reasonable'.[91] A senior advisor to King Faisal said Ghalib 'certainly had no veto over Oman's application to join the league'.[92]

With the next meeting of the Arab League immanent it appeared that with Ghalib's lack of compromise viewed unfavourably against the Sultanate's reasonable offer, diplomatic momentum was very much favour of Qaboos. On 6 September the Sultan's delegation left Muscat for the League meeting. The meeting of 11 September admitted Bahrain and Qatar to membership but decided to continue discussion of Oman's membership on 12 September. The following day, London had still not heard anything and asked Washington for news, their delegation in Cairo reporting 'that further discussions may have been postponed for a longer period'.[93] Chaos continued to reign for days with numerous conflicting reports on the progress of the Omani application. It appeared that the Saudis were not going to support the application, the British Embassy in Jedda reported that in discussions with a senior advisor to King Faisal it had been suggested that the Omani offer should have been made direct to Ghalib and that the Saudis were still concerned to reach a settlement over the issue.[94]

When the Omani delegation arrived back in Muscat it was obvious that they had failed to secure admission to the League. The reason as London had supposed all along was the Saudis. Saudi Prince Saqaaf had raised every possible objection in Cairo. According to the Omani delegation the Syrian delegate had stated in the meeting that 'it was ironical to observe a country like Saudi Arabia uniting with PDRY in opposition to Oman's admission'. In the face of overwhelming support for Oman in the meeting, Prince Saqaaf had even returned to Saudi Arabia during the discussions to see if King Faisal was willing to change his instructions; he was not. As such the League decided to postpone discussions for a further fortnight.[95]

The assessment was made by Ambassador Wincester in Jedda that there was little the British government could do to alter King Faisal's mind and that any attempt would be counter-productive. Al-Kholi, Sadat's envoy, had been in the Kingdom since 14 September however trying to meet with the King. By 27 September the Embassy in Jedda had been unable to work out if al-Kholi had even been able to see the King but reported that a Saudi legal advisor had told them that if the issue was to come up again then 'the Saudis would probably absent themselves', although the Embassy admitted this was difficult to crosscheck.[96]

Elsewhere, another British friend and new member of the League, the deputy Amir of Qatar, Shaikh Khalifah, was making an attempt during a meeting to mediate with Ghalib.[97] The Sultan replied positively to this development and offered further concessions. In conference with Sir Geoffrey Arthur however he expressed his fears that Ghalib 'was nothing but a pretext: the fact was that King Faisal had claims on Omani territory'. The PRPG agreed but said that 'the Sultan's policy should be one of infinite patience'. The Sultan agreed and said that was indeed his policy and that messages he sent to Faisal on national holidays had gone unanswered including one just the previous week. He stated that he found the King 'incomprehensible'. Arthur replied 'we all do!'[98]

By now Saudi reluctance was reportedly beginning to affect Libya and Egypt with the latter moving towards wanting reconciliation between Imam and Sultan.[99] It was something of a surprise to all therefore when on 30 September Oman was admitted to membership of the Arab League. Fourteen countries agreed to Oman's entry, Saudi Arabia had 'reservations' and as expected the PDRY opposed entry.[100] Interestingly, since the Arab League is open to all Arab states in theory without formal votes of entry there was nothing in Oman's way in the first place. But the need to maintain Arab consensus and not offend such generous benefactors as the Saudis meant that applications needed to attract a large degree of consensus.

The success of the Omani application was clearly due to the combination of a lot of hard work by a great number of people. When assessing the British contribution it is again evident that officials around the Arab world worked their contacts assiduously to gain help and information. London was also willing to persuade the Omanis of the importance of patience when required and speed at other times. Without this British help, it is unlikely that Oman would have been able to join the League in 1971. Equally though, the Omanis were flexible enough to change their position when required and to act on British advice. Britain could only take the Omanis so far. Once in the Arab League council Britain could offer no assistance.

Despite success in Cairo, discussions with Ghalib in Doha continued. The Sultan continued to show himself to be flexible and reasonable, offering certain members of the Imam's entourage positions in Omani Embassies abroad and houses in Muscat. The PRPG suggested to Henderson that the Qataris should be encouraged to deal with Oman directly as 'it is better for the Omanis if we do not (not) get between them and other independent Arab states'.[101] The British attitude remained cautious but at the same time Anthony Acland was determined to:

> Get as much information on the Arab League deliberations since this will give us a useful indication of the policies of other Arab states towards Oman... Iraq and Syria seem surprisingly favourable to Oman for reasons that I do not fully understand, and it would be interesting to get more information about their position.[102]

On 2 October Edward Henderson in Doha reported that the Deputy Emir now saw the exercise 'as much changed in character and diminished in importance' since Oman's admission and spoke to Henderson of 'the harshly reactionary ideas of Ghalib's party'.[103]

United Nations/Divided World?

Admission to the Arab League was for both Britain and Oman only half of the story: the United Nations represented a far more significant prize. It had always been accepted that admission to the UN would represent the ultimate recognition of Oman's presence and independence in the world but that the only logical strategy to follow was to first secure accession to the Arab League as a necessary precursor to UN membership, since many states would support Omani membership with few questions if she had been accepted by her neighbours. This did not mean that all British and Sultanate energies were focused on the League application however as there were also considerable hurdles to the UN application.

As mentioned previously, the annual Fourth Committee resolution on the 'colonial' situation in Oman was due to be debated in November 1970. An attempt was made to suspend discussion for a year but this failed and the committee voted as usual to condemn Britain. This resolution was then passed for a further vote at the General Assembly session scheduled for December. Britain was understandably anxious to defeat the motion. As such the word was sent out to Embassies to try and lobby for a vote against the resolution. Unfortunately, with so little time to convince other states of the case, the exercise was pointless and actually had the effect of annoying the British Ambassador in Turkey who wrote a two page letter stating 'this sort of eleventh hour exercise (a) has little chance of achieving the desired result and (b) uses up some of our credit with the Turks.'[104]

Nonetheless the Goodwill Missions to non-Arab states had been well received in early 1971. After a talk with Tariq, David Crawford reported that Tariq's aim was to get Oman entry at the next General Assembly and that 'he plans to lead the Omani delegation at the time of entry himself'. Tariq also stated that he realised that the major obstacle to entry was the Soviet Union and therefore, he did not want to antagonise the Russians. Crawford worried about 'the political implications of discouraging the Omanis from contacts with the Soviet Union even if there are dangers in such contacts'. If the application were to fail because of the Soviets, 'someone might be blamed by Tariq. I have a feeling it might be ourselves'.[105] Acland wrote on this document that the Arab League application must come first and that 'we must consider whether there is a British interest which will lead us to give advice or whether we let Tariq muddle along pl [please] consider'.[106] By 9 March Oman had made its application to join the League, prompting Acland to write 'and muddling along it will be!'[107]

The clear recognition that the Arab League was the priority meant that the challenges faced in that application impacted upon the UN process. The uncertainties created by the Arab League delay meant that if Oman were to secure membership in September then the next session of the General Assembly which was scheduled to begin on 21 September might give rise to 'a tricky point of UN procedure... about the use of the Security Council's [SC] Special Committee on Admissions, to which the Americans attach particular importance.'[108] The background to this U.S. attachment was explained in a telegram sent to Bahrain. Normally 'the provisions of the second and third sentences of rule 59 and of the last two sub-paragraphs of rule 60 were ignored' but in the late 1960s the U.S. came under 'Congressional pressure to do something about the proliferation of very small states in the UN since these states were considered to be in a position to exercise voting power out of all proportion to their financial and general contribution to the UN'. Despite Anglo-American efforts to institutionalise some sort of associate membership for micro-states nothing came of it and so instead Washington decided that 'it might help to deter... if the committee envisaged in rule 59 [the SC Special Committee on Admissions] was reactivated'.[109]

When this new measure was put into effect for Fiji's application in 1970, the Soviets protested and Britain and France ended up voting against the U.S. so as to secure Fiji's membership. Britain and France gave an undertaking to the Americans that they would in future support the use of the committee. Therefore if the Omanis had sufficient Arab backing, the Soviets would wish to 'twist the American tail' and if the Americans continued to insist on the use of the committee 'we would be in a very embarrassing position'.[110] Once again British officials were thinking ahead on behalf of Oman.

Michael Weir therefore suggested discovering what the Sultan's intentions were and 'to try and steer him away from an immediate application to join the UN'.[111] Acland wrote on this letter 'we cd [sic] not hold up Oman on the admissions ctte [sic]... we would have to take the line we took with Fiji.'[112] Weir suggested a possible way out to be an application in July although he realised that membership of the League was seen as an essential condition of Arab support at the UN '(this has been the general attitude of the Arab delegations here)'.[113] He suggested attempting to persuade the league to have an extra meeting. Beaumont in Cairo and Acland were both against this idea on the grounds that 'we might incur criticism for interfering in Arab affairs, and it might not do Oman's position much good if we were seen to be trying to impose an agenda on the Arab League'.[114]

David Crawford was quick to ascertain the Sultan's intentions *viz* joining the UN. It was clear that he wished to join as soon as was practicable and that Tariq and others were even more enthusiastic. But Tariq still had a number of hurdles to overcome. During the Sultan's visit to Britain during the summer of 1971 he was given a full briefing of the difficulties and in separate meetings with Barouni and Sayyid Fahd a copy of Bhutan's application for the UN was given to the Omanis as a model. Officials also explained the importance of proper preparation and securing Arab support in the hope that 'this might either deter them from seeking membership this year, or at least proceed in a rather more businesslike fashion'.[115] Barouni specifically said that the Omanis wanted to be in during 1971 and would try and get their application in with a delegation going to New York by mid-July. Acland told them that they could 'call on you [Weir] for advice and appropriate assistance although we made it clear to them that for obvious reasons, we should not be the front runners in their support'. The Omanis worried that the 'Question of Oman' might be an obstacle but Acland assured them that 'provided the Arab states supported the application and that this was reflected in the Security Council' this would not be a problem. If however the Omanis 'seem to be acting prematurely in New York, we should have to try and discourage them more firmly'.[116]

Along with these fears of haste, there was some frustration at the lack of appreciation of the amount of effort required in order to secure membership. Acland stated that 'failure to get into the WHO [World Health Organisation], to which the Omanis attach much importance, and for which, typically, they have done little or no lobbying or preparation, may oblige them to think again [about their rush for UN membership]'.[117] Luckily for the Omanis they became WHO members later in May.

The Application

On 1 June 1971 Tariq, who had been appointed Omani Minister for Foreign Affairs in addition to his role as Prime Minister sent a letter to the Secretary-General of the UN submitting an application for membership.[118] This was met with a small amount of dismay in London with the Foreign Secretary sending a Telegram to Muscat stating that 'while we do not want to appear to be nannying the Omanis nor must we offend Tariq's susceptibilities, you should tell them' that Tariq or an Omani delegation should 'go to New York without delay to make preliminary contacts'.[119] The application also put the cat among the pigeons in New York with one British official stating 'it clearly took the Arabs (as well as us) by surprise and they have referred it to capitals and asked for instructions'.[120] This was because the standard way of doing things was to conduct extensive lobbying in New York and elsewhere *before* submitting an application.

On 6 June, Imam Ghalib wrote to the Secretary-General to protest at Oman's application and lack of independence. This issue of latent British control was placing in doubt Oman's Arab League aspirations and was also damaging its UN hopes. Arab states such as Egypt[121] advised that closure on the issue was needed before backing would be forthcoming. Meanwhile British officials had been sounding out the U.S. position on the use of the Admissions Committee in the case of Oman's application, things did not look good. The U.S. was adamant about the use of the committee for future consideration of applications.[122] Tariq meanwhile had been busy and met the Russians in Kuwait at the end of July to discuss Oman's UN application.[123] On 5 August he sent a telegram to the UN to ask when the Security Council would be considering Oman's application for membership. Tariq was certainly in a hurry and had been putting in some effort to bring on board those who might oppose the application, except of course the PDRY who had begun a campaign against Oman at the UN.

On 16 August the SC met to consider the Omani and other applications. The Omani application was referred for further reports and examinations to the Admissions Committee. Here something a little unusual happened; writing on 19 August Anthony Parsons stated that:

> It looks therefore... that a new modus vivendi has been reached in which the Americans will be allowed to have their way over the committee for admissions itself but that the deadlines will be conveniently ignored provided the applicant state sees to it in advance that those states, notably the Soviet Union, which have a natural tendency to twist the American tail (or ours for that matter) have been squared in advance... members of the Security Council are only too prone to reiterate the maxim "the Council is master of its own procedures"... this now underlines the necessity... for thorough and effective lobbying in advance... if you can be sure that the important delegations are on board you can achieve almost anything.[124]

It remained essential though for Oman to secure full Arab support and this looked unlikely until admission to the Arab League was secured. But little lobbying was going on at the UN as the Omanis had not sent a delegation since Tariq was on holiday.[125] It was not until the second week of September that the Omani delegation left for New York. Early September also saw the publication of a UN Secretariat working paper on Oman. Some British officials were surprised that the report was not more negative, although Acland was less than impressed. 'There are some slants which aren't helpful and several inaccuracies' he wrote: 'it is pretty pathetic that the UN Secretariat has to lower itself to putting out reports of this kind, admittedly based on press stories'.[126] When the SC met to discuss Qatar's application, it decided to further postpone discussion of Oman's application. By this time the Omani delegation were in New York and meeting anyone who would talk to them. On 17 September a minor victory occurred when the fourth committee suspended consideration of the 'Question of Oman'. This represented real progress since the issue had been doggedly raised at the UN for years and had been used by Communist states and the post-colonial nations as a stick with which to beat Britain. The suspension of discussion of the issue was therefore an important sign that progress was being made and that Oman was moving out of Britain's shadow, further increasing Oman's chances of UN admission.

On the Road Again

After months of encouraging accommodation with the Saudis, British officials were becoming increasingly frustrated with their attitude. Even Winchester in Jedda suggested that it was unlikely to cause 'very serious repercussions on Anglo/Saudi relations if we were to desist from advising caution'.[127] Douglas-Home suggested that there was little either Britain or Egypt could do to influence the Saudis and that it might 'in fact be easier for the Egyptians to tell the Russians that they have no objection to Omani membership'.[128]

On 30 September, just as Arab League membership was announced, Oman's application went before the SC. Although the application had been delayed from 16 August, at the council meeting all representatives including the U.S. agreed to have recourse 'to the last paragraph of rule 60 so that time limits laid down elsewhere in the rules could be waived'.[129] The major hurdle, where the application could have been vetoed by the USSR or China, had now been surmounted, perhaps the Soviets had enjoyed the U.S. having to adapt to not being able to put hurdles in the way of admission. More likely however was that the news from Cairo of Oman's admission to the Arab League and the Syrian representative on the Security Council's wholehearted support for Oman meant that the Soviets had to side with the Arabs. The final obstacle was now the General Assembly. The Omani delegation was bolstered by the arrival of Tariq on 6 October, and the following day the Assembly voted by 117 to 1 (PDRY), with Saudi Arabia and Cuba abstaining, to admit Oman. In a second resolution, taking note of the earlier decision of the fourth committee to suspend discussion on the 'Question of Oman', the vote was won by 115 to 3.

In the end the Omanis had a surprisingly smooth ride to UN membership. They were fortunate to have the support of the Arab contingent of course but a great deal of Anglo-Omani work had been put into gaining this support. It was also beneficial that Bahrain and Qatar happened to be going through the process at the same time, thus creating the impression that Oman was in the same position, making it difficult for those states which took little interest in Gulf affairs to discern the different situation Oman was in and also making it harder to accept Qatar and Bahrain but not Oman.

At the end of October, Tariq tendered his resignation as Minister for Foreign Affairs telling Hawley that his mission had been accomplished. There was more to it than this though as his relations with the Sultan worsened and he was angry about the Sultan giving orders to Oman's new UN representative which he thought countermanded his own.[130]

Omani-Saudi Relations

Saudi attitudes to Oman had run somewhat hot and cold throughout 1971 and their opposition at the Arab League was worrying. Both Qaboos and

Tariq had attempted to get invitations to the Kingdom or to talk to senior Saudis but were consistently rebuffed. Despite the fact that by June both sides seemed to have agreed on the treatment of Ghalib which was causing such difficulties, the first face to face contact only came at the end of June 1971 while Qaboos was in London. He was able to meet with the Saudi Ambassador there thanks to Robert McGregor of the Arabian Department who had assiduously but discreetly lobbied Oman's cause at a Saudi Embassy dinner.[131] In the aftermath of being accepted as members of the Arab League and the UN, King Faisal, capricious as ever, accepted the *fait accompli* and by 11 December Qaboos was in Riyadh being received 'with full honours of a state visit by King Faisal' for a three day visit.[132] Although there had not been an official declaration of recognition, Jedda reported that 'the King's reception of the Sultan is an honour usually accorded only to Heads of States on official state visits'.[133]

In the end Britain's insistence on patience and perseverance with the Saudis paid off. Interestingly, Morris in Jedda noted that a prominent Saudi merchant had been visible in the official motorcade, identifying him as Barouni's emissary to a key Saudi court official from earlier in the year. Morris stated that 'on the face of it he may have been responsible for arranging the invitation to the Sultan'.[134] This is revealing since it shows that while the Omanis had clearly listened to British advice, by the end of 1971 Muscat had developed its own foreign policy processes in line with London's hopes. Britain was, as it had predicted, slowly losing its overt position in the field of Foreign Affairs. Equally though, the appointment of Barouni by Tariq had clearly paid dividends, King Faisal took a liking to Qaboos and a formal statement of recognition was issued on 15 December 1971, with no mention of boundary disputes and with Qaboos addressed as Majesty rather than Highness which had been previous Saudi policy.

The Sultan's visit to Saudi Arabia, culminating in recognition, was in many ways the perfect end to the year. At many points over the preceding months the likelihood of Oman securing entry into the League and UN had looked unlikely under the prevailing circumstances and timescales. This represented a major policy success both for the Sultanate and for the British government. With recognition secured from the most important regional states and the legitimacy bestowed upon Oman through its membership of the UN and Arab League, a major prop of the Sultanate's enemies' propaganda programme was removed. The next problem for officials, both British and Omani was to convert all this newfound goodwill into active help and support in its ongoing war in Dhofar.

External Assistance

In contrast to the earlier position of Saudi Arabia, relations with Jordan and Iran were considerably warmer. The Sultan had planned a trip to Iran during the summer of 1971 but had to cancel. Instead the Shah invited him to Persepolis to celebrate 2,500 years of the Iranian monarchy at the end of October. At the celebrations the Sultan got along very well with the Shah, who had 'shown concern about the situation in Dhofar and had stressed his keen interest in the general security of the area'. He then went on to make the somewhat startling offer 'of military assistance if the Sultan should need it. Army, Air Force and Naval Forces would be put at Qabus' disposal if he requested them'.[135] Hawley strongly suggested to the Sultan that good relations with Iran were desirable, while also taking 'the opportunity of suggesting he [the Sultan] sought expert advice about the median line' of the Strait of Hormuz. Perhaps the Iranians would be willing to be accommodating on this issue too. The whole thing was too good an opportunity to miss. King Hussein had reportedly also been very friendly at Persepolis, and had agreed to send 'three good senior officers for the police and special branch. For his part the Sultan had made a quote modest [cash] contribution unquote to the King'.[136]

Colonel Oldman, the Omani Defence Secretary, in his report of October 1971 about progress in Dhofar since July 1970 stated that great strides had been made in the counterinsurgency. However 'despite all the real advances... in the coastal plain, SAF have made no real progress in wresting from the enemy any part of the rebel environment'.[137] He went on to state that 'all the conditions in Dhofar at present tend to impose a putative stalemate, where SAF is not strong enough to clear out the Communists from the Jebal, and the rebels do not have the strength to capture and hold the Salalah plain and coastal villages'.[138] In spite of this stalemate, the SAF to whom the bulk of the fighting fell, the SAS and the *Firqah* were doing good work and a new strategy to cut rebel supply lines and divide up the *Jebal* into sectors which could then be individually cleared was being developed.[139] Understandably the Iranian aid especially would help facilitate this strategy; indeed British attempts to gain external aid will be explored in the following chapter.

Conclusion

This chapter set out to explore how British policy towards Omani recognition developed and to see the extent of the British involvement in this area. The offers of assistance received by the Omanis from friendly neighbouring states were most welcome both for the Sultanate and the British. But none of this would have been forthcoming without the efforts made by Muscat and London to secure Oman international recognition and respectability. In a little over twelve months Oman went from being a closed and introverted state accused by the UN of being under British colonial control, to being a member of that same organisation. This was only possible because of the co-operation of a number of regional powers, especially Egypt. The importance placed by Britain on involving key states in the region and the startlingly benign view taken by these nations of Britain's role in Oman was to prove especially useful. The unexpectedly accommodating stance of Egypt, Syria and Iraq in particular greatly assisted recognition and surprised British officials.

This transformation from outcast to full member indicates that both Britain and Oman placed a high degree of significance on gaining international recognition. The haste of the Omanis and the caution and planning of British officials offers an interesting contrast but there can be no doubt that both sides shared the same goal. There was moreover a high degree of consistency in British policy and also between British officials themselves. Without having to deal with other Whitehall departments, officials had considerable freedom and demonstrated much common purpose. Even officials working in Foreign Office departments not associated with Oman put in a great deal of effort on Oman's behalf, the only small frictions coming when the FCO got the Embassy in Ankara to lobby without sufficient time and forewarning or indeed anything to offer Turkey diplomatically in return. The Foreign Secretary himself was again much involved and paid close attention to Omani affairs.

With reference to the three questions laid out at the beginning of this chapter it is now clear that while Britain had an important role in Oman's foreign policy sphere, that role slowly diminished over the course of 1971. Oman gradually built a small but useful foreign policy capacity and while British officials sometimes became frustrated with the efficiency, pace and scope of Omani diplomacy, they remained aware of the fact that Oman was an independent state and as such their advice had to be proportionate. The respect for Omani sovereignty is indeed somewhat startling when Britain clearly had *de facto* power over Oman.

That *de jure* recognition was judged to be important and not just the icing on the cake was proved correct by the reaction of the PDRY authorities to Oman's application to the Arab League. They knew that recognition would make winning the war in Dhofar considerably more difficult for them. The Foreign Policy successes of 1971 cannot be put down to Britain alone. Oman was rather fortunate with its timing, but Qaboos and Tariq were also determined and the appointment of Barouni turned out to have very fortunate consequences. Without British advice, logistical support, expertise, information gathering and behind the scenes lobbying though, it is doubtful whether Oman would have achieved so much so soon. The attempts to convert recognition to assistance, both in development and with the conflict in Dhofar were however, the next and more important stage in the process.

CHAPTER 6

BRITISH POLICY, WHITEHALL DEBATES & EXTERNAL AID 1972-74

La parfaite valeur est de faire sans témoin ce qu'on serait capable de faire

La Rochefoucauld, *Maximes*

Introduction

The resignation of Sayyid Tariq as Prime Minister in December 1971, due to disagreements with Qaboos over Oman's future direction, marked the beginning of a new era in Oman. Sultan Qaboos would now hold much greater individual power and the removal of the distraction caused by the frustrating relationship between the two men would, theoretically, aid co-ordination, especially in the development sphere. It would be easy therefore to think that the successes of 1970 and 1971 had in large measure secured Oman's future. Nevertheless, during the next few years, both Sultanate and British officials had to contend with some fundamental difficulties including problematic revenue streams, the thorny issue of defence expenditure versus development, the prosecution of the war in Dhofar and capitalising on the gains made in the foreign relations sphere. For its part Britain had a number of dilemmas of its own to contend with. These included managing the balance between offering sufficient support to the Sultanate and not becoming involved in an escalating and potentially open ended war, attracting and then satisfactorily integrating and controlling the contributions of the new allies and managing the growing interest of the media and other states, in particular the U.S., in Omani affairs, which had for so long been the sole preserve of the British. The British view of other actors in the region and their potential involvement in Oman, as well as their view of the British became increasingly important as Britiain's policy developed, and the extent of British involvement from 1972–74 evolved.

As noted previously, from early 1970 to the end of 1971, a great deal was achieved in the Sultanate. Oman was stabilised, development begun in earnest, counterinsurgency strategy revitalised, increased British military assistance secured and extensive international recognition acquired. Once this initial phase was over however, policymakers faced the challenge of how to build upon these successes in addition to the arrival of a number of new challenges, especially financial troubles, cross border tension with the PDRY, securing additional assistance and managing allies. Overcoming these challenges would necessitate new approaches from Britain. There was to be greater need to focus, in particular, on the nature and level of operations in the Sultanate, but there were also fiscal debates in Whitehall over increased British assistance and the continuing management of a range of external relations which needed continual attention. Meanwhile, the war was progressing and the continuing high level of British influence in Oman was beginning, for the first time, to be challenged by new actors and new relationships. Since the main reason why Britain remained so heavily committed to Oman was because of the threat posed by the rebellion it is important to understand the development of operations there during late 1971 and early 1972 in order to appreciate the broader context of political developments from 1972 onwards.

New Strategy: Dominate the *Jebal*

The end of 1971 saw an upsurge in Sultanate activity in Dhofar and the implementation of a new strategy devised by Brigadier John Graham the Commander of the Sultan's Armed Forces (CSAF). It was clear that PFLOAG's ability to dominate the *jebal* had to be ended by securing a year round SAF presence on high ground. This could then be used as a base for operations, a sanctuary for the *jebali* people from the PFLOAG threat and as a morale boost for the SAF. This operation, codenamed 'Jaguar', began, after the monsoon, in October 1971 with the aim of pacifying the eastern section of the *jebal*.[1] The rebels recognised the danger of a permanent SAF base in their midst and contested the establishment of a base at 'White City', leading to intense fighting. Peterson describes 'Operation Jaguar' as 'signal[ling] a great turning point: it produced the first permanent base on the Jebal, and from it date all SAF offensives in Dhofar, which led to Simba in the west and to eventual victory'.[2] Towards the end of October on the other side of Salalah a complimentary operation, codenamed 'Leopard', was launched, establishing a line of patrol bases down to the sea at Mughsayal. This was designed to interdict supplies to the central and eastern sectors of the *jebal*. While the establishment of bases would seem to be a step in the right direction it also held the danger of giving the rebels clear targets to attack. The use of helicopters, however coupled with these new bases gave the SAF the opportunity to exploit their air superiority and increase the pressure on the insurgents.

While operations in the east of Dhofar were proving successful, in the West the rebels remained relatively unmolested. This had to change. Thus a new operation was called for, the plan being to seize and maintain a base on an important ridge as far to the West as possible. For this Sarfait was chosen since from there barriers could be erected down to the sea thus both interdicting rebel movement and 'diverting the Front's attention away from the pacification operations in the East'.[3] This was accomplished and the Simba line went on to be very successful at preventing rebel movements. The tactic was subsequently used to form the Hornbeam and Damavand lines later in the war. Although costly both in terms of construction and manning, the introduction of this tactic was very significant in ending the war.[4]

Omani Exuberance: British Restraint

In the early summer of 1972 with operations 'Jaguar' and 'Leopard' in full swing an incident was to occur with potentially serious repercussions for both Britain and Oman. On 5 May Ambassador Donald Hawley in Muscat reported that the Sultanate's border fort with the PDRY at Habarut had been attacked for most of the day by mortar and machine gun fire from a fort on the PDRY side of the border. He saw this as a diversionary tactic to draw away resources from SAF's increasing stranglehold over the eastern *jebal*. The attack resulted in the deaths of five SAF soldiers and four wounded.[5] The Sultan, Colonel Hugh Oldman, the Omani Defence Secretary and Brigadier John Graham, CSAF decided that retaliatory action should not be taken immediately and that, the following day, leaflets should be dropped on the PDRY fort demanding a ceasefire and threatening retaliatory action at an unspecified time and location if this was not forthcoming. The following morning the PDRY attack recommenced and continued after the dropping of the leaflets at 11.15 hours. By this time a further SAF member had been killed. Later that day jets from the SOAF bombed the PDRY fort, resulting in, according to Peterson, the destruction of one side of the fort's main tower.[6] This attack though did not halt the bombardment from the Yemeni side of the border and resulted in SAF troops having to abandon their fort and retreat to a more sound position on a ridge behind the fort.[7]

By 8 May the Foreign Secretary, Douglas-Home, was asking Hawley for as much detail as possible, especially confirmation that no British loan personnel had been involved in the air strikes, since Sir Anthony Parsons, assistant under-secretary in the Foreign Office for the Middle East and United Nations, had a prearranged visit by the PDRY Ambassador the same day and the story had broken in that day's newspapers.[8] Hawley was unable to give many details but reported that one of the SAF casualties was an SAS soldier, Trooper Martin, and that the Omanis had made a formal protest about the PDRY actions to the UN Secretary General. He also confirmed that while he had no details of the composition of personnel leading the attack, Oldman was aware of 'our general attitude' towards the use of British loan personnel outside the Sultanate's borders.[9] Britain was concerned not to get drawn into a situation which might necessitate direct British military intervention. Equally though, Hawley[10] was concerned to make sure that at least the Sultanate's side of the story was heard, by asking the British Embassy in Beirut to use its contacts and influence to get the Omani side of the story published in the Lebanese press.[11] Just a day later on 9 May, Hawley was able to send Douglas-Home a full report of what had happened which had been obtained by his Defence Attaché (DA), C.E. Welch, and contained 'detail probably unknown to HQ SAF on account of the inadequacies of their reporting system'.[12] Welch concluded in his report that 'in view of the evident preparation on the PDRY side and their quick fire response [to the air bombardment, which resulted in one of the planes being hit twice] that the incident was deliberately contrived'.[13] The report also confirmed that the attack had been led by a British seconded pilot and that other seconded pilots were involved in the retaliatory action.

Douglas-Home expressed his concern, in a telegram to Hawley:

> We appreciate the need for a speedy Omani response to unprovoked aggression. But the use of seconded personnel in actions against targets within the PDRY could be embarrassing for HMG and you should therefore insist on consultation (under the confidential exchange of letters of 15 December 1971) if further action involving seconded officers crossing the border is to be considered.[14]

With a number of air strikes made against the PDRY fort and protests lodged with the UN and Arab League one would have expected the Omanis to let the matter rest for the time being. The problem was however that while the Omani fort was now heavily damaged, the position itself could not be abandoned 'because of the loss of face that [this] would result in, as well as because of its strategic position on the border and at the confluence of a number of camel trails and the presence of water'.[15] Habarut would clearly have to be reinforced, especially since the PDRY fort continued to fire upon the new SAF positions on the ridge above the damaged Omani fort. On 11 May, Hawley and Welch were invited to a meeting comprising the Defence Secretary, Oldman, CSAF and the heads of the Dhofar Brigade and SOAF. Oldman stated that the Simba position would have to be evacuated sooner than planned and would not now last through the Monsoon. This option would hardly do wonders for the morale of the civilian population or the volatile *firqah* and would also be unpalatable for the Sultan. The only way to sweeten the pill would be a SAF attack on rebel positions inside the PDRY at Hauf, by means of a 48-hour raid, involving land and air forces, targeting rebel supply caches and ships.

The time was perfect for this operation, with PDRY still firing on the SAF and just before the Monsoon season which the guerrillas traditionally used to build up their supplies inside Dhofar. Hawley was understandably concerned about the political sensitivities of such an operation, and while reassured by Oldman that no seconded officers would be involved, still countered with the probability that Britain would get the blame anyway and that PDRY MiGs might attack RAF Salalah. He also stressed the need for greater thought as to how Oman would handle this internationally and that such a decision 'might lead to earlier withdrawal from RAF Salalah than had previously been contemplated'.[16]

The PDRY were slow to release their version of the 'truth' but on 11 May they issued a long statement accusing Britain of launching planes from an aircraft carrier to hit their fort at Habarut.[17] The British Ambassador to Aden was also called in by the PDRY Ministry of Foreign Affairs, although he left the meeting with the impression that 'PDRY feel that things have got out of hand on the eastern border, and they would like to reduce the tension. Their protest seems more in sorrow than in anger'.[18] In Whitehall, concern about the potential attack on Hauf was rising, with the MoD getting wind of it through their own sources, prompting them to write to the FCO stating their concern.[19] Such was the level of alarm in both the MoD and FCO that the Minister of State at the FCO, Mr Joseph Godber, had been approached and had agreed to a dual approach to the Sultan to dissuade him from the attack. This idea, devised by Patrick Wright of the Middle East Department and Richard Lloyd-Jones the head of DS-11 (The Analytical Branch of Defence Intelligence) in the MoD, involved a Ministerial letter direct to the Sultan setting out the political arguments against the use of armed force and a visit by a senior military officer to assess and warn of the military dangers of such an operation, now codenamed 'Operation Aqubah (Punishment)'.[20] Indeed, all of this had been organised on the same day that Hawley had reported what was planned.

If the combined MoD-FCO response had been swift then the Omani one was possibly even quicker. By the end of the same day, Hawley was reporting that the Sultan had agreed to the operation, planning was well underway and that 'the Sultan is proposing to ask the Saudis for a commitment which would be made known to the PDRY, to take offensive action against [them]...in the event of retaliatory action by PDRY'.[21] This was not good news and fears of a major escalation of the Dhofar conflict were not helped by press reports of wild PDRY claims of such things as a British naval invasion of their island province of Socotra.[22]

On 12 May after consultations between MoD and FCO at the highest level, the Foreign Secretary, Douglas-Home, sent a telegram to Hawley in Muscat outlining Whitehall's fears of an attack only having short term benefits. There were also worries that the attack had the potential to alienate Arab states in 'cautiously friendly relations with Muscat'. This would be especially irritating after all the British efforts to secure good regional relations for the new Omani regime. Douglas-Home advised Hawley that both he and the Secretary of State for Defence, Lord Carrington, were planning to advise the Prime Minister, Edward Heath, to send a personal message to the Sultan 'designed to convince [him] of the political disadvantages of going ahead'.[23]

Replying the same day, Hawley appeared to be concerned about such a swift and high level response to the proposed operation. He asked that the Prime Minister's letter be delayed until at least both his political and the DA's military assessment of the proposed operation were complete. Hawley suggested it would be better received 'if we could be constructive e.g. in suggesting viable alternative courses open to him and possibly offering some quid pro quo to help the Sultanate at a critical juncture'.[24] The Sultan believed that the PDRY's continuing aggression at Habarut would actually gain him the sympathy of the majority of Arab states. Vindicating the Sultan's views, the Egyptian Foreign Affairs Minister, Hassan Sabri el-Kholi, said to Ambassador Beaumont in Cairo 'let there be as many British technicians and advisors as we and the Sultan wished but, if there had to be killing "Let Arabs kill Arabs"'.[25]

In the meantime a draft of a potential letter from the Prime Minister had already been prepared. An explanatory letter attached to the draft explained that:

> We have not overlooked the political risks involved [with sending the message]. The Sultan has much of his father's stubbornness. He has already decided to attack Hauf and it is possible that even a message from the Prime Minister will not dissuade him...King

Faisal is obsessed with the idea that we [']handed over['] Aden to the Communists and when he hears that we urged restraint upon the Sultan... he will regard this as an attempt to shore up the PDRY.[26]

Officials had even considered including in the letter the threat to withdraw British seconded officers or other defence assistance if the Sultan were to ignore the 'advice'. It was quickly concluded however that this would be 'most unwise, and if the Sultan decided to go ahead we should have to face the consequences'.[27] Ministers and officials had a narrow margin of error. While the consequences of an attack were possible escalation of the conflict or at minimum much international criticism of Britain's position, even a direct letter from Heath was not guaranteed to prevent such an action. The unwillingness to threaten a reduction of British assistance to Oman seems to indicate less of a desire not to upset the Omanis than the realisation that the threat would have to be carried out if the Sultan failed to heed Whitehall's warning and this could damage wider interests in the region by jeopardising the counterinsurgency efforts.

The DA's assessment of the general situation in Dhofar and the planning for the Hauf operation did not make for pleasant reading. The overall situation was in fact bleaker than first thought. It was reported that 'SAF are presently extremely stretched in every respect – deployment, planning capability, aircraft hours and combat administration. They will need the respite that the monsoon may bring'. The Defence Attaché concluded his report with the cautionary note that events might require SAF to retreat from all but one of its positions on the *jebal* to hold the plain and coastal towns.[28]

There appears to have been some slight annoyance at the resistance to the letter scheme put up by the Ambassador in Muscat. Hawley's suggestion of a quid pro quo for aborting plans for the attack drew the comments that 'it is difficult to see what kind of extra military assistance could be offered. Any request for additional help from the Sultan for additional troops would of course create considerable difficulties here'.[29] It was conceded that while there could be no delay as Hawley had requested, 'Ministers have approved certain amendments to the Prime Minister's message, which will, we hope, overcome the Sultan's opposition to our advice'.

Hawley's response was quick and he was not backing down. He suggested that Colonel Oldman and Brigadier Graham were having second thoughts about the operation, since the likelihood was that it would make holding the Simba position impossible. He suggested that the decision on sending the Prime Minister's letter should be held off 'since it may not be necessary to play this card'.[30] This news seemed to do the trick and Douglas-Home responded saying that provided there was no risk of the

Sultan going ahead with the attack suddenly, the delivery of the message could be suspended.[31]

Having secured himself some time Hawley met with the Sultan on 14 May and exercising all of his diplomatic skills made the case against intervention. In his report of the meeting he stated that 'I took the Prime Minister's letter along in my pocket... I concluded, however, that it was better to leave matters as they are so that the Sultan should feel that the decision to call the operation off was his own'.[32] Hawley reassured the FCO that there was no question of the operation going ahead immediately, indeed having briefed Oldman on the fears of Ministers and giving him the MoD assessment, Oldman 'was somewhat relieved'. Hawley concluded that the Hauf operation was now unlikely to go ahead. It appeared that the Sultan had learnt a great deal, especially from the campaign to gain Omani accession to the UN and Arab League, and was backtracking slowly from his hot headed agreement to the plan on 11 May. The Sultan informed Hawley that he had, since then, presented his case to the UN, Arab League and in personal letters to a number of Arab leaders and was determined that if an attack was to go ahead he would have explicit Arab sympathy, although he hoped that Arab opprobrium directed at Aden would encourage PDRY to restrict its support for the rebels.[33]

The British Ambassador to the UN in New York, Sir Colin Crowe, reported on 15 May that the PDRY delegation had protested against the Omani retaliatory airstrikes at Habarut and that the Omani delegation had not yet released the statement.[34] Crowe stated that if the attack on Hauf was to go ahead and resulted in an official PDRY protest to the Security Council, it would be difficult for Britain in the light of backing a resolution the previous February condemning an Israeli incursion into Lebanon 'to avoid voting in favour of a resolution which confined itself to deploring the Omani action and calling for cease fire and withdrawal'.[35] This was a considerable worry for the FCO, although potential action now appeared to be held in abeyance, since the Sultan had received an Arab League telegram urging caution and promising an initiative to affect a solution. The Sultan had also prepared a detailed press communiqué of his case and sent out missions to the major Arab capitals. Oldman, while remaining attracted by the potential benefits of the raid, had come to see the political consequences of the action as deeply undesirable and was preparing a report detailing his assessment.

In a separate, but closely related development, to those at Habarut and the looming possibility of the Hauf Operation, the MoD began to put in place measures to ensure that seconded officers could not be used outside of Oman's borders without permission from Whitehall. Since neither the terms of secondment nor the December 1971 Memorandum of Understanding on seconded officers spelt out territorial or operational limitations on seconded personnel's activities, this was potentially embarrassing for Her Majesty's Government. The British Ambassador in Muscat had, however, at least secured the Sultan's agreement that there would be consultations before seconded troops served in any operation which might cause embarrassment to either government. The perceived way out of this bind was a special MoD directive issued to CSAF, as was the case with the Commander of the new Union Defence Force of the UAE, specifically prohibiting seconded officers from serving outside the host nation's territory.

It was however recognised that the Omani case was different and that surveillance operations of PDRY airfields which could threaten RAF Salalah, and a general desire not to compromise the effectiveness of the campaign needed consideration.[36] By 16 May a directive for CSAF had been prepared and was to remain secret. This directive informed CSAF that 'neither you nor any British seconded personnel under your command are employed on operations outside Oman, without the prior approval of Her Majesty's Government'. The directive however recognised that there may be times when this was not possible and authorised CSAF to use seconded officers on such missions. It also requested that CSAF ensured that 'loyalty to the Sultan must, however, never appear in doubt'.[37] Contract officers however were a different story and were much freer to take part in cross border raids. The best example of this was an ex-SAS soldier and *firqah* leader recruited by the Sultan who crossed 80 miles into Yemen with two trucks, 500 pounds of gelignite and 80 men and captured the PDRY army fort at Sinau which he promptly blew up. This operation, of which CSAF was unaware, impressed the Sultan greatly although the British commanders were only too aware of Whitehall's sensitivities to cross border operations of this kind.[38]

The use of seconded pilots in the attacks on the PDRY fort had woken the government to the dangers of such personnel operating outside Oman potentially giving cause for embarrassment and risking potential escalation and they were quick to ensure that safeguards were strengthened. Once again fear of international attention and escalation of the conflict damaging British interests led to surprisingly speedy action. Douglas-Home asked Hawley for advice on whether or not Colonel Oldman should know about the new directive. Hawley, always concerned with maintaining good relations with the Omani administration and a good supply of reliable information, was convinced of the need for this, 'since he is always extremely frank with me and I think our interests are always best served by taking him into our confidence'.[39]

The Attack Proceeds

As part of his efforts Hawley had secured movement on the supply of aircraft and helicopters to the Sultanate but much more was needed in terms of assistance. Attitudes in the MoD however were hardening, and a Defence and Overseas Policy Committee document responding to a number of Omani requests for supplies and reinforcements was hardly enthusiastic. Further loan service officers were to be refused, as was the supply of General Purpose Machine Guns. On the plus side RAF airlift and air dispatch equipment would be provided at no extra cost and some payments deferred for transport until the end of the year but that 'no other concessions on payment can be made'.[40] In his telegram informing Hawley of the results of the discussions Douglas-Home, contrary to some commentators' focus on Britain's attempts to prioritise British exports,[41] suggested that 'it would clearly be cheaper for Oman to look for the ammunition elsewhere'.[42]

By 19 May the threat of a raid at Hauf had fallen off the radar. Omani troops had temporarily withdrawn from Habarut on 14 May, but when they returned on 22 May however, they discovered that the Omani fort had been completely levelled and came under immediate heavy mortar and machine gun fire from the PDRY fort. Hawley reported on 23 May that the Sultan had decided that he 'can no longer exercise the restraint urged on him by his friends'.[43] The Hauf operation was firmly back on the agenda. Hawley, fearing that he may have to deliver the Prime Minister's letter, immediately got across his appreciation of the situation stating that 'a modified and up-dated version of the Prime Minister's letter would irritate the Sultan' and that 'the most recent events...have created an entirely new situation'.[44] On this occasion Hawley's recommendations were heeded and he was told merely to stress that seconded officers should not be used in the attack. The plan at this stage was merely for an air and artillery attack on Hauf and not the earlier mooted ground incursion. Hawley managed to disassociate all seconded personnel from the attack, even to the extent of getting CSAF to allow his deputy Colonel Colin Maxwell, a contract officer to sign the orders for the attack. Hawley recommended that while this gave London public deniability 'it would nonetheless be in our interest to discreetly assist the Omani's own information effort when possible'.[45]

The operation was to go ahead on 25 May; the Sultan was concerned about the internal repercussions if he did not respond decisively to the provocation. He had clearly attempted to find a diplomatic solution and assured Hawley that he had full Saudi moral and political support, although Riyadh had not, as had earlier been proposed, agreed to Saudi air action against the PDRY if Salalah was attacked. Hawley ensured the Sultan understood the possible repercussions, there was little more he could do.

Throughout this crisis Hawley had been in a difficult position trying to hold off the Omanis and Whitehall from precipitate moves. In the end, and despite FCO reservations, it was clear that the situation had changed and that there was more to gain than to lose from the operation. The episode shows that Britain's power in Oman was once again much less than the sum of its supposed parts. Ultimately it was the Sultan's decision, and London could not prevent him from taking military action without making threats it would be reluctant to carry through. The affair also indicates the crucial role of the man on the spot. Without Hawley's hard work, Anglo-Omani relations could have been unnecessarily damaged and British influence diminished. Officials in London were, for their part, quick to realise the situation had changed. In a written minute, Anthony Parsons wrote in agreement of Hawley's assessment 'I agree. The situation has changed – (a) the Sultan has obviously decided irrevocably'.[46] Ministers also agreed that nothing more should be done and that seconded officers should not be prevented from acting in an advisory capacity, as this would 'place an unwarranted limitation on our assistance to the Sultan'.[47] Air and artillery bombardment on PFLOAG training camps and stores at Hauf continued over 25 and 26 May and were reported as being reasonably successful, although the sighting of contrails above Salalah caused some concern that the PDRY air force was gathering intelligence for an attack.

Hawley however, believed an attack was more likely on the Simba positions or on Habarut.[48] The possibility of PDRY air strikes created considerable activity and speculation in Dhofar, Muscat and London, resulting in a full assessment of possible targets and defensive measures being completed by CSOAF on 31 May. The attacks on Hauf resulted in increased media interest and a few Parliamentary questions, as well as some activity at the UN but the excitement quickly died down. It is clear that Oman was provoked into taking the action at Hauf, the attacks over the PDRY border were warranted and did not simply represent a broader strategy to cut off PFLOAG supplies. There most certainly was not, as Halliday suggests, 'a land attack on Hauf at the end of May'.[49]

By mid-summer 1972 the PFLOAG was increasingly squeezed by Operations 'Jaguar' and 'Simba'. Desperate to prove they could still strike at will and to boost morale the Front launched what was to be its largest offensive operation of the war on the small coastal town of Mirbat,[50] east of Salalah. It resulted in a battle which has been compared to Rorke's Drift during the Zulu wars.[51] Early in the morning of 19 July 1972 between 200 and 250 guerrillas launched an assault on the town, which was defended by nine SAS soldiers from the BATT (British Army Training Team), who were due to be rotated out of Oman in the coming days, some 40 *firqat* and around 25 Dhofar Gendarmerie. Having surrounded the *Wali's* fort, the Oman Gendarmerie's compound and the BATT's house the rebels pressed home their attack with a savage ferocity. Using Soviet RPG7s and Carl Gustav Rocket Launchers the Gerndarmarie's fort's ancient masonry provided little resistance, its tower crumbling in a 'plume of smoke and dust'.[52] Being the monsoon season the cloud cover was extremely low, at just 150 feet, making air strikes seemingly impossible.[53] In the face of ostensibly overwhelming odds the rebel attack proved unsuccessful, thanks largely to the bravery of the defenders, in particular those SAS troopers manning the gun pit in front of the Oman Gendarmerie Fort and the skill of SOAF pilots, who despite the low cloud cover still managed to strafe and bomb the attackers. The initial assault had the sting taken out of it but it was clear that the battle was by no means over. A real stroke of luck for the defenders was the arrival, by helicopter at 9.15 am, of SAS reinforcements, the very people who were due to take over in the next few days, who had been preparing to go out on a firing exercise but who ended up getting some real practice instead. The rebels had, despite initial superiority and surprise on their side, been decisively defeated in open combat. The defeat seriously depleted the rebel ranks, hugely boosted the SAF and 'gave the Front a crushing psychological blow. It was never again able to mount such a large scale attack'.[54] Halliday, of course, sees the action rather differently, claiming the Front 'launched an attack on the eastern coastal town of Mirbat and held it for fourteen hours in the largest battle of the war, confounding the British and confirming that PFLOAG held the initiative'.[55]

Financial Concerns and Additional Assistance

While victorious on the battlefield, the combination of SAS, SAF, SOAF and the *firqat* was hardly cheap to run. There had been high hopes for oil production but it soon became clear that Oman's reserves were much smaller than those of its neighbours and the combination of defence and development expenditures were placing great strains on the Omani budget. An initial lack of experience and a reluctance to use long term loans to fund development rather than from current earnings, coupled with such large defence expenditures and the fact that oil production and earnings rose only slowly created an increasingly difficult fiscal environment for the Sultanate by 1972. In an economic review of the Omani economy in early May 1972, Donald Hawley reported that while expected oil revenue for 1971 had been £54.5 million, the Sultan had in fact only received £47 million 'and had to spend more that 40 per cent of that on defence'.[56] Hawley described the problem thus faced when departments put forward their budget estimates for 1972 which were well in excess of income. 'The result was that the estimates had to be pruned considerably...even after considerable cuts had been made throughout the public sector [there was still a deficit of] £23 million or 45% of revenue'.[57]

Later in his report Hawley stated that, it is a mater of concern to us 'that for many months now no British contractor has been awarded a major Government contract. Our contractors seem unable to compete on price, and here price is usually the determining factor'.[58] Concern about the competitiveness of British goods was also stressed, since 'with the opening up of the country to businessmen from all over the world it will be a hard struggle for us to maintain our share of Oman's imports'.[59] Britain was thus to be squeezed in both the Omani public and private sector spending and the situation with the Omani Government's finances would only deteriorate over the coming years. John Townsend, the Omani Government's Economic Advisor from 1972–75, demonstrates the problem clearly: In 1971 the government received revenues of 50.1 million Rials and spent 46 million, in 1972[60] they received 53 million Rials and spent 71.6 million, in 1973, 68.5 million spending 92.9 million. By 1975 (even after the oil shock) the government was still spending more than it was earning, receiving 398.1 million Rials, it spent 506.4 million in the financial year 1975–76.[61]

With the Omani budget in such disarray it was little surprise that Whitehall was the first port of call for assistance. On 11 March 1972, Colonel Oldman at the command of the Sultan wrote to Hawley, to 'request your valued assistance to place before your Government, the Sultanate's request for an alleviation of the high rate of capitation charges' paid in respect to seconded personnel.[62] The letter made a careful case for assistance comparing the costs to the Sultanate of seconded and contract officers in SAF and SOAF. Oldman was careful to appeal to the British focus on development issues, precedents of the waiving of charges elsewhere, the practical and tactical benefits to H.M. Armed Forces of operating in Oman in terms of the experience gained and of course an appeal to emotion and high national interests. He did so with the rather poetic phrase: In view of 'your Government's strategic and political interest in the support of Oman as a valiant shield against the spread of Communism in the Gulf'.[63] This plea was well received in the Foreign Office, which wrote to the MoD stating:

> This brings to a head concern which we have felt for some time past...Unless we can go some way towards meeting the Sultan's request, there may be a real danger of the phasing out of British loan personnel, to the detriment of our interests not only in Oman but in the area as a whole.[64]

The issue of the costs of Loan Service Personnel (LSP) was clearly one which irritated many at the Foreign Office who had been on the receiving end of grumblings from other posts as far afield as Singapore, who were considering replacing British LSP with Canadians. A typical example of the depth of feeling can be seen in just a short note between officials at the FCO, referring to the Omani request:

> So Treasury/MOD greed is pricing us out of the market. We must recognise that fact and go into battle on the side of our customers. The plain fact is that we (HMG) want to establish Defence Relations... because of the short and long term benefits to us. If we want the benefits, and that is our only reason for dabbling in Defence Relations, we must make our assistance attractive. We do I believe, make it efficient but then we spoil it all by overcharging. I believe the point has now come when we in FCO must make it clear to Ministers that they must take a look at Defence Relations, see how worthwhile they are and agree that we cannot expect any benefits if at the same time Treasury/MOD are allowed to squeeze every penny they can out of the countries we assist (and out of FCO!)... The only fair charge for all forms of military assistance is 'extra costs'. Cost which HMG would pay for anyway if no assistance were offered must remain a charge to HMG. This is a big question and now, with Oman and Singapore as evidence, is the moment to strike as regards LSP.[65]

The response to Oldman's request from the MoD was not promising. While agreeing with the reasoning and clear British interests behind the request and its backing from the Foreign Office, Richard Lloyd-Jones of the MoD's DS-11 replied:

> I am afraid that the suggestion that we have meetings or working parties to examine capitations rates – presumably in the hope of bringing them down does not appeal to us at all... In short, we would like to help, but I cannot see any prospects of alleviating through accounting methods.[66]

Lloyd-Jones did however suggest that provision should be made in Britain's military assistance funds for greater aid to Oman in future years. The FCO was also concerned by the whole issue and began to rehearse its arguments for securing more money from the Treasury or from MoD budgets. Indeed the situation was about to get much worse, since from 1 April 1972 there was a 19 per cent increase in LSP costs due to a long overdue pay rise.[67] The

Saudis were also accusing Whitehall of not providing enough assistance and were reluctant to give Oman aid until Britain raised its game. The pressure was on to find a solution.[68] After careful negotiations with the MoD, the FCO managed to persuade them that they should look again at the issue 'if unexpectedly, it appeared possible that HMG's inability to help would appreciably damage our political and military relations with Oman'. Lloyd-Jones even offered drafting advice on how best to put the case to the Chiefs of Staff.[69] At least there was some progress, however slight. Hawley, having been told of the slim chance of assistance wrote to Patrick Wright the new Head of the Arabian Department stating: 'I must confess to some disappointment at the apparent inconsistency between the importance we attach to the area and the amount we are able to do in financial terms'.[70]

After a meeting with Oldman in London, the difficulties of securing the £250,000[71] needed from the Treasury or MoD were explained, especially in the light of a recent point blank Treasury refusal to authorise a similar defence package for Malaysia which included significant cost savings. The meeting concluded that an approach to the Treasury should be made anyway but to limit extra assistance to just two years. On a tactical level it was decided that the approach should be made at Secretary of State level 'with a copy to the P.M. with the idea of the P.M. being able to make the offer to the Sultan when he sees him on 22 August'.[72] This was an interesting bureaucratic manoeuvre securing two of the Cabinet's biggest figures and presenting the Prime Minister with an opportunity to appear generous when meeting Qaboos.

In a further meeting on 16 August, involving officials from various FCO departments and the MoD some ideas were raised to help Oman. The meeting however decided against devising some proportionate sharing of the costs of LSP or the creation of a new agreement which might set an unwelcome precedent for other countries which used British LSP. Instead, a combination of cancelling a debt owed to MoD, mainly for SAS ammunition of £563,000, as well as providing further ammunition, the services of the Field Surgical Team (FST) and SAS for free in the next 12 months was proposed as a better way to help the Sultanate cope with rising costs and low revenues. This had an estimated cost of around a further £265,000. The advantage of this combination was seen to be that 'Treasury could not tell us to "find it out of savings" it would have to be new money'. The MoD suggested that the FCO should put the matter to the Treasury since it was driven by political rationale. The FCO note comments that, 'This was a cunning move. Whichever way it goes MoD gets some credit for their generosity... it is really no skin off our nose, it will not come out of our funds with their ceiling, and the important thing is the ability to give aid to Oman'.[73]

In a long submission from the Minister of State at the FCO to the Chief Secretary of the Treasury a few days later, the case was made for more aid to Oman, putting the option of reducing the costs of LSP or the combined option described above. The letter stressed the importance of Oman and its security to Britain's regional commercial interests and national security, as well as the fact that the Foreign Secretary had expressed his strong approval of the plan.[74] The plan was also to secure a strong note of support from Carrington, the Defence Secretary. It worked: when Prime Minister Edward Heath saw the Sultan on 22 August he announced that Britain would be waiving certain charges totalling £850,000. It can be seen that in this instance, the Treasury had been comprehensively outmanoeuvred.[75] The sense of jubilation within the FCO was palpable, as two separate handwritten notes attest. One states: 'My reading of this is that after all the palaver about the impossibility of MoD finding a single cent, they are in fact finding (since they never lost) the whole £850k without difficulty. Excellent!' The other with an eye on future battles states: 'Possible useful ammunition in Def Dept dealings with Treasury and MoD in the future!'[76]

The November Review of Military Assistance

If the Treasury had thought that the Omanis would be satisfied with the gesture made to them in August and that their demands for something to be done over the costs of LSP had been assuaged, they were to be mistaken. The distractions of the Sultan's visit and the negotiations over the additional assistance package meant that Oldman never received a formal reply to his plea for help over the cost of LSP. After a visit by Lord Balniel, the Minister of State at the MoD, to Oman at which he heard an 'impassioned plea' on the issue of LSP, Hawley wrote to Patrick Wright the head of the Middle East Department of the FCO, asking about the matter. Hawley too had spoken to Balniel and in his letter to Wright laid out Oman's case for special consideration. He raised the value of the training, the low rent Britain was paying for the valuable use of Masirah, Oman's financial troubles, the fact that other states were providing aid with no strings, thus providing the possibility 'of our being accused by the Saudis and Iranians of being somewhat skinflint' and finally the importance of stability in Oman.[77] A similar plea was put forward by the Defence Attaché in Muscat who also as part of the review process had to forward the Sultanate's requests for aid to be considered, on this occasion amounting to a further 75 LSP. While Wright was sympathetic to the Omani case for help with LSP costs he recognised that it would be difficult to square this with such a large request for additional LSP.[78]

A review of the Military Assistance to Oman was due in November 1972, comprising CSAF and Ambassador's reports, Omani requests for assistance, a JIC report and a Chiefs of Staff meeting. Hawley submitted a long and detailed report at the end of October which set out the financial problems facing Oman, the cost of LSP, the need for more LSP and the offers of free assistance by Oman's neighbours which were in stark contrast to Britain. He also stressed that since the Chiefs of Staff wished to start negotiations over the relinquishment of RAF Salalah at an appropriate time, without a new visible British financial package, this goal could make the negotiations difficult since Salalah and the vital base at Masirah were part of the same treaty. British 'abandonment' of Salalah would also hardly inspire confidence in those other states assisting Oman. In any case the Sultan would, like his father, be unwilling to relinquish the British presence at RAF Salalah without adequate compensation.[79]

With all required assessments arriving in London and the CoS meeting due for 14 November, Hawley was invited by the Chiefs and encouraged by Wright and Douglas-Home to attend the meeting. There was however still time to co-ordinate the FCO plan for a meeting with MoD officials set for 7 November. The FCO position was spelt out by Patrick Wright in a paper circulated to all FCO officials who would be attending the meeting. The present level of assistance should be continued but this was complicated by two additional demands; firstly, a request for extra LSP and secondly that consideration be given to alleviating the charges levied on the Sultanate for British assistance. The paper made it clear that, while the first additional matter was for the MoD to decide, the FCO should support the idea of reducing the charges for LSP. The Foreign Office was concerned about the increasing help of other nations which made it harder to resist pressure from the Omanis and while pressure should be put upon Saudi Arabia to carry through its promises of aid, there was little optimism that this would be successful without increased British help, since the Saudis saw it as Britain's responsibility to defend Oman. Wright went on to state that while 'a case for further assistance will certainly be resisted by the Treasury... we should try and give more financial help to the Sultanate'. Wright also warned that the MoD were:

> Strenuously resisting the idea that their vote should meet the cost of any concession and indeed F 1 Air (without, apparently, much support from elsewhere in the MOD) are suggesting that MOD's existing concessions (i.e. the charging of SAS and FST at [']extra costs[']) should be stopped.[80]

The FCO team, was therefore to support the continuation of SAS and FST on the current basis, support the sharing of costs for LSP between the Sultanate and HMG, but that this would not be paid for by MoD or FCO and that 'New Money' would therefore be needed. It was suggested that the aim of the meeting should therefore be to gain MoD support for this position and approach the Treasury well before the planned DOPC meeting in December. In the event the MoD approved of all of the FCO's proposals, agreeing in principle to support the FCO's case with the Treasury.[81] The Chief's of Staff meeting on 14 November did not go quite as smoothly. While approving continuation of the current assistance they also decided that a DOPC paper on Britain's future commitment to Oman should be drafted for their meeting the following week. The initial version of the paper was drafted by the MoD, which, while very similar to FCO assessments needed that 'FCO touch' to make some of the assessments more palatable. A good example of this is the change from 'The containment and defeat of the rebels is likely to be a long haul and I am anxious that we should avoid any possibility of our entering into an open ended commitment', to the far less alarming, 'Since the containment and defeat of the rebels is unlikely to be achieved in 1973 I am concerned that we should not become increasingly involved in an open ended commitment'.[82]

Not everyone at the FCO was quite convinced that the plan for securing 'New Money' for Oman was likely to work. A senior FCO finance department official wrote to Patrick Wright stating that, 'I have been following with some interest (and, as the sums have escalated, with increasing alarm) the minuting on this subject'.[83] The letter laid out the concerns that the FCO were now seeking £462,000 per annum rather than the earlier proposed £325,000 per annum for three years and suggested 'In fairness to FCO ministers they must be made aware just how difficult a passage a request to the Treasury...is likely to have at the present time'. The letter set out the background of fiscal problems and the fact that the Prime Minister had personally asked his colleagues 'to hold down the level of expenditure in their departments', as well as listing a number of other requests about to go to the Treasury. The letter noted that, 'The likely Treasury response to this spate of requests can well be imagined'. The official then suggested two ways that FCO could get at least some extra aid to Oman. The first was that the MoD should provide LSP at 'extra cost' only and the second was that the MoD charging for the training that LSP had received in their entire career[84] before posting to Oman should not be charged to the Sultanate. While the suggestions were helpful, they would hardly send the strong message of support to the Sultan that the Middle East Department was looking for.

Much work went into preparing a strong case to maximise the chances of securing DOPC approval for seeking the new money. It is clear from a speaking note prepared for Douglas-Home, that a strong focus on the clear national interests involved was once again used to attempt to convince the committee of the need for the new money:

> The need to preserve stability in the Persian Gulf is as important now as it has ever been. The West is becoming more and more dependent on oil from the Gulf States and Saudi Arabia, and if the Sultan of Oman is overthrown the smaller Gulf States will almost certainly collapse and the security and stability of the whole area could be gravely affected.[85]

Using more poetic but no less concerned language, Sir Anthony Parsons in a note to the Permanent Under Secretary of the FCO made the importance of Oman to British interests even clearer with the words:

> There is no doubt that the continuation in existence of the Sultanic regime is crucial to British interests. If the Sultan were replaced by a radical Arab regime, the poison would rapidly spread to the treasure house of the Persian Gulf States.[86]

The Oman situation was also under review by the (Cabinet) Central Policy Review Staff (CPRS) who also produced a memo for the DOPC meeting on 23 November. This caused some upset for both the Minister of State at the MoD, Lord Balniel, and the Minister of State at the FCO, Julian Amery, who, on 27 November replied to a letter from Lord Balniel with the words, 'I strongly agree... that Oman is the key to the Gulf... The CPRS questions were singularly ill informed – if only we still had Aden!' Against which, some FCO wag has written, 'mmm, rather if only PDRY didn't have it'.[87]

With such strong FCO and MoD support from Ministers it was no surprise that the DOPC meeting went well, with the Prime Minister summing up that: 'The committee has noted that there were good political reasons for examining ways in which to alleviate the burden placed upon Oman's defence budget by the campaign against the rebels.'[88]

Hawley was no doubt pleased with the results of the meeting but continued to push for more. In a letter to Patrick Wright he suggested that the costs of the Field Surgical Team be borne permanently by the MoD on the grounds that they were there to look after other MoD troops and were gaining extremely valuable experience. In addition he suggested that since the Iranians were not charging for their Special Forces, MoD should not charge for the SAS and their ammunition. Wright passed on these concerns, supporting the FST suggestion but not that involving the SAS.[89]

The FCO lost no time in preparing a detailed paper for the Treasury examining a range of options for alleviating LSP costs and sent it to the MoD for comments on 30 November. Option one suggested that Britain shared half of the costs through a formal agreement costing £462,850. Option two proposed that Britain paid for half the costs of what could be considered as training at £231,425. Option three was to pay for all costs associated with the requested 27 additional personnel at £140,700 while option four meant writing off the costs of flying training for 23 men at £92,000. Option five was only charging extra costs for all personnel at £439,823 and option six proposed finding some way of removing income tax charges from the total at a cost of £169,970.[90] The MoD response came a short time later and while generally supportive, quickly ruled out options two to six. Responding to the suggestion in option two, Lloyd-Jones stated 'this hardly seems meaningful. LSPs are fully integrated into SAF how can we distinguish between the training and operational content of their work? We run his army and air force after all'. While option six was seen as a real non-starter, he stated 'we do not see the Treasury agreeing to this'.[91] It was suggested that option one 'seems the most satisfactory'. Lloyd-Jones however expressed his doubts that a formal cost sharing agreement was the best way forward and instead suggested that it would be simpler if the Sultan was offered around £500,000 per annum for 1973–74 and 1974–75 'with no strings attached but with no prospect of any increase or extension. It strikes us that a once and for all cash arrangement would be far easier to explain away to other petitioners than a more formal arrangement.'[92] This was a positive suggestion and when the FCO submitted its request to the Treasury on 18 December they included it and the idea of a more formal cost sharing arrangement.[93]

The Treasury were unhappy with the fact that the Oman request arrived at the same time as two other FCO requests for Thailand and Kenya, making it difficult for the Treasury to judge the priorities to be given to the proposals. It was suggested that the best place to discuss the proposals would be in the new DOP (O) Ancillary Measures Committee, which would meet for the first time in January 1973. A Treasury official told Wright however that he 'should not assume that the Treasury attitude... was "entirely negative" but that they were unlikely to be able to agree the full amount suggested'.[94]

It was not until 2 January 1973 that the Treasury got around to sending a formal reply to the FCO's letter of 18 December. The Treasury were clearly not happy about the requests stating:

> In our view the UK needs to be very cautious in embarking on new projects involving the provision of military capital aid. If exceptional

cases arise where the national interest seems to justify such projects, we think that there should be a full review of existing priorities with a view to implementing offset savings... All other bids, actual or prospective for military aid have to be scrutinised together and an order of priorities established... only then would it be practicable to consider the extent to which it was in the British national interest, and possible to make increased provision.[95]

Clearly the Treasury were not going to make things easy for the Foreign Office. In a briefing note for the meeting, the FCO stated its case on Oman with the words: 'The FCO consider that officials are under ministerial orders on this item, and that the question of priorities does not arise. It should go ahead without reference to the other two cases'.[96] The reply to the Treasury's letter of 2 January made a similar point, stating that the decision of the DOPC on 23 November 'left only the administrative arrangements to be settled'.[97] The FCO also began to make sure that a system for future requests was put in place so that the Treasury could not force them to rank their preferences. This was especially so since, 'this sort of mishap gives the Treasury unnecessary opportunities for probing into our expenditure generally'.[98] The Treasury's somewhat frosty reply stated that:

> If the FCO is satisfied that within the overall balance of priorities it is <u>essential</u> in the British interest (and not just [']desirable[']) to extend financial assistance for yet another year, we are prepared to agree that up to £500,000 of the cost of our Loan Service Personnel in 1973–4 only may be met from public funds.[99]

This was a very reluctant concession from the Treasury and would only cover one year. In their reply the FCO stressed that, 'We must reserve our position about future years. This will be for Ministers to decide'.[100] Of course the FCO knew that if a well crafted case was made to Ministers they would receive a sympathetic hearing. It was only through Ministerial and Prime Ministerial support that they had been able to wring this concession from the Treasury. It is clear that once again the case for British national interests in helping Oman was seen by Ministers as compelling. The role of HM Ambassador Muscat was also an important one; he was dogged in his attempts to make sure that something was done in Whitehall about the costs imposed on Oman for LSP. Without his persistence and compelling arguments in pushing for more resources, it seems unlikely that officials in Whitehall would have gone quite so far to secure 'New Money'. This had been an important victory at a crucial time for

Oman, although there would be many more battles of this kind over the coming years.

Outside Aid

Securing a hard fought victory to receive both additional funding to alleviate the costs of LSP and also some extra personnel to serve with SAF signified important additional progress after the successes of gaining British military assistance in 1970 and 1971 but this only represented one plank of the FCO strategy. It had been formally stated policy since 1971 and informal policy since the coup itself that Britain can 'best contribute to the stability of Oman and to the maintenance of our interests there by... encouraging Oman to establish relations with... friendly countries and to obtain assistance from such... states'.[101] The implementation of this policy however entailed more than merely encouraging Oman to obtain assistance from friendly states, Britain too would have to put in a lot of work both to obtain assistance and then to integrate it with the British efforts in the Sultanate. This work was essential however because, as the difficulty in securing British financial aid from the Treasury suggested little more assistance from that quarter could be expected. The British economy was experiencing difficulties and 'the early 1970s ushered in a period of rapid inflation'.[102] In this environment it is little surprise that some burden sharing was deemed desirable.

Oman was facing a real dilemma: its cash flow problems meant that there was insufficient money for rapid development. Although much improvement had been made in terms of schools, clinics, roads and electrification, the war was absorbing too many resources and needed still more to bring about a resolution to the conflict, allowing the focus to switch to development. Oman clearly could not muster the reserves to finish the war and Britain was proving to be increasingly either unable or indeed unwilling to provide the necessary resources. The only way out of the bind was to seek help elsewhere. With the campaign still remaining on a knife edge, Operations 'Jaguar' and 'Leopard' had demonstrated that the twin tactics of strong-points on the *jebal* and fortified lines dividing up the province and interdicting supply lines could bring about positive results. The only problem was that these winning tactics needed a combination of mobility (chiefly helicopters) to supply the strong-points and men to man the lines dividing up the *jebal*. The Omanis could not find or pay for sufficient personnel to man the lines or afford the helicopters, pilots and ground crew to maintain the strong-points. What were needed were either the troops to fulfil these tasks or better still, a large injection of cash to tip the balance in favour of the SAF. Oman was in this case fortunate. When Britain could not assist sufficiently, it could turn to its neighbours, oil rich states like Saudi Arabia, Iran and Abu Dhabi.

As illustrated in chapter four, both the Jordanians and the Iranians had, with little prompting, made offers of assistance to the Sultan. The Omanis still however, needed British help in dealing with this aid. The Omani Defence Department's first port of call was the British Embassy to ask for information to help draw up rates of pay for the proposed Jordanian Seconded officers. Hawley had to telegram the British Embassy in Amman for further help, receiving from Phillips the British Defence Attaché in the capital a detailed breakdown of the rates of pay and conditions current in the Jordanian Army.[103] It seems rather strange that the Omanis could not have procured this information from the Jordanians themselves and is a clear demonstration of the burden placed upon Britain in co-ordinating the assistance. Later the Jordanians were to ask for British logistic support to transport some of their aid to Oman.[104] King Hussein also offered the Sultan twelve 25 pounder artillery pieces, the gift though presented some problems since there was a shortage of ammunition for the guns and the MoD was extremely reluctant to 'run down British army stocks to an unacceptable level'. The offer of artillery was made in December 1971 but it was calculated that MoD sales would not have any shells to spare for sale until the following December.[105] The MoD therefore suggested that the offer of the guns should be turned down for now but the Arabian Department and the Middle/Near East Department (responsible for Jordan) felt that the gift was most welcome, since from the Arabian Department angle 'Jordanian involvement is preferable to any other Arab involvement, while from our angle [M/NED] we should applaud anything which induces the Sultan to give financial aid to Jordan'.[106]

The 25 pounders, while not the most useful gift, represented something far more important. Jordanian assistance was certainly to be encouraged and Anthony Acland wondered if with the Palestinian uprising of 1970 crushed and Jordan unlikely to 'try conclusions with Israel', Britain should consider 'actively encouraging the Sultan to ask for the maximum military aid from Jordan i.e. personnel, training et al. We could similarly encourage King Hussein. This may be gilding the lily but Jordanian involvement would keep [illegible] off the hook', after all 'the Jordanian forces can't have all that much to do'.[107] Jordanian involvement would indeed be a blessing as it would relieve some of the pressure on Britain to do more and would add a valuable Arab element which would make Britain's lone position in Oman less striking.

The Jordanian solution would not be seen as the most desirable option for long however. While those in the Near East Department wished to maximise the Jordanian military aid with the quid pro quo of financial aid for a stretched and resource poor Jordan, the Arabian Department's Robert McGregor quickly realised that 'Oman cannot afford to give financial aid to Jordan', Acland too realised the problem and the further implications if Oman was to give aid 'they [the Omanis] would only ask us for increased military help at a cut rate – or their resources would be further overstretched and they might have greater difficulty in gaining control over Dhofar. This would certainly not be in British interests'.[108] The Jordanian 'solution' only therefore led policymakers back to the original problem and it was decided that the Omani-Jordanian relationship should evolve naturally rather than being pushed. King Hussein though continued to be very helpful and undertook to sound out King Feisal and the Shah about their possible aid to Oman he also stated that he was 'willing, within his means, to do what he could to give support where there were British withdrawals [in the Gulf]' but would appreciate 'advice or comment' from Britain as to what help would be most useful.[109] By 9 March a Jordanian mission was in Muscat to look at the ways Amman could help. Hawley reported that Oldman and CSAF welcomed Jordanian involvement and would 'undoubtedly work out viable plans which will not cut across anything we are doing ourselves'.[110] The MoD were slightly less happy about the Jordanian involvement and stated that once Oldman, Graham, Welch (the Defence Attaché in Muscat) and Hawley had worked out what the Jordanian involvement would be, 'we envisage that the MoD would examine the recommendations so as to ensure that they were compatible with our own policy requirement'. Indeed, 'it would make good sense for Muscat to communicate with Amman via London'.[111]

The package worked out was mostly technical. According to Hawley the Jordanians 'will not be offered any command or combat posts nor do they want to accept any... the aim is to Omanise and not Jordanise SAF at the expense of the British personnel now serving'.[112] Jordan quickly began to provide intelligence officers, translators, low level staff officers, technical training, and infantry instruction *in situ* as well as further courses in Jordan. By May the Sultan was also asking for a squadron of engineers from Amman. The MoD continued to be wary, suggesting that the proposals should only be agreed to if the instruction was of sufficiently high standard, that Staff and Command training should continue to be carried out in the UK, 'so that they remain UK orientated' and that technical instruction should be based on British weapons 'so that SAF continues to rely on British sales'.[113] This was a rather more cynical approach than that of the FCO. Indeed the Arabian Department believed 'that the modalities of co-operation are essentially for the Jordanians to arrange direct with the Sultanate'. The

MoD attitude was slightly irritating especially when the only assistance forthcoming was Jordanian; the proposed Saudi military mission had again been postponed,[114] although there were rumours that the Saudis might use Jordan as a conduit for aid.[115] With the Jordanians only really able to give some added value and the Saudis running, as ever, hot and cold over aid, Oman still needed men and money and the Shah's Iran could potentially offer both.

The Shah was increasingly concerned about the course of regional events and was beginning to regret somewhat his previous desire for the British to leave the Gulf. As a fellow dynastic state, Iran was keen to co-operate with Oman. Iran had also aided the Royalist[116] fighters in North Yemen for much of the 1960s, providing large quantities of arms and ammunition as well as training.[117] The prospects of Iranian assistance therefore looked much more promising. In late April 1972 Hawley travelled to Tehran and accompanied by the British Ambassador Peter Ramsbotham had a private audience with the Shah who explained his concerns about the USSR and its new Treaty of Friendship with Iraq. He greatly feared this relationship and any Soviet penetration into the Gulf. He was also keen to stress that he wished Britain to maintain a strong presence east of the Strait of Hormuz and for strong intelligence co-operation to be established. On Oman the Shah said that 'Iran was vitally interested in the survival of the Sultan and his regime', and that he intended to suggest to the Saudis that they should take a sympathetic line with Oman. Hawley was quick to inform the Shah that the Saudis were sending civil and military delegations to see what help Oman required. He also gave him a general briefing on the situation.[118] This meeting is seemingly anomalous in light of the FCO's desire to keep Britain's role as low key as possible but when dealing with the Shah and other pro-Western leaders who saw Britain's 'good offices' as a useful way of communicating, the FCO had little choice but to oblige. They too could see the use in this method as a means of overcoming communication problems and moving the process along.

Iranian assistance appeared to be highly desirable, indeed Douglas-Home for one had minuted one telegram concerning Jordanian assistance in May 1972, 'Could the Iranian Government help as well?' In practice this idea was potentially as difficult as the idea of large scale Jordanian help but for rather different reasons. On the day of the British withdrawal from the Gulf at the end of 1971, the Iranians had seized the disputed islands of Abu Musa and the Tumbs, which had aroused widespread Arab anger, leading to Libya breaking diplomatic relations with Britain as she had done nothing to prevent the seizure. When examining the idea of Iranian aid in January 1972 it had been concluded that the presence of Iranian forces in Arabia would be a propaganda gift to the likes of Iraq. Additionally 'the heavy handedness with which the Iranians sometimes operate' could cause further difficulties. It was therefore decided that any Iranian aid should be technical and financial. In May, Patrick Wright the new head of the Arabian Department (now renamed the Middle East Department) suggested that the Sultan should be encouraged to take up the Shah's invitation to visit Iran and that the possibility of an Iranian/Jordanian deal whereby the Shah would assist Jordan in providing troops should be explored.[119] This would have been a neat solution to both problems. Alas it was not to be.

In early summer Qaboos visited Amman amidst rumours of his engagement to a Jordanian princess. King Hussein offered him the loan of strike aircraft, Hercules transport planes and renewed his offer of a Special Forces Battalion for Dhofar.[120] The Sultan though remained wary of other nation's combat troops at this stage for fear of making the situation appear too desperate. It was becoming increasingly clear that the Americans were encouraging the Jordanians to be helpful and that Amman was clearing its proposals with Washington. Ramsbotham in Tehran was annoyed by the prospect of the Iranians discovering that the Americans were pushing the Jordanians as it may give out a signal of lack of trust in Britain, 'seen from here this is another manifestation of the American itch to do something in the Gulf, which has been neither co-ordinated nor thought through'.[121] The whole situation was becoming increasingly complicated with Britain trying to manage the Jordanians, Iranians, Omanis, the UAE and now the Americans.

The Saudis meanwhile were being as inscrutable as ever, while at the same time maintaining that the best place for co-ordination was in Muscat. Hawley while agreeing with the principle of organisation through Muscat was requesting that at least some sort of co-ordination between Britain, the U.S. and Jordan should be worked out quickly and that this should probably happen in Amman for practical reasons. Ramsbotham too stressed the importance of this and echoed Hawley's views a few days later.[122] The Americans were also thinking along similar lines and were strongly in favour of the establishment of a co-ordinating committee in Amman. The suggestion horrified many as it smacked of Western control, while there were also practical disadvantages. The Omanis still did not have an Embassy there and there was also the sheer volume of material the British Ambassador would have to read to fulfil this role. Much better was the prospect of informal contacts and co-ordination from Muscat.[123] This was especially so as the only person who could really represent Oman was Oldman who could not be expected to keep commuting to Amman. The FCO therefore had to attempt to persuade the Americans that the idea was unworkable. Thankfully King Hussein did not like the idea either, stating 'we do not wish to appear as Western stooges'.[124] The formal mechanism which Washington imagined would also draw in the Iranians and Saudis, was clearly a terrible idea and would be unlikely to get the Saudis involved,[125] since it would be 'totally out of character' they were instead reportedly '"co-operating" in their usual independent manner'.[126]

While the wranglings over the issue of co-ordination were continuing, the recently appointed Jordanian go-between Lt General Khammash (Rtd) was rapidly becoming the *de facto* method of co-ordination. He made the trip to Muscat and had extensive tours of Dhofar and long discussions with Oldman. He also had a stopover in Tehran, where he briefed the Shah on the situation in Dhofar and presented 'a shopping list' of equipment, including the much needed helicopters, which the SAF required as soon as possible. The Shah undertook to have the list studied.[127] This was from the British perspective a much more low key and sensible way of getting things done. Although this was by no means the only form of communication. In July 1972 the Shah visited London and held talks with Douglas-Home, Carrington and Heath who reassured him about Britain's continuing commitment to Muscat and stressed the need for discreet co-ordination between the nascent allies.[128] By mid July the U.S. had accepted British reasoning and dropped their hasty idea of a co-ordination committee and Anglo-American policy which throughout had essentially only differed in terms of detail returned to normal.

The Shah was good at his word and by late July had worked out what Tehran could offer (two or three C-130 plane loads of equipment). The Iranian Ambassador in Muscat, Zand, subsequently presented the Sultan with an inventory of what the planes would contain. The Sultan was most gratified and requested that delivery be as speedy as possible. Lack of co-ordination in Muscat however, meant that the Ministry of Foreign Affairs (MFA) knew nothing of this when approached by Zand, in fact the MFA asked the Iranian Ambassador if an explanatory letter could be attached to the supplies. The Iranians then decided to send a plane to Salalah to sort out the practical aspects; they found no Omani ministers conversant with the arrangements. Oldman was back in the UK for briefings and the Iranians were told to call back in a couple of weeks.

The Iranians remained keen to help but were rather bemused considering the earlier urgency urged upon them. The Iranian Foreign Minister consequently approached Ramsbotham, the British Ambassador, during a function in Tehran both to get some information and in the hope that Britain would 'sort out [this] little problem for them'.[129] Britain was therefore forced to step in and sort out the mess. This lack of co-ordination could have been Muscat's undoing, the Iranians could have taken offence and the offer could have been withdrawn. Thankfully though, while reluctant to be too involved the FCO provided Muscat with its usual safety-net. It later transpired that SAF were expecting the Iranian delivery at *Bait al Falaj* and not Salalah. The Iranians for their part wished to deliver to Salalah to keep their involvement low key. To compound the problem, when the inventory was eventually properly examined it was realised that much of what was on offer was not needed nor was some of it compatible with existing equipment. Yet while there was a real need to avoid complicating SAF's supply chain, it was also important to avoid giving offence to the Iranians. This was a further headache for officials. The good news though was that the Iranians were working very swiftly, further supplies were due to begin arriving on 15 August. Better still was the news that the Iranians were offering six vital helicopters and their crews.[130] Thankfully there were no further complications, with all the practical arrangements conducted by the Defence Attaché in Muscat with SAF and FCO Defence Department assistance.

In a meeting with Oldman, Anthony Parsons raised the Shah's recent suggestion of a 150-strong contingent of Iranian Special Forces being sent to Dhofar. Oldman said both he and the Sultan were reluctant to accept this and would prefer sappers instead but both were very pleased with (some) of the helicopters.[131] Parsons stressed the need for the Saudis to be kept informed and that after HMG had worked so hard appealing for aid from friendly countries, Britain could not now have second thoughts and try to discourage the Iranians from sending troops. It would be down to the Omanis to handle the matter. Oldman for his part stated that he thought the Saudis were more important and brought news of their potential offer: £24 million in military aid, £2.9 million of recurrent aid, £12 million for development plus £1 million recurrent and the potential of additional development funding for Musandam. This was an impressive offer indeed and all hoped it would be realised.[132] Oldman stressed that while there had now been offers from Jordan, Iran, Qatar, Saudi Arabia and Abu Dhabi[133] very little had so far come of it and that money was the thing most urgently required. He requested that HMG look at what they could do to help in this regard.[134]

When Hawley saw the Sultan on 9 October, he was informed that despite the previous decision to turn down Jordan's offer of Special Forces, the Sultan had decided to accept the Iranian offer. Hawley gently broached the potential bad press but the Sultan said the news was already out about the helicopters so there was little to lose. He also informed Hawley of the Saudi decision to supply aid and put the delay down to 'people below

King Faisal wanting to control any purchases made of the Sultanate instead of making a specific sum available for the Sultanate itself to spend'.[135] Clearly some Saudi officials saw the potential for kickbacks if they could organise procurement.

The MoD meanwhile was concerned about the Iranian Special Forces, as were the Defence Attachés in Muscat and Tehran. The latter reported that although they had spent six weeks training with British Special Forces in 1970, the SAS reported their standard as being 'pathetically low...they were not physically fit, their map reading was unbelievably bad...and their officers were weak, dull mentally and physically soft'. The Defence Attaché in Tehran stated: 'I shudder to think what will happen to material like this should the Dhofaris get their hands on them...I suggest CSAF give them a very limited role'.[136] The Special Forces were due to disembark on 1 December but ten days later they had still not arrived. CSAF meanwhile had allocated them a role far away from the SAS in the east of Dhofar.

By the end of 1972 assistance was beginning to trickle in but was nowhere near enough to make any sort of impact on the war itself. Britain too had had to put in far more work than was desirable in order to secure much movement. Yet the groundwork laid during 1972 was to pave the way for much larger contributions from Jordan, Iran, Abu Dhabi and Saudi Arabia in the coming years. It was clear policy to encourage such assistance and there was plainly an ever present desire to minimise the British footprint in Oman. While Jordan had clearly been the first choice, financial problems put paid to this plan. With the Saudis being as unpredictable as ever and despite the political problems involved, Muscat and London had no choice but to pursue the Iranian option. While doing the utmost to assist where necessary, London was concerned to play its part from the sidelines, although this was clearly not always going to be possible. Further headaches for London were endeavouring to co-ordinate the aid and as far as possible attempting to assuage fears over potential British loss of influence in Oman (especially in the MoD). This was not the easiest task when many in the FCO shared the same concerns.

As help began to trickle into Oman and foreign interest grew, there began to be a slight but noticeable divergence of opinion within the Foreign Office. While everyone saw the benefits of material support from other nations, the light in which this was seen could differ. Patrick Wright, writing to Sir Stewart Crawford who had now become Deputy to the PUS and who would be representing the FCO at the CoS meeting for the December review, argued that the Saudi and Iranian willingness to give aid was 'probably the most important development since the last review' and that this aid 'makes it important that we should continue to help the Sultan'. This was because:

> The Iranians are so far providing all their military assistance free of charge. I think it is appropriate to get across that we will take every opportunity to impress on the Saudis and Iranians (and others as appropriate) the degree to which we <u>are</u> helping the Sultan.[137]

Wright also wrote in a minute to Parsons, then an Assistant Under Secretary of State, in October 1972 stating that:

> Oman is an independent country and we have continually urged her friends to help her... Foreign military intervention in Dhofar might make the campaign a less tidy business to run but it is in our interests, and the Sultan's that Oman should receive as much help as she can use from her friends.[138]

Wright and others clearly felt that while help was needed and appreciated it was Britain who was doing the most and that if at all possible she should do more. He also believed that Britain should maintain its influence in Oman over other western states in particular, a view which was shared by many, especially those who had served in the Gulf. Anthony Parsons now occupying a more senior position shared these views stating 'we could ill afford to let the French or the American's steal a march on us'.[139]

Others more senior in the FCO and with no record in the Gulf took a rather different view. In reply to Parson's comments, C.M. Le Quesne, a Deputy under Secretary of State wrote:

> It would be very agreeable indeed if we were in a position single-handed to protect our interests in the Gulf and in Southern Arabia... It is clear however... that it is beyond our means, in manpower or in money, to give the Sultan all that he is likely to need or want; indeed his existing requirements already come close to the limit of what is possible, let alone politically desirable for us. In such circumstances I think there is danger in an attempt to maintain for ourselves a <u>chasse gardée</u>. If the Sultan can be ridden off his grandiose ideas [a proposed air defence scheme] so much the better. If, as looks at any rate possible he cannot, I think that we should look seriously at the possibility of ourselves proposing a division of the responsibility and the gravy. I think it was Lord Palmerston who remarked that if a man cannot afford to keep a stable of his own the only sensible course for him is to

sell his horses and go to a livery stable. It seems to me that this is the sort of situation which we are approaching in our defence relationship with the Sultan.[140]

This divergence between those who had served in the Gulf and who wanted Britain to maintain its influence in Oman for as long as possible and those who had served elsewhere and wanted Britain to get other western states involved is marked. One wonders what the point was, if as Le Quesne states, that it was beyond Britain's means to offer more military aid, in Britain being the third highest spender on defence in the world at that time if she lacked the resources to help an important ally, who had so far paid for most of the British help she had received and where British manpower in the country numbered less than 800 men. Rather than turning to western allies then, it is clear why the Saudis, Jordanians and Iranians were seen as ideal replacements. Officials remained wary of too many economic competitors, western economic rivalry, despite the cold war backdrop, remained a factor in the official mind. There was no desire to see French, German, American and Italian firms making too many advances into the Omani market.

Obviously both Jordan and Iran saw benefits in being generous towards Oman. The Shah was motivated in part by both a desire to demonstrate his power but also perhaps to gain some useful counterinsurgency skills for his troops. In addition to this, the offer of aid would also give the Shah a foothold in the Arabian Peninsula and a means of extending influence at the expense of the Saudis. There is no doubt however, that this new aid was facilitated by Oman's successful campaign to join the international community. Britain of course welcomed this help as it gave both more resources which London had trouble providing and also made the war seem less like simply a British endeavour. This aid took a while to arrive and much work to co-ordinate and integrate into the Dhofar campaign but it also sparked other countries into condoning similar benevolence. By the end of 1973 there were contributions both economic and military from Saudi Arabia (£13.2 million in development aid and £20 million in military aid), UAE (£12.3 million in development aid and £2.5 million in military aid), India (secondment of personnel, some development aid and artillery and small arms), Pakistan (naval personnel, medical services and small arms) and Qatar (£625,000 for education and Saladin armoured cars).[141]

The Iranians were praised in a British Chief of Staff report of 1973 with the words, 'a feature of Iranian support for Oman has been the immediate response to requests for aid and the impression that no request, whether for troops or aircraft, would be considered too much'.[142] Iran was to provide during the course of 1973: 150 Special Forces, a helicopter squadron, a battalion with mortars and engineers in addition to joint naval patrols of the Strait of Hormuz and eighteen Hercules supply sorties in July and August alone.[143] The Jordanians too provided what was described as 'considerable military aid, mainly in training assistance, and has also offered to deploy an engineer company to Dhofar'.[144]

While it was undoubtedly the British assistance which turned the tide in the early post-coup period, the role of in particular Jordan and Iran was to prove to be of great significance in the later period of the conflict. Ian Gardiner a seconded officer who fought in Dhofar assesses the Iranian contribution thus: 'Overall, there can be no doubt that the weight they lent to the wheel helped to shorten the war, and the political benefit for the Sultan was incalculable. However, the salient military contribution the Iranians made was the provision of helicopters.'[145] This assessment is endorsed by J.E. Peterson who states that:

> Iranian assistance is noteworthy for the size of its contribution in terms of personnel, plentifulness of supplies and generosity in sharing resources... Iranian forces played a major part in the Western offensives during 1975... at the same time however, Iranian standards of operation were poor... units frequently opened fire indiscriminately at night, even on adjacent Iranian positions.[146]

Gardiner agreed, noting, '[F]or us on the ground, trying to avoid being shot by the *adoo and* the Iranians was one risk more than we would have preferred'.[147]

Increasing U.S. Interest

While attempting to secure assistance for Oman, Britain was by 1972 also beginning to have to deal with Washington. The U.S. had, rather unsurprisingly, in light of their predicament in Vietnam, not taken any real interest in Oman. In 1972 the U.S. appointed its first Ambassador to Oman, William H. Stolzfus Jr.,[148] who told Hawley 'that the US was happy to leave the main political running in the area to Britain as long as we had the will to be actively involved'. Significantly he also told Hawley that 'Commercially... we are rivals'.[149] This situation was to gradually alter. The summer of 1973 saw the beginnings of real change on that score when the U.S. Chargé d'Affaires in Muscat quietly informed the FCO that there had been an increase in American interest in Oman and that 'the low profile policy which had been pursued was being discarded'.[150] Indeed it was even suggested that the U.S. might be willing to help the Omanis, especially with military training. The Foreign Office while welcoming the move told the Americans that it was 'vitally important' to secure proper co-ordination if they were to enter into military assistance with Oman.[151] Washington was told that their support was welcomed, as was their recognition that assistance should be co-ordinated. The Secretary of State for Defence on his visit to Washington was asked to inform the U.S. that the best way it could help would be to 'use their influence to persuade Saudi Arabia to increase their assistance' but that to avoid 'unnecessary duplication of equipment... for the time being it may be premature to send a military mission for direct discussions with the Omanis'.[152]

In consultations with the Americans it became clear that a U.S. military assessment mission might actually give Washington more ammunition to use with the Saudis to persuade them to do more and could also persuade them that 'the British were exerting themselves to the maximum extent possible'.[153] Despite this, there were continuing British concerns, when the State Department made a formal request to the Sultanate for a 10-day visit to be made by a Colonel Maloney. It was quickly realised that the best had to be made of the situation and it was arranged that Maloney would first visit London for extensive briefings. The U.S. Embassy in London told King Charles Street that considerable importance was attached to close co-operation with London and that the visit would be no more than a fact finding trip to lay the ground for possible decisions on assistance. It was also emphasised that Washington had 'no interest in replacing the British role in Oman. Anything which they were to do would be complimentary [to the British role]'.[154] Colonel Maloney's report was very complimentary about the British role in Oman, although somewhat critical of some contract officers. The LSP were considered to be doing a 'superb job'; he did however, suggest that the war could be pursued more aggressively.[155] If officials were worried about loss of influence in Muscat, it was somewhat premature as Hawley was able to secure a copy of the minutes of the private discussion between Maloney and Qaboos. Informing Richard Lloyd-Jones of the outcome of the U.S. visit and enclosing a copy of the minutes, Patrick Wright said: 'naturally we should not let Colonel Maloney know that we have seen it'.[156] Indeed the Sultan told Hawley that he considered Maloney 'in some respects unrealistic' and had informed him that 'SOAF helicopters could not be expended at the same rate as in Vietnam'.[157]

There had been earlier American interest in Oman during 1972, when the U.S. Air Force asked for four F111 aircraft to be able to refuel at Masirah as part of a training flight. There was some unease in the FCO about this but it was agreed on condition that there should be no publicity and as 'a once only visit'. The Sultan agreed to the visit, also on condition of confidentiality. The MoD stated that 'we have recently had information which suggests that the American proposal does not imply any new policies vis-à-vis the Gulf'. In meeting the request 'we shall of course, be helping to maintain the close relationship which exists between RAF and USAF in matters of this kind'.[158] U.S. interest in Oman in this regard was clearly on the rise. In the summer of 1973, with the U.S. conducting carrier operations in the Indian Ocean, there was a strong prospect of a formal request for use of Masirah, for P3 aircraft refuelling and reconnaissance. Douglas-Home expressed his concerns in a telegram to the Washington Embassy, stating that:

> We would not welcome a formal request by the Americans for use of Masirah, the Sultan's reaction is likely to be unfavourable (cf. Oman's participation in the Arab suspension of oil supplies to the United States): nor would we want the RAF facilities at Masirah, which are the only Western facilities of their kind in Arab countries, put at risk.[159]

By 12 November, the Americans had informed London that they would not now be asking for temporary landing rights at Masirah. But the whole episode indicated the increasing U.S. interest in the area.[160] London, though while acceding to the American request in 1972 was far more reluctant to agree in 1973. In the aftermath of the October Arab-Israeli War, a stronger anti-American atmosphere in the Middle East quickly developed and London was therefore fearful of damaging British interests in the Middle East generally and especially disinclined to draw attention to Oman.

With increasing contacts with the Americans, Iranians and Jordanians, the management of Britain's relations with Oman was becoming ever more complex and frequent reviews still had to be held. After the success of the November Review of 1972 however, the summer review of 1973 was designed purely as a military review of the situation and consideration of Sultanate requests for a further 29 LSP. The Chiefs of the Defence Staff (CDS) decided that the current level of support should be maintained and were pleased to note that the campaign in Dhofar was now going much better for SAF:

> Overall the picture is one of continuing improvement. The strength of the hard-core insurgents remains at about 600–700 but in Eastern Dhofar the rebels have lost the initiative...In the West Simba's defences have been strengthened and CSAF intends to hold it throughout the monsoon. A blocking line known as Hornbeam about

60kms further east and manned jointly by SAF and Iranian Special Forces has also succeeded in further limiting rebel supply convoys.[161]

The meeting also recommended that the Secretary of State for Defence, Lord Carrington, approve the additional 29 LSP for the Sultanate. Hawley's review of CSAF's comments for the CDS meeting and general appreciation of the situation was encouraging news, especially when he stated that, 'The Sultan remains generally popular in the country and in the north as well as in Dhofar there is a considerable amount to show for his policy of development and progress.'[162]

The 1973 November Review

These series of reviews were common practice in the Foreign Office. An air of cold rationalism existed at higher levels which meant that 'British policy-makers were constantly reviewing the costs and benefits of Britain's deployment in the Gulf, especially following the 1956 Suez war'.[163] It is difficult to see why Oman should be an exception to this trend. While the review of July was a purely military look at the tactics and prospects for the campaign in Dhofar, the November review was to be a full ministerial affair, preceded by a CoS review, and as such, much work went into the preparations. The review was designed to examine the whole of current policy towards the Sultanate. The FCO had by the end of September prepared a draft submission to the CoS and had sent it to the MoD for suggestions. Richard Lloyd-Jones the head of DS-11 at the MoD replied on 5 October informing David Tatham of the Middle East Department that while the Chiefs of Staff could argue for a policy of disengagement from Oman or of getting out of Salalah. Thankfully though, 'no-one is advancing military reasons of this kind; and I am therefore the more anxious that the Chiefs of Staff should not be given draft conclusions which do not entirely square with the political factors as we find them today'. He suggested that the previous year's guidelines for the review should not be used to frame recommendations and that there should be a fresh start. Omission is a useful tool for convincing Ministers of the necessity of a course of action, or from overcomplicating a situation. Lloyd-Jones stated that 'we agreed that all specific references to a certain non-attributable operation should be omitted from this paper'.[164] What this operation was is unclear but it was evidently best not to unnecessarily worry Ministers.

The draft paper began, as usual with a restatement of the three key British political and economic interests in the area: 'a) the promotion of stability and peace b) the preservation of British and the limitation of communist and other hostile influence c) the maintenance and expansion of UK trade and economic interests, including the uninterrupted flow of oil on reasonable terms'.[165] Lloyd-Jones' redrafts included references to the use of oil as a weapon and the fact that Oman's neighbours 'rightly or wrongly regard it as Britain's duty to support the Sultan'. He also stated that 'The U.S. Government have made it clear their wish that HMG should continue with their policy of assistance to Oman'. Lloyd-Jones further stressed the importance of Masirah as a 'major UK defence interest' in Oman, stating its purposes as being 'a) a staging post on the route to the Far East b) a forward deployment and dispersal base for UK CENTO declared forces c) a base for surveillance d) a site for a BBC wireless station and an RAF radio station'. The MoD conclusion was that, 'There is no slack in SAF's capacity; and we agree with CSAF's deduction that, in the light of the resources likely to be available to him, the correct assumption is that the rebels must be overcome by a process of attrition: and that the campaign must continue for another two years at least.'[166]

The FCO were generally very pleased with the MoD redrafts. It was even more promising when the CoS asked both CSAF and HM Ambassador Muscat to attend the meeting on 27 November. The review went well and British assistance to the Sultanate was to continue for another year. The report for the November Review of 1973 still supported British assistance to Oman, and was optimistic at the prospects for a successful resolution to the conflict. Its overall tone however, was much more cautious, pensive even and took a longer term view than in previous years, using phrases such as 'it should be our aim to reduce the extent of our commitment'.[167] The report saw that increasing assistance from Oman's neighbours was reducing Britain's influence, 'as the Sultan becomes more at home on the international stage, he is turning to new friends for advice and assistance'. The report took on something of the tone of a parent realising that their child is growing up rapidly and that their presence is not as essential as it once was:

> Foreign advice has induced him [the Sultan] to pursue the idea of an air defence scheme [and] press for attacks on PDRY... it might therefore be considered appropriate to increase the level of our support to the Sultan merely to ensure that our influence is not diluted, but we take the view that such an increase in support would not be justified; if our relations are carefully handled.[168]

When the Sultan visited London in September 1973 he asked that RAF planes be allowed to carry out air-strikes in support of specific operations on the *jebal*. After much consideration Sir Alec Douglas-Home replied to the

Sultan on 18 December 1973 with an answer: sorry but no, military objections and the possibility of the employment of RAF aircraft being used for propaganda purposes by the rebels and a public controversy which would damage both British and Omani interests were cited as the reasons for the rejection.[169]

Conclusion

This chapter set out to explore the evolution of British policy during the final two years of the Heath government's period in office. As observed, British policy from 1972–74 essentially consisted of three pillars: to prevent escalation of the fighting (thus minimising British exposure) especially during the potential escalation at Habarut, attempting to get British financial assistance to help with the Sultan's problematic finances and, as this proved difficult, trying to secure the assistance of neighbouring nations. The extent of British material involvement was clearly relatively large and continued to grow but was becoming increasingly constrained by the limits of what was politically and financially acceptable. The Habarut incident meanwhile demonstrated that the extent of British political involvement in Oman was limited both in terms of the influence that could be wielded and the extent to which Hawley was willing to use that influence. Hawley's role in this incident also demonstrates the continuing importance of the man on the spot in adjusting policy to suit the climate.

Britain's attempts to attract both economic and military aid to Oman can be seen as a reaction to the limits of Britain's own willingness and ability to assist Oman directly during this period. Britain increasingly saw the role that other regional actors could play as essential. Jordan and Iran on the other hand, as the incident with the delivery of supplies indicated, viewed the British role in Oman as absolutely necessary and saw the British as 'honest brokers'.

With Oman's growing stature and the increasing influence of external actors in close relations with Washington, an increasing interest on the part of the U.S. in the Sultanate became inevitable. As Maloney's report indicated though, the U.S. believed that Britain was doing a good job in Oman. Washington clearly stated that it had no interest in usurping Britain's role. London's perceptions of the U.S.' role were more mixed however, while wishing to secure the maximum assistance, London remained wary of the American's request for landing rights, not wishing to be seen to be introducing the U.S. into the Sultanate.

None of these policies of preventing escalation, giving financial aid and guidance and securing external assistance were easy to implement but with

Britain facing increasing economic difficulties of her own and with political caution noticeable, these policies represented the only way that Britain could ensure that the war in Dhofar was won, while maintaining her influence. In the light of changing economic and political times policy was bound to evolve differently under a Labour government who were keener on cuts in defence expenditure and less enthusiastic about foreign adventurism than the Conservatives.

CHAPTER 7

CONTINUITY AND CHANGE: THE LABOUR GOVERNMENT AND DEFENCE REVIEWS

> The first, the supreme, the most far-reaching act of judgement that the statesman and the commander have to make is to establish... the kind of war on which they are embarking and why
>
> Von Clausewitz

Introduction

The arrival of a Labour government in spring 1974 came when the situation in Oman was improving markedly. The deadlock of 1971-72 had been broken and although there was a long way still to go, the outlook was positive. The arrival of this new government though, created some apprehension among officials. The Labour party had, after all, been the government which had announced Britain's withdrawal 'East of Suez' and was ideologically much less inclined to support overseas adventurism than the Conservatives, who had consistently viewed Oman's requests in a favourable light. However, the situation was now more opaque. The new Prime Minister, Harold Wilson, had, when elected previously in October 1964, stated in the House of Commons that: 'I want to make it quite clear that whatever we may do in the field of cost effectiveness... we cannot afford to relinquish our world role – our role which for shorthand purposes, is sometimes called our "East of Suez role"'.[1] While in 1967–68 he had had to make a choice between, on the one hand defence expenditure and Britain's world role, and on the other, the stability of a fragile British economy resulting in major defence cuts and withdrawal 'East of Suez', he was clearly a man who wanted Britain to exercise global influence.

Yet being a Labour leader meant the priority was the economic imperative, and more than that, investment in public services within Britain. This was clearly crucial for Labour. During the earlier Labour government from 1964-70, while defence expenditure fell by five per cent, social expenditure rose by 25 per cent. As Saki Dockrell states, 'the defence ceiling was a self imposed one... it was not one that was imposed on the government by Britain's financial predicament'.[2] The period of the second Wilson government is an important one for Oman and for British policy towards the Sultanate. The impact of the Labour government upon policy towards Oman however, continued to be underpinned by perceptions of national interest.

An important effect of Labour policy was the debate on the future of both RAF Salalah and Masirah, which led to increasing tensions between the Foreign Office and the Ministry of Defence.[3] This in turn, was linked to the fact that the impact of increased American involvement in the Gulf was also beginning to be felt during this period. Despite these changes though, one of the most important policymaking debates during the final years of the war and beyond was the dilemma for officials of fulfilling Britain's need to increase her commercial interests in Oman, while not appearing to be overexploiting the Sultan's dependence on Britain. All of this was playing out in the context of the need to justify Britain's continuing assistance to Oman.

The 'Salalah Hook'

Since the chapter is in large part concerned with the future of the RAF bases at Salalah and Masirah and the impact of the new government it is important in the first instance to examine how the Heath government viewed the future of the British bases. While Masirah was key to the 'eastabout' route and was seen as vital for Britain's commitment to the Five Power Defence Agreement in South East Asia, Salalah was seen differently even during the Conservative years.

In the aftermath of the air-strikes on Hauf in May 1972 there were increased fears that RAF Salalah could become a target for PDRY strikes as a form of political retaliation. Plans for the defence of the base were revised[4] and PDRY airfields were repeatedly reconnoitred for the rest of the campaign, especially when the prospect of the PDRY obtaining Russian MiG 21s arose. When the initial panic calmed, Hawley assessed that an attack was actually rather unlikely. The Sultan on the other hand had been convinced of the need for a comprehensive Air Defence Scheme (ADS) for his country.

In a meeting with Lord Carrington the Secretary of State for Defence on 12 April 1973, the issue of an ADS was raised, with Carrington warning that any scheme 'would prove complex and consequently very expensive' and that 'taken as a whole it would be "the hell of an undertaking"'. Qaboos agreed with Carrington, stressing that 'it would not be enough for the capital cost paid; there would also be the operating costs'.[5] Carrington agreed however to arrange for an evaluation of the project and for a team of MoD experts to visit and write a report.

By July 1973 the team had completed this task which estimated that the capital costs of the scheme would be £60 million with £11 million annual running costs and that 'these figures could be conservative'. They recommended that the scheme should be implemented in phases and that it would require 'the provision of some hundreds of highly skilled men'. None of this was what anyone wanted to hear with money so tight and difficulties in providing LSP, even though Abu Dhabi was proposing to bear most of the costs. On the other hand, the CoS worried about the 'risks involved if another country, possibly France' should be asked to provide a system in the face of British reluctance.[6] Even CSAF was reluctant about the ADS stating in an MoD meeting that it was, 'essentially a status symbol and that the Sultan was being pushed into it by other Arab nations'.[7]

Under the 1958 Agreement concerning the RAF bases at Masirah and Salalah, Britain was obliged to pay a peppercorn rent of £15,000 for the use of Masirah and to provide defence and civil aviation facilities at Salalah. The arrangements at Salalah should continue to be provided as long as Britain leased part of Masirah, in effect tying the RAF to Salalah.[8] In 1972 the Chiefs of Staff had decided that it should be a long term aim to try and relinquish RAF Salalah, since it had no real value to Britain and was a constant target for rebel attacks. During the November 1972 Review it was suggested that the additional aid could be used as a way of renegotiating the Salalah commitment, or getting off the 'Salalah Hook' as it became known in official circles. Hawley recommended that at that stage he should merely raise with the Sultan the future possibility of transferring the administration of the airfield to a civilian firm. Patrick Wright worried that 'any attempt to get off the Salalah hook might lead to demands for a much higher rent for Masirah. In putting up a marker Mr Hawley would have to take extreme care to avoid arousing suspicions in the Sultan's mind that we were trying to default on our present commitment.'[9] Hawley considered that the RAF presence at Salalah 'itself provides a considerable deterrent to PDRY launching any air attack on Salalah'.[10] The CoS did not discuss the Salalah hook in the July 1973 review, but it did appear in the November review of that year, with the MoD recommending that 'for political reasons... the present arrangements continue as long as we need Masirah'.[11] One of the political reasons for not attempting to renegotiate the 1958 Agreement was the fact that when Lord Carrington met with the Sultan in September 1973 he told him that:

> We do not consider that the financial and manpower expense of such a system [of Air Defence] was justified by the PDRY air threat. This was unwelcome advice, and if it was immediately followed by an attempt to reduce our commitment to Salalah, the Sultan might well become more insistent on the need for an air defence scheme.[12]

In addition to this there was the fear that this would be 'mal vu by Iran and Saudi Arabia, and might well result in a reduction in their assistance', although the FCO conceded that 'it is a definite long-term objective that the administration of the airfield should be taken over by SOAF or by a contract company (preferably British)'.[13] This seemed especially important since it had become apparent to the FCO during the autumn of 1973 that 'the Americans, the Iranians and the Saudis all suspect that [SAF] are not taking a sufficiently aggressive line in the conduct of operations in Dhofar' and this viewpoint would fit nicely with another rumour doing the rounds of the Gulf, namely that Britain could end the war in Dhofar at any time but prefers to let it simmer on either because she wants to use it as a training ground or because she hopes to sell military equipment... and continue charging enormous sums for the use of her seconded personnel.[14]

Now was clearly not the time to broach the issue of getting off the hook. In talks held on 14 September 1973, Sir Alec Douglas-Home stressed his agreement with Carrington's views on air defence. The Sultan said that while he accepted this advice, he thought that Salalah should have some type of air defence such as radar. This would 'give the Omanis confidence... [and] might provide a deterrent to some extent to PDRY'.[15] On 17 November 1973 the Sultan again raised the issue of the ADS with Hawley, who reported that the Sultan 'still felt that it was imperative... his present thinking was that he would like our assistance over the provision of anti-aircraft guns and radar', but that the Sultan had stressed 'he was making no specific request at this time'.[16]

The Conservative government, through the DOPC, had authorised the MoD and FCO decision to aim to withdraw from RAF Salalah as a long term policy goal, although it was clear that the consensus was that this should not be attempted until the war was over. The issue of the air defence scheme is also interesting in that despite the clear economic interest, especially with Britain's struggling economy, in securing a very large defence contract both ministers and officials had serious doubts about the need for such an elaborate scheme and the detrimental effect this could have on Oman's finances.

Qaboos though was very keen on the ADS. After a talk with him in early May 1974, Hawley reported that, 'he was most grateful for our help and it was in recognition of and in gratitude for, this that he had decided to buy British aircraft and equipment rather than shopping elsewhere. A firm and conscious decision to buy British, and to continue to do so, had been taken.'[17] The Sultan went on to stress that he was particularly keen to have Rapier missiles to be followed up with a purchase of Jaguars. He also 'made a point of saying that he wished the RAF presence in Salalah to continue' even though civil development of the airfield would soon be starting. It seemed that despite official and ministerial efforts, there would be no dissuading the Sultan.

The Labour Defence Review

During 1973 the Conservative Government faced mounting problems at home, including the declaration of a State of Emergency due to the Energy Crisis as a result of the October (Yom Kippur) War and increasing industrial unrest, culminating in the imposition of the three day week at the end of the year and a miners strike early in 1974. The Prime Minister requested the dissolution of Parliament on 7 February and elections at the end of the month led to a hung parliament with Labour as the biggest party by four MPs. On 4 March after failed Conservative attempts to secure a coalition with the Liberals, Labour leader Harold Wilson became Prime Minister. Facing continued strikes, a huge deficit in trade and the problem of stagflation, the years ahead were to be very challenging indeed. This was in turn to impact on London's relations with Oman.[18]

The new Labour government quickly set about finding ways of saving money and on 21 March 1974 initiated a Defence Review; Britain had still, despite the previous Labour government's drastic cuts in defence expenditure, the third highest expenditure on defence in the world.[19] The government pledged to 'achieve savings of several hundred million pounds per annum while maintaining a modern and effective defence system'.[20] Clearly the announcement of this far reaching review and the likelihood of cuts in defence spending may well have had implications for policy towards Oman. Indeed many of the initial proposals strongly indicated a retrenchment from the Conservative position on 'East of Suez', a position which had been already heavily downgraded from Britain's role in the 1960s. Proposals included ceasing to commit forces to the South East Asian Treaty Organisation and to CENTO and at one point withdrawal from the Sovereign Base Areas of

Cyprus, although this was heavily opposed and was subsequently rejected following the Turkish invasion of late 1974.[21] The general trend was clear however: further cutbacks and withdrawals were the name of the day.

Officials were somewhat wary of the probable consequences of the Defence Review generally and in particular both its impact on and the likely commitment to Oman of the Labour government. They need not have been unduly worried, as until the DOPC meeting in September 1974 the only people in the Labour government to know the extent of British involvement were the Prime Minister, Harold Wilson, the Foreign Secretary Jim Callaghan and the Defence Secretary, Roy Mason and relevant ministers within the MoD and FCO.[22] The scheduled May 1974 review was made into a draft OPD paper in preparation for full DOPC examination but the FCO successfully made the argument that since it was a continuation of existing policy, there was no need or point in putting it to the full DOPC in advance of the outcome of the Defence Review.[23] This was clearly important as the Defence Review would take some time, thus effectively leaving British policy and assistance towards Oman unchanged for the rest of 1974. The new government was in fact to develop good relations with the Omani government; the Omani Minister of State for Foreign Affairs, Qais al Zawawi, visited London in May and met the Foreign Secretary and the Sultan met the Prime Minister later in the year. It is also interesting to note that during the first months of the Labour government the temporary loan for six months of four British helicopters and crew was authorised.[24]

There were some concessions to the mood of the times however. The early Overseas Policy and Defence (OPD(74)23) document which was agreed by Wilson, Mason and Callaghan, came to the conclusion that, 'We should continue to aim at ending our direct assistance to the Sultan's armed forces in the war against the rebels as soon as the military situation points at a way acceptable to the Iranians, Saudi Arabians and Americans. The loss of the airfield and facilities at Masirah would have to be accepted.'[25] This last phrase which was included in the final version of the OPD paper caused consternation in parts of the FCO with Michael Weir writing, 'I was horrified to read...I do not know what reasons were advanced for this conclusion but the result looks like a complete reversal of what we had previously understood the consensus in the Defence Review Working Party to be'. As Weir understood it, only the direct assistance to the Sultan's forces in the campaign against the rebels should be aimed to be reduced. In the new paragraph, 'the loss of Masirah would be [seen as] a corollary of our ceasing to provide assistance in the Dhofar campaign. As I see it this is a misapprehension'. Indeed Weir thought that the danger was that 'the abandonment of Masirah may come to be seen as a desirable objective rather than an unwelcome consequence'. Weir was also perplexed by the fact that despite the inclusion of political arguments in the paragraphs about other territories, 'such considerations are not even mentioned in this paper' in the section on Oman, especially since 'a defeat in Dhofar could undermine the stability of the Gulf from which Britain draws over two-thirds of its oil supplies'.[26] The understanding of the reliance upon oil was undoubtedly reinforced by the fact that the energy crisis had become so bad that there was only one electric light bulb allowed to illuminate the entire Middle East Department (some 20 people including archivists and secretaries). This situation was described as 'very depressing' by the Assistant Head of the Department, Terrence Clark.[27]

In the light of the earlier OPD paper, the MoD was keen to get more clarity on future policy towards Oman and began preparing a draft paper on Oman examining the current deployment of British forces there, the possible reactions to withdrawal and proposed broad guidelines for the reductions in British force levels. This paper would then be submitted to the CoS and subsequently Ministers. The MoD also suggested that a negotiating line to take with interested parties on the effects of the Defence Review on Oman would also have to be worked out by the FCO. A.J. Cragg, of the MoD's DS-11, in his covering letter to the first draft of the paper stated, 'I have drafted on the basis that Ministers would wish to consider proposals for reducing our commitment; but bearing in mind the Aden analogy, I have sought to avoid too firm or detailed a timetable'.[28]

The MoD draft paper for the September meeting of the DOPC laid out the background to Britain's involvement in Oman and was not shy in stressing the connection with 'our precipitate withdrawal from Aden' and using phrases such as, supporting the Sultanate 'in their attempts to contain Aden-based aggression'. The paper further emphasised the role of LSP and the fact that this cost Britain nothing and that direct British assistance 'costs us only some £[3] million a year'. The paper too highlighted the potential serious implications to British national interests from a rebel victory and was careful to state that 'a precipitate withdrawal of British assistance...could well prejudice the successful outcome which now appears to be in prospect'.[29] No longer were officials fighting to secure extra resources for Oman, it now appeared that they were directing all their attention to securing the continuation of British assistance. Annex B of the draft paper, containing options for the withdrawal of British forces, carefully made no mention of withdrawing the SAS or the FST, only giving the options of the Royal Engineers, RAF Salalah, the defences for Salalah and potentially Masirah. While the MoD views were broadly similar to those of the FCO some issues were increasingly problematic, not least the fact that the MoD did not make clear enough distinctions between aspects of British assistance.

While the first draft prepared by the MoD clearly focused on the need for continued British assistance and stressed this case, Patrick Wright while agreeing with the general thrust of the paper, provided six pages of amendments. Wright wished to separate out the three separate elements of the British military 'involvement' (his quotation marks) in Oman. Masirah he stressed with its associated facilities 'is not directly involved with our "assistance" to the Sultan'. Then there was the issue of direct assistance at Salalah and elsewhere and finally the supply of LSP for which the Sultan paid in full and were 'not therefore strictly subject to review under the heading of Defence Expenditure'.[30] Wright also stressed that it should be RAF withdrawal from Masirah mentioned (if at all) and not the withdrawal of intelligence facilities or the BBC relay station, as well as reserving the FCO's option to decide on a suitable date for any withdrawal for a future date.

The whole question of Masirah worried the FCO greatly. In the FCO Defence Review Steering Committee it was suggested that the last sentence of the OPD decision 'erroneously suggests that the ending of our military involvement in Oman would automatically entail our withdrawal from Masirah'. It was stressed that 'a total withdrawal from Masirah would not only require the negotiated termination of our 1958 Lease but would also mean the closing of valuable broadcasting facilities'. While it was conceded that the airfield would be unlikely to be used for the Eastabout route, with the coming withdrawal of declared British forces from CENTO, 'it will still be useful to have minimum staging facilities there'. On assistance more generally the group stated that while some direct assistance could be withdrawn in 1975 and more still in 1976 especially at Salalah, 'it is unlikely that the Sultan will be able to dispense with SAS help for several years'.[31]

These views were passed on to the MoD whose redraft while not taking into account all of the FCO suggestions, was enough to satisfy Wright. The FCO even conceded that 'the main RAF element at Masirah could and should be reduced discreetly as soon as the proposed reductions east of Suez allow'.[32] By mid September though, the MoD clearly favoured relinquishing their facilities at Masirah because soon they would no longer be required to support British forces in the Far East.[33] Although quite why the MoD were so convinced of the need to get out of Masirah is somewhat unclear, it seems likely that cost was the main driver. While Masirah only represented expenditure of £1.5–£2 million per annum, savings from the Indian Ocean were needed of around £8 million, of which retreat from Masirah would make a healthy contribution.[34]

FCO reluctance to terminate the Masirah agreement might appear to arise from the likely message that this would send to allies, especially those neighbouring states helping in Dhofar[35] or possible damage to the relationship with the Omanis. Other issues such as the future of the BBC relay station, the chance that the MoD might still need staging facilities in the future or the sheer diplomatic difficulty of negotiating an end to the agreement and the potential financial costs arising from compensation claims all look like convincing reasons to remain at Masirah. While all of these are plausible explanations for the FCO reluctance, there is another possible reason. All of the documents discussing this have sentences and whole paragraphs removed but it can be surmised that Masirah was home to some kind of intelligence assets. Since the FCO incorporates GCHQ, it would (and they) would likely have been reluctant to lose such a valuable asset.[36] Indeed these other 'facilities' depended upon the RAF base for supply on the barren island of Masirah, which in turn provided appropriate cover.

By October 1974 much consideration had been given to how best to consult with allies over the implications of the Defence Review. This was especially the case with regard to Oman. It was decided that the brief for the U.S. should be written 'on the basis that our aim would be withdrawal from Oman and Masirah as soon as conditions permitted; but that we could not announce this now since this could prejudice our chances of early withdrawal'.[37] Over time both DS-11 of the MoD and the FCO produced consultation briefs. The MoD draft assumed total withdrawal from Masirah. The FCO draft on the other hand stated, 'we do not intend to make any firm decisions about our future use of the staging facilities so long as the Dhofar campaign continues on its present course.' Indeed, aside from terminating the small advisory team based at Sharjah the FCO stated that 'apart from some small savings in numbers, our policy in the Gulf and Oman for the time being remains as it is at present'.[38] By the beginning of October 1974, the time for consulting Ministers on the proposals was drawing near and the FCO were increasingly keen to get their position on Masirah accepted. While agreeing that the RAF commitment to Masirah should be reduced, the FCO desired the inclusion of the phrase, 'it will however be important to carry out any such reduction without prejudicing the continuing use of Masirah'.[39] The FCO wanted no decisions to be taken on Masirah until the campaign was over.

Meanwhile Anglo-Omani relations were still excellent and British policy continued largely as normal. With a proposed visit to Britain by the Sultan in November 1974 and his desire to meet the new Prime Minister, there was an urgent need for a briefing paper for Wilson. Should the Sultan ask about the effects of the Defence Review, the Foreign Office decided that no mention of Masirah should be made and if the Sultan were to raise the point then the phrase 'we may reduce our staging requirements' be used.[40] The FCO was still taking the line that no decision on Masirah should be taken until after full consultations with the Americans; this was just a tactic however, since it was clear that they wished to retain some semblance of facilities there (and were sure that the Americans would dislike the idea of a British withdrawal). In an attempt to demonstrate Oman's importance, Wright wrote a submission for the Permanent Under Secretary who was the FCO representative on the Steering Committee tasked with suggesting how the Prime Minister should respond to the Sultan's questions on the Defence Review, stating that:

> If there is any disposition to question the need for speaking to the Sultan at this stage I suggest that the Permanent Under Secretary might point out the that the Sultan deserves some special consideration in view of the very large contract which he has recently signed for the supply of Jaguar and Rapier (to a value of about £71m).[41]

Despite the best efforts of Wright and his team, the MoD were still talking in terms of a complete withdrawal from Masirah. At the OPD Meeting on 23 October at which a draft Cabinet Paper was approved, the FCO made it clear that they were still unhappy about the proposed retreat from Masirah. With the paper due to undergo Cabinet consideration on 31 October, Terrance (Tony) Clark wrote to Westbrook of the FCO's Defence Department stating that, 'while we will not now get a sight of the final text, I gather that it presumes that a decision has been taken on the future of Masirah. This is not satisfactory from the FCO point of view and I would like the Secretary of State to make this point at the Cabinet meeting'.[42] The Cabinet decided that Britain's military commitment to Oman would be unchanged and that a general statement to the House of Commons on 3 December would give brief details on the progress of the Defence Review including a mention of Oman.[43] The position on Masirah was not outlined in the statement but Ministers had reached the provisional conclusion that there should be a withdrawal 'as soon as this could be done without upsetting the delicate political situation in the area'.[44]

As part of the consultation process with allies, which began in November, Washington was of course part of the process. It quickly became clear that they were concerned about the idea of a retreat from Masirah. In their eyes, the FCO had been right to fight hard for a continuation of the status quo that existed. On 28 November the U.S. Embassy in London hand delivered a statement of their views:

> We believe that the decision to withdraw the British presence from Masirah island following termination of the Dhofar rebellion has

potentially serious ramifications. As a result of its strategic position near the mouth of the Persian Gulf, this facility could be important in providing for the security of petroleum supplies to the NATO area... there are no realistic prospects that a comparable arrangement could be established by any western nation in the area... in the event of a British withdrawal... We would urge that a final British decision on Masirah be reconsidered.[45]

The U.S. was clearly rather concerned about the sudden British indication that it was planning eventual withdrawal from Masirah.[46] Washington had slowly begun to take an interest in Oman in 1972. Halliday states that, America had urged 'Iran to play an important role in the Gulf and the Indian Ocean'[47] seeing the Iranians as U.S. proxies. The Shah though had quite enough interests of his own in intervening in Oman and needed little American encouragement. U.S. interest in Masirah came to fruition during the Sultan's visit to Washington in January 1975 when the Secretary of State made a request for U.S. occasional use of the facilities at Masirah to which the Sultan agreed in principle. A telegram from the Embassy in Washington suggested that the U.S. was interested in acquiring 'more general and lasting facilities to compensate for our withdrawal'. The FCO responding to the U.S. request for use of what were after all RAF facilities which was rather belatedly made to London, asked for more details but the feeling was that, 'I doubt if we shall be able to refuse a request which on the face of it is a limited one and to which the Sultan has already agreed in principle'. While the FCO were glad that the American concerns would at least now have to be addressed, thus putting a hold on withdrawal from Masirah, they worried that:

> Once the Americans have a toe-hold on Masirah it is possible to envisage a situation in which they stepped up their requests to a point where we could be exposed to considerable embarrassment in our relations with the Arab world... Were the Americans to be left on the island after our departure much of the credit we might have expected to gain from leaving in a post-Dhofar situation could be dissipated.[48]

In return for the Sultan's agreement to the U.S. request, Washington was willing to supply on a commercial basis TOW missiles.[49] The U.S. was clearly making plans for when the British would pull out of the island. The Foreign Office having disliked the withdrawal from the start but not being able to effectively resist the MoD campaign to do so, had seen Washington as allies in either slowing or reversing the progress of the MoD's plan to withdraw but ended up having to deal with the likely problems of U.S. moves to secure their own interests.

Defence Review in 1975

The defence review was a lengthy process and continued into the following year. In early January 1975 the Middle East Department of the FCO had written a draft paper on the future of Masirah to be used as a basis for a reply to the Americans. This was then circulated to interested FCO departments, all of which agreed with the thrust of the document although all suggested additions. The North America Department suggested that some possibility of eventual withdrawal should be given in the paper, while 'continuing to pay rent and retaining certain specified rights over the use of facilities in certain circumstances'. This should go 'some substantial way towards meeting some American objections'.[50] The Defence Department worried about the potential MoD view of who would pay the costs for the continuing RAF presence. After all, the FCO vote was already stretched and no-one wanted the burden to fall on their department. The Information Administration Department worried that the fact that the RAF base gave the BBC transmitter security and logistic support was not stressed strongly enough.[51] The Foreign Secretary, Callaghan, informed Muscat of these developments but requested that no approach be made to the Sultan just yet, since the first draft of the Defence White Paper was still under discussion and made no mention of withdrawal from Masirah, American fears must first be assuaged. Indeed the Middle East Department's desire was to have just one short sentence on Oman in the White Paper; 'we do not think that it would be right in the present circumstances to make any change in the arrangements we have with the Sultan of Oman'.[52] This was very similar in tone to the Parliamentary Statement on the Defence Review made in the Commons on 3 December 1974.

The U.S. intervention had caused quite a stir in Whitehall and the earlier and continuing extreme reluctance of the FCO to agree to complete withdrawal from Masirah combined with this U.S. request for reconsideration effectively meant that the idea would be shelved. In a telegram to the Embassy in Washington, the Foreign Secretary explained that the importance the U.S. attached to the issue had been recognised and while there may be some reduction in the number of British personnel on the island, there was no need to upset the delicate balance of the area. Indeed, 'since we have not discussed and will not disclose our long term intention to withdraw from Masirah to anyone other than the United States government we have not limited our freedom [of action]'.[53] The Foreign Office had got its own way, for now, but the fault lines remained and the general atmosphere and provisional ministerial decision that withdrawal should occur when the time was right, suggested that the MoD was still in a strong position.

The final Defence White Paper was due to go to the Cabinet for consideration on 27 February. The MoD was expecting any opposition to Defence Review decisions to concentrate on the major non-NATO commitments including Masirah. An FCO Heads of Department circular stated 'Mr Mason will defend these but, since political considerations predominate in each case, he will look for support from the Secretary of State'.[54] As such the FCO prepared a short note outlining where Britain stood on Oman and why. The short piece was careful to stress the importance of the area 'to our vital economic interests', the U.S.' representations on the issue and relations with Iran and Saudi Arabia. It also stated that the issue was kept under review with the intention of reducing direct military assistance 'as and when we can' and that reductions in RAF deployment to Masirah was the aim and not withdrawal.[55] The White Paper was approved, Masirah was safe for now and there were no major changes in policy towards the Sultanate. In the statement of defence estimates the section on Oman finally read:

> [W]e do not therefore think it would be right in the present circumstances to make any change in the arrangements we have with the Sultan of Oman. We shall, however, make some economies as our need for staging facilities at Masirah declines, and shall continue to keep the level of our military assistance to the Sultan under review.[56]

The final part of the statement was to be fulfilled surprisingly quickly. With the conflict in Dhofar going well, there was no longer any real threat from the rebels to Salalah or the RAF camp there. It was therefore decided by the Chiefs of Staff in their routine review of operational progress early in 1975 that the Royal Artillery detachment, known as the Cracker Battery, and part of the RAF Regiment detachment would be withdrawn in the first week of April 1975. In a meeting with the Chief of Staff on 2 March, the Sultan had 'accepted the general case for reductions and is prepared in particular for the early withdrawal of the RA detachment'.[57] The Sultan was much less happy when he was informed that the rest of the RAF Regiment detachment would not be replaced when their tour ended in June. He had expected the withdrawal to come in stages of several months apart and hoped that the detachment could stay until after the monsoon. He was therefore only reluctantly persuaded to acquiesce by the new CSAF, Ken Perkins, and the new Ambassador Jim Treadwell, who had served in Oman previously.[58]

The Labour Government and Oman

The withdrawals which took place in April and June 1975 were in effect quite minor, having been approved of by all three Omani service chiefs (all LSP) and the Sultan while having no effect on Britain's commitment to Oman. While the outcome of the Defence Review was a positive one for the Sultanate there is no doubt that the change of government early in 1974 had some effects. Whereas in previous years the arguments had been about how much extra support to give to Oman, under the new government it is telling that the existing levels of support had to be justified. In addition it is also interesting that the full extent of British involvement in Oman was only revealed to Wilson, Callaghan and Mason, during Labour's early months in office, and that these three were so convinced of the case for involvement that they authorised the continuation of assistance without reference to the full DOPC. But the overall background of political and economic strife in Britain, including troubles in Northern Ireland, strikes, inflation and the effects of the energy crisis, all meant savings had to be made in government expenditures though.

There was a real change of atmosphere under the new government. While the continuation of British assistance was approved, the goal was always to 'aim at ending our direct assistance to the Sultan's armed forces in the war against the rebels as soon as the military situation permits'.[59] The Labour government, more through the change of atmosphere created by this statement of policy, was able to push this as the main aim for officials, even though many did not seem to much like the change of pace. A good example of the general change in atmosphere was the upsurge in correspondence received about Oman and questions asked in the house which necessitated much hard work in the preparation of answers, briefings and letters. Much of this upsurge came from constituency Labour parties and trade union branches. This was often directed towards 'Comrade' Wilson himself with many letters demanding an explanation for British colonialist attitudes and the cessation of support for the 'Sultan's despotic rule'. This forced Wilson and other senior government figures to reply (often through secretaries of course) to refute the allegations and try and explain what was really happening in Oman. Naturally, these explanations did little to quieten the discontent 'of honest socialists' who continued to decry the continuation of 'reactionary, oppressive, colonialist Tory policies'.[60] Against this background of dissent it is easy to see why the general atmosphere changed and why the Labour government had to tread a difficult path between the winding down of British involvement and ensuring national interests were secured.

Influence, Economic Interests and the Progress of the Campaign

It would be easy to conclude that, during this period, the Foreign Office was preoccupied with Whitehall disputes and that with the flood of, in particular, Iranian assistance and the campaign progressing increasingly well, there was no need for Britain to be as involved as before. This was certainly not the case. Taking just three examples from autumn 1974 to spring 1975 alone should dispel this notion. Thinking of the future, in autumn 1974 the FCO in consultation with the Sultan asked the Foreign Office officials, Sir Gawain Bell and Anthony Ashworth, to prepare a plan for the establishment of an organisation to administer the areas of the *jebal* which had been taken from the rebels and in addition to 'consider the future role of the *firqah* in the social structure of Dhofar'.[61] However, by the end of 1974, Oman was experiencing a cash flow crisis requiring $40 million to be raised by the end of February and $45 million by the end of March 1975.[62] Unless this was secured the Economic Advisor, John Townsend, informed the Embassy that from March salaries would not be able to be paid. The FCO arranged for a team of bankers to visit Oman with a view to raising a longer term loan of $400 million. In addition to this, Ivor Lucas, who replaced Patrick Wright as the head of the Middle East Department in January 1975, suggested that decisions needed to be taken to restrict government expenditure. 'Mr Townsend is trying to do this but is having to contend with the vested interests of "the mafia"', the cabal of advisors who had secured influence in Muscat. He instructed Treadwell 'to do all he can to discreetly strengthen Mr Townsend's hand'.[63] If these two critical examples of British assistance were not enough, the Omanis were also continuing to seek more detailed information from the FCO, e.g. 'on suitable grass seed for the jebal'.[64]

Now that the British monopoly in Oman had largely been broken by other powers, concern in the Foreign Office and on the ground in Muscat was also turning towards ensuring that the British economy could derive more benefit from Britain's position and that British influence in Oman would remain strong. Early in 1974 Hawley reported that there was a feeling,

> [I]n some Omani quarters – which was really quite predictable – that though they were in the past perforce closely tied to the British their new-found wealth puts them in a new position and they want to diversify. One need not complain about this in principle... none the less, we naturally want to get as many slices of the new cake as is reasonable.[65]

There were increasing fears that the new 'Mafia' were gaining influence. The Sultan's new foreign advisors who were in some respects replacing the British were led by what Hawley called 'the Libyan "Don" of the Omani "Mafia"' Yahya Omar. He used a Kipling poem to say the rest:

> Who shall doubt the secret hid
> Under Cheops Pyramid
> Was that the contractor did
> Cheops out of several million quid

The influence of this mafia was important and Hawley believed that 'there was undoubtedly at one stage some attempt by the "mafia" to curtail our influence and certain large defence contracts might have gone to the Americans or the French', although the influence of CSAF and Hawley prevailed and Britain got the Air Defence Scheme contracts and others.[66] Hawley also reported that the Sultan became increasingly inaccessible and meetings were a little less frequent than in previous years, though 'our personal relationship remained as close as ever'.[67]

Britain then, despite a loss of some influence still had easy enough access to the Sultan and a warm relationship with Oman. Major contracts were secured and Britain remained the largest supplier to the Sultanate, with British exports rising by 90 per cent in a single year, reaching a value of £41.5 million. This was an underestimate since more British goods came indirectly via Dubai and Abu Dhabi. Hawley also reported that British consultants remained paramount and that 'British contractors have some £150 million currently on hand and the prospect of more to come'.[68] Despite fears, British influence and commerce was still more than holding its own in Oman.

In other areas too things were looking increasingly hopeful for Oman. After a successful state visit to Tehran the Shah agreed to guarantee Omani airspace until their own air defences were up and running. The Hornbeam line was proving successful and arrival of the Imperial Iranian Task Force at the beginning of 1974 enabled the clearing of the Midway road across the *jebal* of insurgents. Development in the cleared areas took off and the Shah gave the Sultan another 2,900 troops as a 'birthday present' at the end of the year. In addition, Abu Dhabi provided troops to guard the north of Oman to free more of the SAF for the fight in Dhofar. On the political front too there was some progress with talks on frontiers beginning with both the Saudis and Abu Dhabi. Tensions on the southern border remained high however. An Arab League Mission of Mediation visited in an attempt to at least calm the situation, the PDRY refused the mission admission to their territory, a major error on their part, which only added to Oman's case in the eyes of other Arab states. Finally a formal agreement was signed with the Iranians on the median line in the Straits of Hormuz. This was a generous agreement for Oman and was important for future stability. As Hawley noted, 1974 was 'a year of great progress'.[69]

It was also a year in which earlier British policies and groundwork began to pay off. The FCO's decision to focus on securing external assistance for Oman had had a rough beginning, bearing very little fruit in 1972. The following year saw the arrival of a battalion of Iranian troops and some financial aid but it was not until 1974 that the foundations prepared earlier and the switch in strategy really began to pay off. It would have been relatively easy for officials to keep Muscat reliant on London for everything but despite fears of a loss of influence, officials were keen that Oman should diversify its support as London became less willing, especially under the new Labour government, to provide resources even when payment was offered. Indeed not only were the Iranians to provide substantial aid but because of their close relationship with China, the Shah was in fact able to persuade the Chinese to withdraw much of their material support for the PFLOAG rebels. However, this was quickly replaced by East German and Soviet aid.[70]

Withdrawal from Salalah

With the campaign progressing better than expected by 1975 and the Labour policy of withdrawals as and when the military situation allowed firmly in place, it was no surprise that there was a renewed insistence on a swift exit from RAF Salalah. While getting off the 'Salalah hook' had always been the objective of officials and the previous government it had been put on hold. As the situation around the airfield calmed and some withdrawals began to take place the temptation quickly arose to think about terminating the British presence there completely, with the MoD being especially keen. The new Ambassador Jim Treadwell wrote a long letter at the beginning of March 1975, considering the problems and possibilities to the new head of the Middle East Department, Sir Ivor Lucas.[71] He replied with the rebuke:

> When you propose to [']think aloud['] in this way it would be preferable from our point of view if you did not copy the correspondence to the Ministry of Defence... We have problems with the MOD over Masirah, from which they would like us to make a far hastier exit than we consider politically prudent. Your and our preliminary

reconnaissances of this territory are accordingly better kept within the family in order to avoid prolonged wrangles with the MOD.[72]

The rush for the exit at Salalah however, was already on. The Chiefs of Staff Committee – Defence Operational Staff – had already produced a report on the future requirement of RAF Salalah, which concluded that there was no operational or technical reason why SAF could not take over the running of the airfield. It suggested that the FCO instruct HM Ambassador Muscat to open consultations with the Sultan on the transfer of the base. If the Sultan agreed then there should be a six month handover period with Britain 'leaving at Salalah if necessary, sufficient personnel to meet any request by the Sultan for a deterrent British presence'.[73] Despite FCO reluctance the MoD remained insistent on the issue and in the new political atmosphere prevailed. The FCO opened negotiations with the Sultan on the matter in June 1975 which were eventually concluded amicably a few months later. Although British withdrawal did not take place within the expected six months, Ministers were forced to agree a continuing presence there until 31 March 1977, but with the Sultan having to pay for their presence after October 1976 until the point of departure at a cost of £465,000.[74]

The End of Major Operations: Dhofar is Safe for Development

During 1975, the war continued to progress well for the Sultanate. Indeed, as the new Ambassador reported in his Annual Review for that year, 'By far the biggest surprise of the year was the collapse early in December of organised resistance to the Sultan's authority in Western Dhofar'.[75] Most of the rebels, having had their supplies cut by the network of manned lines dividing the *jebal*, lost the support of the population to the liberal use of oil wealth as inducements[76] and the impressive development of Dhofar, retreated into PDRY territory. After receiving the news on 4 December 1975 that 'Dhofar was secure for civil development',[77] the Sultan was so confident that the rebellion was all but over, 'that he presided over a massive victory Eid parade in Muscat stadium on 11 December. His people turned up in their thousands to cheer and exult him'.[78] According to Treadwell the ultimate factor which made possible the victory was the dropping of a line from Sarfait across the coastal strip 'in full view of the PDRY town of Hauf, thus sealing once and for all the principle rebel supply route into Oman'.[79] While this was clearly important, the CSAF, General Ken Perkins, also put the victory down, in part, to his and the Sultan's willingness, despite British fears, to bomb PDRY positions which were shelling Oman.[80]

While the Iranian role, was somewhat downplayed by General Akehurst, the Commander of the Dhofar Brigade, in his book, and the SAS role was over emphasised by Tony Jeapes in his,[81] Iranian aid was seen as being much more important by CSAF, Perkins and Treadwell. Indeed, Treadwell stated that while 'the Iranians did not win the war, it could not have been won so quickly without them...the sheer weight of their numbers assisted greatly in overwhelming the opposing forces'.[82] It is also clear that their provision of helicopters from late 1972 was also significant.

Of course this jubilation did not actually mean that the war was finally over. The PDRY continued to support the rebels and shell Omani territory, and pockets of rebel activity remained in western Dhofar. A ceasefire was negotiated in March 1976, but 'implied no acknowledgement by PDRY or PFLOAG that they were beaten. Indeed fighting continued on and off for years.'[83] The Iranian troops did not leave Oman until 1979 and the SAS remained until September 1976. Skeet believes that the formal end to the war did not come about until the signing of a normalisation agreement in November 1982, between the PDRY and the Sultanate.[84] This agreement is put down to Saudi efforts at getting the PDRY to act more moderately,[85] effectively buying South Yemen off in the process.[86] According to General Sir Charles Huxtable, the Commander of the Dhofar Brigade from August 1976–78, three British officers and one from New Zealand were lost in skirmishes with rebels during his period of command. It was hard work mopping up the remaining rebels.

General Huxtable planned operations based on intelligence, on one occasion staking out waterholes for two weeks before ambushing a party of rebels in possession of a large amount of cash, destined to be used to attempt to reignite the rebellion. These senior British LSP are also keen to point out that there was no question of them accepting direction from Whitehall. Ken Perkins stated that he had 'a completely free hand' in running the campaign (although little say in weapons procurement) and was more than willing to fly air reconnaissance missions and conduct raids over the PDRY border against Whitehall's wishes.[87] General Huxtable recalls his predecessor John Akehurst's advice to, 'just remember who pays the piper'.[88] Ambassador Treadwell however, was keen to note the importance of continuing to supply good quality LSP like these, despite the reduction in hostilities. He considered that 'this will go a long way towards ensuring the paramountcy of our commercial position and strengthen the Sultan's reliance on us as wise political counsellors.' However, he also considered it inevitable that 'our loan service personnel should take their leave of Oman when they are no longer needed.[89]

The Annual Review of 1975 painted an encouraging picture concerning British commercial successes in Oman. Reporting that 'despite the modest size of the Embassy's specialist staff British exports from January to October shot up to a record total of £81.9m; a gain of 90.9% on the figures for the whole of 1974.' Treadwell warned that some of this lead was down to defence sales and that:

> Those in charge should begin to exercise restraint and diversify their demands, though this would oblige us to work all the harder to sell cars and pumps and factories rather than get the easy money by giving the green light for newer and shinier missiles (which however the French would sell if we refused).[90]

Some British manufacturers were able to respond to the challenge of increasing diversification of supply however, with Black and Decker selling partly modified bench drills for squashing dates down slightly so that they would fit into the packaging.[91] The year 1975 had proven to be a successful time both commercially and militarily. Now some were waiting in the wings to take advantage of this nascent economic boom.

With the effective end of the conflict there was no reason why the Masirah issue should remain on ice. With the Labour government looking for more expenditure cuts and especially in defence, Masirah, with annual running costs of £1.9 million, was a natural target. Consequently, the FCO could not hold up the decision for much longer and instead secured a lengthened withdrawal date of April 1977. It was therefore left to the FCO to negotiate the withdrawal with the Sultan and win round the U.S. who again mounted strenuous protests against the idea.[92] Despite these difficulties the RAF withdrawal went ahead and a once 'vital' defence interest was abandoned in the face of a reassessment of national interests and a final rundown of the majority of defence commitments 'East of Suez'. The Treasury were overjoyed, stating in a letter to the MoD that, 'We were pleased to learn, from your Secretary of State's announcement on 19th July, that our RAF stations at Salalah and Masirah in Oman will be withdrawn at the end of March 1977'. An FCO hand has underlined the words 'We were pleased to learn' and written 'No doubt!!' encapsulating the bureaucratic enmities which had been present throughout this period. The Treasury letter was actually writing to enquire just what the value of the surplus moveable equipment and fixed assets to be gifted to the Sultan was, perhaps with the purpose of removing it from MoD/FCO votes in the coming financial year.[93]

Conclusion

The years after 1971 had been difficult but in most spheres had brought great successes. In just six short years Oman had become a peaceful, prosperous and rapidly developing state which was recognised internationally. Britain had played a large part in this transformation and while Britain had always been wary of publicising its role too widely, the decision to support the Sultanate had paid huge strategic and growing financial dividends.

The continuation of British support after the election of a Labour government would on the face of things seem to be a little unexpected. But the Labour leadership having been in government during the withdrawal from Aden had clearly drawn lessons from the experience and could not deny the clear national interest in supporting the Sultan. That by spring 1974 the campaign was going better than expected, thanks in part to the huge Iranian and lesser Jordanian support, was also undoubtedly a factor in securing continued British assistance under a Labour government. While there are clear similarities between the Conservative and Labour governments, there are also clear differences in style and approach. The Conservatives were manifestly more comfortable with the necessity of providing support to the Sultan and were willing (within reason) to provide more if necessary. Overall though, the evolution of British policy during the period of Labour government exhibited many more continuities than changes. The broad outlines of policies remained the same as they had under the Conservatives. The Wilson government could see the same national interests in remaining in Oman as the Heath government had. Consequently emphasis remained upon the role of the SAS, the importance of development and the supply of LSP.

Officials had clearly expected Britain to lose influence over time as the Sultanate and the Sultan emerged onto the international stage, yet Britain was able, despite the rise of 'the mafia' to continue to assist the Sultan and of course to secure some very lucrative defence and development contracts. Against considerable international competition, she was able to obtain her fair share of the cake that Oman's new oil wealth was beginning to provide. Despite this though, there were also signs that the Sultan, while still deeply valuing his British connection, was also looking for new partners and to cut his own dash on his new stage. The U.S. was of course the natural new partner for an Anglophile Sultan looking for a new security guarantee in the dangerous currents of east-west confrontation and intra-Arab rivalry.

Prior to 1973, Washington had been content to let Britain make the running in Oman. However, in the post-oil shock world the U.S. began to wake up to Oman's strategic position and its pro-Western Sultan. Yet despite the delay to the decision on Masirah, the U.S. exerted remarkably little influence upon Britain's Oman policy. This is mostly due to the fact that British policy was well established and that the U.S. arrived rather late and had been more than willing for Britain to take care of Oman. As the British retreated though, it was only natural for the Americans to begin to take over; this though was a very slow process. The first U.S. involvement was possibly conducted through their Iranian proxy, although this is not at all clear since the Iranians had more than enough reasons of their own for becoming involved, including a desire to expand their influence, to prevent a hostile anti-monarchist force sharing the Strait of Hormuz[94] and to provide combat training for Iranian troops especially in counterinsurgency techniques. As such, Iranian troops were rapidly rotated through Dhofar to expose the maximum number.[95] Later the U.S. became much more directly involved in Oman with the signing in 1980 of the Facilities Access Agreement.[96]

In the end though, it was the officials, who behind the scenes created the conditions for the continued British assistance which was so vital to the successful prosecution of the Dhofar campaign. These officials and the British and Omani troops on the ground deserve much of the credit. Without officials' vision of what was needed, their dogged pursuit of the means to assist (even if that led to conflict with other departments) and their clearly formulated conceptions of the national interest, which were so useful in convincing others, it is doubtful whether so much progress in helping Oman could have been made in such a short time. The role of officials in shaping policy detail, this time under a Labour government, which remained committed, albeit less enthusiastically, to the British role in securing Oman's future was vital.

CONCLUSION

THEMES AND IMPLICATIONS

> Le gain de notre étude, c'est en être devenu meilleur et plus sage
> Montaigne, *Essais*

The nature of Britain's involvement in Oman during the 1970s has always been somewhat oblique and has tended to be overshadowed by a popular focus on the exploits of the SAS. The backdrop to this involvement is usually briefly explained in the most simplistic terms, yet Britain's role in Oman consisted of much more than just the supply of the SAS to fight a Communist insurgency during the third decade of the Cold War. While traditional Cold War concerns were of principal importance, Britain's role in Oman was more vital than simply propping up an anti-Communist leader in the way that leaders, such as Mobutu in Zaire and Pinochet in Chile, were supported by the west. Britain had far more complex motives for committing itself and its resources to the Sultanate. Having witnessed the anarchy in South Yemen, which led to a Marxist state in Arabia, it was paramount that this did not happen when Britain withdrew from the Gulf. In order to ensure a better outcome in this case however, much more than naked force would have to be used.

British strategy therefore rested upon a number of pillars, which combined were considerably more effective and subtle than overwhelming the guerrillas with British force of arms. In order to leave the Gulf in a stable and peaceful condition and maintain British influence, an entire modern state had to be constructed in the Sultanate almost from scratch. This was a strategy which had been tried earlier; its roots can clearly be seen in the 1958 Exchange of Letters and similar policies, with a focus on development, which was also prominent in Britain's dealings with neighbouring Gulf States. What this strategy needed however was sufficient funds and will. Oman had largely lacked these two prerequisites until the export of oil from 1967 onwards and the arrival of Qaboos who shared the vision of a modern developed state. The creation of this state alone would have been a hard task but when combined with an insurgency, looked like an impossible dream. Oman therefore represents much more than just another proxy conflict of the Cold War. Its strategic location and fears of a 'domino' effect in the oil-producing states of the Gulf meant that no mistakes could be made. The combination of the implementation of a new counterinsurgency strategy, fast paced development programme, the establishment of more efficient governance mechanisms and the campaign to gain international recognition and respectability make the task in Oman look much more like a modern exercise in statebuilding *viz* Afghanistan, Sierra Leone or Bosnia than a Cold War proxy conflict. Britain's statebuilding role in Oman was undoubtedly key; no other western power was in a position to take on the task, and without British assistance in so many areas it is unlikely that the Sultan would have achieved so much progress in all these spheres so quickly or indeed that the insurgency would have actually been suppressed.

This book's primary aim was to explore British decision-making concerning Oman and to investigate the extent of British involvement in the Sultanate during a critical period. In the light of the British decision to withdraw from the Gulf, a large and seemingly contradictory British involvement in Oman was authorised for a number of key reasons. Memories of the results of the withdrawal from Aden and the Conservative desire to retain more influence in the Gulf, and 'East of Suez' more generally, clearly played a part. But by far the most significant reason was the importance of Oman and the Gulf to Britain's fundamental national interests. In order to be able to depart from the Gulf it was essential that modern, stable states, friendly to Britain were left behind. Before this could be assured though, the Dhofar conflict had to be ended satisfactorily and Oman turned into a modern state.

The driving forces behind British policymaking on Oman were diverse but often complimentary during the period. The new Conservative government led by Heath, sections of the bureaucracy and individuals on the ground all played important roles. The role of officials in reshaping counterinsurgency policies – including the commitment of the SAS, in demonstrating the growing power of the insurgency and raising awareness of the importance of Oman to Britain were clearly vital. This led to a bid to finally push Sultan Sa'id to change the way in which the counterinsurgency was fought. The work, which was conducted by officials predominantly in the early months of 1970, gave the Conservatives an inbuilt strategy for dealing with Oman when they were elected in June of that year. The Conservatives also evidently thought differently than Labour about 'East of Suez' issues, Heath's tour of the Gulf in 1969 clearly highlighting the distinction. This willingness to engage with Oman was also demonstrated through an examination of military and financial policy towards the Sultanate from June 1970 to the end of 1971, when the new government was willing to swiftly authorise military intervention both in Dhofar and Musandam. The importance of key Conservative ministers – Heath, Douglas-Home and Carrington – and the interest they displayed in Oman was important in shaping policy and in ensuring its implementation. Yet throughout this period the role of officials, who in the Heath government, found willing allies and a sympathetic ear for their case, remained vital. The government though, while remaining sympathetic to the cause, was especially concerned to prevent any escalation of the conflict and saw the importance of securing other sources of assistance for Oman. What this book highlights was that for the main part, officials were able to take the lead in developing policy towards Oman but they needed an understanding government to agree to their implementation. While officials can raise issues, suggest (and indeed stress) courses of action and deal with matters as important as advisors for regimes, they still need ministerial approval for the commitment of British troops.

It is clear that the Conservative government inherited the beginnings of a more active policy which had been worked out by officials. Without the interest in these matters shown by Heath, Douglas-Home and Carrington it would have been much harder to secure as much help for Oman from Britain as was eventually forthcoming. The role of officials though is key; it was they who took care of day to day issues, they who shaped the debates and they who made sure Oman's importance was understood by all. What is remarkable though is the level of interconnectedness on the part of officials. Many of those dealing with Oman, either on the ground in the Gulf or in Whitehall had some kind of previous relationship. In many cases this was through the Sudan Political Service. Hawley, as an obvious example, knew through his service in Sudan – Hugh Oldman and Sir William Luce, from FCO postings he had excellent relations with Sir Geoffrey Arthur, Colin Maxwell (Deputy CSAF) as well as Acland, Parsons and Wright. His earlier stint as liaison between the FCO and the MoD Joint Planning Staff meant he was friends with the Chief of the General Staff, Mike Carver. In addition, the Deputy under Secretary (Policy) at the MoD, Pat Nairne, was an old school friend.[1] These formative relationships can only have made things easier for Hawley and he was by no means alone in these networks. The shared backgrounds and experiences of officials undoubtedly gave them similar outlooks and it was their determination that Britain should do its duty in Oman that kept the issue on the agenda.

One of the key tools used in decision-making at all levels is the notion of the national interest. Perceptions of the national interest rarely changed during the period and played a large role in informing policymaking. Therefore, it was important to examine how officials identified what Britain's national interests in Oman were and how they used them to inform their decision-making. Indeed so obvious were these interests that officials seemed to see little need to state them formally to each other. In chapter three we saw how it was left to Luce to clearly outline Britain's national interests in the area for the DOPC, a conception which was then used to frame policy but which anyway essentially matched the largely unspoken understandings of officials. The concept of national interests and those particular British interests identified in the case of Oman were simply used as tools to support policy recommendations, their bold statement making it virtually impossible to argue about their importance. The restatement of this outline of national interests was made at the start of each review of policy. Thus throughout the Heath government the perceptions of national interest in this case did not change. Even under the Wilson government there was a continuing reliance upon the same conception of national interest. Chapter seven shows how Wilson, Callaghan and Mason accepted unquestioningly the statement of interests when agreeing to the continuation of British assistance to Oman during their first months in power. This did not change much throughout their time in government. While the broad thrust of these interests appeared immutable there was also some change and flexibility, this is especially evident with the issue of the RAF base at Masirah which went from being a 'vital' national interest to something which was disposed of as rapidly as possible in 1977. The concept of the national interest is a very important tool in policymaking, but not all of those things identified as being in the national interest are destined to remain so. That said though, the overall stability of Oman and the Gulf in any context was and remains a clear national interest.

British policy towards Oman and how it evolved over the period clearly reflected how importantly Oman was viewed in the hierarchy of national interest, which was in turn decided by the perceived threat to the stability and pro-British nature of the Sultanate. British policy towards Oman became much more engaged after the crisis over Buraimi, developing through the Imamate rebellion and the *Jebal Akhdar* campaign which involved regular British troops into the policy encapsulated by the 1958 Exchange of Letters. Despite the ups and downs of British involvement in Oman, this policy of modernisation of the Omani Armed Forces and extensive civil development remained essentially the same basis of policy throughout the period. What changed was the extent of British assistance. Frustration with the pace of change under Sultan Sa'id and the continual hunt for 'savings' meant that Britain gradually retreated from Oman during the late 1960s; the British subsidy was withdrawn in 1967 and any assistance Britain offered was to be paid for. As the rebellion in Dhofar became more serious though, officials re-engaged with the Sultanate and urged change more forcefully. The changes of government in both London and Muscat in 1970 facilitated this re-engagement and while it is unlikely that a full picture of the background to the coup will emerge soon, if ever, Britain clearly approved of the change. What followed was the full scale implementation of a three pronged plan to make Oman into a viable state. The most important part of this was a complete rethink of the counterinsurgency tactics in Dhofar to focus on 'hearts and minds' and the undermining of rebel support. This necessitated the use of specialised British Forces and especially the SAS who were ideally suited to their role of intelligence gathering and running the *firqat*. It was also vital to prevent the spread of subversion in the rest of the country and so operations were launched in northern Oman and in the Musandam Peninsula, with the latter using quite extensive British armed force. The second priority was to show Omani citizens that the new era could provide more than just hope, and with British government help extensive plans were laid for development. The third pillar was to secure international recognition for the Sultanate and to cement its legitimacy, something that was achieved remarkably quickly.

Throughout this period though, the Sultan still had to pay for almost all of the help he received, either on an 'extra costs' basis or in full. As it became clear that the cash flow crisis in the Sultanate was becoming chronic, officials attempted to find ways in which Britain could relieve some of the burden, no easy task given Britain's own economic malaise. This was supplemented by a drive to internationalise the conflict by drawing in both financial and material aid from those neighbouring states with a vested interest in preventing the spread of communism in Arabia. Fortunately this was largely achieved before the return to office of a Labour government in 1974, by which time it was no longer possible to think about increasing British aid, and the focus switched to trying to find ways to disengage from the Sultanate as and when the situation permitted. The change in government though, overall resulted in little more than a change of emphasis and, as has been demonstrated, there was a great deal of continuity in policy between Conservative and Labour governments.

The extent of British involvement (military, political and economic) in Oman naturally varied along with policy. While this was at times substantial, principally from 1970–76, it was considerably less than the American commitment to Vietnam. In terms of its military contribution, Britain had for most of the period just 80 SAS troops, a field surgical team, some Royal Engineers, about 100 RAF regiment soldiers, RAF ground teams running Salalah airfield and a Royal Artillery battery. This was supplemented by around 200 LSP, including the heads of all the services, and a similar number of contract officers.[2] On the civilian side, British companies and contractors did much work in development and planning. Yet chapter four displays the care taken so that permanent British advisors in the Ministries were kept to a minimum, never numbering more than a dozen,[3] quality not quantity were the order of the day. Where Britain made its impact was not in sheer numbers but in ideas and leadership. Those advisors which were in place were of very high quality and British LSP tended to be among the 'best and brightest' keen to gain valuable experience. Britain's role emerged as that of a facilitator helping Oman to reach goals laid out by the Sultan; what began as a tutor-pupil relationship quickly evolved through mentoring into a partnership.

There has been much written in recent years about the changing nature of insurgency and counterinsurgency, sparked in large measure by the poor performance of British and American troops in Iraq and Afghanistan, which has led some to rightly re-examine the best ways of 'doing COIN'. Britain's retreat from empire and its many counterinsurgency campaigns after 1945 have consistently been held up by much of the literature as 'best practice' or the 'ideal type'. The six core principles of British COIN have frequently being enumerated as: a) co-ordinated government machinery, b) minimum force, c) adhere to the law, d) clear and hold not search and destroy, e) importance of intelligence, and f) defeat the insurgent subversion and not the insurgent *per se* – the final hallmark of success is a political settlement.[4] There is now a growing body of literature which challenges both the extent to which any of these techniques was properly applied during Britain's varied counterinsurgency campaigns[5] and questions the applicability and success of the 'dominant paradigm'.[6]

Clearly in the case of Oman and the Dhofar War the 'ideal type' of counterinsurgency campaign was fought and was based upon earlier British practice. When deciding whether or not to commit the SAS to Dhofar in an active role alongside running the *firqah* during the 1971 offensive, the top brass' concern with the very political nature of COIN was evident when it was stated:

> We agree with the objectives of the 1971 Dhofar campaign and consider there is a reasonable chance of military success with the forces proposed. Nevertheless the possibility cannot be excluded at this stage that some British combat troops may, in the event, be needed.

We would emphasise that... military operations without effective political measures designed to win over the Dhofaris would ultimately be futile.[7]

While the 1971 offensive was less successful than had been hoped, it marked the beginning of the end of the Dhofar War and there was no need for the commitment of British combat troops. The war itself represents the culmination of the lessons learnt during earlier British counterinsurgency campaigns adhering to the six main principles of British COIN doctrine. This new literature suggests that brutality and large scale use of force characterised British COIN.[8] While no war is ever 'clean', the campaign in Dhofar was not characterised by brutality or excessive force and the principles of British COIN summed up in the term 'hearts and minds' were applied quite assiduously. The counterinsurgency effort in Oman was remarkably successful but it was not this alone which led to British success in the Sultanate.

In the political sphere, throughout the period, Britain attempted to maintain as low key a role as possible. Much energy was expended in presenting the right image to world, devising 'lines to take' and generally attempting to keep out of the limelight as much as possible. The reasons for this were twofold: firstly, so as not to attract too much attention at home and secondly, so as not to tarnish Oman's legitimacy. Hand in hand with this approach went a remarkable degree of respect for Omani sovereignty from a country which essentially had *de facto* control over the Sultanate. Officials were very careful not to force the Sultan into decisions or action and indeed were sometimes surprised by their level of influence. This fact clearly does not fit with the image of the Anglo-Omani relationship portrayed by Halliday in his chapter entitled 'The Sultanate of Oman – A British Colony'.[9]

Such a low key role meant that Britain increasingly had to draw in other actors, both to help with development and legitimacy, and especially in the ever man power intensive field of counterinsurgency in putting boots on the ground. Initially, due to adverse attention at the UN, the British role in Oman was largely viewed by external actors as malign. Yet in the Gulf, those states with experience with Britain were pleased with London's commitment to Muscat. Gradually though, with Omani persistence and charm, and British advice and backup, most states were brought around to Oman's new status and accepted the British role. London for its part always saw regional states as key to its strategy, first of recognition and then to securing additional assistance. Saudi Arabia was seen from the very beginning as key, and British officials did much to encourage the Omanis to focus on nurturing good relations with Riyadh. The U.S. though had surprisingly little impact upon British policy towards Oman throughout this period, being largely content to allow Britain to run the show as long as the business playing field remained a level one. Only their concerns about withdrawal from Masirah led them to voice a protest, which delayed rather than reversed Labour policy.

This book then has provided a systematic re-examination of the Anglo-Omani relationship during the critical years of transformation from isolated, undeveloped state into a modern outward looking nation. Since there have been no impartial, in-depth studies of this period which have had access to a wide range of primary source documents, this work has shown the evolution of a careful, considered and sometimes parsimonious policy, far from the deterministic, callous and rapacious image presented by Halliday. It has also shown those, like Kelly, that Britain adopted this low key approach to Oman, not solely because of lack of will or resources but because it was the policy which was the most appropriate for statebuilding in the post colonial world.

Britain pursued a determined but reasoned policy towards Oman based on a clear appreciation of the national interest. The evidence presented in this book has shown that, while Britain did have an enormous amount of control in Oman during the initial post-coup period, by 1975–76 this control was considerably diminished. However, this presented relatively few concerns, since Britain's regard for Oman's sovereignty remained surprisingly high from the very beginning of Qaboos' reign. Britain's relations with Oman were not those of pure dominance presented by Halliday but were based on a high degree of mutual regard. By showing both the complexity of Anglo-Omani relations and the detail of British policymaking this book contributes to the historiography in a number of ways. Firstly, and most importantly, by being the first to examine the newly released archival record, it has been able to show for the first time many of the details and debates in Whitehall concerning British policy towards Oman, thus filling a large void in the existing literature on Anglo-Omani relations during this period. Secondly, by explaining why Britain decided to commit itself to the protection of the Omani regime while, at the same time, withdrawing from the Gulf and seeking membership of the European Economic Community it challenges notions of Britain's loss of will. It has furthermore highlighted the reluctance of the U.S. to take over from Britain in the Gulf region and has also questioned the extent to which the foreign policy of the Heath government was based on refocusing Britain's efforts on Europe. In this way it has contributed to the literature on Britain's decline in the second half of the twentieth century by demonstrating that any loss of will was by no means complete, especially when vital national interests were at stake. It has also shown that even whilst Britain was moving further into the European Circle, responsibilities in the old Commonwealth/World Circle were still being willingly fulfilled, thus challenging the notion of Britain becoming purely a European power.

The debacle at Suez and the 'scuttle' from Aden are often seen as symptomatic of either British loss of will to protect its interests or lack of ability to do so. These events are viewed as being indicative of Britain's decline from pre-eminence, yet these two events have shifted attention from the more numerous occasions when Britain has been more than willing and able to stand up for its interests and create the conditions which when it withdrew would ensure that its interests would continue to be served. In what almost appears to be something of a trend, Britain was involved in the Malaya 'Emergency', the 1953 coup in Iran, Buraimi, the *Jebal Akhdar* campaign, the 1958 operation to support King Hussein of Jordan, the 1961 operation to support Kuwait, the mercenary operation in the Yemen, the Indonesian 'Confrontation' and Oman 1970–76. Even in more recent times Britain has not lacked the will to defend its interests in the Falklands, to send warships to the Gulf to defend tankers during the Iran-Iraq war or 42,000 troops to participate in operation Desert Storm. Britain has never truly ended its 'East of Suez' role, indeed as the 1998 Strategic Defence Review stated: 'our vital interests are not confined to Europe...our national security and prosperity thus depend on promoting international stability'.[10] Britain removed the most visible aspects of its role in the Gulf while modernising its relations with the Gulf States, and it was its successful involvement in Oman that made that possible.

NOTES

Introduction
Oman: Between the *Pax Britannica* and the World

1. The words Persian and Arabian when attached to the Gulf are highly contentious. Generally, and simply because it was the usage in the archival documents, Persian Gulf is the most frequently used nomenclature in this book.
2. Anthony Cordesman, *Bahrain, Oman, Qatar and the UAE: Challenges of Security* (Boulder, CO.; Oxford: Westview Press, 1997), p.128.
3. John Duke Anthony, 'Oman, The Gulf and the United States', In B.R. Pridham (Ed.), *Oman: Economic, Social and Strategic Developments* (London: Croom Helm, 1987), p.178.
4. Francis Hughes, 'Oil in Oman: A Short Historical Note', In B.R. Pridham (Ed.), *Oman: Economic, Social and Strategic Developments*, pp.174–175.
5. Ian Skeet, *Oman: Politics and Development* (Basingstoke: Palgrave Macmillan, 1992), p.34.
6. The works of Mao were in fact the more influential. See: Fred Halliday, *Arabia Without Sultans* (London: Saqi Books, 2002), pp.361–391.
7. David Reynolds, *Britannia Overruled: British Policy and World Power in the 20th Century* (London: Longman, 2000), p.225.
8. Paul Kennedy, *The Rise and Fall of the Great Powers: Economic Change and Military Conflict 1500–2000* (London: Fontana, 1989), p.xxii.
9. B.W.E. Alford, *Britain in the World Economy Since 1880* (London: Longman, 1996), p.71.
10. Alec Cairncross, *The British Economy Since 1945* (Oxford: Blackwell, 1995), p.297.
11. Roger Tooze, 'Economic Security and Order', In Michael Smith, Steve Smith and Brian White (Eds.), *British Foreign Policy: Tradition, Change and Transformation* (London: Unwin Hyman, 1988), p.137.
12. Ritchie Ovendale, *British Defence Policy Since 1945* (Manchester: MUP, 1994), pp.6–7.
13. *Ibid*, pp.13–14.
14. John Darwin, *The End of the British Empire* (Oxford: Blackwell, 1991), p.4.
15. *Ibid*, p.44.
16. *Ibid*, p.43.

17. P.J. Cain and A.G. Hopkins, *British Imperialism 1688–2000* (London: Longman, 2002), p.658.
18. Darwin, *The End of the British Empire*, p.53.
19. Darwin, *The End of the British Empire*, p.13.
20. *Ibid*, p.13.
21. *Ibid*, pp.34–35.
22. *Ibid*, p.57.
23. Darwin, *The End of the British Empire*, p.63.
24. *Ibid*, p.68.
25. *Ibid*, p.110.
26. John Darwin, *Britain and Decolonisation: The Retreat From Empire in the Post-War World* (Basingstoke: Macmillan, 1988), p.24.
27. Wm Roger Louis and Ronald Robinson, 'The Imperialism of Decolonisation' In Wm Roger Louis, *The Ends of British Imperialism* (London: I.B.Tauris, 2006), p.451.
28. *Ibid*, p.501.
29. *Ibid*, p.502.
30. See for example: Robin Neillands, *A Fighting Retreat: The British Empire 1947–1997* (London: Coronet Books, 1997).
31. Reynolds, *Britannia Overruled*, p.309.
32. Wm Roger Louis, *The British Empire in the Middle East 1945–1951* (Oxford: Clarendon, 1984), p.viii.
33. Elizabeth Monroe, *Britain's Moment in the Middle East* (London: Chatto & Windus, 1981), pp.201–202.
34. Simon C. Smith, *Britain's Revival and Fall in the Gulf* (London: RoutledgeCurzon, 2004), p.6.
35. Ritchie Ovendale, *Britain, The United States and the Transfer of Power in the Middle East, 1945–1962* (London: Leicester University Press, 1996), p.178.
36. Keith Kyle, *Suez* (London: Weidenfield & Nicholson, 1991), p.526. See also p.560.
37. Tore T. Petersen, *The Middle East between the Great Powers* (Basingstoke: Macmillan, 2000), p.75.
38. *Ibid*, p.74.
39. Gordon Martell, 'Decolonisation after Suez: Retreat or Rationalisation?', *Australian Journal of Politics and History*, Vol. 46, No. 3, (2000), pp.403–417.
40. *Ibid*, p.417.
41. Darwin, *The End of the British Empire*, p.71.
42. Wm Roger Louis, 'The British Military Withdrawal from the Gulf 1967–71', *The Journal of Imperial and Commonwealth History*, Vol. 31, No. 1, (2003), p.84.
43. Fred Halliday, 'Arabia Without Sultans Revisited', *MERIP Reports*, No. 204, (July/September 1997), [http://www.merip.org/mer/mer204/halliday.htm].
44. According to the U.S. Library of Congress the existing literature on Oman 'is scarce and varies in quality. Most works were published in the late 1970s or 1980s and concentrate on contrasting the periods before and after Qabus ibn Said came to power'. U.S. Library of Congress [http://lcweb2.loc.gov/frd/cs/omtoc.html].
45. J.B. Kelly, *Arabia, the Gulf and the West* (New York: Basic Books, 1980), p.143.
46. Fred Halliday, *Arabia Without Sultans* (London: Saqi, 2002), pp.361–392.

47. John Young, 'The Heath Government and Britain's Entry into the European Community' In Ball & Seldon (Eds.), *The Heath Government 1970–1974* (London: Longman, 1996), p.260.
48. Sanders, *Losing an Empire, Finding a Role*, p.158.
49. Edward Heath, *The Course of My Life* (London: Coronet Books, 1999), pp. 354–395.
50. For notable exceptions see: Walter C. Ladwig III., 'Supporting Allies in Counterinsurgency: Britain and the Dhofar Rebellion', *Small Wars & Insurgencies*, Vol. 19, No. 1, (2008), pp.62–88 and: Geraint Hughes, 'A "Model Campaign" Reappraised: The Counter-Insurgency War in Dhofar, Oman, 1965–1975', *Journal of Strategic Studies*, Vol. 32, No. 2, (2009), pp.271–305.
51. Robert Thompson, *Defeating Communist Insurgency: Experiences from Malaya and Vietnam* (London: Chatto & Windus, 1966).
52. Frank Kitson, *Low Intensity Operations: Subversion, Insurgency, Peacekeeping* (London: Faber & Faber, 1971) and *Gangs and Counter-Gangs* (London: Barrie & Rockliff, 1960).
53. See: *The Journal of Statebuilding and Intervention* [http://www.tandf.co.uk/journals/risb].
54. Charles Tilley, 'Western-State Making and Theories of Political Transformation', In Charles Tilley (Ed.), *The Formation of National States in Western Europe* (Princeton, NJ.: Princeton University Press, 1975), p.70.
55. Max Weber, The Theory of Social and Economic Organization (New York: Free Press, 1947). For a good article examining the state in the Middle East see: Lisa Anderson, 'The State in the Middle East and North Africa', *Comparative Politics*, Vol. 20, No. 1, (1987), pp.1–18.
56. T.E. Lawrence, 'Twenty Seven Articles' *The Arab Bulletin*, 20 August 1917.
57. Joseph Frankel, *International Relations in a Changing World* (Oxford: OUP, 1988), p.93.
58. Fred Sondermann, 'The Concept of the National Interest', *Orbis*, (Spring 1977), p.121.
59. Scott Burchill, *The National Interest in International Relations Theory* (Basingstoke: Palgrave Macmillan, 2005), p.3.
60. Jutta Weldes, Quoted In: Scott Burchill, *The National Interest in International Relations Theory*, p.3.
61. Sondermann, 'The Concept of the National Interest', p.126.
62. Frankel, *International Relations in a Changing World*, p.94.
63. Simon Jenkins and Anne Sloman, *With Respect Ambassador: An Inquiry into the Foreign Office* (London: British Broadcasting Corporation, 1985), p.91.
64. There is a vast literature on Realism in all its forms but one of the best single volume introductions is: Jack Donnelly, *Realism and International Relations* (Cambridge, CUP, 2000).
65. K.J Holsti, *International Politics: A Framework for Analysis*, 7th Edition (Englewood Cliffs, NJ.: Prentice-Hall International, 1995), p.84.
66. Clive Jones, *Britain and the Yemen Civil War* (Brighton: Sussex Academic Press, 2004), p.18.
67. Jenkins and Sloman, *With Respect Ambassador*, p.110.

Chapter 1
The Context of Oman's Importance to Britain

1. Brian White, 'East-West Relations', In Michael Smith, Steve Smith and Brian White (Eds.), *British Foreign Policy: Tradition, Change and Transformation* (London: Unwin Hyman, 1988), pp.159–160.
2. Joseph S. Nye (Jr.), *Soft Power: The Means to Success in World Politics* (New York: Public Affairs Press, 2004).
3. K.J. Holsti, *International Politics: A Framework for Analysis*, 7th Edition (Englewood Cliffs NJ.: Prentice-Hall International, 1995), p.107.
4. Brian White, 'British Foreign Policy', In Roy Macridis (Ed.), *Foreign Policy in World Politics* (London: Prentice Hall International, 1992), p.8.
5. White, 'British Foreign Policy', In Roy Macridis (Ed.), *Foreign Policy in World Politics*, p.9.
6. Ritchie Ovendale, *Anglo-American Relations in the Twentieth Century* (Basingstoke: Palgrave, 1998), p.130.
7. White, 'British Foreign Policy', In Roy Macridis (Ed.), *Foreign Policy in World Politics*, p.18.
8. *Ibid*, p.19.
9. Ovendale, *Anglo-American Relations in the Twentieth Century*, p.133.
10. White, 'British Foreign Policy', In Roy Macridis (Ed.), *Foreign Policy in World Politics*, p.17.
11. *Ibid*, p.17.
12. Donald Maclean, *British Foreign Policy Since Suez 1956–1968* (London: Hodder And Stoughton, 1970), p.94.
13. White, 'British Foreign Policy', In Roy Macridis (Ed.), *Foreign Policy in World Politics* p.21.
14. White, 'British Foreign Policy', In Roy Macridis (Ed.), *Foreign Policy in World Politics*, p.20.
15. Cain and Hopkins, *British Imperialism: Crisis and Deconstruction, 1914–1990*, p.281.
16. David Allen, 'Western Europe', In Michael Smith, Steve Smith and Brian White (Eds.), *British Foreign Policy: Tradition, Change and Transformation*, p.170.
17. White, 'British Foreign Policy', In Roy Macridis (Ed.), *Foreign Policy in World Politics*, p.20.
18. As Verrier states 'Unless a member of the permanent government was an extreme radical he would take it for granted that Russia menaced the Empire at every point', Anthony Verrier, *Through The Looking Glass: British Foreign Policy in the Age of Illusions* (London: Jonathan Cape, 1983), p.174.
19. See: Ian F.W. Beckett and John Pimlott (Eds.), *Armed Forces and Modern Counter-Insurgency* (New York: St. Martins Press, 1985).
20. Holsti, *International Politics: A Framework for Analysis*, 7th Edition, p.85.
21. For an excellent insight into the problems of colonial control faced by Britain and France in the region and their complex responses see: Martin Thomas, *Empires of Intelligence: Security Services and Colonial Disorder after 1914* (Berkeley, CA.: University of California Press, 2007).
22. Glenn Balfour-Paul, *The End of Empire in the Middle East* (Cambridge: CUP, 1991), p.8.

23. Ovendale, *Britain, The United States and the Transfer of Power in the Middle East 1945–1962*, p.2.
24. *Ibid*, p.1.
25. Wm Roger-Louis, *The British Empire in the Middle East 1945–1951* (Oxford: Clarendon Press, 1984), p.238.
26. *Ibid*, pp.334–335.
27. Ovendale, *Britain, The United States and the Transfer of Power in the Middle East 1945–1962*, p.15.
28. For American Anti-Colonialism See: Wm Roger Louis, 'American Anti-Colonialism, Suez, and the Special Relationship' In *Ends of British Imperialism* (London: I.B.Tauris, 2006), pp.589–608.
29. Ovendale, *Anglo-American Relations in the Twentieth Century* (Basinstoke: Palgrave, 1998), p.45
30. Lloyd C. Gardner and Warren F. Kimball, 'The United States Democratic Diplomacy', In David Reynolds *et al.* (Eds.), *Allies at War: The Soviet, American and British Experience 1939–1945* (Basingstoke: Macmillan, 1994), p.399.
31. Ovendale, *Britain, The United States and the Transfer of Power in the Middle East 1945–1962*, p.3.
32. *Ibid*, p.15.
33. For more on Allied planning in the Middle East see, Michael J. Cohen, *Fighting World War Three from the Middle East: Allied Contingency Plans 1945–54* (London: Cass, 1997).
34. See: James Cable, *Intervention at Abadan: Plan Buccaneer* (Basingstoke: Palgrave Macmillan, 1991).
35. J.H Bamberg, *The History of the British Petroleum Company: Volume 2* (Cambridge: CUP, 1994), p.418.
36. *Ibid*, p.492.
37. For more on the Iranian Crisis see: Christopher Woodhouse, *Something Ventured* (St Albans: Granada, 1982) and Stephen Kinzer, *All The Shah's Men: An American Coup and the Roots of Middle East Terror* (Hoboken, NJ.: John Wiley, 2004).
38. FO 371/90144, No. 365, Stevenson To Morrison, 16 October 1951.
39. J.H. Hail, *Britain's Foreign Policy in Egypt and Sudan 1947–1956* (Reading: Ithaca Press, 1996), p.75.
40. Ovendale, *Britain, The United States and the Transfer of Power in the Middle East 1945–1962*, p.109.
41. Zach Levey, *Israel and the Western Powers 1952–1960* (Chapel Hill, NC.: University of North Carolina Press, 1997), p.16.
42. Ovendale, *Britain, The United States and the Transfer of Power in the Middle East 1945–1962*, p.135.
43. Wm Roger Louis, 'The Dissolution of the British Empire in the Era of Vietnam' In *Ends of British Imperialism*, p.585.
44. Keith Kyle, *Suez* (London: Weidenfield & Nicholson, 1991), p.224 and pp.243–4.
45. *Ibid*, p.124.
46. Zachary Karabell, *Parting the Desert: The Creation of the Suez Canal* (London: John Murray, 2003), pp.262–263.

47. Kyle, *Suez*, p.314.
48. Levey, *Israel and the Western Powers 1952–1960*, pp.35–54.
49. Kyle, *Suez*, pp.314–331.
50. Kyle, *Suez*, p.500.
51. Wm Roger Louis, 'The Crisis of 1958' In *Ends of British Imperialism*, pp.792–793.
52. *Ibid*, pp.796–804.
53. See: Malcolm Hooper Kerr, *The Arab Cold War: Gamel 'Abd Al-Nasir and His Rivals, 1958–70* (Oxford: OUP, 1972).
54. Parker T. Hart, *Saudi Arabia and the United States: Birth of a Security Partnership* (Bloomington, Ind.: Indiana University Press, 1998), p.150.
55. See: Salim Yaqub, *Containing Arab Nationalism: The Eisenhower Doctrine and the Middle East* (Chapel Hill, NC.: University of North Carolina Press, 2004).
56. Clive Jones, *Britain and the Yemen Civil War* (Brighton: SAP, 2004), p.9.
57. This was later in its revised version codenamed 'Bellringer'. Anthony Verrier, *Through the Looking Glass: British Foreign Policy in the Age of Illusions*, p.188.
58. Tore T. Petersen, *The Decline of the Anglo-American Middle East 1961–1969* (Brighton: Sussex Academic Press, 2006), pp.28–29.
59. Laura James, *Nasser at War: Arab Images of the Enemy* (Basingstoke: Palgrave Macmillan, 2006), pp.69–87.
60. Jones, *Britain and the Yemen Civil War*, p.30.
61. *Ibid*, p.171.
62. David Smiley, *Arabian Assignment* (London: Leo Cooper, 1975), p.113.
63. *Ibid*, p.113.
64. Jonathan Walker, *Aden Insurgency – The Savage War in South Arabia 1962–67* (Staplehurst: Spellmount, 2005), pp.75–133.
65. Jones, *Britain and the Yemen Civil War*, p.9.
66. Balfour-Paul, *The End of Empire in the Middle East*, p.78.
67. Walker, *Aden Insurgency – The Savage War in South Arabia 1962–67*, p.288.
68. Jones, *Britain and the Yemen Civil War*, p.190.
69. *Ibid*, p.193.
70. J.B Kelly, *Arabia, the Gulf and the West*, p.46.
71. Tore T. Petersen, *The Decline of the Anglo-American Middle East 1961–1969*, p.87.
72. Michael Carver, *War Since 1945* (London: Weidenfield & Nicholson, 1980), p.81.
73. Kelly, *Arabia, the Gulf and the West*, p.42.
74. *Ibid*, p.47.
75. Balfour-Paul, *The End of Empire in the Middle East*, p.124.
76. Kelly, *Arabia, the Gulf and the West*, p.47.
77. *Ibid*, p.49.
78. Balfour-Paul, *The End of Empire in the Middle East*, p.124.
79. Saki Dockrill, *Britain's Retreat from East of Suez: The Choice between Europe and the World* (Basingstoke: Palgrave Macmillan, 2002), p.217.
80. *Ibid*, p.218.
81. The best telling of the story of Britain's attempts to form the UAE can be found in Simon C. Smith, *Britian's Revival and Fall in the Gulf: Kuwait, Bahrain, Qatar and the Trucial States* (London: RoutledgeCurzon, 2004).
82. Ira M. Lapidus, *A History of Islamic Societies* (Cambridge: CUP, 2002), p.576.

83. For a full account of the Ibahdis and the Imamate tradition, see: Hussein Ghubash, *Oman – The Islamic Democratic Tradition* (Abingdon: Routledge, 2006) and J.C. Wilkinson, *The Imamate Tradition of Oman* (Cambridge: CUP, 1987).
84. J.E. Peterson, *Oman in the Twentieth Century*, p.20.
85. Uzi Rabi, *The Emergence of States in a Tribal Society: Oman under Sa'id Bin Taymur* (Brighton: Sussex Academic Press, 2006), p.26.
86. *Ibid*, p.27.
87. J.E. Peterson, *Oman in the Twentieth Century*, p.27.
88. For more on this period see: M. Reda Bhacker, *Trade and Empire in Muscat and Zanzibar – The Roots of British Domination* (Abingdon: Routledge, 1992).
89. Peterson, *Oman in the Twentieth Century*, p.27.
90. For the text of the Treaty see: Ian Skeet, *Muscat and Oman: The End of an Era*, (London: Faber, 1985), pp.213–215.
91. Bhacker, *Trade and Empire In Muscat and Zanzibar*, p.31.
92. *Ibid*, p.35.
93. Peterson, *Oman in the Twentieth Century*, p.27.
94. Bhacker, *Trade and Empire in Muscat and Zanzibar*, p.180.
95. Skeet, *Muscat and Oman: The End of an Era*, p.48.
96. Peterson, *Oman in the Twentieth Century*, p.28.
97. Bhacker, *Trade and Empire in Muscat and Zanzibar*, p.189.
98. Peterson, *Oman in the Twentieth Century*, p.30.
99. For the full text of the Treaty see: Rabi, *The Emergence of States in a Tribal Society: Oman under Sa'id Bin Taymur*, p.31.
100. Skeet, *Muscat & Oman: The End of an Era*, p.99.
101. Peterson, *Oman in the Twentieth Century*, p.31.
102. Uzi Rabi, *Oman under Sa'id bin Taymur, 1932–1970: The Emergence of States in a Tribal Society*, Unpublished Version of Manuscript, 2005, p.56.
103. Kelly, *Arabia, the Gulf and the West*, p.71.
104. *Ibid*, p.71.
105. *Ibid*, p.71.
106. This was the country's formal name and encapsulated the division between interior and coast. Soon after coming to power Qaboos abolished this antiquated name and as if to sum up the new, more unified, era gave his country the official name of the Sultanate of Oman.
107. Halliday, *Arabia Without Sultans*, p.281.
108. Ovendale, *Britain, the United States, and the Transfer of Power in the Middle East, 1945–1962*, p.127.
109. Balfour-Paul, *The End of Empire in the Middle East*, p.114.
110. It is clear that the Buraimi problem played a role in the revival of the Imamate problem as did the exploration for oil which was proceeding in the interior of Oman. The Sultan sought to establish his sovereignty more clearly in these domains and the Saudis did their best to undermine him. It is not surprising that this situation, combined with a new Imam, proved combustible. See Rabi, *The Emergence of States in a Tribal Society: Oman under Sa'id Bin Taymur*, pp.71–98.
111. Rabi, *The Emergence of States in a Tribal Society: Oman under Sa'id Bin Taymur*, p.72.
112. John C. Wilkinson, *The Imamate Tradition of Oman* (Cambridge: CUP, 1987), p.315

113. Halliday, *Arabia Without Sultans*, p.282.
114. Ovendale, *Britain, the United States, and the Transfer of Power in the Middle East, 1945–1962*, p.128.
115. This journey is evocatively described in Jan Morris, *Sultan in Oman* (London: Sickle Moon Books, 2002).
116. Skeet, *Oman Before 1970: The End of an Era*, p.142.
117. Miriam Joyce-Haron, 'Britain and the Sultan of Muscat & Oman and Dependencies, 1958–1959', *Diplomacy & Statecraft*, Vol. 4, No. 1, (1993), p.90.
118. Rabi, *Oman under Sa'id bin Taymur, 1932–1970*, p.81.
119. Joyce-Haron, 'Britain and the Sultan of Muscat & Oman and Dependencies, 1958–1959', p.91.
120. Smiley, *Arabian Assignment*, p.50.
121. Ovendale, *Britain, The United States, and the Transfer of Power in the Middle East, 1945–1962*, p.143.
122. Peterson, *Oman's Insurgencies: The Sultanate's Struggle for Supremacy* (London: Saqi, 2007), p.86. This book gives the best and most complete account of the campaign.
123. Rabi, *Oman under Sa'id bin Taymur, 1932–1970*, p.47.
124. Joyce-Haron, 'Britain and the Sultan of Muscat & Oman and Dependencies, 1958–1959', p.100.
125. Rabi, *Oman under Sa'id bin Taymur, 1932–1970*, p.98.
126. *Ibid*, p.106.
127. *Ibid*, p.109.
128. Halliday, *Arabia Without Sultans*, p.276.
129. Rabi, *Oman under Sa'id bin Taymur, 1932–1970*, p.111.
130. *Ibid*, p.117.
131. *Ibid*, p.118.
132. Tore Petersen, *The Middle East between the Great Powers*, p.74.

Chapter 2
Events and Policy Surrounding Britain's Increasing Involvement in Oman

1. J.E. Peterson, *Defending Arabia* (London: Croom Helm, 1986), p.99.
2. *Ibid*, p.100.
3. Halliday, *Arabia Without Sultans*, pp.320–321.
4. *Ibid*, p.321.
5. See for example: Daniel Yergin, *The Prize: The Epic Quest for Oil, Money and Power* (London: Simon & Schuster, 1991).
6. G.R. Berridge, *Diplomacy: Theory and Practice* (Basingstoke: Palgrave Macmillan, 2002), p.77.
7. British and Foreign State Papers 1957–58, H.M.S.O., 1966.
8. Miriam Joyce, *Ruling Shaikhs & Her Majesty's Government, 1960–1969* (London: Frank Cass, 2003), p.94.
9. *Ibid*, p.94.
10. Halliday, *Arabia Without Sultans*, p.284.

11. FO 371/16285, Letter, Luce To Walmsley, 16 May 1962, Quoted In Joyce, *Ruling Shaikhs*, p.96.
12. A process which was progressing successfully elsewhere in the Gulf States. See for example: Rosemarie Said Zahlan, *The Making of the Modern Gulf States* (Reading: Ithaca Press, 1998), Ian R. Netton, (Ed.), *Arabia and the Gulf from Traditional Society to Modern States* (Beckenham: Croom Helm, 1986), Miriam Joyce, *Kuwait, 1945–96: An Anglo-American Perspective* (London: Frank Cass, 1998), Donald Hawley, *The Emirates – Witness to a Metamorphosis* (Norwich: Michael Russell, 2007) and Simon C. Smith, *Kuwait, 1950–1965: Britain, The Al-Sabah and Oil* (Oxford: OUP, 1999).
13. John Townsend, *Oman: The Making of the Modern State* (London: Croom Helm, 1977), p.66.
14. For more detail on these difficulties see: Sir Hugh Boustead, *The Wind of Morning: An Autobiography* (Fresno, CA.: Linden Publishing, 2002).
15. Townsend, *Oman: The Making of the Modern State*, p.66.
16. *Ibid*, p.65.
17. *Ibid*, pp.66–67.
18. Ian Skeet, *Oman Before 1970: The End of an Era*, p.163.
19. David Smiley, *Arabian Assignment*, p.41.
20. Townsend, *Oman: The Making of the Modern State*, p.68.
21. For good surveys of the population and geography of Dhofar see in particular: Ian Skeet, *Oman Before 1970* (London: Faber & Faber, 1985), Fred Halliday, *Arabia Without Sultans* (London: Saqi Books, 2001), J.E. Peterson, *Oman in the Twentieth Century* (London: Croom Helm, 1978), Miranda Morris, 'Dhofar What Made It Different?' In B.R. Pridham (Ed.), *Oman: Economic, Social and Strategic Developments* (London: Croom Helm, 1987) and J.E. Peterson, 'Oman's Diverse Society: Southern Oman', *Middle East Journal*, Vol. 58, No. 2, (2004), pp.254–269.
22. Dhofar is of course also known as the Land of Frankincense, for more information on the Frankincense trade and its impact on Dhofar and beyond see: Abdul Qadar Al-Ghassany, *Dhofar: The Land of Frankincense*, 2nd Edition, Pamphlet (2008).
23. See: Jones, *Britain and the Yemen Civil War*.
24. J.E. Peterson, *Oman's Insurgencies: The Sultante's Struggle for Supremacy* (London: Saqi Books, 2007), p.189.
25. D.L. Price, 'Oman: Insurgency and Development', *Conflict Studies*, No. 53, January 1975, p.4.
26. Joyce, *Ruling Shaikhs*, p.97.
27. DEFE 13/779, Dhofar Campaign, Summary of Events Period One.
28. General Assembly Resolution 2073 (XX), [www.un.org/documents/ga/res/20/ares20.htm].
29. General Assembly Resolution 2238 (XXI), [www.un.org/documents/ga/res/21/ares21.htm].
30. FCO 8/1075, United Nations General Assembly Resolution 2302 (XXII).
31. FCO 8/1075, Telegram, FCO To UKMisNY, 14 December 1968.
32. FCO 8/1075, Telegram, Lane (UKMisNY) To Papadopoulos (UN Dept FCO), 11 December 1968.
33. *Ibid*.

34. FCO 8/1417, Muscat & Oman Annual Review 1969.
35. For examples of these exchanges see: FCO 8/1075 and FCO 8/1076.
36. DEFE 13/779, Dhofar Campaign, Summary of Events Period One.
37. DEFE 13/779, Dhofar Campaign, Summary of Events Period Two (May 1965 – December 1967).
38. The best readily accessible account of this incident can be found in J.E. Peterson, 'Oman: The 1966 Assassination Attempt on Sultan Sa'id b. Taymur', *Arabian Peninsula Background Note*, No. APBN-004, [www.jepeterson.net], August 2004.
39. Joyce, *Ruling Shaikhs & Her Majesty's Government, 1960–1969*, p.99.
40. *Ibid*, p.99.
41. Townsend, *Oman: The Making of a Modern State*, pp.11–12.
42. Halliday, *Arabia Without Sultans*, pp.274–275.
43. Rabi, *Oman under Sa'id bin Taymur, 1932–1970*, p.206.
44. *Ibid*, p.112.
45. Dale F. Eickelman and M.G. Dennison, 'Arabizing the Omani Intelligence Services: Clash of Cultures?', *International Journal of Intelligence and Counterintelligence*, Vol. 7, No. 1, (1994), pp.8–9.
46. Francis Owtram, *A Modern History of Oman* (London: I.B.Tauris, 2004), pp.104–105.
47. Owtram, *A Modern History of Oman*, p.105.
48. DEFE 13/779, Dhofar Campaign, Summary of Events Period One.
49. See: FO 1016/800, Consequences If Sultan of Muscat And Oman Dies Suddenly, 1968.
50. For information on Qaboos' years in Britain and Salalah see for example: John Beasant and Christopher Ling, *Sultan in Arabia: A Private Life* (Edinburgh: Mainstream Publishing, 2004) and John Townsend, *Oman: The Making of the Modern State*.
51. FCO 8/576, Minute, 14 February 1968.
52. Joyce, *Ruling Shaikhs*, p.100.
53. DEFE 13/779, Dhofar Campaign, Summary of Events Period Two.
54. Halliday, *Arabia Without Sultans*, p.318.
55. *Ibid*, p.320.
56. Joyce, *Ruling Shaikhs*, p.101.
57. Halliday, *Arabia Without Sultans*, p.320.
58. DEFE 13/779, Dhofar Campaign, Summary of Events Period Two.
59. See for example: Simon C. Smith, *Britain's Revival and Fall in the Gulf* (London: RoutledgeCurzon, 2005).
60. Joyce, *Ruling Shaikhs*, p.101.
61. DEFE 13/779, Dhofar Campaign, Summary of Events Period Two.
62. Francis Hughes, 'Oil in Oman', In B.R. Pridham (Ed.), *Oman: Economic, Social and Strategic Developments* (London: Croom Helm, 1987), pp.173–175.
63. Townsend, *Oman*, p.67.
64. DEFE 13/779, Dhofar Campaign, Summary of Events Period Two.
65. J.B. Kelly, *Arabia, the Gulf and the West*, p.47.
66. FCO 8/31, Report, G. Roberts To Foreign Secretary G. Brown, 17 November 1967.

67. *Ibid.*
68. *Ibid.*
69. FCO 8/31, Report, G. Roberts To Foreign Secretary G. Brown, 17 November 1967.
70. *Ibid.*
71. See: Kelly, *Arabia, the Gulf and the West* for a scathing indictment of the nature of the British withdrawal from the FSA.
72. Halliday, *Arabia Without Sultans*, p.320.
73. See: Saki Dockrill, *Britain's Retreat from East of Suez* (Basingstoke: Palgrave Macmillan, 2002).
74. Balfour-Paul, *The End of Empire in the Middle East*, p.124.
75. FCO 8/33, Report, S. Crawford (PRPG) To Foreign Secretary G. Brown, 27 January 1968.
76. FCO 8/33, Report, S. Crawford (PRPG) To Foreign Secretary G. Brown, 27 January 1968.
77. *Ibid.*
78. FCO 49/10, Report, 'Long-term Policy In The Persian Gulf', 28 September 1967.
79. The JIC were also beginning to become concerned about the potential impact of the withdrawal upon the security of Britain's oil supplies and other interests in the region. See: POWE 63/449 (JIC (68) 24), JIC Report On The Implications For Oil Supplies And British Oil Interests In The Middle East), 9 September 1968.
80. FCO 49/53, FO Planning Staff Background Paper 'Withdrawal From The Persian Gulf', 29 April 1968.
81. FO 371/174489, Dispatch, Sir William Luce (PRPG) To Foreign Secretary Gordon Walker, 11 November 1964.
82. FCO 8/576, Letter, D.J. McCarthy To M.S. Weir, 2 October 1968.
83. Elizabeth Monroe, *Britain's Moment in the Middle East 1914–1971*, p.216.
84. FCO 8/574, Letter, S. Crawford To M.S. Weir, 14 February 1968.
85. Joyce, *Ruling Shaikhs*, pp.102–104.
86. For the full text of this document see: Townsend, *Oman: The Making of the Modern State*, pp.192–198.
87. Townsend, *Oman: The Making of the Modern State*, p.194.
88. *Ibid*, p.195.
89. Townsend, *Oman: The Making of the Modern State*, pp.67–68.
90. Joyce, *Ruling Shaikhs*, p.103.
91. Halliday, *Arabia Without Sultans*, p.366.
92. Halliday, *Arabia Without Sultans*, p.366.
93. *Ibid*, p.367.
94. Halliday, *Arabia Without* Sultans, p.331.
95. *Ibid*, p.367.
96. FCO 8/1418, Doc. 21, Telegram No. 86, 25 February 1970.
97. FCO 1016/790, Sultanate Balance Sheet, First Quarter 1969, 14 April 1969.
98. FCO 8/1075, Doc. 41, Handwritten Note, J.L. Blackley To J. Edes, 7 October 1968.
99. FCO 1016/798, D.C. Carden (Muscat) To O'Bryen Tear (Bahrain), 18 April 1970.
100. FCO 8/1418/21, Telegram No. 86, 25 February 1970.
101. FCO 1016/798, The Sultan of Muscat – Review or Remonstrance, 5 March 1970.

102. FCO 1016/798, Letter And Report – Policy Towards The Sultanate of Muscat & Oman, A.A. Acland (FCO) To S. Crawford (Bahrain) & D.G. Crawford (Muscat), 18 February 1970.
103. FCO 8/1436, Telegram No. 88, FCO To Bahrain & Muscat, 12 March 1970.
104. This was vital given the need for force rotation, rest and recovery and to maintain two battalions in northern Oman.
105. FCO 1016/798, Telegram No. 76, 10 March 1970. A similar statement is also made in FCO 1016/798, Letter – Review of Policy – Dhofar, D.G. Crawford (Muscat) To S. Crawford (Bahrain), 30 March 1970.
106. FCO 1016/798, Doc. 24, 20 March 1970.
107. FCO 1016/798, Telegram No. 58, Bahrain To FCO, 24 February 1970.
108. FCO 1016/798, Telegram No. 56, Bahrain To FCO, 23 February 1970.
109. FCO 8/1425, Telegram No. 58, Bahrain To FCO, 24 February 1970.
110. FCO 8/1436, Doc. 53, Letter, S. Crawford (Bahrain) To A.A. Acland (FCO), 3 March 1970.
111. FCO 8/1436, Doc. 59, Letter, S. Crawford (Bahrain) To A.A. Acland (FCO), 24 March 1970.
112. The first mention of the SAS in the archives comes towards the end of 1969 and by February 1970 planning and discussion of their deployment is quite extensive. In a CoS report examinig their potential deployment the overall British strategy for the counterinsurgency campaign is made clear: 'If the peace is to be won it will be necessary to win over the hostile tribes of the jebel as well. All this would require the economic development of the area and eventually a political accommodation with its inhabitants. The latter might be approached initially through a "hearts and minds" campaign for which at present the Sultan shows little enthusiasm, particularly if it were to entail military personnel controlling civil activities'. Clearly British policy envisaged a key but limited role for the SAS within a wider framework for the counterinsurgency campaign grounded in traditional British ways of conducting such a campaign. FCO 46/609, Annex To CoS 1166/6/3/70, 'The Employment of An SAS Squadron In Dhofar', 26 February 1970.
113. FCO 8/1436, Doc. 59, Letter, S. Crawford (Bahrain) To A.A. Acland (FCO), 24 March 1970.
114. FCO 8/1437, Doc. 72, An Outline Plan To Restore The Situation In Dhofar Using Special Air Service Regiment Troops, 7 April 1970, p.2.
115. FCO 8/1437, Doc. 72, An Outline Plan To Restore The Situation In Dhofar Using Special Air Service Regiment Troops, 7 April 1970.
116. These included: Robert Thompson, *Defeating Communist Insurgency: Experiences from Malaya and Vietnam* (London: Chatto & Windus, 1966), Julian Paget, *Counter Insurgency Campaigning* (London: Faber & Faber, 1967) and Frank Kitson, *Low Intensity Operations: Subversion, Insurgency, Peacekeeping* (London: Faber & Faber, 1971).
117. It is worth noting that of the four intelligence officers in Oman there was only one intelligence officer for the whole of Dhofar at this point. FCO 46/609, Air Vice Marshall Philpott, 'Confidential Annex To CoS 8th Meeting/70', 17 March 1970, Point 10.
118. FCO 46/609, CoS Defence Operational Planning Staff, July 1970.

119. FO 1016/798, G.G. Arthur (PRPG) To S. Crawford (FCO), 7 April 1970.
120. Reynolds, *Britannia Overruled*, p.214.
121. Interview, Lord Hurd, House of Lords, 5 February 2008.
122. FCO 8/979, Doc. 60, Letter, D.J. McCarthy To Sir S. Crawford, 8 May 1969.
123. *Ibid.*
124. FCO 8/979, Doc. 70, D.J. McCarthy (Head, Arabian Department), June 1970.
125. Interview, Lord Hurd, House of Lords, 5 February 2008.
126. Alec Douglas-Home, Statement To Parliament, 1 March 1971.
127. Interview, Lord Hurd, House of Lords, 5 February 2008.
128. Ray Kane, Mail on Sunday, 2 July 2002.
129. FCO 46/609, J.J. Bannerman To Edes (Arabian Depratment), 'H.H. Sayyid Said bin Taimur', 29 July 1970.
130. Townsend, *Oman: The Making of the Modern State*, pp.74–75.
131. FCO 8/1425, Telegram No. 46, 26 July 1970. See also the BBC Radio 4 Document programme broadcast 23 November 2009 in which I was initially asked to participate.
132. It seems unlikely that they knew more than a few months in advance as during a CoS meeting in March General Harrington had said that 'in his view the Sultan's son was unlikely to stage a Palace coup', FCO 46/609, 'Confidential Annex To CoS 8th Meeting/70', 17 March 1970, Point 9.
133. FCO 46/609, A.A. Acland 'Sultanate of Muscat and Oman: Possibility of a Coup'.
134. FCO 46/609, Telegram No. 340 Bahrain To London, 13 July 1970.
135. FCO 46/609, J.J. Bannerman To Edes (Arabian Depratment), 'H.H. Sayyid Said bin Taimur', 29 July 1970.
136. FCO 46/609, P.J. Bayne (CoS Committee) To CoS, referring to Sir S. Crawford (PRPG) Bahrain Dispatch 3/7, 12 May 1970, On 4 June 1970. Although by 4 July there are references to 'an evacuation plan for Muscat and Oman (military-assisted) which covers American citizens in case U.S. authorities were to request it; and the Ministry of Defence have a plan of their own for the evacuation of the RAF from Salalah if necessary...[we do] not expect such action will be necessary' FCO 46/609, Doc. 5, R.M. Tesh (Defence Department, FCO) To Sir E. Peck (FCO), 2 July 1970.
137. Glenn Balfour-Paul, *Bagpipes in Babylon: A Lifetime in the Arab World and Beyond* (London: I.B.Tauris, 2006), pp.190–201.
138. Interview, Peter Hinchcliffe, Former Ambassador To Jordan and FCO Official in the UAE, Le Meridien Hotel, Amman, 12 June 2006.
139. See for example: Elizabeth Monroe, *Britain's Moment in the Middle East 1914–1971*, 2nd Ed. (Oxford: OUP, 1981).

Chapter 3
The Conservative Ascendancy: Getting the Troops In

1. Kelly, *Arabia, the Gulf and the West*, pp.78–79.
2. CAB 148/101, Foreign Policy Issues, 29 June 1970.

NOTES TO PAGES 80–86   243

3. Luce described the decision 'as morally wrong, unwise and unnecessary'. Kelly, *Arabia, the Gulf and the West*, p.81.
4. *Ibid*, p.81.
5. *Ibid*, p.82.
6. See: Miriam Joyce, *Kuwait, 1945–96: An Anglo-American Perspective* (London: Frank Cass, 1998) and Jill Crystal, *Oil and Politics in the Gulf: Rulers and Merchants in Kuwait and Qatar* (Cambridge: CUP, 1995).
7. Douglas Hurd, *Memoirs* (London: Abacus, 2003), p.200.
8. Kelly, *Arabia, the Gulf and the West*, p.83.
9. CAB 148/101, Presentation of Defence Policy, 14 October 1970, pp.3–4.
10. *Ibid*, p.4.
11. Skeet, *Oman: Politics and Development*, p.38.
12. Kelly, *Arabia, the Gulf and the West*, p.141.
13. Skeet, *Oman: Politics and Development*, p.38.
14. Kelly, *Arabia, the Gulf and the West*, p.141.
15. FCO 1016/791, Annual Review 1969, 30 December 1969, p.4.
16. FCO 8/1437, Doc. 72, An Outline Plan To Restore The Situation In Dhofar Using Special Air Service Regiment Troops, 7 April 1970.
17. DEFE 25/186, Folio No. 21, Visit of the Military Secretary to the Sultan of Muscat and Oman, 'Flag E', 12 October 1970.
18. DEFE 25/186, Folio No. 21, Visit of the Military Secretary to the Sultan of Muscat and Oman, 'Flag E', 12 October 1970.
19. Given the fact that a role for the SAS in training the SAF in northern Oman and potential in the 'Hearts and Minds' role in Dhofar had been considered extensively from late 1969 plans for the training role had already been approved and were awaiting the formal Sultanate request in July 1970. FCO 46/609, CoS Defence operational Planning Staff, 'The Situation in Muscat and Oman', July 1970.
20. DEFE 25/186, Folio No. 1, M.S. Weir To FCO, 5 August 1970.
21. DEFE 25/186, Folio No. 4(i), Woolford To Birkett, 6 August 1970.
22. DEFE 25/186, Folio No. 5, VCGS To CLFG, 7 August 1970.
23. *Ibid*.
24. DEFE 25/186, Folio No. 7(i), Minute From VCGS, 13 August 1970.
25. DEFE 25/186, Note, Baker (MoD) To Hall (FCO), 17 August 1970.
26. DEFE 25/186, Folio No. 8(i), Minute From D.A.J. West To APS of S of S, 24 August 1970.
27. DEFE 25/186, Note, Douglas-Home To Secretary of State for Defence, SAS Assistance To The Sultanate of Oman, 4 September 1970.
28. DEFE 25/186, Folio No. 4, Telegram No. 373, Douglas-Home To Bahrain Residency, 7 August 1970.
29. DEFE 25/186, Note, C.W. Roberts (Downing Street) To J.A.N. Graham (FCO), 7 September 1970.
30. DEFE 25/186, Minute, Lord Balniel (MoD) To S of S (MoD), 11 September 1970.
31. FCO 8/979, Letter, D.J. McCarthy To Sir S. Crawford, 8 May 1969.
32. John Ramsden, 'The Prime Minister and the Making of Policy', In Ball and Seldon (Eds.), *The Heath Government 1970–74* (Harlow: Addison Wesley Longman, 1996), p.21.

33. J.E. Peterson, *Oman in the Twentieth Century*, pp.27–28.
34. T 317/1859, Doc. 18, Letter, Lucas (Treasury) To Gent (FCO), 11 July 1966.
35. T 317/1859, Doc. 20, Letter, Gent (FCO) To Lucas (Treasury), 12 August 1966.
36. T 317/1859, Doc. 25, Letter, Wall (Gulf) To Gent (FCO), 24 November 1967.
37. T 317/1859, Doc. 40, Letter, Gordon (Treasury) To McGregor (FCO), 12 August 1970.
38. T 317/1859, Doc. 41, Letter, McGregor (FCO) To Gordon (Treasury), 24 August 1970.
39. T 317/1859, Doc. 40, Letter, Gordon (Treasury) To McGregor (FCO), 12 August 1970.
40. FO 1016/798, Letter, G.G. Arthur To S. Crawford, 7 April 1970.
41. FCO 8/1431, Telegram No. 127, S. Crawford To FCO, 9 August 1970.
42. FCO 8/1431, Letter, D.G. Crawford To A.A. Acland, 3 August 1970.
43. FCO 8/1431, Telegram No. 146, D.G. Crawford To Arabian Department, 18 August 1970.
44. FCO 8/1431, Telegram No. 149, D.G. Crawford To S. Crawford, 20 August 1970.
45. The Tariq administration's formation is examined in the following chapter.
46. FCO 8/1431, Telegram No. 414, S. Crawford To J.M. Edes, 19 August 1970.
47. FCO 8/1431, Telegram No. 127, Douglas-Home To D.G. Crawford, 21 August 1970.
48. FCO 8/1431, Telegram No. 420, M.S. Weir To FCO, 21 August 1970.
49. FCO 8/1431, Letter, G.G. Arthur To A.A. Acland, 8 December 1970.
50. DEFE 25/186, Folio No. 22(i), JIC Weekly Intelligence Report No 43/70, 2 November 1970.
51. DEFE 25/186, Folio No. 22(i), JIC Weekly Intelligence Report No 43/70, 2 November 1970.
52. DEFE 25/186, Folio No. 23, CBFG To MoD, 4 November 1970.
53. DEFE 25/186, Folio No. 23(i), CBFG To MoD 'Appreciation of the Musandam Situation', 11 November 1970.
54. DEFE 25/186, Folio No. 24, CBFG To MoD, 14 November 1970.
55. DEFE 25/186, Folio No. 24(ii), D.G. Crawford To G.G. Arthur, 18 November 1970.
56. DEFE 25/186, Folio No. 24(iii), Telegram No. 593, M.S. Weir To S. Crawford & W. Luce, 22 November 1970.
57. DEFE 25/186, Folio No. 29, VCDS To CDS & S of S for Defence, 25 November 1970.
58. DEFE 25/186, Folio No. 32, Musandam, DOP Note 718/70, 25 November 1970.
59. DEFE 25/186, Folio No. 30, E5621, D.J. Brewster (MoD), 25 November 1970.
60. DEFE 25/186, Folio No. 36, Supplementary Brief for VCDS Meeting With CBFG On 30 November, 27 November 1970.
61. DEFE 25/186, Folio No. 37, Chief of Defence Staff To S of State, 27 November 1970.
62. DEFE 25/186, Folio No. 41, Telegram No. 256, Douglas-Home To Bahrain, 30 November 1970.
63. CAB 148/101, DOP (70) Meeting 11, Cabinet, Item 4, 30 November 1970.

64. DEFE 25/186, Folio No. 44, Telegram No 259, Muscat To FCO, 3 December 1970.
65. DEFE 25/186, Folio No. 48, Telegram No 261, Muscat To FCO, 4 December 1970.
66. DEFE 25/186, Douglas-Home To Prime Minister, 8 December 1970.
67. DEFE 25/186, Folio No. 62, CBFG To MoD, 19 December 1970. It was estimated that the rebel gang consisted of less than a dozen men.
68. DEFE 25/186, Folio No. 71, Telegram No. 650Z, CBFG To MoD, 5 January 1971.
69. CAB 148/102, DOP (70) Meeting 44, Cabinet, Note By Secretary of State For Foreign & Commonwealth Affairs – Policy In The Persian Gulf, 8 December 1970.
70. Sir Donald Hawley believed that British National Interests were so well understood by officials in the FCO that they hardly felt the need to state them formally. Although the degree of importance ascribed to Omani oil is an interesting debate. Hawley sees Omani oil as desirable but the Hormuz connection as being key. Sir Terrence Clark who was Hawley's Chancellor from 1972–73 and Assistant Head of the Middle East Department from 1974–76 sees Omani oil as being much more important in a world where the Biafran war had interrupted Nigerian supplies. With the oil shock, Omani oil assumed even greater importance despite most of the exports going to the Far East, more oil was clearly always very welcome. Interviews, 14 January 2008 (Hawley) and 26 November 2007 (Clark).
71. Hawley also emphsises the fears current at the time of a 'Domino Effect' in the Gulf. Interview, 14 January 2008.
72. CAB 148/102, DOP (70) 44, Policy In The Persian Gulf, 8 December 1970.
73. CAB 148/102, DOP (70) Meeting 44, Cabinet, Note By Secretary of State For Foreign & Commonwealth Affairs – Policy In The Persian Gulf, 8 December 1970, p.11.
74. DEFE 25/186, Folio No. 21, Visit of Colonel Oldman, 14 October 1970.
75. DEFE 25/186, Folio No. 71, Telegram No. 20, CDS To CBFG, 31 December 1970.
76. DEFE 25/186, Folio No. 71(ii), CBFG To CDS, 9 January 1970.
77. DEFE 25/186, Folio No. 76(i), D.G. Crawford To T.J. Everard (Bahrain), 17 January 1971.
78. DEFE 25/186, Folio No. 91, CDS To CBFG, 5 February 1971.
79. The Omani authorities were however still very keen to gain RE assistance.
80. DEFE 25/186, Folio No. 77, Telegram No. 665, CGS To MoD, January 1971.
81. For examples of these leaflets and posters see: David Arkless, *The Secret War: Dhofar 1971/2* (London: William Kimber, 1988), pp.201–2 and Halliday, *Arabia Without Sultans*, p.349.
82. DEFE 25/186, Folio No. 108, PsyOps – Updating Sit Rep, 19 March 1971.
83. DEFE 25/186, Folio No. 88, Letter, Douglas-Home To Carrington, 4 February 1971.
84. DEFE 25/186, Folio No. 93, Letter, P.J.S. Moon (No. 10) To FCO & MoD, 9 February 1971.
85. DEFE 25/186, Folio No. 76, British Military Assistance To The Sultanate of Oman: Joint Theatre Plan (Gulf) – Operation Mahonia, 14 February 1971.
86. DEFE 24/575, Draft Submission To The Secretary of State [For Defence], 14 December 1971.

Chapter 4
Britain & Oman's Internal/External Legitimacy Dilemma

1. FCO 8/1680, Valedictory Dispatch D. Crawford To G.G. Arthur (PRPG – Bahrain), 24 April 1971, p.8.
2. Halliday, *Arabia Without Sultans*, p.336.
3. Ian Skeet, *Oman: Politics and Development* (Basingstoke: Palgrave Macmillan, 1992), pp.40–41.
4. Uzi Rabi, *The Emergence of States in a Tribal Society* (Eastbourne: Sussex Academic Press, 2006), p.209.
5. FCO 8/1426, Letter D.G. Crawford (Muscat) To J.M. Edes (Arabian Dept), 19 August 1970.
6. Uzi Rabi, *The Emergence of States in a Tribal Society*, p.138, and J.E. Peterson *Oman in the Twentieth Century* (London: Croom Helm, 1978), p.201.
7. *Ibid*, p.198.
8. FCO 8/1425, Doc 31, Telegram BFG To JIC, JIC Gulf Weekly Report, 27 July 1970, p.1.
9. John Townsend, *Oman: The Making of the Modern State* (London: Croom Helm, 1977), p.79.
10. J.E. Peterson, *Oman in the Twentieth Century*, p.202.
11. *The Times*, 3 August 1970.
12. J.E. Peterson, *Oman in the Twentieth Century*, p.204.
13. FCO 8/1426, Doc. 12, Telegram No. 403, D.G. Crawford (Muscat) To FCO, 7 August 1970, p.1.
14. FCO 8/1426, Doc. 12, Telegram No. 403, D.G. Crawford (Muscat) To FCO, 7 August 1970, p.2.
15. J.E. Peterson, *Oman in the Twentieth Century*, p.204.
16. FCO 8/1426, Doc. 12, Telegram No. 403, D.G. Crawford (Muscat) To FCO, 7 August 1970, p.2.
17. *Ibid*, p.2.
18. *Ibid*, p.3.
19. FCO 8/1426, Doc. 12, Telegram No. 403, D.G. Crawford (Muscat) To FCO, 7 August 1970, p.2.
20. FCO 8/1426, Doc. 99, Hallows (Bank of England) To A.A. Acland (Arabian Dept), 5 September 1970.
21. 95 per cent of Oman's income came from oil at this point. Townsend, *Oman*, p.81.
22. Jill Crystal, *Oil and Politics in the Gulf* (Cambridge: CUP, 1995), pp.22–9.
23. FCO 8/1426, Doc. 104, J.C. Kay (Muscat) To M.S. Weir (Bahrain), 7 August 1970.
24. FCO 8/1426, Doc. 104, J.C. Kay (Muscat) To M.S. Weir (Bahrain), 7 August 1970.
25. FCO 8/1426, Doc. 106, J.C. Kay & D. Crawford (Muscat) To M.S. Weir (Bahrain), 18 September 1970.
26. *Ibid*.
27. Townsend, *Oman*, p.82.

28. FCO 8/1426, Doc. 113, M.S. Weir (DPRPG Bahrain) To A.A. Acland (FCO), 30 September 1970, p.6.
29. FCO 8/1426, Doc. 115, C.J. Treadwell (Abu Dhabi) To M.S. Weir (Bahrain), 5 October 1970.
30. *Ibid.*
31. Townsend, *Oman*, p.83.
32. FCO 8/1426, Doc. 113, M.S. Weir (DPRPG Bahrain) To A.A. Acland (FCO), 30 September 1970, p.6.
33. FCO 8/1669, Annual Review For Oman 1970, p.8.
34. FCO 8/1669, Doc. 185, Report On Visit To Oman By Engineer In Chief (Army) 23-26 October 1970, p.1.
35. FCO 8/1669, Doc. 185, Report On Visit To Oman By Engineer In Chief (Army) 23-26 October 1970, pp.2-3.
36. FCO 8/1669, Doc. 184, A.A. Acland To J.M. Edes (Arabian Dept), 5 November 1970.
37. FCO 8/1669, Doc. 183, Telegram No. 170, Douglas-Home To D.G. Crawford, 9 November 1970.
38. FCO 8/1026. Doc. 86, 'Sultanate Scene', D.G. Crawford To M.S. Weir, 17 August 1970, p.1
39. FCO 8/1026. Doc. 86, 'Sultanate Scene', D.G. Crawford To M.S. Weir, 17 August 1970, p.2
40. *Ibid*, p.2.
41. FCO 8/1026, Doc. 125, 'Sultanate of Oman', D.G. Crawford To M.S. Weir, 5 November 1970, p.1.
42. *Ibid*, p.1.
43. *Ibid*, p.2.
44. *Ibid*, p.2.
45. FCO 8/1026. Doc. 86, 'Sultanate Scene', D.G. Crawford To M.S. Weir, 17 August 1970, p.1
46. FCO 8/1026. Doc. 86, 'Sultanate Scene', D.G. Crawford To M.S. Weir, 17 August 1970, p.3
47. *Ibid*, p.3.
48. FCO 8/1026. Doc. 125, A.A. Acland, Handwritten Note On 'Sultanate of Oman', D.G. Crawford To M.S Weir, 2 November 1970, p.1.
49. FCO 8/1026. Doc. 135, 'Sultan's Official Birthday', D.G. Crawford To M.S. Weir, 21 December 1970, p.2.
50. Skeet, *Oman: Politics and Development*, pp 40-41.
51. FCO 8/1026. Doc. 125, 'Sultanate of Oman', D.G. Crawford To M.S. Weir, 2 November 1970, p.1.
52. FCO 8/1680, R. McGregor (Arabian Dept) To R.A. Lloyd-Jones (DS-11 MoD), 24 March 1971.
53. FCO 8/1680, J.M. Blackley, The Sultanate of Oman, HMG's Policy, 20 March 1970, pp.1-2.
54. FCO 8/1680, J.M. Blackley, The Sultanate of Oman, HMG's Policy, 20 March 1970, p.2.
55. *Ibid*, p.6.

56. *Ibid*, p.6.
57. FCO 8/1680, J.M. Blackley, The Sultanate of Oman, HMG's Policy, 20 March 1970, p.8.
58. Fred Halliday, *Revolution and Foreign Policy: The Case of South Yemen 1967–1987* (Cambridge: CUP, 1990), p.23.
59. FCO 8/1680, J.M. Blackley, The Sultanate of Oman, HMG's Policy, 20 March 1970, pp. 7–10.
60. *Ibid*, p.17.
61. FCO 8/1680, J.M. Blackley, The Sultanate of Oman, HMG's Policy, 20 March 1970, pp.22–23.
62. FCO 8/1680, Handwritten Note, R. McGregor To A.A. Acland, 14 April 1971.
63. *Ibid*.
64. FCO 8/1680, Doc. 5, A.A. Acland To A. Parsons, 20 April 1971.
65. FCO 8/1680, Doc. 6, A. Parsons To W. Luce, 21 April 1971.
66. FCO 8/1670, Doc. 22, 'Conditions In Oman', G.G. Arthur To A.A. Acland, 13 April 1971.
67. *Ibid*, p.1.
68. FCO 8/1670, Doc. 36, Telegram No. 186, D.G. Crawford To G.G. Arthur, 11 April 1971.
69. FCO 8/1670, Doc. 22, 'Conditions In Oman', G.G. Arthur To A.A. Acland, 13 April 1971, p.2.
70. FCO 8/1680, Doc. 6, A. Parsons To W. Luce, 21 April 1971.
71. *Ibid*.
72. FCO 8/1680, Doc. 10, D.G. Crawford To G.G. Arthur, 24 April 1971, p.3.
73. FCO 8/1680, Doc. 10, D.G. Crawford To G.G. Arthur, 24 April 1971, p.6.
74. *Ibid*, pp.2–3.
75. *Ibid*, p.5.
76. FCO 8/1680, Doc. 10, G.G. Arthur To Douglas-Home, 26 April 1971, p.3.
77. FCO 8/1680, Doc. 12, G.G. Arthur To Douglas-Home, 30 April 1971.
78. FCO 8/1680, Doc. 10, G.G. Arthur To Douglas-Home, 26 April 1971, p.9.
79. FCO 8/1680, Doc. 10, D.G. Crawford To G.G. Arthur, 24 April 1971, p.3.
80. FCO 8/1680, Doc. 14, P.J. Dun (Arabian Department) To D.G. Allen (Arabian Department), 24 May 1971.
81. FCO 8/1680, Doc. 7, Draft Policy Paper, 27 April 1971, p.2.
82. FCO 8/1680, Doc. 14, P.J. Dun (Arabian Department) To D.G. Allen (Arabian Department), 24 April 1971.
83. FCO 8/1680, Doc. 15, G.G. Arthur To A.A. Acland, 04 May 1971, p.3.
84. FCO 8/1680, Doc. 15, G.G. Arthur To A.A. Acland, 04 May 1971, pp.4–5.
85. *Ibid*, p.1.
86. FCO 8/1680, Doc. 21, A.A. Acland To G.G. Arthur, 25 May 1971.
87. FCO 8/1680, Doc. 17, D.G. Allen To R.A. Lloyd-Jones (DS 11 – MoD), 18 May 1971.
88. FCO 8/1680, Doc. 18, D.G. Allen To J.C. Rowley, 18 May 1971.
89. FCO 8/1680, Doc. 19, J.C. Rowley To D.G. Allen, 26 May 1971.
90. FCO 8/1680, Doc. 23, B.G.T. Stanbridge (MoD) To R.M. Tesh (Defence Dept, FCO), 27 May 1971.
91. FCO 8/1680, Doc. 31, M.J. Harte To D.G. Allen, 3 June 1971, p.1.

92. *Ibid*, p.3.
93. FCO 8/1680, Doc. 33, A.A. Acland To D.F. Hawley, 16 June 1971.
94. See: Tony Jeapes, *SAS Secret War* (Glasgow: HarperCollins, 1996).
95. FCO 8/1670, Doc. 31, D.G. Crawford To G.G. Arthur, 23 April 1971, p.2.
96. FCO 8/1670, Handwritten Note, A.A. Acland, 23 May 1971.
97. FCO 8/1670, Doc. 44, G.G. Arthur To A.A. Acland, 2 June 1971.
98. Sir Donald Hawley, the incoming Ambassador, however had a different attitude to Tariq and got along well with him, playing tennis with him once a week. He put great effort into persuading him not to resign. Tariq did in fact later return to become head of the Omani Central Bank. Interview, Little Cheverell, Wilts, 14 January 2008.
99. FCO 8/1681, Doc. 32, HMG's Policy Towards The Sultante of Oman, 15 June 1971, p.1.
100. Fred Halliday, *Arabia Without Sultans*, p.271.

Chapter 5
The Search for International Recognition: Britain's Role in Securing Legitimacy

1. Peterson, *Oman in the Twentieth Century*, p.205.
2. For more on Franco-Omani relations see: *L'Oman et la France: Quelques Elements d'Histoire*, Ministère des Affaires Étrangères, Paris.
3. The U.S. had in 1958 signed a 'Treaty of Amity, Economic Relations & Consular Rights' replacing an earlier agreement of 1833. See Skeet, *Oman: Politics & Development*, p.81.
4. Joseph Kéchichian, *Oman and the World: The Emergence of an Independent Foreign Policy* (California: Rand, 1995), p.129.
5. Miriam Joyce, 'Britain and the Sultan of Muscat & Oman and Dependencies, 1958–9', *Diplomacy & Statecraft*, Vol. 4, No. 1, (March 1993), p.97.
6. Skeet, *Muscat & Oman: The End of an Era*, p.154.
7. Kéchichian, *Oman and the World*, p.130.
8. Jürgen Osterhammel, 'Britain & China, 1842–1914' In A. Porter (Ed.), *The Oxford History of The British Empire, Vol. III, The Nineteenth Century* (Oxford: OUP, 1999), pp.148–149.
9. Kéchichian, *Oman and the World*, p.130.
10. *Ibid*, p.130.
11. Francis Owtram, *A Modern History of Oman. Formation of the State Since 1920* (London: I.B.Tauris, 2004), p.16.
12. Halliday, *Arabia Without Sultans*, p.271.
13. Adam Roberts and Benedict Kingsbury (Eds.), *United Nations, Divided World* (Oxford: Clarendon, 1993), p.104.
14. FCO 8/1425, Telegram No. 346, Douglas-Home To Bahrain, 24 July 1970.
15. FCO 8/1425, J.M. Edes, Coup In The Sultanate of Muscat & Oman, 24 July 1970, p.3.
16. FCO 8/1425, P.T. Hayman, Note Attached To, Coup In The Sultanate of Muscat & Oman, 24 July 1970, p.4.

17. FCO 8/1425, Telegram No. 390, D.G. Crawford (Muscat) To Bahrain, 3 August 1970.
18. FCO 8/1427, Telegram No. 2, Phillips (Amman) To FCO & Muscat, 8 August 1970.
19. FCO 8/1427, Telegram No. 61, Falle (Kuwait) To Bahrain, 18 August 1970.
20. FCO 8/1427, Telegram No. 562, Tehran To FCO, Bahrain & Muscat, 12 August 1970.
21. FCO 8/1427, Telegram No. 101, FCO To Tehran, Bahrain & Muscat, 12 August 1970.
22. FCO 8/1427, Doc. 75, M.C.S. Weston (New York) To S.L. Egerton (FCO), 12 August 1970.
23. FCO 8/1427, Telegram No. 197, M.S. Weir (Bahrain) To Muscat, 15 August 1970.
24. FCO 8/1427, Telegram No. 424, D.G. Crawford To Bahrain, 16 August 1970.
25. FCO 8/1427, Ian McCluney (FCO) To Downing Street, 19 August 1970.
26. FCO 8/1427, Ian McCluney (FCO) To Downing Street, 19 August 1970.
27. FCO 8/1427, Telegram No. 111, Douglas-Home To Muscat, 21 August 1970.
28. FCO 8/1427, Telegram No. 6, Muscat To Jedda, 2 September 1970.
29. Skeet, *Oman: Politics and Development*, pp.55–56.
30. FCO 8/1427, Telegram No. 481, J.C. Kay (Muscat) To Bahrain, 16 September 1970.
31. FCO 8/1427, Telegram No. 134, Douglas-Home To Muscat, 17 September 1970.
32. See chapter two for more details.
33. FCO 8/1427, Telegram No. 134, Douglas-Home To Muscat, 17 September 1970.
34. The Palestinian uprising against the Hashemite Kingdom.
35. FCO 8/1427, Telegram No. 482, M.S. Weir (Bahrain) To FCO, 18 September 1970.
36. FCO 8/1427, Telegram No. 624, Sir Dennis Wright (Tehran) To Muscat, 21 September 1970.
37. FCO 8/1427, P.R.H. Wright (Cairo) To Arabian Department & Muscat, 21 October 1970.
38. Skeet, *Oman: Politics and Development*, p.57.
39. FCO 8/1427, Oman Goodwill Missions, D.G. Crawford (Muscat) To Bahrain, 25 November 1970.
40. FCO 8/1427, Telegram No. 658, D.G. Crawford To Bahrain, 30 December 1970.
41. FCO 8/1851, Doc. 9, The Saudis & The Fall of The Ibadhi Imamate In Oman, 29 April 1972.
42. A small donation was made to the UN Relief and Works Agency for Palestine (UNRWA).
43. FCO 8/1693, Status of the Mission in Muscat, Geoffrey Arthur (Bahrain) To Anthony Acland (Arabian Department), 13 April 1971.
44. FCO 8/1693, Embassy In Muscat, J.M. Edes (FCO) To Mr Donald (Personnel Policy Department), 18 March 1970. A grade 1 post would usually be Paris or Washington.
45. FCO 8/1693, Status of the Mission in Muscat, Geoffrey Arthur (Bahrain) To Anthony Acland (Arabian Department), 13 April 1971.
46. *Ibid.*

47. FCO 8/1693, Telegram No. 153, Hawley (Muscat) To FCO, 13 April 1971.
48. FCO 8/1693, Diplomatic Report No. 429/71, Presentation of Credentials, 2 August 1971.
49. FCO 8/1693, Telegram No. 269, Greaves (Muscat) To FCO, 24 August 1971.
50. FCO 8/1681, HMG's Policy Towards The Sultanate of Oman, 16 June 1971, p.4.
51. *Ibid*, p.4.
52. *Ibid*, p.4.
53. FCO 8/1681, HMG's Policy Towards The Sultanate of Oman, 16 June 1971, pp.7–8.
54. *Ibid*, p.8.
55. FCO 8/1676, Telegram No. 2, Phillips (Amman) To Muscat, 2 February 1971.
56. FCO 8/1676, Telegram No. 2, Phillips (Amman) To Muscat, 2 February 1971.
57. FCO 8/1676, Telegram No. 156, Geoffrey Arthur (Bahrain) To FCO, 9 March 1971.
58. *Ibid*.
59. FCO 8/1676, Telegram No. 313, Beaumont (Cairo) To FCO, 11 March 1971.
60. FCO 8/1676, Telegram No. 326, Beaumont (Cairo) To FCO, 12 March, 1971.
61. FCO 8/1676, Telegram No. 236, Beaumont (Cairo) To FCO, 27 February 1971.
62. FCO 8/1676, Telegram No. 248, Beaumont (Cairo) To FCO, 1 March 1971.
63. FCO 8/1676, Letter, A.A. Acland (Arabian Department) To D.L. Stewart (Cairo), 11 March 1971.
64. FCO 8/1676, Letter, Beaumont (Cairo) To A.A. Acland (Arabian Department), 17 March 1971.
65. FCO 8/1676, Telegram No. 302, Balfour-Paul (Baghdad) To FCO, 16 March 1971.
66. Hawley reported in February 1972 that the Syrians had been given a gift of $4 million, both as a reflection of their help at the UN and also in the hope that they may be helpful in any possible negotiations with PDRY. Hawley said, 'No doubt he paid rather too high a price...[this] reflects his own inexperience and the lack of expertise among those around him when dealing with wily men from Damascus', FCO 8/2019, Letter, Hawley To Wright, 28 February 1973, p.2.
67. See: Michael B. Oren, *Six Days of War: June 1967 and the Making of the Modern Middle East* (London: Penguin, 2002), p.13.
68. FCO 8/1676, Doc. 7, Middle East News Agency Press Release, 15 March 1971.
69. FCO 8/1676, Telegram No. 337, R.A. Beaumont (Cairo) To FCO, 16 March 1971.
70. FCO 8/1676, Doc. 11, A. Kellas (Aden) To Robert McGregor (Arabian Department), 17 March 1971.
71. FCO 8/1676, Telegram No. 141, D.G. Crawford (Muscat) To Bahrain, 22 March 1971.
72. FCO 8/1676, Doc. 15, Donald Hawley (Baghdad) To Anthony Acland (Arabian Department), 13 March 1971.
73. FCO 8/1676, Telegram No. 367, R.A. Beaumont (Cairo) To FCO, 23 March 1971.
74. FCO 8/1676, Telegram No. 511, R.A. Beaumont (Cairo) To FCO, 26 April 1971.
75. *Ibid*.
76. FCO 8/1676, Doc. 27, D.G. Allen (Arabian Department) To A.A. Acland, 30 April 1971.

77. FCO 8/1674, Doc. 14, Letter: R.A. Beaumont (Cairo) To A.A. Acland, 7 April 1971.
78. FCO 8/1676, Doc. 36, J.R. Young (Cairo) To FCO, 16 June 1971.
79. FCO 8/1676, Telegram No. 287, Edden (Beirut) To FCO, 5 July 1971.
80. FCO 8/1697, Record of Conversation Between Foreign Secretary And The Sultan of Oman, Monday 14 June 1971, 4pm, p.5.
81. Officials in Kuwait were reporting that the Imam had in fact no idea of the offer. FCO 8/1676, Doc. 40, Paddy de Courcy-Ireland (Kuwait) To D.G. Allen (Arabian Department), 5 July 1971.
82. FCO 8/1676, Doc. 39, Oman & The Arab League, D.G. Allen (Arabian Department) To Donald Hawley (Muscat), 8 July 1971.
83. FCO 8/1676, Doc. 42, J.R. Young (Cairo) To Near East Department, 28 July 1971.
84. FCO 8/1676, Doc. 42, J.R. Young (Cairo) To Near East Department, 28 July 1971.
85. FCO 8/1676, Telegram No. 367, McGurk (Kuwait) To FCO, 3 August 1971.
86. FCO 8/1676, Telegram No. 987, Beaumont (Cairo) To FCO, 12 August 1971.
87. FCO 8/1676, Telegram No. 262, Greaves (Muscat) To FCO, 18 August 1971.
88. FCO 8/1676, Telegram No. 628, Morris (Jedda) To FCO, 20 August 1971.
89. FCO 8/1676, Telegram No. 191, Douglas-Home To Muscat, 20 August 1971.
90. FCO 8/1676, Telegram No. 277, Greaves (Muscat) To FCO, 29 August 1971.
91. FCO 8/1676, Telegram No. 413, McGurk (Kuwait) To FCO, 26 August 1971.
92. FCO 8/1676, Telegram No. 667, Morris (Jedda) To FCO, 28 August 1971.
93. FCO 8/1676, Telegram No. 1012, Crowe (New York) To FCO, 12 September 1971.
94. FCO 8/1676, Telegram No. 729, Winchester (Jedda) To FCO, 16 September 1971.
95. FCO 8/1676, Telegram No. 305, Greaves (Muscat) To FCO, 19 September 1971.
96. FCO 8/1676, Telegram No. 768, Winchester (Jedda) To FCO, 27 September 1971.
97. FCO 8/1676, Telegram No. 179, Henderson (Qatar) To FCO, 27 September 1971.
98. FCO 8/1676, Telegram No. 654, G.G. Arthur To FCO, 29 September 1971.
99. FCO 8/1676, Telegram No. 776, Winchester (Jedda) To FCO, 29 September 1971.
100. FCO 8/1676, Telegram No. 1255, Beaumont (Cairo) To FCO, 30 September 1971.
101. FCO 8/1676, Telegram No. 662, G.G. Arthur (Bahrain) To Henderson (Qatar), 1 October 1971.
102. FCO 8/1676, Note: Arab League Consideration of Oman's Application, A.A. Acland To R. McGregor, 22 September 1971.
103. FCO 8/1676, Telegram No. 139, Henderson (Qatar) To Bahrain, 2 October 1971.
104. FCO 8/1674, Doc. 1, Letter, R. Sarell (Ankara) To FCO, 15 December 1970.
105. FCO 8/1674, Doc. 5, Oman's Entry Into The UN, D.G. Crawford (Muscat) To P.R.H. Wright (Bahrain), 2 March 1971.
106. *Ibid.*
107. FCO 8/1674, Note: Oman & The Arab League, R. McGregor To A.A. Acland, 9 March 1971.

108. FCO 8/1674, Doc. 13, Oman and UN Membership, M.S. Weir (New York) To A.A. Acland (FCO), 26 March 1971.
109. FCO 8/1674, Telegram No. 515, Parsons (New York) & Douglas-Home To Bahrain, 19 August 1971.
110. FCO 8/1674, Doc. 13, Oman & UN Membership, M.S. Weir (New York) To A.A. Acland (FCO), 26 March 1971.
111. FCO 8/1674, Doc. 13, Oman & UN Membership, M.S. Weir (New York) To A.A. Acland (FCO), 26 March 1971.
112. *Ibid.*
113. FCO 8/1674, Doc. 13, Oman & UN Membership, M.S. Weir (New York) To A.A. Acland (FCO), 26 March 1971.
114. FCO 8/1674, Doc. 14, Letter, R.A. Beaumont (Cairo) To A.A. Acland (FCO), 7 April 1971.
115. FCO 8/1674, Doc. 16, A.A. Acland (FCO) To M.S. Weir (New York), 6 May 1971.
116. FCO 8/1674, Doc. 16, A.A. Acland (FCO) To M.S. Weir (New York), 6 May 1971.
117. *Ibid.*
118. FCO 8/1674, Telegram No. 585, Jamieson (New York) To FCO, 1 June 1971.
119. FCO 8/1674, Telegram No. 101, Douglas-Home To Muscat, 2 June 1971.
120. FCO 8/1674, Doc. 26, M.C.S. Weston (New York) To FCO, 8 June 1971.
121. Beaumont in Cairo reported that the Egyptians were 'irritated at what they consider to be misguided Omani tactics', FCO 8/1674, Telegram No. 772, 28 June 1971.
122. FCO 8/1674, Telegram No. 673, Jamieson (New York) To FCO, 22 June 1971.
123. FCO 8/1674, D.F. Hawley To FCO, 29 July 1971.
124. FCO 8/1675, Telegram No. 515, Douglas-Home To Bahrain, 19 August 1971.
125. FCO 8/1675, Letter, J.G.T. Shipman (Muscat) To P.J. Dun (Arabian Department), 21 June 1971.
126. FCO 8/1675, Doc. 65, A.A. Acland, Handwritten Note, 20 September 1971.
127. FCO 8/1675, Telegram No. 744, Winchester (Jedda) To FCO, 19 September 1971.
128. FCO 8/1675, Telegram No. 637, Douglas-Home To New York, 21 September 1971.
129. FCO 8/1675, Security Council Report, 30 September 1971.
130. FCO 8/1679, Telegram No. 358, D.F. Hawley (Muscat) To FCO, 28 October 1971.
131. FCO 8/1679, Letter, R. McGregor (Arabian Department) To D.F. Hawley (Muscat), 24 June 1971.
132. FCO 8/1679, Telegram No. 943, Morris (Jedda) To FCO, 14 December 1971.
133. FCO 8/1679, Telegram No. 944, Morris (Jedda) To FCO, 14 December 1971.
134. *Ibid.*
135. FCO 8/1677, Telegram No. 353, Hawley (Muscat) To FCO, 23 October 1971.
136. *Ibid.*
137. FCO 8/1671, The Dhofar Rebellion An Evaluation By The Defence Secretary Of The Sultanate of Oman, Colonel H.R.D. Oldman, OBE., MC., October 1971, p.2.

138. *Ibid*, p.9.
139. For more details on this see: Tony Jeapes, *SAS Secret War* (Glasgow: HarperCollins, 1996).

Chapter 6
British Policy, Whitehall Debates & External Aid 1972–74

1. Operation Jaguar Plans, Graham Papers, St Antony's Archives, Oxford.
2. Peterson, *Oman's Insurgencies*, p.276.
3. *Ibid*, p.288.
4. Ken Perkins, CSAF, 1975–7, Interview, By Telephone, 12 November 2007.
5. FCO 8/1860, Doc. 1, Telegram No. 260, Hawley To FCO, 5 May 1972.
6. Peterson, *Oman's Insurgencies*, p.291.
7. *Ibid*, p.291.
8. FCO 8/1860, Doc. 5, Telegram No. 169, Douglas-Home To Hawley, 8 May 1972.
9. FCO 8/1860, Doc. 7, Telegram No. 273, Hawley To FCO, 8 May 1972.
10. FCO 8/1860, Doc. 9, Brief For Meeting With PDRY Ambassador, Patrick Wright To Sir Anthony Parsons, 8 May 1972, p.2.
11. Lebanon being one of the states least subject to censorship in the region, thus meaning that its press enjoyed a position of trust and a wide readership in the Arab world, similar to the position of Al-Jazeera today.
12. FCO 8/1860, Doc. 12, Telegram No. 275, Hawley To FCO, 9 May 1972, p.1.
13. *Ibid*, p.3.
14. FCO 8/1860, Doc. 15, Telegram No. 174, Douglas-Home To Hawley, 9 May 1972.
15. Peterson, *Oman's Insurgencies*, p.291.
16. FCO 8/1860, Doc. 19, Telegram No. 283, Hawley To FCO, 11 May 1972.
17. FCO 8/1860, Doc. 21, Telegram No. 173, Boswell (Aden) To FCO, 11 May 1972.
18. FCO 8/1860, Doc. 22, Telegram No. 174, Boswell (Aden) To FCO, 11 May 1972.
19. FCO 8/1860, Doc. 23a, R.N. Noyes (MoD) To D.E. Tatham (ME Dept, FCO), 11 May 1972.
20. FCO 8/1860, Doc. 23b, Note, Wright To Lloyd-Jones (MoD), 11 May 1972.
21. FCO 8/1860, Doc. 23c, Telegram No. 285, Hawley To FCO, 11 May 1972.
22. *The Times*, 12 May 1972, *The Guardian*, 12 May 1972, *Daily Express*, 12 May 1972.
23. FCO 8/1860, Doc. 32, Telegram No. 182, Douglas-Home To Hawley, 12 May 1972.
24. FCO 8/1860, Doc. 34, Telegram No. 297, Hawley To FCO, 12 May 1972.
25. FCO 8/1860, Doc. 45, Telegram No. 734, Beaumont (Cairo) To FCO, 14 May 1972.
26. FCO 8/1860, Doc. 36a, FCO To Lord Bridges (No 10), 12 May 1972.
27. *Ibid*.
28. FCO 8/1860, Doc. 37, Telegram No. 15, DA (Muscat) To MoD & FCO, 12 May 1972.
29. FCO 8/1860, Doc. 39, Telegram No. 184, Wright To Hawley, 13 May 1972.

30. FCO 8/1860, Doc. 42, Telegram No. 293, Hawley To FCO, 13 May 1972.
31. FCO 8/1860, Doc. 44, Telegram No. 187, Douglas-Home To Hawley, 13 May 1972.
32. FCO 8/1860, Doc. 46, Telegram No. 298, Hawley To FCO, 14 May 1972.
33. Ibid.
34. Indeed it later emerged that they knew nothing about it at this stage. FCO 8/1860, Doc. 54, Telegram No. 684, Crowe (New York) To FCO, 16 May 1972.
35. FCO 8/1860, Doc. 48, Telegram No. 681, Crowe (New York) To FCO, 15 May 1972.
36. FCO 8/1860, Doc. 23d, Chief of The Defence Staff To Secretary of State For Defence, 10 May 1972.
37. FCO 8/1860, Doc. 56, Telegram No. 194, Douglas-Home To Hawley, 16 May 1972.
38. Tony Geraghty, *Who Dares Wins: The Special Air Service 1950–1992* (London: Abacus, 2002), pp.202–3.
39. FCO 8/1860, Doc. 63, Telegram No. 312, Hawley To FCO, 17 May 1972.
40. FCO 8/1861, Doc. 75, ACDS (Ops), Annex A, 17 May 1972, p.5.
41. Townsend, *Oman: The Making of the Modern State*, p.147.
42. FCO 8/1861, Doc. 80, Telegram No. 209, Douglas-Home To Hawley, 19 May 1972.
43. FCO 8/1861, Doc. 82, Telegram No. 331, Hawley To FCO, 23 May 1972.
44. FCO 8/1861, Doc. 84, Telegram No. 330, Hawley To FCO, 23 May 1972.
45. FCO 8/1861, Doc. 86, Telegram No. 332, Hawley To FCO, 24 May 1972.
46. FCO 8/1861, Doc. 88, Wright (Head of MED) To Parsons, 24 May 1972.
47. FCO 8/1861, Doc. 95, Telegram No. 217, Douglas-Home To Hawley, 23 May 1972.
48. FCO 8/1862, Doc. 117, Telegram No. 363, Hawley To FCO, 31 May 1972.
49. Halliday, *Arabia Without Sultans*, p.338.
50. For the best descriptions of the battle see: Tony Jeapes, *SAS Secret War*, pp.145–161, and Tony Geraghty, *Who Dares Wins*, pp.189–198.
51. Geraghty, *Who Dares Wins*, p.191.
52. Ibid, p.193.
53. Ibid, p.195.
54. Peterson, *Oman's Insurgencies*, p.301.
55. Halliday, *Arabia Without Sultans*, p.339.
56. FCO 8/1855, Doc. 2, Oman Economy, Hawley To Wright, 8 May 1972, p.2.
57. Ibid, p.2.
58. Ibid, p.4.
59. FCO 8/1855, Doc. 2, Oman Economy, Hawley To Wright, 8 May 1972, p.5.
60. 1 OR = $2.65 in 1972. From 1973 the Riyal was pegged to the U.S. Dollar.
61. Townsend, *Oman: The Making of the Modern State*, p.151.
62. FCO 46/947, Doc. 1, Letter, Oldman To Hawley, 11 March 1972, p.1.
63. Ibid, p.2.
64. FCO 46/947, Doc. 2, Letter, Allen (Arabian Dept) To Lloyd-Jones (DS-11 MoD), 28 March 1972.
65. FCO 46/947, Doc. 3, Note, T.E.F. Pooley (FCO) To R.M. Tesh (FCO), 6 April 1972.
66. FCO 46/947, Doc. 4, Letter, Lloyd-Jones (MoD) To Allen (FCO), 24 April 1972.

67. FCO 46/947, Doc. 8, Letter, Wright To Hawley, 11 May 1972.
68. FCO 46/947, Doc. 14, Telegram No. 352, Hawley To FCO, 28 May 1972.
69. FCO 46/947, Doc. 22, Letter, Lloyd-Jones (MoD) To Wright, 22 June 1972.
70. FCO 46/947, Doc. 23, Letter, Hawley To Wright, 9 July 1972.
71. This £250,000 was a seemingly insubstantial amount of money, although it seems slightly more significant when one considers that in the early 1970s the entire Defence Budget only amounted to £1,900 million, the £250,000 represented half of the costs of LSP in 1971 and was the best offer the Defence Department thought realistically achievable. FCO 46/947, Doc. 21, R.F. Skilbeck (Defence Department) To David Tatham (Middle East Department).
72. FCO 46/947, Doc. 27, Handwritten Note 'Aid To Oman', 7 August 1972.
73. FCO 46/947, Doc. 28, Handwritten Note, 'Aid To Oman', 17 August 1972.
74. FCO 46/947, Doc. 29, Draft Letter, Minister of State (FCO) To Chief Secretary of the Treasury, 17 March 1972.
75. FCO 46/947, Doc. 30, Telegram No. 336, Douglas-Home To Hawley, 25 August 1972.
76. FCO 46/947, Doc. 31, Handwritten Notes, Letter, Wright To Allen, 21 August 1972.
77. FCO 46/947, Doc. 34, Letter, Hawley To Wright, 15 October 1972.
78. FCO 46/947, Doc. 37, Telegram No. 493, DA Muscat To FCO, 24 October 1972.
79. FCO 8/1865, Doc. 14, Report, Hawley To FCO, 23 October 1972, pp.12–18.
80. FCO 8/1865, Doc. 27, Paper: Assistance To Oman, Wright To Crawford & Parsons, 6 November 1972, p.5.
81. FCO 8/1865, Doc. 29, Records of FCO-MoD Meeting, 7 November 1972.
82. FCO 8/1865, Doc. 31, Draft DOPC Paper, 16 November 1972.
83. FCO 8/1865, Doc. 31b, E.N. Smith (FCO Finance Dept) To Wright, 16 November 1972.
84. Interview, Sir Donald Hawley, Little Cheverill, Wiltshire, 14 January 2008.
85. FCO 8/1865, Doc. 32, Speaking Notes For Douglas-Home, 23 November 1972.
86. FCO 8/1865, Doc. 38, Note – Defence Assistance To The Sultanate of Oman, Parsons To PUS, 23 November 1972.
87. FCO 8/1865, Doc. 39, Letter, Julian Amery To Lord Balniel, 27 November 1972.
88. FCO 8/1865, Doc. 40, Draft FCO Paper, 30 November 1972.
89. FCO 8/1865, Docs. 41 & 43. Hawley To Wright To Lloyd-Jones (MoD), 26 November and 6 December 1972.
90. FCO 8/1865, Doc. 39, Letter, Wright To Lloyd-Jones (MoD), 30 November 1972, pp.4–5.
91. FCO 8/1865, Doc. 44, Letter, Lloyd-Jones (MoD) To Wright, 11 December 1972, pp.2–3.
92. *Ibid*, p.2.
93. FCO 8/1865, Doc. 48, Letter, Wright To H.S. Lee (Treasury), 18 December 1972.
94. FCO 8/1865, Doc. 50, Memo, Wright To Tatham (FCO), 18 December 1972.
95. FCO 46/955, Doc. 1, Letter, E.H. Boothroyd (Treasury) To C.M. Rose (FCO), 2 January 1973.
96. FCO 46/955, Doc. 3, Letter, B.O. White (Defence Dept FCO) To C.M. Rose (FCO), 3 January 1973.

NOTES TO PAGES 181–187 257

97. FCO 46/955, Doc. 5, Letter, C.M. Rose (FCO) To E.H. Boothroyd (Treasury), 3 January 1973.
98. FCO 46/955, Doc. 14, Letter, D.C. Tebbit (FCO) To PUS (FCO), 17 January 1973.
99. FCO 46/955, Doc. 9, Letter, E.H. Boothroyd (Treasury) To C.M. Rose (FCO), 11 January 1973.
100. FCO 46/955, Doc. 15, Letter, C.M. Rose (FCO) To E.H. Boothroyd (Treasury), 18 January 1973.
101. FCO 8/1681, HMG's Policy Towards The Sultanate of Oman, 16 June 1971, p.4.
102. Alec Cairncross, 'The Heath Government and the British Economy' In Ball and Seldon (Eds.), *The Heath Government 1970–74*, p.107.
103. FCO 8/1858, Doc. 2, Phillips (DA Amman) To Hawley, 13 January 1972.
104. FCO 8/1858, Doc. 66, Douglas-Home To MED, 12 July 1972.
105. Oldman later secured shells for the guns from India and Pakistan.
106. FCO 8/1858, Doc. 5a, Evans (M/NED) To McGregor, 21 January 1972.
107. FCO 8/1858, Doc. 6, Handwritten Note, A.A. Acland, 26 January 1972.
108. FCO 8/1858, Doc. 7, Handwritten Notes, R. McGregor & A.A. Acland, 28 January 1972.
109. FCO 8/1858, Doc. 11, Phillips (DA Amman) To FCO, 6 March 1972.
110. FCO 8/1858, Doc. 17, Hawley To FCO, 9 March 1972.
111. FCO 8/1858, Doc. 25, R.A. Lloyd-Jones (MoD) To D.G. Allen, 4 April 1972.
112. FCO 8/1858, Doc. 30, DA Muscat To FCO, 9 April 1972.
113. FCO 8/1858, Doc. 32, R.M.H. Vickers (MoD) To Defence Dept FCO, 14 April 1972.
114. The mission eventually arrived in mid May 1972.
115. FCO 8/1858, Doc. 41, Briefing, D.G. Allen To R.M. Le Quesne, 15 May 1972. (The Saudis would later decide to deal direct with Muscat but this was not clear until months later.)
116. The Royalists were followers of the Zeidi Imam, Zeidism is a branch of Shia Islam.
117. Jones, *Britain and the Yemen Civil War*, p.219.
118. FCO 8/1858, Doc. 42b, Record of Conversation, H.M. Ambassador Muscat & H.I.M The Shahanshah, 26 April 1972.
119. FCO 8/1858, Doc. 42a, Patrick Wright To Le Quesne (FCO), 16 May 1972.
120. FCO 8/1858, Doc. 53, Hawley To FCO, 2 July 1972.
121. FCO 8/1858, Doc. 43, Ramsbotham (Tehran) To FCO, 16 May 1972.
122. FCO 8/1858, Docs. 48 & 49, Hawley & Ramsbotham To FCO, 22 & 25 May 1972.
123. FCO 8/1858, Doc. 55, Wright To Allen (FCO), 27 June 1972.
124. FCO 8/1858, Doc. 58, Champion (Amman) To FCO, 5 July 1972.
125. A good example of Saudi independence is the fact that more than two months after the Saudi military mission left Muscat the Omanis had had no further news about its intentions.
126. FCO 8/1858, Doc. 62, Rothnie (Jeddah) To FCO, 8 July 1972.
127. FCO 8/1858, Doc. 67a, D.F. Murray (Tehran) To Wright, 6 July 1972.
128. FCO 8/1858, Doc. 67, Douglas-Home To Tehran, 12 July 1972.

129. FCO 8/1859, Doc. 77, Ramsbotham (Tehran) To FCO, 25 July 1972.
130. Three 206 helicopters and three 205s.
131. The three 206 helicopters were later rejected as having too small a payload.
132. FCO 8/1859, Doc. 84, Record of Meeting, Oldman and Parsons, 7 August 1972.
133. Abu Dhabi eventually gave £3 million in 1972 and 6 million Omani Riyals in 1973 alone.
134. FCO 8/1859, Doc. 92, Wright To Private Secretary, 8 August 1972. (The Sultan was in London for meetings and was due to call on the Secretary of State that day).
135. FCO 8/1859, Doc. 110, Hawley To FCO, 9 October 1972.
136. FCO 8/1859, Doc. 116, DA Tehran To DA Muscat, 20 October 1972.
137. FCO 8/1865, Letter, Wright To S. Crawford, 14 November 1972.
138. FCO 8/1859, Wright To Parsons, Iranian Special Forces In Oman, 10 October 1972.
139. FCO 8/2010, Quoted In, Le Quesne To A.J. Coles (& Parsons), 5 July 1973.
140. FCO 8/2010, Letter, Le Quesne To A.J. Coles, 5 July 1973.
141. DEFE 5/197/14, Appendix 5 of Annex A To Chief of Staff 46/73, December 1973.
142. DEFE 5/197/14, Chiefs of Staff Committee, Military Activity In Oman, June – October 1973, p.8.
143. DEFE 5/197/14, Chiefs of Staff Committee, Future U.K. Defence Activity In Oman, December 1973, p.9.
144. *Ibid*, p.9.
145. Ian Gardiner, *In the Service of the Sultan* (Barnsley: Pen & Sword, 2006), p.155.
146. Peterson, *Oman's Insurgencies*, pp.330–331.
147. Gardiner, *In the Service of the Sultan*, p.155.
148. A non-resident Ambassador based in Kuwait.
149. Donald Hawley, Interview, Little Cheverell, Wilts, 14 January 2008.
150. FCO 8/2010, Doc. 1, Memo, D. Tatham To Wright, 7 June 1973.
151. FCO 8/2010, Doc. 3, Memo: U.S. Interest In Oman, Wright To Hunt, 5 July 1973.
152. FCO 8/2010, Doc. 8, Speaking Notes For Defence Secretary, 24 July 1973.
153. FCO 8/2010, Doc. 11, Letter, Tony Reeve (Washington Embassy) To Wright, 25 July 1973.
154. FCO 8/2010, Doc. 38, Telegram No. 441, T. Clark (Muscat) To FCO, 22 September 1973.
155. FCO 8/2010, Doc. 1, Memo, Tatham To Wright, 7 June 1973.
156. FCO 8/2010, Doc. 51, Letter, Wright To Lloyd-Jones (MoD), 11 October 1973.
157. FCO 8/2010, Doc. 60, Letter, Hawley To Wright, 8 November 1973.
158. FCO 46/868, Doc. 54, USAF Request, R.N. Noyes (MoD) To Secretary of State, 26 April 1972.
159. FCO 46/1050, Doc. 30, Telegram No. 2213, Douglas-Home To Washington, 2 November 1973.
160. FCO 46/1050, Doc. 40, Telegram No. 331, Douglas-Home To Muscat, 12 November 1973.
161. FCO 8/2019, Doc. 56, Chief of The Defence Staff To Secretary of State For Defence, 17 July 1973.
162. FCO 8/2020, Doc. 62, Memorandum, Hawley To Wright, 10 June 1973, p 8.

163. Smith, *Britain's Revival and Fall in the Gulf*, p.4.
164. FCO 8/2020, Doc. 102, Memorandum, Lloyd-Jones (MoD) To Tatham (FCO), 5 October 1973.
165. FCO 8/2020, Doc. 102, Memorandum, Annex A, Lloyd-Jones (MoD) To Tatham (FCO), 5 October 1973.
166. FCO 8/2020, Doc. 102, Memorandum, Annex B, Lloyd-Jones (MoD) To Tatham (FCO), 5 October 1973, p.1.
167. *Ibid*, p.3.
168. *Ibid*, p.3.
169. FCO 8/2020, Doc. 123, Telegram No. 379, Douglas-Home To Muscat, 18 December 1973.

Chapter 7
Continuity and Change:
The Labour Government and Defence Reviews

1. Saki Dockrell, *Britain's Retreat from East of Suez: The Choice between Europe and the World?* (Basingstoke: Palgrave Macmillan, 2002), p.2.
2. Dockrell, *Britain's Retreat from East of Suez*, p.217.
3. This chapter draws partly upon previously published work: James Worrall, 'Britain's Last Bastion In Arabia: The End of the Dhofar War, the Labour Government and the Withdrawal from RAF Salalah and Masirah, 1974–1977' In Tore T. Petersen (Ed.), *Challenging Retrenchment: The United States, Great Britain and The Middle East 1950–1980* (Trondheim: Tapir Academic Press, 2010), pp.115–140.
4. FCO 46/868, Future of RAF Bases in Muscat & Oman, 1972.
5. FCO 8/2019, Doc. 63, Record of Conversation, Qaboos & Carrington, 12 April 1973, p.3.
6. FCO 8/2019, Doc. 70, CoS Meeting Report, 17 July 1973, pp.7–8.
7. FCO 8/2020, Doc. 94, Record of Meeting, CSAF & DMO (MoD), 12 July 1973.
8. FCO 8/2020, Doc. 93, Letter, R. Skilbeck (Defence Dept FCO) To Lt. Col. Napier (MoD), 3 September 1973, p.2.
9. FCO 8/1865, Doc. 28, Memorandum, P.R.H. Wright To Sir Stewart Crawford, 14 November 1973, pp.2–3.
10. FCO 8/2020, Doc. 62, Memorandum, D.F. Hawley To P.R.H. Wright, 10 June 1973, p.6.
11. FCO 8/2020, Doc. 102, Memorandum, Annex A, R.A. Lloyd-Jones (MoD) To D.E. Tatham (FCO), 5 October 1973, p.7.
12. FCO 8/2020, Doc. 93, Letter, R. Skilbeck (Defence Dept FCO) To Lt Col. Napier (MoD), 3 September 1973, p.3.
13. FCO 8/2020, Doc. 93, Letter, R. Skilbeck (Defence Dept FCO) To Lt Col. Napier (MoD), 3 September 1973, p.3.
14. FCO 8/2020, Doc. 96, Letter, D.E. Tatham (FCO) To A.J. Cragg (MoD), 1 October 1973.
15. FCO 46/868, Doc. 23, Record of Conversation, Douglas-Home & H.M. Sultan Qaboos, 14 September 1973.

16. FCO 46/1050, Doc. 41, Letter, D.F. Hawley To P.R.H. Wright, 17 November 1973.
17. FCO 8/2221, Doc. 14, Telegram No. 175, D.F. Hawley To FCO, 9 May 1974.
18. Ball and Seldon (Eds.), *The Heath Government 1970–74*, pp.402–404.
19. Dockrell, *Britain's Retreat from East of Suez*, p.218.
20. Ritchie Ovendale, *British Defence Policy Since 1945* (Manchester: Manchester University Press, 1994), p.151.
21. FCO 8/2240, Effect of UK Defence Review On Oman, 1974.
22. FCO 8/2239, Doc. 4, A.J. Cragg (DS-11 MoD) To FCO etc, 30 August 1974.
23. FCO 8/2239, Doc. 25, N.T. Bagnall (Secretary CoS) To CoS, 30 September 1974.
24. FCO 8/2221, Doc. 12, Brief For Callaghan For Visit Of Al-Zawawi, 3 May 1974.
25. FCO 8/2239, Doc. 1, A.J. Cragg (DS-11 MoD) To FCO etc, 20 August 1974.
26. FCO/8/2239, Doc. 10, M.S. Weir To Thomson (MoD), 15 July 1974.
27. Interview, Sir Terrence Clark, Assistant Head Middle East Department 1974–76, Telephone, 26 November 2007.
28. FCO 8/2239, Doc. 1, A.J. Cragg (DS-11 MoD) To FCO etc, 20 August 1974.
29. FCO 8/2239, Doc. 1, Draft OPD Paper, Military Assistance To Oman, 20 August 1974. p.2.
30. FCO 8/2239, Doc. 2, Letter, P.R.H. Wright To A.J. Cragg (MoD), 26 August 1974.
31. FCO 8/2239, Doc. 4, FCO Defence Review Steering Committee, 3 September 1974.
32. FCO 8/2239, Doc. 8, Defence Review Non-NATO Commitments, 16 September 1974, p.3.
33. FCO 8/2239, Doc. 15, Preparation For Briefs (MoD), 26 September 1974, p.5.
34. FCO 8/2240, Doc. 69, S. Webb (DS-11) To DS6 (MoD), 17 December 1974, p.5.
35. The Shah was especially keen for the British to remain just over the horizon.
36. FCO 8/2239, Doc. 18, P.R.H. Wright To J.E. Jackson (Defence Department FCO), 30 September 1974, pp.1–2.
37. FCO 8/2239, Doc. 19, Defence Review Official Level Meeting, 2 October 1974.
38. FCO 8/2239, Doc. 21, Wright To Jackson (Defence Department FCO), 7 October 1974.
39. FCO 8/2239, Doc. 24, P.R.H. Wright To A.J. Cragg (DS-11 MoD), 8 October 1974.
40. FCO 8/2240, Doc. 34, J.E. Jackson (Defence Department FCO) To M.S. Weir (FCO), 16 October 1974.
41. FCO 8/2240, Doc. 35, P.R.H. Wright To M.S. Weir (FCO), 16 October 1974.
42. FCO 8/2240, Doc. 45, T.J. Clark To Westbook (Defence Department FCO), 29 October 1974.
43. FCO 8/2240, Doc. 53, Telegram No. 343, Callaghan To D.F. Hawley, 27 November 1974.
44. FCO 8/2475, Doc. 9, J.A. Thomson (FCO) To H.F.T. Smith (Cabinet Office), 20 January 1975.
45. FCO 8/2240, Doc. 60, U.S. Department of Defense To FCO, 28 November 1974.
46. Sir Terrence Clark (Assistant Head of Middle East Department FCO, 1974–76) stated that there was by 1974–75 a tacit understanding between the U.S. and

Britain that the northern Gulf was America's responsibility and that the southern Gulf was Britain's. This news made it seem more likely that the U.S. would be forced to take over Britain's responsibilities. Interview, 26 November 2007.
47. Halliday, *Arabia Without Sultans*, p.484.
48. FCO 8/2475, Doc. 18, Letter, T.J. Clark To M.S. Weir, 21 January 1975.
49. *Ibid*.
50. FCO 8/2475, Doc. 3, G.N. Smith (North America Department) To T.J. Clark, 8 January 1975.
51. FCO 8/2475, Doc. 5, L.J. Watling (Information Administration Department FCO) To T.J. Clark, 8 January 1975.
52. FCO 8/2475, Doc. 16, P.A. Raferty (Middle East Department) To Doble (Defence Department), 24 January 1975.
53. FCO 8/2475, Doc. 25, Telegram No. 377, Callaghan To Washington, 6 February 1975.
54. FCO 8/2476, Doc. 32, J.E. Jackson (Defence Department FCO) To FCO Heads of Department, 25 February 1975.
55. *Ibid*.
56. Ovendale, *British Defence Policy since 1945*, p.153.
57. FCO 8/2476, Doc. 40, Telegram No. 110, Callaghan To C.J. Treadwell, 23 March 1975.
58. FCO 8/2476, Doc. 48, Telegram No. 152, C.J. Treadwell To FCO, 1 April 1975.
59. FCO 8/2239, Doc. 1, A.J. Cragg (DS-11 MoD) To FCO etc, 20 August 1974.
60. FCO 8/2460, Doc. 54, Resolution of Dorking Labour Party About Oman & Seven Replies, June 1975.
61. Sir Gawain Bell, *An Imperial Twilight* (London: Lester Crook, 1989), p.183.
62. FCO 8/2460, Doc. 4a, Telegram No. 82, D.E. Tatham (Muscat) To FCO, 17 February 1975.
63. FCO 8/2460, Doc. 4, UK/Oman Relations, I.T.M. Lucas, 18 February 1975.
64. FCO 8/2460, Doc. 1, Letter, T.J. Clark (MED) To D.E. Tatham (Muscat), 3 January 1975.
65. FCO 8/2227, Doc. 6, Letter, D.F. Hawley To P.R.H. Wright, 16 February 1974.
66. This was in part funded by Abu Dhabi's gift of 60 million Omani Riyals.
67. FCO 8/2454, Doc. 2, Oman – Annual Review 1974, D.F. Hawley To Secretary of State, 7 January 1975, pp.2–6.
68. *Ibid*, pp.2–6.
69. FCO 8/2454, Doc. 2, Oman – Annual Review 1974, D.F. Hawley To Secretary of State, / January 1975, p.1.
70. Interviews, Sir Donald Hawley, British Ambassador To Oman 1971–75, 26 November 2007 and 14 January 2008.
71. Lucas had replaced Patrick Wright who had moved to become Foreign Affairs Advisor at No. 10, a position he no doubt used to stress Oman's importance to the Prime Minister. Ivor Lucas, *A Road To Damascus* (London: Radcliffe, 1997), p.138.
72. FCO 8/2476, Doc. 54, Letter, I.T.M. Lucas (Middle East Department FCO) To C.J. Treadwell, 4 April 1975.
73. FCO 8/2476, Doc. 63, Chiefs of Staff Committee, Defence Operational Staff Report On RAF Salalah, May 1975.

74. FCO 46/1403, Doc. 49, Telegram No. 101, Foreign Secretary (Crosland) To Muscat, 12 May 1976.
75. FCO 8/2687, Doc. 1, Oman: Annual Review 1975, 2 January 1976, p.7.
76. The role of inducements is ascribed by General Sir Charles Huxtable (Commander Dhofar Brigade 1976–78) as being a key factor in victory, along with the *firqat*. Interview 19 November 2007.
77. Skeet, *Oman: Politics and Development*, p.50.
78. FCO 8/2687, Doc. 1, Annual Review 1975, 2 January 1976.
79. *Ibid*.
80. Interview, Ken Perkins, CSAF 1975–77, 12 November 2007.
81. John Akehurst, *We Won a War: The Campaign in Oman 1965–1975* (Salisbury (Wilts): Michael Russell, 1982). Tony Jeapes, *SAS Secret War* (Glasgow: HarperCollins, 1996).
82. FCO 8/2687, Doc. 1, Annual Review 1975, 2 January 1976 and Interviews.
83. Skeet, *Oman: Politics and Development*, p.50.
84. *Ibid*, p.50.
85. FCO 8/2687, Doc. 1, Annual Review 1975, 2 January 1976.
86. Interview, Ken Perkins, CSAF 1975–7, 12 November 2007.
87. FCO 8/2460, Doc. 58, Brief For S of S (Callaghan) Visit To The Gulf, November 1975.
88. Interview, Ken Perkins, CSAF 1975–77, 12 November 2007 and Interview Sir Charles Huxtable, Commander Dhofar Brigade 1976–78, 19 November 2007.
89. FCO 8/2687, Doc. 1, Annual Review 1975, 2 January 1976.
90. *Ibid*.
91. Interview, Terry Morgans-Slader, Former BP Internal Travel Department and one of the first post-coup tourists in Oman, 22 December 2006.
92. FCO 46/1403, Withdrawal of UK Forces From Salalah, Muscat & Oman, 1976.
93. FCO 46/1404, Doc. 67, Letter, M.T. Folger (Treasury) To A.G. Rucker (MoD), 26 July 1976.
94. FCO 8/2218, Doc. 8, Trip Report On Department of Defense Visit To Oman, Colonel Maloney, September 1973, p.11.
95. Owtram, *A Modern History of Oman*, p.134.
96. Kéchichian, *Oman and the World: The Emergence of an Independent Foreign Policy*, pp.147–150.

Conclusion
Themes and Implications

1. Sir Donald Hawley, *Desert Wind and Tropic Storm* (Norwich: Michael Russell, 2000), pp.156–210 and Interview, Little Cheverell, Wilts, 14 January 2008.
2. J.E. Peterson, *Oman's Insurgencies*, p.328.
3. Interview, Sir Donald Hawley, Little Cheverell, Wilts, 14 January 2008.
4. D. Betz and A. Cormack, 'Iraq, Afghanistan and British Strategy', *Orbis*, Vol. 53, No. 2, (2009), p.321; John A. Nagel, *Learning to Eat Soup With a Knife. Counterinsurgency Lessons from Malaya and Vietnam* (Chicago: Chicago University Press, 2005).

5. See for example: John Newsinger, *British Counterinsurgency from Palestine to Northern Ireland* (Basingstoke: Palgrave Macmillan, 2002); Paul Dixon, '"Hearts and Minds"? British Counter-insurgency from Malaya to Iraq' *Journal of Strategic Studies*, Vol. 32, No. 3, (2009), pp.353–381; Ashley Jackson, 'British Counter-Insurgency in History: A Useful Historical Precedent?' *British Army Review*, No. 139, (2006); John Newsinger, 'Review of T.R. Mockaitis, 'British Counterinsurgency 1919–1960' *Race and Class*, Vol. 34, No. 2, (1992), pp.96–98; David French, *The British Way in Counter-Insurgency 1945–67* (Oxford: OUP, 2011).
6. David Kilcullen, 'Counterinsurgency *Redux*', *Survival*, Vol. 48, (2006), pp.111–130.
7. FCO 46/609, DOP Note 705/70, CoS Defence Operational Planning Staff, 'The Situation In Muscat & Oman', p.4.
8. Newsinger, *British Counterinsurgency from Palestine to Northern Ireland* (Basingstoke: Palgrave Macmillan, 2002)
9. Halliday, *Arabia Without Sultans*, pp.265–303.
10. 'The Strategic Defence Review', Cmd. 3999 (London: The Stationary Office, July 1998), p.7.

BIBLIOGRAPHY

Primary Sources

National Archives

Cabinet – CAB Series 130, CAB Series 148
Foreign Office – FO Series 93, FO Series 248, FO Series 1016
Foreign & Commonwealth Office – FCO Series 8, FCO Series 46, FCO Series 51
Ministry of Defence – DEFE Series 4, DEFE Series 5, DEFE Series 11, DEFE Series 13, DEFE Series 24, DEFE Series 25, DEFE Series 68
Overseas Development – OD Series 34, AY Series 11
Ministry of Power – POWE Series 63
Prime Minister's Office – PREM 15
Treasury – T Series 317
War Office – WO Series 32, WO Series 181

Churchill College Cambridge

British Diplomatic Oral History Programme (BDOHP)

Coles, Sir (Arthur) John, GCMG (b.1937) – DOHP 46
Gray, Sir John Walton David, KBE CMG (1936–2003) – DOHP 76
Henderson, Sir Nicholas, GCMG KCVO (b.1919) – DOHP 32
Hurd, The Rt Hon The Lord Hurd of Westwell CH CBE (b.1930) – DOHP 90
Lamb, Sir Albert Thomas (Sir Archie), KBE CMG DFC (b.1921) – DOHP 59
Lucas, Ivor Thomas Mark, CMG (b.1927) – DOHP 93
Parsons, Sir Anthony Derrick, GCMG, LVO, MC (1922–1996) – DOHP 10
Ramsbotham, Hon Sir Peter, GCMG (b.1919) – DOHP 44
Walker, Sir Harold Berners, KCMG (b.1932) – DOHP 16
Wright, Sir Denis, GCMG (1911–2005) – DOHP 67
Wright, Patrick Richard Henry, Lord Wright of Richmond, GCMG (b.1931) – DOHP 48

St Antony's College Oxford

Graham Papers (GB165-0327)
Hawley Papers (GB165-0338)
Skeet Papers (GB165-0329)
Smiley Papers (GB165-0336)
Sultan's Armed Forces Association Papers (GB165-0333)

Interviews

Sir Terrence Clark KBE, CMG, CVO (Assistant Head Middle East Department 1974-6), By Telephone, 26 November 2007.
Sir Donald Hawley KCMG, MBE, QC (British Ambassador To Oman 1971-5), 26 November 2007 and 14 January 2008, Little Cheverell, Wiltshire.
Peter Hinchcliffe CMG, CVO (Former Ambassador to Jordan and FCO Official In UAE), Le Meridien Hotel, Amman, 12 June 2006.
Rt Hon Lord Hurd of Westwell CH, CBE (ran Edward Heath's Private Office 1968-70, Political Secretary, Downing Street 1970-74), House of Lords, 5 February 2008.
General Sir Charles Huxtable KCB, CBE (Commander Dhofar Brigade 1976-8), By Telephone, 19 November 2007.
Terry Morgans-Slader (Former BP Internal Travel Department and one of the first post-coup tourists in Oman), Paphos, Cyprus, 22 December 2006.
Major General Ken Perkins CB, MBE, DFC (CSAF 1975-7), By Telephone, 12 November 2007.

United Nations Documents

General Assembly Resolution 2073 (XX).
[www.un.org/documents/ga/res/20/ares20.htm]
General Assembly Resolution 2238 (XXI).
[www.un.org/documents/ga/res/21/ares21.htm]
Question of Oman 1966.
[http://daccessdds.un.org/doc/RESOLUTION/GEN/NR0/218/36/IMG/NR021836.pdf?OpenElement]
Question of Oman 1967.
[http://daccessdds.un.org/doc/RESOLUTION/GEN/NR0/005/41/IMG/NR000541.pdf?OpenElement]
Question of Oman 1968.
[http://daccessdds.un.org/doc/RESOLUTION/GEN/NR0/236/37/IMG/NR023637.pdf?OpenElement]
Question of Oman 1969.
[http://daccessdds.un.org/doc/RESOLUTION/GEN/NR0/236/37/IMG/NR023637.pdf?OpenElement]
Question of Oman 1970.
[http://daccessdds.un.org/doc/RESOLUTION/GEN/NR0/256/93/IMG/NR025693.pdf?OpenElement]

Question of Oman 1971.
[http://daccessdds.un.org/doc/RESOLUTION/GEN/NR0/349/67/IMG/NR034967.pdf?OpenElement]
Letter dated 24 May 1971 from the Prime Minister and Minister for Foreign Affairs of the Sultanate of Oman addressed to the Secretary-General.
[http://daccessdds.un.org/doc/UNDOC/GEN/N71/112/83/PDF/N7111283.pdf?OpenElement]
Security Council official records, 26th year, 1587th meeting, 30 September 1971, New York.
[http://daccessdds.un.org/doc/UNDOC/GEN/NL7/100/04/PDF/NL710004.pdf?OpenElement]
Letter dated 30 September 1971 from the Permanent Representative of the People's Democratic Republic of Yemen to the United Nations addressed to the President of the Security Council.
[http://daccessdds.un.org/doc/UNDOC/GEN/N71/160/24/PDF/N7116024.pdf?OpenElement]
Report of the Security Council Committee on the Admission of New Members concerning the application of Oman for membership in the United Nations.
[http://daccessdds.un.org/doc/UNDOC/GEN/N71/197/22/PDF/N7119722.pdf?OpenElement]
Security Council Resolution 299 (1971) On Admission of Oman to Membership of the United Nations – Adopted by the Security Council at its 1587th meeting of 30 September 1971.
[http://daccessdds.un.org/doc/RESOLUTION/GEN/NR0/261/59/IMG/NR026159.pdf?OpenElement]
Admission of Oman to Membership in the United Nations.
[http://daccessdds.un.org/doc/RESOLUTION/GEN/NR0/327/70/IMG/NR032770.pdf?OpenElement]
Letter dated 21 September 1972 from the Permanent Representative of Oman to the United Nations Addressed to the President of the Security Council.
[http://daccessdds.un.org/doc/UNDOC/GEN/N72/185/18/PDF/N7218518.pdf?OpenElement]
Letter dated 19 November 1973 from the Charge d'Affaires of Oman to the United Nations Addressed to the Secretary-General.
[http://daccessdds.un.org/doc/UNDOC/GEN/N73/265/33/PDF/N7326533.pdf?OpenElement]
Agreement concerning delimitation of the continental shelf (with annexed map). Signed at Tehran on 25 July 1974.
[http://untreaty.un.org/unts/1_60000/27/11/00052504.pdf]
Letter dated 24 December 1975 from the Charge d'Affaires of the People's Democratic Republic of Yemen to the United Nations Addressed to the Secretary-General.
[http://daccessdds.un.org/doc/UNDOC/GEN/N76/002/06/PDF/N7600206.pdf?OpenElement]

Published Government Documents

'British and Foreign State Papers 1957–8', HMSO, 1966.
L'Oman et la France: Quelques Elements d'Histoire, Ministère des Affaires Étrangères, Paris: MAE, 1988.

'The Strategic Defence Review', Cmnd. 3999, London: The Stationary Office, July 1998.

Statement on the Defence Estimates 1966 Part I 'The Defence Review', Cmnd 2901, HMSO, February 1966.

Statement on the Defence Estimates 1966 Part I 'Defence Estimates 1966–7', Cmnd 2902, HMSO, February 1966.

Secondary Sources

Books

Alford, B.W.E., *Britain in the World Economy: Since 1880* (London: Longman, 1996).

Akehurst, John., *Generally Speaking: Then Hurrah for the Life of a Soldier* (Norwich: Michael Russell, 1999).

Akehurst, John., *We Won a War: The Campaign in Oman 1965–1975* (Salisbury: Michael Russell, 1982).

Allen, Calvin H., *Oman: The Modernisation of the Sultanate* (London: Routledge, 1987).

Allen, Calvin H., and Rigsbee, W. Lynn., *Oman Under Qaboos: From Coup to Constitution, 1970–1996* (London: Frank Cass, 2000).

Allen, Charles., *The Savage Wars of Peace* (Harmondsworth: Penguin, 1990).

Allen, Mark., *Arabs* (London: Continuum, 2006).

Allfree, P.S., *Warlords of Oman* (London: Hale, 2008).

Al-Qasimi, Sultan M., *Les relations entre Oman et la France* (Paris: L'Harmattan, 1995).

Arkless, David C., *The Secret War: Dhofar, 1971–72* (London: William Kimber, 1990).

Ashton, S.R. and Louis, Roger, W.M. (Eds.)., *British Documents on the End of Empire, Series A, Volume 5, East of Suez and the Commonwealth 1964–1971 Parts I-III* (London: The Stationary Office, 2004).

Atkinson, Fred and Hall, Steven., *Oil and the British Economy* (London: Croom Helm; New York: St. Martin's Press, 1983).

Balfour-Paul, Glenn., *Bagpipes In Babylon: A Lifetime in the Arab World and Beyond* (London: I.B.Tauris, 2006).

Balfour-Paul, Glenn., *The End of Empire in the Middle East* (Cambridge: CUP, 1994).

Ball, Stuart and Seldon Anthony (Eds.)., *The Heath Government 1970–1974: A Reappraisal* (London: Longman, 1996).

Bamburg, J.H., *The History of the British Petroleum Company. Vol. 2, The Anglo-Iranian Years, 1928–1954* (Cambridge: CUP, 1994).

Barth, Frederick., *Sohar: Culture and Society in an Omani Town* (Baltimore MD.: Johns Hopkins University Press, 1983).

Baylis, John and Smith, Steve (Eds.)., *The Globalisation of World Politics*, Second Edition (Oxford: OUP, 2001).

Beasant, John., *Oman: The True-Life Drama and Intregue of an Arab State* (Edinburgh: Mainstream Publishing, 2002).

Beasant, John and Ling, Christopher., *Sultan in Arabia: A Private Life* (Edinburgh: Mainstream Publishing, 2004).

Beckett, F.W. and Pimlott, John., *Armed Forces and Modern Counter-Insurgency* (New York: St. Martin's Press, 1985).

Bell, Sir Gawain., *An Imperial Twilight* (London: Lester Cook, 1989).

Berridge, G.R., *Diplomacy: Theory and Practice*, Second Edition (Basingstoke: Palgrave, 2002).

Bhacker, M. Rheda., *Trade and Empire in Muscat and Zanzibar: The Roots of British Domination* (Abingdon: Routledge, 1992).
Bloch, Jonathan and Fitzgerald, Patrick., *British Intelligence and Covert Action* (London: Junction Hill Books, 1983).
Booth, Alan., *The British Economy in the Twentieth Century* (Basingstoke: Palgrave Macmillan, 2001).
Boustead, Sir Hugh., *The Wind of Morning: An Autobiography* (Fresno, CA.: Linden Publishing, 2002).
Brenchley, Frank., *Britain and the Middle East an Economic History 1945–87* (London: Lester Crook Academic, 1989).
Brown, Carl L. (Ed.)., *Diplomacy in the Middle East: The International Relations of Regional and Outside Powers* (London: I.B.Tauris, 2001).
Brown, Chris., *Understanding International Relations* (Basingstoke: Palgrave Macmillan, 2001).
Bulloch, John., *The Persian Gulf Unveiled* (New York: Congton & Weed, 1984).
Burchill, Scott., *The National Interest in International Relations Theory* (Basingstoke: Palgrave Macmillan, 2005).
Burrows, Bernard., *Footnotes in the Sand: The Gulf in Transition 1953–1958* (Salisbury: Michael Russell, 1990).
Butt, Gerald., *The Lion in the Sand: The British in the Middle East* (London: Bloomsbury, 1995).
Cable, James., *Intervention at Abadan: Plan Buccaneer* (Basingstoke: Palgrave Macmillan, 1991).
Cain, P.J. and Hopkins, A.G., *British Imperialism: Crisis and Deconstruction, 1914–1990* (London: Longman, 1993).
Cairncross, Alec., *The British Economy Since 1945: Economic Policy and Performance, 1945–1990* (Oxford: Blackwell Publishers, 1995).
Cannadine, David., *Ornamentalism: How The British Saw Their Empire* (Oxford: OUP, 2001).
Carver, Michael., *War Since 1945* (London: Weidenfield & Nicholson, 1980).
Chautard, Sophie., *Guerres et conflits du XXe siècle* (Paris: Libio, 2004).
Clark, Sir Terrence., *Underground To Overseas: The Story of Petroleum Development Oman* (London: Stacey International, 2007).
Clarke, Michael and White, Brian (Eds.)., *Understanding Foreign Policy: The Foreign Policy Systems Approach* (Aldershot: Edward Elgar, 1989).
Clements, Frank A., *Oman: The Reborn Land* (London: Longman, 1980).
Cohen, Michael J., *Fighting World War Three from the Middle East: Allied Contingency Plans, 1945–1954* (London: Frank Cass, 1997).
Connor, Ken., *Ghost Force: The Secret History of the SAS* (London: Weidenfeld & Nicholson, 1998).
Cordesman, Anthony H., *Bahrain, Oman, Qatar and the UAE: Challenges of Security* (Boulder, CO.; Oxford: Westview Press, 1997).
Croft, S., Dorman, A., Rees, W. and Uttley, M. (Eds.)., *Britain and Defence 1945–2000: A Policy Re-Evaluation* (Harlow: Pearson, 2001).
Crystal, Jill., *Oil and Politics in the Gulf: Rulers and Merchants in Kuwait and Qatar* (Cambridge: CUP, 1995).
Curtis, Mark., *The Ambiguities of Power: British Foreign Policy Since 1945* (London: Zed Books, 1995).

Darwin, John., *Britain and Decolonisation: The Retreat from Empire in the Post-War World* (Basingstoke: Macmillan, 1988).
Darwin, John., *The End of the British Empire* (Oxford: Blackwell, 1991).
De La Billiere, Peter., *Looking for Trouble: SAS to Gulf Command* (London: HarperCollins, 1995).
Dickie, John., *Inside The Foreign Office* (London: Chapmans, 1992).
Dickie, John., *The British Consul: Heir to a Great Tradition* (London: Hurst & Co, 2007).
Dockrill, Michael., *British Defence Since 1945* (Oxford: Blackwell, 1988).
Dockrill, Saki., *Britain's Retreat from East of Suez* (Basingstoke: Palgrave Macmillan, 2002).
Donnelly, Jack., *Realism and International Relations* (Cambridge, CUP, 2000).
Dorell, Chris., *MI6: Fifty Years of Special Operations* (London: Fourth Estate, 2001).
Dumortier, Brigitte and Lavergne, Marc., *L'Oman Contemporain: État, Territoire, Identité* (Paris: Karthala, 2002).
Eickelman, Christine., *Women and Community in Oman* (New York: New York University Press, 1984).
Eickleman, Dale F. and Piscatori, James., *Muslim Politics* (Princeton, N.J.: Princeton University Press, 1996).
Fiennes, Ranulph., *Where Soldiers Fear To Tread* (London: Hodder & Stoughton, 1975).
Finney, Patrick, (Ed.)., *International History* (Basingstoke: Palgrave Macmillan, 2005).
Frankel, Joseph., *International Relations in a Changing World*, 4th Edition (Oxford: OUP, 1988).
Frankel, Joseph., *National Interest* (London: Pall Mall Press, 1970).
French, David., *The British Way In Counter-Insurgency 1945–67* (Oxford: OUP, 2011).
Gardiner, Ian., *In The Service of The Sultan: A First Hand Account of the Dhofar Insurgency* (Barnsley: Pen & Sword, 2006).
Geraghty, Tony., *Who Dares Wins: The Special Air Service 1950–1992* (London: Abacus, 2002).
Geraghty, Tony., *Guns for Hire: The Inside Story of Freelance Soldiering* (London: Piatkus, 2007).
Ghubash, Hussein., *Oman: The Islamic Democratic Tradition* (Abingdon: Routledge, 2006).
Gorst, Anthony and Kelly, Sally (Eds.)., *Whitehall and the Suez Crisis* (London: Frank Cass, 2000).
Graz, Liesl., *The Omanis: Sentinels of the Gulf* (London: Longman, 1982).
Hail, J.H., *Britain's Foreign Policy in Egypt and Sudan 1947–1956* (Reading: Ithaca, 1996).
Hall, Richard., *Empires of the Monsoon: A History of the Indian Ocean and its Invaders* (London: HarperCollins, 1996).
Halliday, Fred., *Arabia Without Sultans* (London: Saqi Books, 2001).
Halliday, Fred., *Mercenaries: Counter Insurgency in the Gulf* (Nottingham: Spokesman, 1977).
Halliday, Fred., *Revolution and Foreign Policy: The Case of South Yemen 1967–1987* (Cambridge: CUP, 1990).
Hamoudi, Hadi. H., *Oman Prosperity Today: The State and Development* (London: S.A.R.S., 2006).
Harclerode, Peter., *Fighting Dirty: The Inside Story of Covert Operations from Ho Chi Minh to Osama Bin Laden* (London: Cassell & Co, 2001).

Hart, Parker T., *Saudi Arabia and the United States: Birth of a Security Partnership* (Bloomington, In.: Indiana University Press, 1998).
Hawley, Sir Donald., *Desert Wind and Tropic Storm: An Autobiography* (Norwich: Michael Russell, 2000).
Hawley, Sir Donald., *The Emirates: Witness to a Metamorphosis* (Norwich: Michael Russell, 2007).
Hawley, Sir Donald., *Oman and its Renaissance* (London: Stacey International, 1977).
Healey, Denis., *The Time of My Life* (London: Michael Joseph, 1989).
Heath, Edward., *The Course of My Life* (London: Coronet, 1999).
Henderson, Edward., *Arabian Destiny* (London: Motivate Publishing, 1999).
Hill, Christopher., *Cabinet Decisions on Foreign Policy: The British Experience, October 1938 – June 1941* (Cambridge: CUP, 1991).
Hill, Christopher., *The Changing Politics of Foreign Policy* (Basingstoke: Palgrave Macmillan, 2003).
Holsti, K.J., *International Politics: A Framework for Analysis* – Seventh Edition (Englewood Cliffs, NJ.: Prentice-Hall International, 1995).
Hooper Kerr, Malcolm., *The Arab Cold War: Gamel 'Abd Al-Nasir and His Rivals, 1958–70* (Oxford: OUP, 1972).
Hoskins, Alan., *A Contract Officer in the Oman* (Tunbridge Wells: Costello, 1988).
Hurd, Douglas., *Memoirs* (London: Abacus, 2003).
James, Laura M., *Nasser at War: Arab Images of the Enemy* (Basingstoke: Palgrave Macmillan, 2006).
Jenkins, Simon and Sloman, Ann., *With Respect, Ambassador: An Inquiry Into The Foreign Office* (London: British Broadcasting Corporation, 1985).
Jones, Clive., *Britain and the Yemen Civil War, 1962–1965: Ministers, Mercenaries and Mandarins – Foreign Policy and the Limits of Covert Action* (Brighton: Sussex Academic Press, 2004).
Jones, Clive., *Soviet Jewish Aliyah, 1989 to 1992: Impact and Implications for Israel and the Middle East* (London: Frank Cass, 1996).
Jones, Jeremy., *Negotiating Change: The New Politics of the Middle East* (London: I.B. Tauris, 2006).
Jones, Matthew., *Conflict and Confrontation in South East Asia 1961–1965: Britain, the United States and the Creation of Malaysia* (Cambridge: CUP, 2002).
Joyce, Miriam., *Kuwait, 1945–96: An Anglo-American Perspective* (London: Frank Cass, 1998).
Joyce, Miriam., *Ruling Shaikhs & Her Majesty's Government 1960–1969* (London: Frank Cass, 2003).
Joyce, Miriam., *The Sultanate of Oman: A Twentieth Century History* (Westport, Conn.: Praeger, 1995).
Kapiszewski, Andrzej *et al* (Eds.)., *Modern Oman: Studies on Politics, Economy, Environment and Culture of the Sultanate* (Cracow: Ksiegarnia Akademicka, 2006).
Karabell, Zachary., *Parting the Desert: The Creation of the Suez Canal* (London: John Murray, 2003).
Keay, John., *Sowing the Wind: The Mismanagement of the Middle East 1900–1960* (London: John Murray, 2004).
Kéchichian, Joseph A., *Oman and the World: The Emergence of an Independent Foreign Policy* (Santa Monica, CA.: Rand, 1995).
Kéchichian, Joseph A., *Political Participation & Stability in the Sultanate of Oman* (Dubai: Gulf Research Centre Research Papers, 2006).

Kelly, J.B., *Arabia, the Gulf and the West* (New York: Basic Books, 1980).
Kemp, Anthony., *The SAS Savage Wars of Peace – 1947 to the Present* (London: John Murray, 1994).
Kennedy, Paul., *The Rise and Fall of the Great Powers: Economic Change and Military Conflict from 1500 to 2000* (London: Fontana Press, 1989).
Keohane, Robert O. and Milner, Helen V., *Internationalization and Domestic Politics* (Cambridge: CUP, 1996).
Keohane, Robert O., *Neo-Realism and its Critics* (New York: Columbia University Press, 1986).
Kinzer, Stephen., *All The Shah's Men: An American Coup and the Roots of Middle East Terror* (Hoboken, NJ.: John Wiley, 2004).
Kitson, Frank., *Gangs and Counter-Gangs* (London: Barrie & Rockliff, 1960).
Kitson, Frank., *Low Intensity Operations: Subversion, Insurgency, Peacekeeping* (London: Faber & Faber, 1971).
Kyle, Keith., *Suez* (London: Weidenfield & Nicholson, 1991).
Lapidus, Ira M. *A History of Islamic Societies*, Second Edition (Cambridge: CUP, 2002).
Larres, Klaus and Lane, Ann (Eds.)., *The Cold War: The Essential Readings* (Oxford: Blackwell Publishers, 2001).
Le Cour Grandmaison, Bruno and Colette., *Contribution to a General Bibliography of Oman* (Muscat: Ministry of National Heritage and Culture, 1980).
Levey, Zac., *Israel and the Western Powers 1952–1960* (Chapel Hill, NC.: University of North Carolina Press, 1997).
Limbert, Mandana., *In the Time of Oil: Piety, Memory & Social Life in an Omani Town* (Stanford, CA.: Stanford University Press, 2010).
Little, Richard and Smith, Michael (Eds.)., *Perspectives on World Politics* (London: Routledge, 1991).
Louis, Wm Roger., *Ends of British Imperialism* (London: I.B.Tauris, 2006).
Louis, Wm Roger., *The British Empire in the Middle East, 1945–1951: Arab Nationalism, the United States and Postwar Imperialism* (Oxford: Clarendon, 1984).
Lucas, Sir Ivor., *A Road To Damascus: Mainly Diplomatic Memoirs from the Middle East* (London: The Radcliffe Press, 1997).
McLeod Innes, Neil., *Minister in Oman* (Cambridge: Oleander Press, 1987).
McMahon, Robert J., *The Cold War* (Oxford: OUP, 2003).
Mackintosh-Smith, Tim., *Yemen: Travels in Dictionary Land* (London: Picador, 1999).
Maclean, Donald., *British Foreign Policy Since Suez, 1956–68* (London: Hodder & Stoughton, 1970).
Macridis, Roy C. (Ed.)., *Foreign Policy in World Politics* (London: Prentice Hall International, 1992).
Marshall, Peter., *Positive Diplomacy* (Basingstoke: Palgrave Macmillan, 1999).
Milton-Edwards, Beverly and Hinchcliffe Peter., *Jordan: A Hashemite Legacy* (Abingdon: Routledge, 2002).
Mockaitis, Thomas., *British Counterinsurgency in the Post-Imperial Era* (Manchester: Manchester University Press, 1995).
Monroe, Elizabeth., *Britain's Moment in the Middle East 1914–1971* (London: Chatto & Windus, 1981).
Morris, Jan., *Sultan in Oman* (London: Sickle Moon Books, 2002).
Nagel, John A., *Learning to Eat Soup with a Knife: Counterinsurgency Lessons from Malaya and Vietnam* (Chicago: Chicago University Press, 2005).

Neillands, Robin., *A Fighting Retreat: The British Empire 1947–1997* (London: Coronet Books, 1997).
Netton, Ian R. (Ed.)., *Arabia and the Gulf from Traditional Society to Modern States* (Beckenham: Croom Helm, 1986).
Newsinger, John., *British Counterinsurgency from Palestine to Northern Ireland* (Basingstoke: Palgrave Macmillan, 2001).
Niblock, Tim., *Saudi Arabia: Power, Legitimacy and Survival* (Abingdon: Routledge, 2006).
Nye, Joseph S. (Jr.)., *Bound to Lead: The Changing Nature of American Power* (New York: Basic Books, 1990).
Nye, Joseph S. (Jr.)., *Soft Power: The Means to Success in World Politics* (New York: Public Affairs, 2004).
Nzongola-Ntalaja, Georges., *The Congo from Leopold to Kabila: A People's History* (London: Zed Books, 2002).
Oren, Michael B., *Six Days of War: June 1967 and the Making of the Modern Middle East* (London: Penguin, 2002).
Ovendale, Ritchie., *Anglo-American Relations in the Twentieth Century* (Basingstoke: Palgrave Macmillan, 1998).
Ovendale, Ritchie (Ed.)., *British Defence Policy Since 1945* (Manchester: Manchester University Press, 1994).
Ovendale, Ritchie., *Britain, The United States, and the Transfer of Power in the Middle East, 1945–1962* (Leicester: Leicester University Press, 1996).
Owtram, Francis., *A Modern History of Oman: Formation of the State Since 1920* (London: I.B.Tauris, 2004).
Paget, Julian., *Counter Insurgency Campaigning* (London: Faber & Faber, 1967).
Parsons, Anthony., *They Say the Lion – Britain's Legacy to the Arabs: A Personal Memoir* (London: Jonathan Cape, 1986).
Perkins, Ken., *A Fortunate Soldier* (London: Brassey's, 1988).
Perkins, Ken., *Khalida* (London: Quartet, 1991).
Petersen, Tore T., *The Decline of the Anglo American Middle East 1961–1969* (Brighton: Sussex University Press, 2006).
Petersen, Tore T., *The Middle East between the Great Powers: Anglo-American Conflict and Cooperation, 1952–7* (Basingstoke: Macmillan, 2000).
Peterson, J.E., *Defending Arabia: Air Power & Gulf Security* (London: Croom Helm, 1986).
Peterson, J.E., *Oman's Insurgencies: The Sultanate's Struggle for Supremacy* (London: Saqi Books, 2007).
Peterson, J.E., *Oman in the Twentieth Century: Political Foundations of an Emerging State* (London: Croom Helm, 1978).
Phillips, Wendell., *Oman: A History* (London: Longman, 1967).
Plekhanov, Sergey., *A Reformer on the Throne: Sultan Qaboos Bin Said Al Said* (London: Trident Press, 2004).
Potter, Lawrence G. and Sick, Gary G. (Eds.)., *Security in the Persian Gulf: Origins, Obstacles and the Search for Consensus* (Basingstoke: Palgrave Macmillan, 2002).
Pridham, B.R. (Ed.)., *Oman: Economic, Social and Strategic Developments* (London: Croom Helm, 1987).
Purdon, Corran., *List the Bugle: Reminiscences of an Irish Soldier* (Antrim: Greystone, 1993).

Rabi, Uzi., *The Emergence of States in a Tribal Society: Oman under Sa'id Bin Taymur, 1932–1970* (Brighton: Sussex Academic Press, 2006).
Ray, Bryan., *Dangerous Frontiers: Campaigning in Somaliland and Oman* (Barnsley: Pen & Sword, 2008).
Reynolds, David., *Britannia Overruled: British Policy and World Power in the Twentieth Century*, Second Edition (London: Longman, 2000).
Reynolds, David, Kimball, Warren and Chubarain, A.O. (Eds.)., *Allies at War: The Soviet, American and British Experience, 1939–1945* (Basingstoke, Macmillan, 1994).
Riphenburg, Carol J., *Oman: Political Development in a Changing World* (Westport, Conn.: Praeger, 1998).
Risso, Patricia., *Oman and Muscat: An Early Modern History* (London: Routledge, 1986).
Roberts, Adam and Kingsbury, Benedict., *United Nations, Divided World: The UN's Roles in International Relations* (Oxford: Clarendon, 1993).
Rosecrance, Richard., *The Rise of the Trading State: Commerce and Conquest in the Modern World* (New York: Basic Books, 1986).
Said, Edward W., *Orientalism* (London: Penguin, 2003).
Said Zahlan, Rosemarie., *The Making of the Modern Gulf States* (Reading: Ithaca Press, 1998).
Sanders, David., *Losing an Empire Finding a Role: British Foreign Policy Since 1945* (Basingstoke: Macmillan, 1990).
Searle, Pauline., *Dawn Over Oman* (London: Allen & Unwin, 1979).
Seldon, Anthony., *The Foreign Office* (London: Harper Collins, 2000).
Sindelar, Richard III. and Peterson J.E. (Eds.)., *Crosscurrents in the Gulf* (London: Routledge, 1988).
Sirriyeh, Hussein., *United States Policy in the Gulf, 1968–77: Aftermath of British Withdrawal* (London: Ithaca, 1984).
Skeet, Ian., *Oman Before 1970: The End of an Era* (London: Faber & Faber, 1985).
Skeet, Ian., *Oman: Politics and Development* (Basingstoke: Palgrave Macmillan, 1992).
Smiley, David., *Arabian Assignment* (London: Leo Cooper, 1975).
Smith, Michael, Smith, Steve and White, Brian (Eds.)., *British Foreign Policy: Tradition, Change and Transformation* (London: Unwin Hyman, 1988).
Smith, Simon C., *Britain's Revival and Fall in the Gulf: Kuwait, Bahrain, Qatar and the Trucial States, 1950–1971* (London: RoutledgeCurzon, 2004).
Smith, Simon C., *Kuwait, 1950–1965: Britain, the Al-Sabah and Oil* (Oxford: OUP, 1999)
Tempset, Paul (Ed.)., *An Enduring Friendship: 400 Years of Anglo-Gulf Relations* (London: Stacey International, 2006).
Thesiger, Wilfred., *Arabian Sands* (London: Penguin, 1984).
Thomas, Martin., *Empires of Intelligence: Security Services and Colonial Disorder after 1914* (Berkeley, CA.: University of California Press, 2007)
Thompson, Julian (Ed.)., *The Imperial War Museum Book of Modern Warfare* (London: Sidgwick & Jackson/Macmillan, 2002).
Thompson, Robert., *Defeating Communist Insurgency: Experiences from Malaya and Vietnam* (London: Chatto & Windus, 1966).
Thwaites, Paul., *Muscat Command* (London: Leo Cooper/Pen & Sword, 1995).
Townsend, John., *Oman: The Making of the Modern State* (London: Croom Helm, 1977).
Venn, Fiona., *Oil Diplomacy in the Twentieth Century* (Basingstoke: Macmillan, 1986).

Verrier, Anthony., *Through The Looking Glass: British Foreign Policy in the Age of Illusions* (London: Jonathan Cape, 1983).
Vine, Peter., *The Heritage of Oman* (London: Immel, 1995).
Viotti, Paul R. and Kauppi, Mark V., *International Relations Theory: Realism, Pluralism, Globalism* (New York: Macmillan, 1987).
Walker, Jonathan., *Aden Insurgency: The Savage War in South Arabia 1962–67* (Staplehurst: Spellmount, 2005).
Weber, Cynthia., *International Relations Theory: A Critical Introduction* (London: Routledge, 2005).
Weber, Max., *The Theory of Social and Economic Organization* (New York: Free Press, 1947).
Wikan, Unni., *Behind the Veil in Arabia* (Chicago, Il.: University of Chicago Press, 1991).
Wilkinson, John C., *The Imamate Tradition of Oman* (Cambridge: CUP, 1987)
Woodhouse, Christopher M., *Something Ventured: An Autobiography* (St Albans: Granada, 1982).
Yaqub, Sali., *Containing Arab Nationalism: The Eisenhower Doctrine and the Middle East* (Chapel Hill, NC.: University of North Carolina Press, 2004).
Yergin, Daniel., *The Prize: The Epic Quest for Oil, Money and Power* (London: Simon & Schuster, 1991).
Young, John W., *Britain and the World in the Twentieth Century* (London: Arnold, 1997).

Chapters in Edited Books

Balfour-Paul, Glenn., 'Britain's Informal Empire in the Middle East', In Brown, Judith M. & Roger Louis, W.M. (Eds.)., *The Oxford History of the British Empire, Vol. IV, The Twentieth Century* (Oxford: OUP, 1999).
Clayton, Anthony., '"Deceptive Might": Imperial Defence and Security, 1900–1968', In Brown, Judith M. & Roger Louis, W.M. (Eds.)., *The Oxford History of the British Empire, Vol. IV, The Twentieth Century* (Oxford: OUP, 1999).
Darwin, John., 'Decolonisation and the End of Empire', In Winks, Robin W. (Ed.)., *The Oxford History of the British Empire, Vol. V, Historiography* (Oxford: OUP, 1999).
Eickelman, Dale F., 'Intelligence in an Arab Gulf State', In Roy Godson (Ed.)., *Comparing Foreign Intelligence: The U.S., the USSR, the U.K. and the Third World* (London: Brassey's, 1988).
Hollis, Rosemary., 'Britain's Strategic Approach to the Gulf', In The Emirates Center for Strategic Studies & Research, *International Interests in the Gulf Region* (Abu Dhabi: ECSSR, 2004).
Jones, Clive., 'From the Deniable to the Acceptable? Britain, Intelligence and Covert Action in Yemen and Oman 1962 – 1976' In Tore T. Petersen (Ed.)., *Challenging Retrenchment: The United States, Great Britain and The Middle East 1950–1980* (Trondheim: Tapir Academic Press, 2010).
Osterhammel, Jürgen., 'Britain & China', In Porter, Andrew (Ed.)., *The Oxford History of the British Empire, Vol. III, The Nineteenth Century* (Oxford: OUP, 1999).
Robinson, Francis., 'The British Empire and the Muslim World', In Brown, Judith M. & Roger Louis, W.M. (Eds.)., *The Oxford History of the British Empire, Vol. IV, The Twentieth Century* (Oxford: OUP, 1999).
Sluglett, Peter., 'Formal and Informal Empire in the Middle East', In Winks, Robin W. (Ed.)., *The Oxford History of the British Empire, Vol. V, Historiography* (Oxford: OUP, 1999).

Tilley, Charles., 'Western State Making and Theories of Political Transformation', In Tilley, Charles (Ed.)., *The Formation of National States in Western Europe* (Princeton, NJ: Princeton University Press, 1975).
Worrall, James., 'Britain's Last Bastion in Arabia: The End of the Dhofar War, the Labour Government and the Withdrawal from RAF Salalah and Masirah, 1974–1977' In Tore T. Petersen (Ed.)., *Challenging Retrenchment: The United States, Great Britain and The Middle East 1950–1980* (Trondheim: Tapir Academic Press, 2010).

Articles

Anderson, Lisa., 'The State in the Middle East and North Africa', *Comparative Politics*, Vol. 20, No. 1, (1987), pp.1–18.
Betz, David and Cormack, Anthony., 'Iraq, Afghanistan and British Strategy', *Orbis*, Vol. 53, No. 2, (2009), pp.319–36.
Brewer, William D., 'Yesterday and Tomorrow in the Persian Gulf', *Middle East Journal*, Vol. 23, No. 2, (1969), pp.149–58.
Cecil, Charles O., 'Oman's Progress Toward Participatory Government', *Middle East Policy*, Vol. XIII, No. 1, (Spring 2006), pp.60–8.
Clements, Frank., 'The Islands of Kuria Muria: A Civil Aid Project in the Sultanate of Oman Administered from Salalah, Regional Capital of Dhofar', *British Journal of Middle Eastern Studies*, Vol. 4, No. 1, (1977), pp.37–9.
Dixon, Paul., '"Hearts and Minds"? British Counter-Insurgency from Malaya to Iraq', *Journal of Strategic Studies*, Vol. 32, No. 3, (2009), pp.353–81.
Eickelman, Christine., 'Fertility and Social Change in Oman: Women's Perspectives', *Middle East Journal*, Vol. 47, No. 4, (1993), pp.652–66.
Eickleman, Dale F., 'From Theocracy to Monarchy: Authority & Legitimacy in Inner Oman, 1935–1957', *International Journal of Middle East Studies*, Vol. 17, No. 1, (February 1985), pp.3–24.
Eickelman, Dale F., 'National Identity and Religious Discourse in Contemporary Oman', *International Journal of Islamic and Arabic Studies*, Vol. 6, No. 1, (1989), pp.1–20.
Eickelman, Dale F. and Dennison, M.G., 'Arabizing the Omani Intelligence Services: Clash of Cultures?', *International Journal of Intelligence and Counterintelligence*, Vol. 7, No. 1, (Spring 1994), pp.1–28.
Gauze, F. Gregory III., 'Systemic Approaches to Middle East International Relations', *International Studies Review*, Vol. 1, No. 1, (Spring 1999), pp.11–31.
Halliday, Fred., 'Arabia Without Sultans Revisited', *Middle East Report*, No. 204, (July-September 1997), pp.27–9.
Halliday, Fred., 'Counter-Insurgency in Oman', *Gulf Studies*, No. 1, (April 1976), pp.13–35.
Hensel, Howard M., 'Soviet Policy Towards the Rebellion in Dhofar', *Asian Affairs*, Vol. 13, No. 2, (1982), pp.183–207.
Hopwood, Derek., 'Earth's Proud Empires Pass Away: Britain's Moment in the Middle East', *British Journal of Middle Eastern Studies*, Vol. 29, No. 2, (2002), pp.109–21.
Hughes, Geraint., 'A "Model Campaign" Reappraised: The Counter-Insurgency War in Dhofar, Oman, 1965–1975', *Journal of Strategic Studies*, Vol. 32, No. 2, (2009), pp.271–305.
Ismail, Abdul Fatah., 'How We Liberated Aden', *Gulf Studies*, No. 1, (April 1976), pp.3–11.

Jackson, Ashley., 'British Counter-Insurgency in History: A Useful Historical Precedent?', *British Army Review*, No. 139, (2006), pp.12–22.
Jones, Clive and Stone, John., 'Britain and the Arabian Gulf: New Perspectives on Strategic Influence', *International Relations*, Vol. 13, No. 4, (1997), pp.1–24.
Joyce-Harron, Miriam., 'Britain and the Sultan of Muscat & Oman 1958–1959', *Diplomacy and Statecraft*, Vol. 4, No. 1, (1993), pp.90–103.
Katz, Mark N., 'Assessing the Political Stability of Oman', *Middle East Review of International Affairs*, Vol. 8, No. 2, (September 2004).
Kelly, J.B., 'Hadramaut, Oman, Dhufar: The Experience of Revolution', *Middle East Studies*, Vol. 12, No. 2, (May 1976), pp.213–30.
Kelly, J.B., 'The Legal and Historical Basis of the British Position in the Persian Gulf', *St Antony's Papers No 4:* Middle Eastern Affairs No 1, (1958), pp.119–38.
Kilcullen, David., 'Counterinsurgency *Redux*', *Survival*, Vol. 48, (2006), pp.111–30.
Ladwig, Walter C. III., 'Supporting Allies in Counterinsurgency: Britain and the Dhofar Rebellion', *Small Wars & Insurgencies*, Vol. 19, No. 1, (2008), pp.62–88.
Louis, Wm Roger., 'The British Withdrawal from the Gulf', *The Journal of Imperial and Commonwealth History*, Vol. 31, No. 1, (January 2003), pp.83–108.
Martell, Gordon., 'Decolonisation after Suez: Retreat or Rationalisation?', *Australian Journal of Politics and History*, Vol. 46, No. 3, (2000), pp.403–417.
Martin, L.W., 'British Defence Policy: The Long Recessional', *Adelphi Paper*, No. 61, (November 1969).
Mawby, Spencer., 'From Tribal Rebellions to Revolution', *The Electronic Journal of International History*, Article 5.
Newsinger, John., 'Review of T.R. Mockaitis, 'British Counterinsurgency 1919–1960' *Race and Class*, Vol. 34, No. 2, (1992), pp.96–98.
Olson, William J., 'Air Power in Low-Intensity Conflict in the Middle East', *Air University Review*, (March-April 1986).
O'Reilly, Mark., 'Omanibalancing: Oman Confronts an Uncertain Future', *Middle East Journal*, Vol. 52, No. 1, (1998), pp.70–84.
Peterson, J.E., 'Britain and "The Oman War": An Arabian Entanglement', *Asian Affairs*, Vol. 63, No. 3, (1976), pp.285–298.
Peterson, J.E., 'Guerrilla Warfare and Ideological Confrontation in the Arabian Peninsula: The Rebellion in Dhufar', *World Affairs*, Vol. 139, No. 4, (1977), pp.278–295.
Peterson, J.E., 'Legitimacy and Political Change in Yemen and Oman', *Orbis*, Vol. 27, No. 4, (1984), pp.971–998.
Peterson, J.E., 'Oman's Diverse Society: Northern Oman', *Middle East Journal*, Vol. 58, No. 1, (2004), pp.31–51.
Peterson, J.E., 'Oman's Diverse Society: Southern Oman', *Middle East Journal*, Vol. 58, No. 2, (2004), pp.254–269.
Peterson, J.E., 'Oman: Three and a Half Decades of Change and Development', *Middle East Policy*, Vol. XI, No. 2, (2004), pp.125–137.
Peterson, J.E., 'The Emergence of Post-Traditional Oman', *Durham Middle East Papers*, No. 78, Sir William Luce Fellowship Paper No. 5, 2004.
Peterson, J.E., 'The Revival of the Ibadi Imamate and the Threat to Muscat, 1913–1920', *Arabian Studies*, Vol. 3, (1976), pp.165–188.
Peterson, J.E., 'Tribes and Politics in Eastern Arabia', *Middle East Journal*, Vol. 31, No. 3, (1977), pp.297–312.
Price, David Lynn., 'Oman: Insurgency and Development', Institute for the Study of Conflict, *Conflict Studies*, No. 53, (1975), 19 Pages.

Rabi, Uzi., 'Britain's 'Special Position' in the Gulf: Its Origins, Dynamics and Legacy', *Middle Eastern Studies*, Vol. 42, No. 3, (May 2006), pp.351–364.

Rabi, Uzi., 'Majlis al-Shura and Majlis al-Dawla: Weaving Old Practices and New Realities in the Process of State Formation in Oman', *Middle Eastern Studies*, Vol. 38, No. 4, (October 2002), pp.41–60.

Rabi, Uzi., 'Oil Politics and Tribal Rulers in Eastern Arabia: The Reign of Shakhbut 1928–1966', *British Journal of Middle Eastern Studies*, Vol. 33, No. 1, (May 2006), pp.37–50.

Rabi, Uzi., 'Oman and the Arab-Israeli Conflict: The Reflection of a Pragmatic Foreign Policy', *Israel Affairs*, Vol. 11, No. 3, (July 2005), pp.535–551.

Rubin, Barry., 'China's Middle East Strategy', *Middle East Review of International Affairs*, Vol. 3, No. 1, (March 1999).

Smith, Steve., 'The Development of International Relations as a Social Science', *Millennium*, Vol. 16, No. 2, (1987), pp.189–206.

Sondermann, Fred., 'The Concept of the National Interest', *Orbis*, (Spring 1977), pp.121–138.

Thornton, Rod., 'Countering Arab Insurgencies: The British Experience', *Contemporary Security Policy*, Vol. 28, No. 1, (2007), pp.7–27.

Tremayne, Penelope., 'Guevara Through the Looking Glass: A View of the Dhofar War', *RUSI Journal*, Vol. 119, No. 3, (1974), pp.39–43.

Tremayne, Penelope., 'Seven Years On: Dhofar', *RUSI Journal*, Vol. 127, No. 3, (1982), pp.45–46.

Valeri, Marc., 'High Visibility, Low Profile: The Shi'a in Oman under Sultan Qaboos', *International Journal of Middle East Studies*, Vol. 42, (2010), pp.251–268.

Valeri, Marc., 'Nation-Building and Communities in Oman since 1970: The Swahili-Speaking Omani in Search of Identity', *African Affairs*, Vol. 106, No. 424, (July 2007), pp.479–496.

Walcott, Colonel Tom., 'The Trucial Oman Scouts 1955 to 1971: An Overview', *Asian Affairs*, Vol. XXXVII, No. 1, (March 2006), pp.34–47.

'The Anglo-American Special-Relationship', *Diplomatic History*, No. 13, (1989), pp.479–498.

'Symposium on Oman', *Middle East Policy*, Vol. IV, No. 3, (1994–95).

Unpublished Works/Pamphlets

Al-Ghassany, Abdul Qadar., *Dhofar: The Land of Frankincense*, Second Edition, (2008), Pamphlet From: The World of Frankincense Museum, Salalah, Oman.

Rabi, Uzi, *Oman under Sa'id bin Taymur, 1932–70: The Emergence of States in a Tribal Society* (Unpublished Draft Manuscript, 2005).

Timpe, G. Lawrence., *British Foreign Policy towards the Sultanate of Oman 1954–59* (Unpublished PhD Thesis, University of Exeter, 1991).

Newspapers

The Daily Express
The Daily Mail
The Daily Telegraph
Financial Times

The Guardian
The Independent
International Herald Tribune
The Mirror
Le Monde
Le Monde Diplomatique
The Sunday Times
The Times
The Times of Oman

Internet Sources

Anglo-Omani Society
  [http://www.oman.org.uk/]
Arabian Peninsula and Persian Gulf Database – Oman and Dhofar
  [http://www.acig.org/artman/publish/article_202.shtml]
Britain's Small Wars
  [http://www.britains-smallwars.com/Desert_song/index.htm]
Ian Gardiner
  [http://www.iangardiner.com/]
J.E. Peterson's Website
  [http://www.jepeterson.net/]
The British-Yemeni Society
  [http://www.al-bab.com/bys/Default.htm]
The Historical Association of Oman
  [http://www.hao.org.om/]
The Insurgency In Oman, 1962–1976
  [http://www.globalsecurity.org/military/library/report/1984/CSA.htm]
The Jebal Akhdar War 1954–59
  [http://www.globalsecurity.org/military/library/report/1985/MJB.htm]
The Journal of Statebuilding and Intervention
  [http://www.tandf.co.uk/journals/risb]
Oman Information Portal
  [http://www.al-bab.com/arab/countries/oman.htm]
Oman Studies Centre
  [http://www.oman.org/]
Photographs of the Sultanate of Oman & The Sultan's Armed Forces 1974–76
  [http://www.kdesign.info/oman/index.htm]
Strait of Hormuz
  [http://www.dataxinfo.com/index.htm]
Sultan's Armed Forces Association
  [http://www.oman.org.uk/]
U.S. Library of Congress
  [http://lcweb2.loc.gov/frd/cs/omtoc.html]

CHRONOLOGY OF THE DHOFAR WAR

1940s	Dhofaris begin to move to other countries of the Gulf in search of work and education.
1960 (approx.)	A Dhofari branch of the Arab Nationalists' Movement (ANM) is established.
1962	Differences appear between ANM leadership in the Levant and the Dhofari branch; some Dhofaris break away to form the Dhofar Benevolent Society (DBS).
1962, August	Talib bin 'Ali al-Hina'i of the Oman Revolutionary Movement (of northern Oman) attempts to enlist Dhofari exiles in anti-Sultanate activities.
1963, April	Musallim bin Nufal and followers from the Kathir tribe attack a John Mecom oil-company truck on Salalah-Midway road, killing an Omani escort; after carrying out two further attacks, Musallim travels to Saudi Arabia to seek support.
1963, 1 May	A Land-Rover belonging to the Royal Air Force station at Salalah is blown up by a landmine.
1964	Musallim bin Nufal makes a second trip to Saudi Arabia, where he receives arms and ammunition from Talib bin Ali al Hindi. He returns across the Rub' al-Khali Desert with thirty four followers and caches the arms, which are soon discovered by Sultanate forces.
1964	Another group of Dhofari dissidents begins training at al-Mansurah in northern Iraq.
1964, August-September	Several people are killed by a number of mines laid on the Salalah-Raysut road and Musallim bin Nufal and his followers attack the John Mecom camp at Raysut.

1964, December	The Sultan's Armed Forces (SAF) are allowed to operate in Dhofar for the first time when a company from the Northern Frontier Regiment (NFR) travels overland from northern Oman to Dhofar to search for Musallim bin Nufal.
1965, February	Musallim bin Nufal returns to Dhofar, followed in March by another group of Dhofari dissidents led by Amir bin Ghanim.
1965, May	Operation Rainbow sends two companies of the Muscat Regiment (MR) to Dhofar to stop dissident activities.
1965, May	A dhow intercepted by the Iranian Navy in the Shatt al-Arab contains armed Dhofari dissidents and arms.
1965, 1–9 June	The various dissident groups meet in Wadi al-Kabir of central Dhofar and agree to merge into the Dhofar Liberation Front.
1965, 9 June	The new DLF attacks an oil-company lorry on the Salalah-Midway road and shoots the driver; the rebels regard this incident as the official start of the Dhofar War.
1965, 9 June	Aircraft of the Sultan of Oman's Air Force (SOAF) fire their guns and drop bombs on the opposition for the first time, as Provosts support MR elements operating in the Najd of Dhofar.
1965, 18 June	The Muscat Regiment carries out a cordon-and-search operation in Salalah, arresting thirty to thirty-five suspects identified by information from the May 1965 dhow capture.
1965, August	Another group of rebels uses the Rub' al-Khali Desert to enter Dhofar with eight vehicles and a supply of arms and mines.
1965, October-November	Rebel attacks increase, including attacks on the coastal towns of Taqah and Mirbat.
1966	External support for the DLF begins to shift from Saudi Arabia to Egypt and Iraq.
1966, February	Musallim bin Nufal returns to Dhofar with another convoy of arms and is wounded during an attack on an NFR patrol on 8 February.
1966, February	The increasingly serious situation prompts the SAF to send a second company of the NFR to reinforce the company already in Dhofar, as well as the new Red Company, elements of the Oman Artillery, air cover from the SOAF and the Coastal Patrol's dhow.
1966, 9 March	Three soldiers from the NFR die after their patrol base on *Jebal* Dhofar is attacked.
1966, 13 March	A Company of the NFR is ambushed in Wadi Nahiz and two soldiers and Captain Woodman are killed; Woodman is the first British officer to die in Dhofar.
1966, 26 April	*Jebbali* members of the Dhofar Force attempt to assassinate Sultan Sa'id during an inspection at Razat camp outside Salalah.

Chronology of the Dhofar War

1966, 24 May	B Company of the NFR is ambushed on *Jebal* Dhofar and eight soldiers, including the British company commander, and ten opposition members, including Amir bin Ghanim, are killed.
1966, October	British forces conduct a cordon-and-search operation in Hauf, across the border from Dhofar, and capture a number of Dhofari fighters.
1967, Early	Operations along the border in a temporarily successful effort to deny resupply to the rebels on *Jebal* Dhofar.
1967, April	Brigadier Corran Purdon replaces Colonel Tony Lewis as commander of the Sultan's Armed Forces.
1967, November	Sultan Sa'id orders construction to begin on a fort on the border at Habarut.
1967, 30 November	Aden and the Protectorate receive their independence and the People's Republic of Southern Yemen (PRSY; later the People's Democratic Republic of Yemen (PDRY); also known as South Yemen) is declared.
1968, January	A series of rebel attacks, using mines, rifles, light machine guns and mortars, indicates that they are being resupplied from South Yemen.
1968, June	The SAF establishes forward bases at Januk and Difa' in the Western Sector.
1968, July-August	Northern Omani members of the ANM meet in Dubai and establish the Popular Revolutionary Movement (PRM).
1968, 10 August	Salalah is attacked for the first time when mortar bombs fired from the mouth of Wadi Jarsis land near RAF Salalah.
1968, 1–20 September	The DLF's second congress is held at Wadi Hamrin in Central Dhofar; the radicals gain control and oust the nationalists from the Front's leadership and the name is changed to the Popular Front for the Liberation of the Occupied Arabian Gulf (PFLOAG).
1969	The People's Republic of China provides the PFLOAG with arms, equipment and training facilities, including some training in China.
1969, 25–28 May	Operation Lance is launched to penetrate the Shirshitti cave complex in western Dhofar but meets fierce resistance and the SAF suffer serious casualties.
1969, August	Raykut falls to the enemy, eliminating the last Sultanate presence in western Dhofar.
1970, 6 January	Fifty Front fighters attack Taqah using mortar and rocket support.
1970, February	Colonel Pat Waterfield retires as defence secretary and is replaced by retired Colonel Hugh Oldman, a former commander of the Sultan's Armed Forces.
1970, April	Brigadier R.F. Semple leads a British military team to Oman to discuss the possibility of using the SAS in the Dhofar War.

1970, April	Brigadier John Graham replaces Brigadier Corran Purdon as commander of the Sultan's Armed Forces.
1970, May	The SAF's last position on *Jebal* Dhofar, overlooking the Salalah-Midway road, is withdrawn as not useful.
1970, 11/12 June	The new National Democratic Front for the Liberation of the Occupied Arabian Gulf (NDFLOAG; formerly known as the Popular Revolutionary Movement) launches an attack on the army camp at Izki and fails to explode a bomb at the camp in Nizwa; an NFR party is soon able to capture or kill all the Izki attackers.
1970, 21 June	The Sultan of Oman's Navy, incorporating the Coastal Patrol, is established within the Sultan's Armed Forces, with a contract officer, Commander Douglas Williams, as the first commander.
1970, 23 July	Sultan Sa'id bin Taimur is deposed in Salalah by his son Qaboos bin Sa'id, but the event is not announced to the public until 26 July.
1970, 30 July	The Sultan Qaboos arrives in Muscat, and is followed by his uncle, Sayyid Tariq bin Taimur, who becomes prime minister on 4 August. Among the first decisions taken by Sultan Qaboos are a commitment to accelerated socio-economic development throughout the country, a truce in Dhofar and the expansion of the SAF to allow them to deal with the Dhofar situation properly. Despite the change in government, the Front continues to carry out attacks throughout Dhofar.
1970, August	The first SAS elements arrive in Oman to train a bodyguard for the Sultan and to prepare the next SAF battalion due to move to Dhofar.
1970, September	Elements of the SAS deploy into Dhofar as the British Army Training Team (BATT).
1970, 12 September	*Jebbalis* in eastern Dhofar attempt a counterrevolution against the Front but are brutally suppressed with many killed, which encourages defections to the government.
1970, 12 September	An opposition attack on the fort at Taqah is driven off by SOAF Strikemaster aircraft.
1970, December	A cell of the Arab Action Party is discovered near Bukha in the Musandam and is subsequently evicted by British and Sultan's Armed Forces elements.
1970, December	Musallim bin Nufal surrenders to the government.
1971, January	The SAF return to the offensive, as the Desert Regiment (DR) recommences operations on *Jebal* Dhofar while SOAF and Artillery strikes are carried out against enemy concentrations and supply points. Meanwhile, the NFR establishes itself at Haluf in order to allow operations against the enemy from the north side of the *jebal*. This is the first time a complete battalion is based on the *jebal*.

Chronology of the Dhofar War

1971, January	A small headquarters for the Dhofar Area, the forerunner of the Dhofar Brigade, is established in Umm al-Ghawarif camp at Salalah.
1971, January	The first *firqah* is raised with the help of the BATT and begins training at Mirbat under the name of Firqah Salah al-Din.
1971, February	Headquarters Dhofar is established at Umm al-Ghawarif camp in Salalah with Colonel Mike Harvey as the first commander, Dhofar Area.
1971, 23 February	Operation Everest results in recapture of Sadh by the Firqah Salah al-Din and its BATT, supported by a company of the MR and Coastal Patrol dhows.
1971, March	The number of surrendered opposition personnel (SEP) reaches 201 from September 1970.
1971, May	The NFR moves to a new base at Akut, permitting it to mount the first battalion operations into the treeline of the Western Sector in two years.
1971, 8–9 June	The Front celebrates its anniversary of the 'revolution' with Taqah and Mirbat, and follows up with more attacks on coastal towns in the following weeks.
1971, 1–3 September	NDFLOAG involvement is detected in the demonstrations taking place in Muscat, Matrah and Ruwi, but these are contained without major incident by the new police supported by SAF elements.
1971, 11 September	A Strikemaster is the first aircraft to be brought down by enemy fire.
1971, October	The end of the Monsoon, the expansion of both the BATT and the *firqat*, the arrival of helicopters and improvements in logistics and command and control, SAF are now ready for offensive operations on the *jebal*.
1971, 2 October	Operation Jaguar, led by a number of *firqat* and two squadrons of the SAS, is launched in the east to establish a permanent base on the *jebal* and pacify the Eastern Sector.
1971, November	Heliborne forces are used in Operation Leopard to set up a line of picquets running from Mughsail across the mountains to the Najd in an attempt to prevent enemy resupply from the west.
1971, November	An incursion of armed men into northern Oman from Ras al-Khaimah is repulsed.
1971, 14–20 December	A Front conference at Ahlaysh in Central Dhofar merges the PFLOAG and NDFLOAG to form the Popular Front for the Liberation of Oman and the Arabian Gulf, and some northern Omanis are added to the new Front's committees.
1972, Early	Soviet weapons and supplies appear on the *jebal* as the Front's relations with China begin to deteriorate.
1972, January-March	Successful operations are carried out in the east to consolidate gains and to clear Wadi Darbat of the opposition.

1972, 16 April	Operation Simba, an ambitious attempt to deny the rebels resupply from Yemen, begins with the seizure of Sarfait on the border. Bad weather delays the move down the escarpment to seal off supply routes and then a strong enemy response and developments elsewhere force a withdrawal back to Sarfait.
1972, 5–6 May	South Yemeni troops attack the Sultanate fort at Habarut and force the Dhofar Gendarmerie to withdraw, following which the fort is destroyed.
1972, 7 May	As a result of monsoon redeployments, the Tawi 'Atayr and Leopard treeline positions are abandoned but White City is reinforced, marking the first time that the SAF are able to hold positions throughout the monsoon on both the eastern and western *jebal*.
1972, 25–26 May	Sultan Qaboos orders the SAF to carry out Operation Aqubah in retaliation for Habarut: Artillery and SOAF air trikes are carried out against Front targets in Hauf.
1972, 8 June	The Front celebrates the 9 June anniversary by firing rocket rounds onto RAF Salalah; one strikes the officers' mess and seriously wounds two people.
1972, 19 July	The Front launches its biggest ever operation in an attack on Mirbat but is repulsed after several hours of fighting with heavy opposition casualties.
1972, August	At least 1,000 armed opposition members have been killed, wounded or captured in battle since July 1970, in addition to 570 SEPs, while the SAF losses in all Oman during the same period total ninety dead and 266 wounded (including traffic accidents).
1972, August	Colonel Jack Fletcher takes over as commander, Dhofar Area.
1972, August	After CSAF briefs the Iranian ambassador in Salalah, Iran sends some sixty loads of supplies on C-130 Hercules aircraft.
1972, September	Major General Tim Creasey replaces Brigadier John Graham as commander of the Sultan's Armed Forces.
1972, September	The first Iranian helicopters with pilots and ground crews arrive in Dhofar.
1972, 22 September	Operation Hornbeam begins by sending patrols onto the *jebal* above Mughsail as a preliminary step to establishing the Hornbeam Line as a series of picquets, linked by a barrier of barbed wire and mines, between Mughsail and the northern side of the *jebal*.
1972, November	The first Iranian Special Forces Unit arrives in Dhofar and is deployed on the Hornbeam Line.
1972, 23 December	Operation Jason begins in northern Oman and captures nearly eighty members of the National Democratic Front for the Liberation of the Occupied Arabian Gulf (NDFLOAG), who are preparing to open a second front in the north and planning to overthrow the government.

Chronology of the Dhofar War

1973	The main operational base of the Sultan of Oman's Air Force moves from the old airfield at Bait al-Falaj to new facilities adjacent to Sib International Airport.
1973	The Sultan of Oman's Navy moves into its new Sultan bin Ahmad base at Mukalla Cove in Muscat Harbour, brings its first Fast Patrol Boats into service and receives its first seconded commander, Captain Philip Brooke-Popham.
1973	The Royal Guard becomes a separate entity outside the Sultan's Armed Forces.
1973, 17 March	The National Defence Council meets for the first time.
1973, 26–27 March	The first two Diana positions are established on the *jebal* overlooking Salalah Plain to prevent rocket attacks on RAF Salalah.
1973, 26 April	Headquarters Northern Oman is formed to take overall command of the various units in the north.
1973, 1 May	The position of defence secretary is abolished on the retirement of Sir Hugh Oldman; Sayyid Fahr bin Taimur is named deputy defence minister and Brigadier R.F. Semple is appointed as director general of defence administration.
1973, 30 June	Sultan Qaboos lays down three priorities for Dhofar: defence of the coastal plain, especially Salalah; the continued maintenance of a position at Sarfait; and continued operations on the eastern *jebal*.
1973, Summer	Government forces remain in strength on the *jebal* throughout the monsoon for the first time.
1973, October–January 1974	The Oman Gendarmerie unit in Suhar is relieved for duty in Dhofar by two rifle squadrons of the Abu Dhabi Defence Force.
1973, 18 November	A South Yemeni Air Force 11–28 Beagle aircraft drops eight bombs near Makinat Shihan in northwest Dhofar, in the only instance during the war in which the SAF is bombed from the air.
1973, 19–29 December	The Salalah-Thamrit (Midway) road is reopened permanently by government forces, the bulk of which are provided by an Imperial Iranian Battle Group, moving simultaneously from Salalah and Thamrit.
1974	The director of intelligence, Brigadier Malcolm Dennison, becomes adviser to the Sultan on security and tribal affairs as the Oman Research Department is formed.
1974, January–March	The success of Operation Jason leads to further arrests and arms discoveries in the UAE, Bahrain, Qatar and Kuwait.
1974, 4 April	The first squadron of Royal Jordanian Engineers arrives at Thamrit.
1974, 10–12 May	An Arab League mediation committee visits Muscat but is refused admission to South Yemen. PFLOAG insists that the committee comes to 'liberated Dhofar'.

1974, 29 June	The Hornbeam Line, begun on 4 December 1973 to stop opposition resupply between western and central Dhofar, is finished.
1974, July	A PFLOAG congress, marked by disputes between Dhofari and other Gulf members, ends with the truncation of the Front's name to the Popular Front for the Liberation of Oman (PFLO) and the decision to concentrate military activity on Dhofar.
1974, August	Brigadier John Akehurst takes over command of forces in Dhofar headquarters are moved from Umm al-Ghawarif camp to SOAF Salalah.
1974, October	Hammer positions are established midway between the Hornbeam Line and the Salalah-Thamrit road.
1974, 29 October	A Land-Rover with five PFLO members exchanges fire with a SAF picquet near Rustaq and one opposition member is killed and the others are captured; additional arrests prevent a PFLO attempt to disrupt Omani National Day celebrations in what becomes the final PFLO-related incident in northern Oman.
1974, November-April 1975	The Oman Gendarmerie unit in Sohar is again relieved for April 1975 duty in Dhofar by a detachment of the Abu Dhabi Defence Force.
1974, 14 November	The Iranian Task Force is increased in size from battalion to brigade strength and is deployed to Mansion in preparation for a major offensive in western Dhofar.
1974, 2 December	Operation Nadir begins with SAF diversions before an Iranian attack on the Shirshitti caves complex in the west; when Iranian forces suffer heavy losses in the face of strong resistance, their objective is redefined as the capture of Raykut.
1975, January	The Civil Aid Department is established.
1975, 4 January	Operation Darb is launched by the SAF to relieve pressure on the Iranian drive on Raykut and to renew the attempt to capture the Shirshitti caves complex.
1975, 5 January	Operation Darb forces suffer a serious reverse not far from Shirshitti and plans to capture the caves are abandoned. Operation Darb continues until 20 January and results in the establishment of key positions at Stonehenge and Gunlines.
1975, 6 January	Iranians succeed in capturing Raykut and establish the Damavand Line.
1975, February	Major General Ken Perkins replaces Major General Tim Ceasey as commander of the Sultan's Armed Forces.
1975, February	King Hussain of Jordan presents thirty-one Hawker Hunter combat aircraft to the Sultan of Oman's Air Force.
1975, 21 February	Operation Himar is launched to engage the opposition's 9 June Regiment in the west, and is followed by major operations in the centre and east.

Chronology of the Dhofar War

1975, 1 March-15 September	Jordan's 91 Special Forces Battalion relieves Omani troops guarding the Salalah-Thamrit road; a patrol on 8 March is ambushed in Wadi Nahiz, losing one soldier killed and two wounded, and three more Jordanian soldiers are killed when their Land-Rover is ambushed on 3 July.
1975, 13 August	Operations Wagid Badri and Badri are mounted as the opening diversionary moves of the Final Push in the west to capture all remaining rebel-held territory in Dhofar.
1975, 19 August	The opposition fires a SAM-7 missile for the first time, shooting down a Strikemaster aircraft; another Strikemaster is brought down on 29 September and an AB-205 helicopter is downed on 31 October.
1975, 11 September	Jordan's 91 Special Forces Battalion hands responsibility for the Salalah-Thamrit road back to the SAF and subsequently returns to Jordan.
1975, October	The Sultan of Oman's Air Force begins receiving the Jordanian gift of thirty-one Hawker Hunter combat aircraft.
1975, 15 October	The first of two diversionary operations is launched in preparation for Operation Hadaf, the main thrust of the Final Push. The move down the escarpment from Sarfait is so successful that the entire plan for the Final Push is quickly and drastically revised.
1975, 17 October	Operation Sa'id, the second diversion before Operation Hadaf, is launched by Iranian forces to the west of Raykut.
1975, 17 October	The SAF use Hawker Hunter aircraft and 5.5-inch guns to attack enemy bases at Hauf and Jadib in South Yemen in retaliation for heavy enemy shelling of Sultanate territory; the attacks are called off on 21 November after having lost two Hunters.
1975, 22 October-18 November	Operation Hadaf by the Frontier Force succeeds in clearing the treeline along the north side of Wadi Sayq and capturing the Shirshitti caves.
1975, 28 November	Operation Hilwah begins to clear Dara Ridge, the last remaining territory under opposition control.
1975, 2 December	The Frontier Force party clearing Dara Ridge meets up with elements of the Muscat Regiment coming from Sarfait, marking the end of organized opposition resistance in Dhofar and permitting the commander of the Sultan's Armed Forces to inform the Sultan that Dhofar is secure for civil development.
1975, 11 December	Sultan Qaboos declares in Muscat that the Dhofar War officially is over.
1976, 1 January	The Front smuggles a bomb aboard a Boeing 720 aircraft belonging to Middle East Airlines en route from Beirut to Muscat, which explodes over Saudi Arabia and kills eighty one passengers.
1976, 10 March	The Sultanate announces a ceasefire along the border with South Yemen one day after Saudi Arabia establishes diplomatic relations with Aden.

1976, April–September	A number of contacts are made with scattered opposition members in eastern Dhofar; these are accompanied by the July surrender of the principal Front leader in Dhofar.
1976, 30 April	The Front fires its weapons across the border at Sarfait for the last time.
1976, September	The Front's Special Force crosses the border, but as a result of captures and surrenders, only two members achieve their objective of infiltrating eastern Dhofar.
1976, September–December	Major operations are launched in the east to round up the fifty or so remaining rebels.
1976, 14 September	Operation Storm, the codename for the activities of SAS squadrons in Dhofar, ends after recording twelve SAS deaths during the six years of its operation.
1976, 24 November	An Iranian F-4 Phantom aircraft is struck over South Yemeni territory by a SAM-7 missile and crashes into the sea off Jadib; one crew member is killed and the other is captured; with the help of Saudi mediation, an Iranian merchant ship is able to recover most of the aircraft in December.
1977, April	RAF Salalah (along with RAF Masirah) is turned over to the Sultanate for dual use as SOAF Salalah and a civil airport.
1977, 1 May	The last squadron of Royal Jordanian Engineers departs Dhofar.
1977, 5 June	An opposition group launches a stand-off attack against a Southern Regiment platoon position in eastern Dhofar; there are no casualties and all the attackers escape.
1978, 31 January	An SOAF helicopter flying in Sultanate territory near Sarfait is fired upon by South Yemeni positions but is not hit.
1978, 2 June	The bodies of five British employees of Airwork Services are found at Khawr Rawri near Taqah; they had been shot dead by an opposition group.
1978, 7 June	An artillery convoy on the Salalah-Thamrit road is ambushed by a rebel group; two soldiers are killed and eight are wounded.
1979, 9 May	An operation on *Jebal* Aram in eastern Dhofar results in a contact with four opposition members; three are killed but the fourth retreats into a cave and kills an SAF company commander before surrendering.
1979, 19–20 May	A soldier and one opposition member are killed in a skirmish north of Mirbat on 19 May, while another opposition member is killed on the following day in a separate contact.
1979, 8 August	SAF soldier killed in the Eastern Sector
1979, 21 October	A soldier in a Southern Regiment patrol in the Eastern Sector is killed by an opposition group.

1980, 28 March In the final contact of the war, a Southern Regiment ambush in the east results in one opposition member killed and a second probably wounded.

Compiled from J.E. Peterson *Oman's Insurgencies: The Sultanate's Struggle for Supremacy* (London: Saqi Books, 2007) and DEFE 13/779, Dhofar Campaign, Summary of Events.

KEY PERSONALITIES

Britain

Prime Minister
Harold Wilson (L) – 16 October 1964–19 June 1970
Edward Heath (C) – 19 June 1970–4 March 1974
Harold Wilson (L) – 4 March 1974–5 April 1976
Jim Callaghan (L) – 5 April 1976–4 May 1979

Chancellor of the Exchequer
Jim Callaghan (L) – 16 October 1964–30 November 1967
Roy Jenkins (L) – 30 November 1967–19 June 1970
Ian Macleod (C) – 19 June 1970–25 July 1970
Anthony Barber (C) – 25 July 1970–4 March 1974
Denis Healey (L) – 4 March 1974–4 May 1979

Foreign Secretary
George Brown (L) – 11 August 1966–16 March 1968
Michael Stewart (L) – 16 March 1968–19 June 1970
Sir Alec Douglas-Home (C) – 19 June 1970–4 March 1974
Jim Callaghan (L) – 4 March 1974–8 April 1976
Anthony Crosland (L) – 9 April 1976–19 February 1977
David Owen (L) – 22 February 1977–4 May 1979

Minister of Defence
Denis Healey (L) – 16 October 1964–19 June 1970
Lord Carrington (C) – 20 June 1970–8 January 1974
Ian Gilmour (C) – 8 January 1974–4 March 1974
Roy Mason (L) – 5 March 1974–10 September 1976
Frederick Mulley (L) – 10 September 1976–4 May 1979

Key Players in the FCO
Anthony Acland – Head of the Arabian Department, Foreign and Commonwealth Office, 1970–1972. He was Principal Private Secretary to the Foreign Secretary, 1972–1975

Key Personalities

Geoffrey Arthur – Ambassador to Kuwait, 1967–70; Political Resident in the Persian Gulf, 1970–1971;. Deputy Under-Secretary of State FCO, 1973–75

Terence Clark – Assistant Political Agent, Dubai, 1965–68; Belgrade [Yugoslavia], 1969–71; Head of Chancery, Muscat, 1972–73; Assistant Head of Middle East Department, Foreign and Commonwealth Office, 1974–76

Stewart Crawford – Political Resident, Persian Gulf, 1966–70; Deputy Under-Secretary of State, FCO, 1970–73

Donald Hawley – Counsellor (Commercial), Baghdad, 1968; Consul-General, Muscat, 1971; Ambassador to Oman, 1971–75; Assistant Under Secretary of State, Foreign and Commonwealth Office, 1975–77

Ivor Lucas – Foreign Office, 1966–68; Counsellor, Aden, 1968–69 (Chargé d'Affaires, August 1968-February 1969); Deputy High Commissioner, Kaduna, Nigeria, 1969–71; Counsellor, Copenhagen, 1972–75; Head of Middle East Department, Foreign and Commonwealth Office, 1975–79; Ambassador to Oman, 1979–81

Anthony Parsons – Political Agent, Bahrain, 1965–69; Counsellor and Head of Chancery, UK Mission to UN, 1969–71; Ambassador to Iran, 1974–79

Michael Weir – Deputy Political Resident in Bahrain, 1968–71, Head of Chancery UKMISNY, 1971–74; Assistant Under-Secretary of State FCO, 1974–79

Denis Wright – Ambassador to Iran, 1963–71

Patrick Wright – First Secretary and Head of Chancery, Cairo, 1967–70; Deputy Political Resident, Bahrain, 1971–72; Head of Middle East Dept, FCO, 1972–74; Private Secretary (Overseas Affairs) to Prime Minister, 1974–77

JIC Chairmen
Sir Stewart Crawford – 1970–73
Sir Geoffrey Arthur – 1973–75
Sir Anthony Duff – 1975–79
Sir Anthony Acland – 1979–82
Sir Patrick Wright – 1982–84

Chiefs of the Defence Staff
Marshal of the RAF Sir Charles Elworthy – August 1967 – April 1971
Admiral of the Fleet Sir Peter Norton Hill – April 1971 – October 1973
Field Marshal Sir Michael Carver – October 1973 – October 1976

Vice Chiefs of the Defence Staff
Vice Admiral Sir Ian Hogg – 1967–70
Air Marshal Sir John Barraclough – 1970–72
Lieutenant General Sir John Gibbin – 1972–73
Air Marshal Sir Peter Le Cheminant – 1973–75
Vice Admiral Sir Henry Leach – 1975–77

Chiefs of the General Staff
General Sir Geoffrey Baker – 1968–71
General Sir Michael Carver – 1971–73
General Sir Peter Hunt – 1973–76

In the Gulf and Sultanate

Political Resident Persian Gulf
Sir William Luce – 1961–66
Sir Robert Stewart Crawford – 1966–70
Sir Geoffrey Arthur – 1970 – 15 Aug 1971

British Consul-General – Muscat
Derrick Carden – October 1965 – September 1969
David Crawford – September 1969 – May 1971
Donald Hawley – May 1971 – July 1971

Ambassador – Muscat
Donald Hawley – July 1971 – February 1975
Jim Treadwell – February 1975–1979

Oman

Omani Military Secretary, became Defence Secretary in 1970
Brigadier Pat Waterfield – 1958–70
Colonel Hugh Oldman – 1970–73

Minister of Defence
H.H. Sultan Qaboos 1973–present

Deputy Minister of Defence
Sayyid Fahr bin Taimour Al Sa'id – 1973–79

Director General of Defence Administration
R.F. Semple – 1973–76

Command Positions In Oman

Commander Sultan's Armed Forces
Colonel David Smiley – 1958–61
Colonel Hugh Oldman – 1961–64
Colonel Tony Lewis – 1964–67
Brigadier Corren Purdon – 1967–70
Brigadier John Graham – 1970–72
Major General Tim Creasey – 1972–75
Major General Ken Perkins – 1975–77

Deputy Commander Sultan's Armed Forces
Brigadier Colin Maxwell – 1958–76

Commander Sultan of Oman's Air Force
Wing Commander Brian Entwhisle – 1964–67
Squadron Leader Alan Bridges – 1967–70
Wing Commander Curly Hurst – 1970–73

Group Captain L.W. Phipps – 1973–74
Air Vice Marshal Erik Bennett – 1974–90

Commander Sultan of Oman's Navy
Commander Douglas Williams – 1971–73
Captain Philip Brooke-Popham – 1973–76
Commodore Harry Mucklow – 1976–80

Commander Dhofar Brigade
General John Akehurst – 1974–76
General Charles Huxtable – 1976–78

INDEX

25 Pounders 183

Abdullah al-Khalidi 40
Aberdeen, Lord 37
Abu Dhabi 38, 48, 60, 61, 75, 109, 112, 132, 183, 188, 189, 201, 214
Abu Musa 185
Acheson, Dean 4, 28
Acland, Anthony A. 73, 109, 110, 113, 118, 121, 122, 123, 124, 125, 136, 140, 143, 144, 147, 151, 152, 153, 154, 155, 183, 184, 223
Aden 11, 12, 22, 32, 33, 34, 36, 44, 48, 51, 56, 57, 63, 67, 68, 70, 80, 82, 89, 117, 145, 165, 167, 168, 179, 205, 219, 222, 229
Aden Club 89, 91, 111
Adoo 192
Afghanistan 13, 22, 226
Ahmed bin Sa'id 36
Akehurst, General John 217
Al Bu Sa'id 36, 37, 38, 61
Aldous, Mr. (Financial Advisor, Proposed) 91, 115
Allen, D.G. (Arabian Department, FCO) 147
Amery, Julian 17, 179
Amman 142, 183, 184, 186
Anglo-Egyptian Treaty (1936) 26
Anglo-Iranian Oil Company (*See also* BP) 27, 28, 32
Anglo-Iraqi Treaty (1930) 26
Aqubah, Operation 165

Arab League 40, 116, 128, 136, 142, 143, 145, 146, 147, 148, 149, 150, 151, 152, 153, 154, 155, 156, 157, 159, 164, 168, 214, 285
Arabian Department (FCO) 51, 73, 87, 89, 90, 95, 108, 110, 113, 116, 118, 119, 121, 123, 124, 126, 128, 132, 134, 140, 147, 148, 157, 175, 183, 184, 186
ARAMCO 2, 39, 41
Arthur, Geoffrey 90, 118, 119, 120, 121, 122, 123, 124, 125, 126, 139, 140, 142, 143, 150, 223
Ashworth, Anthony 213
Asim, Dr Jamili 142
Australia 132
Austria 133

Badri, Operation 287
Baghdad 38, 46, 48, 116, 144, 145
Baghdad Pact 26, 29
Bahrain 37, 48, 51, 73, 85, 89, 90, 92, 93, 115, 116, 118, 119, 122, 130, 132, 133, 135, 136, 139, 149, 152, 156
Bait al Falaj 188, 285
Balfour-Paul, Glenn 75, 144
Balniel, Lord 176, 179
Bannerman, J.J. (Middle East Sec. FCO) 74
Batinah Force 40
Beaumont, R.A. (British Ambassador, Cairo) 143, 144, 145, 146, 153, 166

INDEX

Bell, Sir Gerwain 213
Beveridge Report 25
Blackley, J.M. (Ian) 116, 117, 118, 124
Borneo 68, 69
Boustead, Col. Hugh 46, 47
Breik bin Hamoud, Sheikh 73
British Ambassador Muscat 181, 196, 216
British Army Training Team (BATT) 171, 282, 283
British Embassy Ankara 159
British Empire 4, 6, 8, 9, 26, 70
British Petroleum (BP) *See* Anglo-Iranian Oil Company
Brown, George (Foreign Secretary, Labour) 37, 57, 59
Buraimi 38, 39, 40, 42, 45, 55, 58, 59, 60, 137, 224, 229, 236

Cairo 29, 32, 33, 45, 46, 47, 48, 51, 136, 143, 144, 145, 146, 148, 149, 151, 153, 156, 166
Canada 26, 132
Canning Award 37, 86
Carden, Bill (British Consul-General, Muscat) 54, 87
Carrington, Lord (Conservative Defence Secretary, 1970–74) 84, 85, 93, 98, 99, 100, 101, 166, 176, 187, 195, 201, 202, 223
Carver, General Mike (Chief of General Staff) 223
Central Treaty Organisation (CENTO) 196, 203, 206
Chamoun, Camille 31
China 2, 8, 30, 64, 96, 130, 156, 215, 281, 283
Churchill, Sir Winston 21, 23, 26, 28
Clark, Terence 205, 208, 245
Clutterbuck, Major-General R.I. (Royal Engineers) 110
Communist 2, 17, 24, 29, 30, 35, 41, 44, 47, 55, 63, 64, 76, 96, 97, 117, 155, 158, 167, 196, 221,
Compagnie Française des Pétroles (CFP) 28
Conservative Government (1970–74) 19, 23, 33, 72, 75, 76, 77, 78, 79, 80, 81, 83, 86, 95, 96, 98, 202, 203, 205, 219, 222, 223, 235
Conservative Opposition (1964–70 and 1974–79) 44, 69, 70
Counterinsurgency (COIN) 2, 13, 14, 15, 18, 35, 64, 66, 67, 67, 68, 69, 103, 131, 158, 162, 167, 191, 220, 221, 222, 225, 236, 237, 241
Cracker Battery 101, 211
Crawford, David (Consul-General, Muscat) 73, 83, 89, 92, 99, 101, 103, 107, 110, 111, 114, 115, 119, 120, 121, 123, 124, 125, 126, 133, 139, 152, 153
Crawford, Sir Stewart 59, 61, 74, 86, 89, 189
Crossman, Anthony 34
Crowe Memorandum 21
Crowe, Sir Colin 168
Cuba 24, 156

Damascus 133
Damavand Line 163, 286
Dammam 45
Darb, Operation 286
Darwin, John 68, 69
De Gaulle, Charles 23
Defence Attache (Amman) 183
Defence Attache (Muscat) 164, 167, 176, 183, 184, 188, 189
Defence and Overseas Policy Committee (DOPC) 68, 79, 81, 94, 96, 170, 178, 179, 181, 202, 204, 205, 212, 224
Defence Review (1966–67) 60
Defence Review (1974–75) 19, 199, 203, 204, 205, 206, 207, 208, 210, 211, 212
Denmark 133
Dennison, Malcolm 106, 285
Development Programme 14, 15, 18, 41, 42, 45, 46, 47, 52, 53, 54, 55, 56, 61, 62, 63, 64, 65, 66, 67, 68, 72, 74, 75, 86, 89, 99, 101, 102, 105, 106, 107, 109, 110, 111, 112, 113, 114, 115, 118, 119, 120, 122, 126,

127, 128, 131, 132, 135, 138, 160, 161, 162, 172, 173, 182, 188, 191, 195, 203, 214, 216, 219, 221, 222, 224, 225, 226, 227
Dhofar (Terrain/History) 47
Dhofar Liberation Front (DLF) 43, 44, 48, 51, 54, 55, 63, 65, 280, 281
Diana 285
Doha 151
Dorchester, The, London 74
Douglas-Home, Sir Alec (Foreign Secretary 1970–74) 51, 74, 79, 84, 85, 90, 93, 95, 97, 98, 99, 101, 132, 134, 135, 47, 148, 156, 164, 166, 167, 169, 170, 177, 179, 185, 189, 194, 196, 202, 223
DS-11 (MoD) 165, 174, 193, 195, 205, 207
Dubai 56, 106, 131, 132, 214, 281
Dulles, John Foster 28, 40
Dye, Major General J.B. 67

East India Company 37
'East of Suez' 3, 6, 10, 11, 18, 35, 44, 58, 66, 71, 78, 79, 80, 82, 86, 132, 199, 200, 203, 218, 222, 223, 229
Eden, Anthony 9, 30
Edes, J.M. (FCO) 132
Egypt/Egyptians 10, 25, 26, 27, 29, 30, 31, 32, 33, 47, 55, 67, 133, 136, 138, 139, 143, 144, 145, 150, 154, 156, 159, 166
Eisenhower, President 28, 30, 31
Empty Quarter/Rub al Khali 279, 280
Everest 283

Fabrique Nationale (FN) 66
Fahud, *Jebal* 56
Field Surgical Team (FST) 101, 175, 177, 178, 179, 205, 226
Firqah/Firqat 76, 125, 158, 165, 168, 170, 172, 213, 225, 226, 283
France 21, 24, 30, 31, 70, 129, 132, 153, 201

Germany 25, 47, 54, 70, 106, 107, 111, 132
Ghalib bin Ali al-Hani (Imam) 40, 45, 48, 137, 143, 144, 145, 146, 147, 148, 149, 150, 151, 154, 157

Gibbs, General Roly (Commander British Forces Gulf) 67, 85, 93
Glubb, Sir John 31
Godber, Joseph 165
Graham, Brigadier John (CSAF) 73, 106, 162, 163, 167, 184, 282

Habarut 163, 165, 168, 170, 171, 193, 281, 284
Halliday, Fred 11, 12, 13, 39, 46, 52, 54, 55, 58, 63, 64, 127, 128, 131, 171, 172, 209, 227, 228
Hammer Line 286
Hart, Judith 45
Hashemite 31, 32
Hauf 55, 56, 165, 166, 167, 168, 170, 171, 200, 216, 281, 284, 287
Hawley, D.F. (British Ambassador, Muscat) 115, 122, 123, 124, 125, 137, 139, 140, 147, 156, 158, 163, 164, 165, 166, 167, 168, 169, 170, 171, 172, 173, 175, 176, 177, 179, 183, 184, 185, 186, 188, 192, 193, 195, 197, 200, 201, 202, 203, 213, 214, 215, 223, 245, 251
Healey, Denis 34
Heath, Edward 70, 71, 78, 80, 81, 86, 95, 97, 98, 100, 101, 166, 167, 176, 187, 197, 200, 219, 222, 223, 224, 228
Hilwah, Operation 287
HMG 96, 117, 118, 121, 132, 140, 164, 174, 175, 196
Hornbeam Line 214, 284, 286
Hunter 92, 93, 286, 287
Hurd, Douglas 70, 80
Hussein, King 32, 133, 134, 142, 152, 158, 183, 184, 186, 187, 229
Huxtable, Sir Charles 217

Ibadi/Ibadism 36
Imam (Ibadi) 36, 37, 38, 40, 48, 53, 143, 148, 149, 150, 151, 154
Imam (North Yemen) 33
Imamate 36, 38, 39, 40, 41, 42, 44, 236
Imamate (Rebellion) 45, 46, 47, 48, 49, 52, 53, 54, 137, 224

INDEX

India 25, 36, 37, 38, 47, 86, 129, 135, 139, 140, 191
Indian Ocean 1, 2, 36, 194, 206, 209
International Monetary Fund (IMF) 58, 90
Intradon, Operation 92, 94, 95, 96, 98, 101
Iran/Iranians 2, 9, 25, 27, 28, 29, 70, 80, 133, 135, 136, 138, 158, 176, 179, 183, 185, 186, 187, 189, 190, 191, 192, 194, 195, 197, 202, 204, 209, 211, 213, 214, 215, 217, 219, 220, 229, 280, 284, 205, 286, 287, 288
Iraq 10, 13, 25, 26, 29, 31, 32, 33, 36, 38, 47, 91, 117, 133, 144, 148, 151, 159, 185, 186, 226, 229, 279, 280
Iraq Petroleum Company 38
Israel 26, 29, 30, 31, 63, 168, 183, 194

Jaguar, Operation 162, 163, 171, 182, 283
Jaguars (Aircraft) 203, 208
Japan 133
Jason, Operation 284, 285
Jeapes, Tony 217
Jebal Akhdar Campaign 106, 224, 229
John Mecom Oil Comapny 48, 279
Joint Intelligence Committee (JIC) 60, 91, 177, 240
Jordan/Jordanians 25, 26, 31, 32, 133, 135, 138, 142, 146, 158, 183, 184, 185, 186, 187, 188, 189, 191, 192, 194, 197, 219, 229, 285, 286, 287, 288

Kelly, J.B. 12, 34, 35, 57, 80, 81, 238
Kennedy, President 22
Khareef 48
King Faisal (Saudi Arabia) 50, 134, 135, 147, 149, 150, 157, 166, 189
Kuria Muria Islands 55
Kuwait 32, 33, 35, 37, 48, 60, 70, 72, 80, 133, 146, 147, 148, 149, 154, 229

Labour Government (1964–70) 5, 10, 34, 60, 61, 66, 67, 70, 72, 75, 76, 79, 80, 86, 95, 200
Labour Government (1974–79) 198, 199, 200, 203, 204, 212, 215, 218, 219, 220, 225
Landon, Timothy 72, 140

Lawrence, T.E. 15
Le Quesne, C.M. (Deputy Under Secretary of State, FCO) 190, 191
Lebanon 31, 146, 168, 254
Leopard Line/Operation 162, 163, 182, 283, 284
Lloyd, Selwyn (Conservative Foreign Secretary 1960s) 53
Lloyd-Jones, Richard (DS-11 MoD) 165, 174, 193, 195, 205, 207
Loan Service Personnel (LSP) 66, 174, 175, 176, 177, 178, 180, 181, 182, 193, 194, 195, 201, 205, 206, 212, 217, 219, 226, 256
Lucas, Sir Ivor 213, 215
Luce, Sir William 46, 71, 79, 80, 96, 97, 101, 102, 118, 119, 121, 122, 134, 136, 146, 223, 224

Macmillan, Harold 17, 22, 31, 40
Mahonia, Operation 100
Malaya 13, 17, 24, 44, 57, 68, 69, 229
Maloney, Col. (U.S. Army) 193, 197
Maria Theresa Thaler 37, 108
Marxist 2, 11, 43, 44, 127, 221
Masirah 70, 99, 116, 117, 118, 123, 124, 176, 179, 193, 194, 196, 200, 201, 202, 204, 205, 206, 207, 209, 210, 211, 215, 218, 219, 224, 228, 288
Mason, Peter (British Bank of the Middle East) 106
Mason, Roy (Secretary of State for Defence, Labour 1974–76) 204, 211, 212, 224
Matrah 54, 62, 65, 82, 108, 287
Middle East Department (FCO) 165, 176, 181, 186, 195, 205, 210, 213, 215, 245
Mirbat, inc. Battle of 171, 172, 180, 283, 284, 288
Monroe, Elizabeth 9
Morrison, Herbert 29
Moscow 24
Mossadeq, Mohammed 27, 28
Mughsail 283, 284
Musandam Peninsula 1, 91, 92, 94, 95, 96, 182, 223, 225, 282

Nairne, Pat 223
Nasser, President Gamal Abdal 30, 31, 32, 33, 34, 45, 47, 48, 49, 55, 136, 138, 143, 144
National Interest(s) 3, 4, 11, 15, 16, 17, 18, 21, 23, 24, 44, 60, 76, 77, 78, 86, 96, 97, 100, 102, 104, 115, 125, 127, 128, 173, 179, 181, 200, 205, 212, 218, 219, 220, 222, 224, 228
NATO 5, 27, 29, 58, 81, 202, 211
NDFLOAG 82, 92, 282, 283, 284
Netherlands 132
New York 49, 51, 133, 153, 154, 155, 168
New Zealand 133, 217
Nizwa 40, 82, 119, 128, 182

Ogram, Major 46
Oil 2, 10, 14, 17, 26, 27, 28, 29, 33, 38, 39, 41, 47, 82, 92, 96, 116, 173, 179, 196
Oil (Oman) 40, 41, 43, 44, 46, 48, 53, 56, 57, 62, 71, 76, 87, 92, 107, 108, 111, 114, 115, 130, 144, 172, 173, 194, 196, 205, 216, 219, 222
Oldman, Col. Hugh (Oman Defence Secretary) 67, 73, 74, 82, 89, 99, 106, 107, 108, 111, 120, 126, 133, 139, 158, 163, 164, 165, 167, 168, 169, 173, 174, 175, 176, 184, 186, 187, 188, 223
Oman Rebel Movement (ORM): Northern Oman 40, 49, 137
Ovendale, Ritchie 9, 10

Pakistan 29, 133, 135, 191
Palestine 9, 10, 25, 26
Parsons, Sir Anthony 118, 119, 121, 122, 123, 124, 132, 135, 164, 171, 179, 188, 190, 223
Perkins, Ken 211, 216, 217, 286
Persepolis 158
Petersen, Tore T. 9
Peterson, J.E. 12, 106, 162, 163, 192
Petroleum Development (Oman), (PD(O)) 2, 40, 104, 106

Political Resident Persian Gulf (PRPG) 46, 59, 118
Popular Front, PFLO, PFLOAG 44, 63, 64, 82, 84, 103, 162, 171, 172, 215, 217, 281, 283, 286
Portsmouth Treaty (1948) 26
Portuguese/Portugal 36
Provost 280

Qaboos 3, 14, 54, 61, 72, 73, 74, 75, 88, 90, 92, 98, 102, 104, 105, 106, 107, 108, 109, 111, 112, 113, 114, 115, 125, 126, 127, 131, 133, 135, 136, 137, 138, 142, 145, 146, 149, 156, 157, 158, 159, 161, 175, 186, 193, 201, 203, 222, 228, 236, 239, 282, 285, 287
Qais al-Zawawi 204
Qatar 37, 48, 56, 131, 132, 149, 150, 151, 155, 156, 188, 191
Queen Victoria 55

Rabi, Uzi 53
RAF Salalah 51, 65, 73, 98, 101, 165, 169, 177, 200, 201, 202, 205, 215, 216
Rainbow, Operation 280
Rapier Missiles 190, 196, 200, 201, 202, 203, 208, 214
Ras al-Khaimah 58, 91, 94, 283
Raykyut 281, 286, 287
Review of Policy 65, 66, 67, 69, 79, 82, 104, 116, 119, 122, 124, 125, 126, 127, 139, 140, 172, 176, 177, 179, 181, 189, 194, 195, 196, 199, 201, 203, 204, 224
Rhodesia 22
Riyadh 39, 137, 147, 157, 170, 227
Riyal 255, 258, 261
Roberts, Goronwy 34, 57, 58, 59
Roger Louis, Wm 8, 9, 10
Royal Dutch Shell 2, 28, 43, 46
Royal Engineers (Operation Tenable) 98, 99, 101, 110, 205, 226
Royal Irish Regiment 92
Rustaq 36, 40, 286

INDEX

Sa'id bin Taimur 3, 38, 40, 45, 48, 52, 54, 57, 61, 62, 65, 67, 73, 74, 75, 82, 105, 106, 129, 131, 139, 143
Sadat, President Anwar al- 138, 144, 145, 146, 150
Salalah 45, 51, 54, 60, 61, 62, 64, 65, 67, 69, 73, 83, 97, 98, 99, 101, 104, 110, 123, 134, 158, 162, 165, 169, 170, 171, 177, 187, 188, 195, 200, 201, 202, 203, 205, 206, 211, 215, 216, 218, 226, 242, 279, 280, 281, 282, 283, 284, 285, 287, 288
Salih bin Himyar al-Nabhani 40
Salih bin Isa 40
Salim, Imam 37
Sandhurst 54, 72
Saqaaf, Prince (Saudi Arabia) 149, 150
Sarfait 163, 216, 284, 285, 287, 288
Saudi Arabia 2, 31, 32, 38, 39, 40, 41, 45, 50, 70, 134, 135, 136, 137, 138, 141, 147, 149, 150, 156, 157, 158, 177, 179, 183, 188, 189, 191, 193, 202, 204, 211, 227, 279, 280, 287
Second World War (WWII) 4, 5, 7, 8, 17, 21, 27, 35
Secretary of State for Defence 92, 94, 95, 166, 193, 195, 201
Seeb/Sib 38, 40, 285
Semple, Brigadier (Commander SAS Group) 84, 281, 285
Sevrès 30
Shah 27, 28, 79, 133, 136, 158, 184, 185, 186, 187, 188, 191, 209, 214, 215, 260
Shakhbut, Sheikh (Abu Dhabi) 75
Sharjah 41, 91, 98, 207
Shirshitti 281, 286, 287
Simba, Operation 162, 163, 165, 167, 171, 194, 284
Singapore 32, 82, 116, 174
Skeet, Ian 2, 12, 38, 104, 114, 115, 127, 128, 135, 136, 217
Skyvan 66
Smith, Ian 22
Sohar 36, 38
Special Air Service (SAS) 41, 67, 68, 74, 76, 82, 83, 84, 85, 92, 96, 97, 98, 99, 100, 101, 122, 124, 125, 158, 164, 169, 171, 172, 175, 177, 178, 179, 189, 205, 206, 217, 219, 221, 222, 225, 226, 241, 243, 281, 282, 283, 288
Stanbridge, Air Commodore Brian (Secretary of the Chiefs of Staff, MoD) 124
Statebuilding 13, 14, 15, 66, 104, 222, 228
Sterling/Pound 5, 6, 23, 27, 31, 35, 58, 61, 116, 203
Stevenson, Sir Ralph 29
Stewart, Sir Michael (Foreign Secretary, Labour) 33, 65
Strait of Hormuz 1, 2, 92, 158, 185, 192, 215, 220
Strang, Sir William 28
Strikemaster 282, 283, 287
Sudan 26, 29, 223
Suez Canal 1, 9, 25, 26, 30, 32
Sultan bin Ahmed 36
Sultan of Oman's Air Force (SOAF) 163, 165, 171, 172, 173, 193, 202, 280, 282, 284, 286, 288
Sultan of Oman's Navy (SON) 64, 66, 282, 285, 293,
Sultan *See* Qaboos and Sa'id
Sultan's Armed Forces (SAF) 41, 45, 51, 59, 60, 62, 63, 64, 65, 66, 67, 68, 72, 73, 74, 75, 82, 83, 84, 91, 92, 99, 100, 103, 104, 106, 110, 114, 115, 116, 117, 123, 125, 126, 158, 162, 169, 170, 172, 173, 177, 180, 182, 184, 187, 188, 189, 190, 195, 196, 202, 204, 212, 214, 216, 280, 281, 282, 284, 285, 286, 287, 292
Sultan Taimur bin Faisal 38
Syria 31, 32, 133, 144, 146, 149, 151, 156, 159, 251

Talib, bin Ali al-Hani (Brother of Imam Ghalib) 40, 137, 149, 279
Taqah 280, 281, 282, 283, 288
Tariq, bin Taimur 18, 47, 61, 89, 92, 94, 102, 106, 107, 108, 109, 111, 112,

113, 115, 120, 122, 125, 126, 127,
131, 134, 135, 136, 137, 138, 139,
142, 145, 146, 147, 152, 153, 154,
155, 156, 157, 159, 161, 249, 282
Tatham, David (Middle East
  Department, FCO) 195
Tehran 133, 185, 186, 187, 189, 214
Thamrit 64, 103, 285, 286, 288
TOW Missiles 209
Townsend, John (Economic Advisor,
  Muscat) 47, 57, 62, 106, 109, 173,
  213
Treadwell, C.J. (Jim) 109, 211, 213, 215,
  216, 217, 218
Treasury 69, 86, 87, 88, 91, 101, 174,
  175, 176, 177, 178, 180, 181, 182,
  218
Treaty of Friendship, Commerce and
  Navigation (1951) 130
Treffry, David 89, 90
Trevaskis, Sir Kennedy (Governor of
  Aden) 89
Trucial Oman Scouts (TOS) 91, 92
Trucial States *See also* United Arab
  Emirates (UAE) 92, 96, 100, 117,
  132
Truman, President 25, 28
Turkey 29, 152, 159

United Arab Emirates (UAE) *See also*
  Trucial States 35, 37, 50, 72, 117,
  169, 186, 191, 285
United Nations 30, 49, 50, 51, 122, 128,
  132, 142, 151, 164
United Nations General Assembly 49,
  50, 51, 94, 152, 156
United Nations Relief and Works
  Agency (UNRWA) 250
United Nations Security Council 39, 40,
  50, 152, 153, 154, 155, 156, 168
United States of America (U.S.) 2, 4, 7,
  9, 10, 13, 21, 26, 27, 69, 76, 129,
  132, 152, 153, 154, 156, 161, 186,
  187, 192, 193, 194, 196, 197, 207,
  208, 209, 210, 211, 218, 219, 220,
  227, 228, 242, 249, 261
USSR 2, 156, 185

Vietnam 22, 24, 44, 192, 193, 225

Wadi 110, 280, 281, 283, 287
Wali 51, 73, 112, 172
Washington 23, 25, 27, 28, 29, 30, 32,
  33, 35, 39, 90, 149, 152, 186, 187,
  192, 193, 194, 197, 208, 209, 210,
  219
Weir, Michael 83, 90, 109, 133, 135,
  136, 139, 153, 204, 205, 291
Welch, Col. C.E. (Defence Attaché,
  Muscat) 164, 167, 176, 184, 188,
  189
White City 162, 284
Whitehall 16, 18, 19, 25, 55, 75, 76, 84,
  86, 88, 94, 95, 102, 105, 118, 126,
  130, 159, 161, 162, 165, 166, 167,
  168, 169, 171, 173, 175, 181, 210,
  213, 217, 223, 228
Wilson, Harold 10, 22, 23, 34, 35, 69,
  71, 199, 200, 203, 204, 207, 212,
  219, 224, 290
World Health Organisation (WHO) 140
Wright, Patrick 165, 175, 176, 177, 178,
  179, 180, 186, 189, 190, 193, 201,
  206, 208, 213, 223, 261, 291

Yahya, Omar 214
Yemen *See also* PDRY and PRSY 1, 2, 11,
  33, 34, 49, 55, 58, 63, 64, 92, 117,
  136, 143, 144, 145, 146, 148, 150,
  154, 156, 159, 161, 162, 163, 164,
  165, 166, 167, 168, 169, 170, 171,
  179, 196, 200, 201, 202, 214, 216,
  217, 221, 281, 284, 285, 287, 288

Zahedi, Fazlollah 28
Zanzibar 37, 87, 101
Zanzibar Subsidy 86, 88, 101
Zayid/Zaid, Sheikh (Abu Dhabi) 61, 109

www.ingramcontent.com/pod-product-compliance
Lightning Source LLC
Chambersburg PA
CBHW061426300426
44114CB00014B/1559